TOWERING JUDGES

In *Towering Judges: A Comparative Study of Constitutional Judges*, Rehan Abeyratne and Iddo Porat lead an exploration of a new topic in comparative constitutional law: towering judges. The volume examines the work of nineteen judges from fourteen jurisdictions, each of whom stood out individually among their fellow judges and had a unique impact on the trajectory of constitutional law. The chapters ask: what makes a towering judge; what are the background conditions that foster or deter the rise of towering judges; are towering judges, on balance, positive or detrimental for constitutional systems; how do towering judges differ from one jurisdiction to another; how do political and historical developments relate to this phenomenon; and how does all of this fit within global constitutionalism? The answers to these questions offer important insight into how these judges were able to shine to an uncommon degree in a profession where individualism is not always looked on favourably.

Rehan Abeyratne is an associate professor of law and the executive director of the Centre for Comparative and Transnational Law at the Chinese University of Hong Kong. His research focuses on comparative constitutional law. His published works have appeared in leading peer-reviewed journals and in edited volumes from Cambridge University Press and other scholarly publishers.

Iddo Porat is an associate professor of law at the College of Law and Business, Israel. He specialises in constitutional law, comparative constitutional law and legal theory. His books include *Proportionality and Constitutional Culture* (with Moshe Cohen-Eliya; Cambridge University Press, 2013).

T0382238

COMPARATIVE CONSTITUTIONAL LAW AND POLICY

Series Editors

Tom Ginsburg *University of Chicago*
Zachary Elkins *University of Texas at Austin*
Ran Hirschl *University of Toronto*

Comparative constitutional law is an intellectually vibrant field that encompasses an increasingly broad array of approaches and methodologies. This series collects analytically innovative and empirically grounded work from scholars of comparative constitutionalism across academic disciplines. Books in the series include theoretically informed studies of single constitutional jurisdictions, comparative studies of constitutional law and institutions, and edited collections of original essays that respond to challenging theoretical and empirical questions in the field.

Books in the Series

Towering Judges

A COMPARATIVE STUDY OF CONSTITUTIONAL JUDGES

Edited by

REHAN ABEYRATNE

The Chinese University of Hong Kong

IDDO PORAT

College of Law and Business, Israel

CAMBRIDGE
UNIVERSITY PRESS

CAMBRIDGE
UNIVERSITY PRESS

University Printing House, Cambridge CB2 8BS, United Kingdom

One Liberty Plaza, 20th Floor, New York, NY 10006, USA

477 Williamstown Road, Port Melbourne, VIC 3207, Australia

314-321, 3rd Floor, Plot 3, Splendor Forum, Jasola District Centre, New Delhi - 110025, India

103 Penang Road, #05-06/07, Visioncrest Commercial, Singapore 238467

Cambridge University Press is part of the University of Cambridge.

It furthers the University's mission by disseminating knowledge in the pursuit of education, learning and research at the highest international levels of excellence.

www.cambridge.org
Information on this title: www.cambridge.org/9781108794145
DOI: 10.1017/9781108879194

First published 2021
First paperback edition 2022

A catalogue record for this publication is available from the British Library

Library of Congress Cataloging in Publication data
NAMES: Abeyratne, Rehan, author. | Porat, Iddo, author.
TITLE: Towering judges : a comparative study of constitutional judges / edited by Rehan Abeyratne, The Chinese University of Hong Kong; Iddo Porat, College of Law and Business (Israel).
DESCRIPTION: Cambridge, United Kingdom ; New York, NY : Cambridge University Press, 2021. | Series: Comparative constitutional law and policy | Includes index.
IDENTIFIERS: LCCN 2020028702 (print) | LCCN 2020028703 (ebook) | ISBN 9781108840217 (hardback) | ISBN 9781108879194 (epub)
SUBJECTS: LCSH: Judges. | Constitutional courts. | Constitutional law.
CLASSIFICATION: LCC K3367 .A24 2021 (print) | LCC K3367 (ebook) | DDC 347/.03534–dc23
LC record available at https://lccn.loc.gov/2020028702
LC ebook record available at https://lccn.loc.gov/2020028703

ISBN 978-1-108-84021-7 Hardback
ISBN 978-1-108-79414-5 Paperback

For Anna and Eila – Rehan Abeyratne
For my Natalie – Iddo Porat

Contents

Acknowledgements

We first developed the idea for this book over a coffee at Melbourne Law School in 2017, when we were both visiting scholars. We are grateful to Melbourne Law School for hosting us and providing us with the opportunity to meet. The Chinese University of Hong Kong Faculty of Law organised a conference on Towering Judges in early 2019 from which this book emerged. We thank CUHK LAW for funding the travel and accommodation of all our contributors and for hosting the conference in its Graduate Law Centre. We are grateful to our contributors for their patience, creativity and willingness to fit their research into our framework. We feel very fortunate to have worked with such a strong group of comparative constitutional law scholars. Ran Hirschl expressed initial enthusiasm for this project and worked with us on the book proposal, which he generously considered for his co-edited series on Comparative Constitutional Law and Policy. We thank him, Tom Ginsburg and Zachary Elkins for including this book in that series. Finally, we thank the editors at Cambridge University Press for their hard work in getting this volume into publishable shape.

Contributors

Rehan ABEYRATNE is an associate professor of law and the executive director of the Centre for Comparative and Transnational Law at the Chinese University of Hong Kong.

Gabrielle APPLEBY is a professor and director of the Judiciary Project, Gilbert + Tobin Centre of Public Law, University of New South Wales Faculty of Law.

BUI Ngoc Son is an assistant professor of law at the Chinese University of Hong Kong.

Tom Gerald DALY is an associate professor and deputy director of the Melbourne School of Government and an associate director of the Edinburgh Centre for Constitutional Law.

Dennis M DAVIS is Judge President of the Competition Appeal Court of South Africa.

Rosalind DIXON is a professor of law and director of the Gilbert + Tobin Centre of Public Law, University of New South Wales Faculty of Law.

Alon HAREL is the Phillip and Estelle Mizock Chair in Administrative and Criminal Law at the Hebrew University of Jerusalem Faculty of Law.

Rosemary HUNTER is Professor of Law and Socio-Legal Studies at Kent Law School, University of Kent.

David LANDAU is the Mason Ladd Professor and Associate Dean for International Programs at Florida State University College of Law.

CL LIM is the Choh-Ming Li Professor of Law at the Chinese University of Hong Kong; Hon. Senior Fellow, BIICL, and Visiting Professor, King's College, London.

Andrew LYNCH is a professor at the Gilbert + Tobin Centre of Public Law, University of New South Wales Faculty of Law.

Mara MALAGODI is an assistant professor of law at the Chinese University of Hong Kong.

Jaclyn L NEO is an associate professor at the National University of Singapore Faculty of Law.

Iddo PORAT is an associate professor at the College of Law and Business, Israel.

Erika RACKLEY is a professor of law at Kent Law School, University of Kent.

Kevin YL TAN is an adjunct professor at the Faculty of Law, National University of Singapore and a professor at the S Rajaratnam School of International Studies, Nanyang Technological University.

Gábor Attila TÓTH is the Alexander von Humboldt Senior Fellow at Humboldt University, Berlin.

Mark TUSHNET is the William Nelson Cromwell Professor of Law Emeritus at Harvard Law School.

Sergio VERDUGO is an associate professor of law at Universidad del Desarrollo, Chile.

Introduction: Towering Judges – A Conceptual and Comparative Analysis

Rehan Abeyratne and Iddo Porat

This volume is a collection of essays on a new topic in comparative constitutional law: towering judges. The volume discusses nineteen judges of apex and constitutional courts from fourteen jurisdictions. Within their particular political, historical, and institutional settings, each of these judges made a significant impact on the trajectory and development of constitutional law. These judges towered over their peers to distinguish themselves in the local context and, in some cases, globally. Some of these judges became well-known public figures, cultural icons, or political leaders. Some acted in crucial moments in their country's constitutional history or led their court in a new direction. Others acted in less fraught times and were known primarily within the legal profession. Some were uncontrovertibly respected and valued, while others were complex figures that were subject to debate and criticism. All of them, however, were able to shine individually to an uncommon degree in a profession where individualism is not always looked on favorably.

That there are such judges, we think, is indisputable. Everyone can intuit the "towering" judges in their own jurisdiction. But this is the first in-depth study of this phenomenon within the field of comparative constitutional law. The term "towering judge" and the questions we pose about these judges are novel. What makes for a towering judge and what are the possible parameters for assessing their "towering-ness"? What are the background conditions that foster or deter the rise of towering judges? Are towering judges, on balance, positive or detrimental for a constitutional system? How do towering judges differ from one country to another and what are the comparative and global effects on towering judges? How do historical and social development relate to this phenomenon, and is it part of "global constitutionalism"? These questions will be at the center of this volume, and are answered by the rich, varied chapters that comprise it.

In this introduction, we outline in Section I the contours of the phenomenon that we aim to investigate; its naming; and its definition. We then preview all the chapters (Section II). Section III provides an overview of the existing literature and explains how this volume contributes to it. Sections IV and V discuss different dimensions of

1

toweringness (political, institutional, and doctrinal) and the various contexts that
promote or deter towering judges (institutional, political, and historical). Sections
VI, VII, and VIII discuss additional aspects of toweringness (personal traits, relations
with other judges, and transnational/global relations among judges). We conclude
(Section IX) with a discussion of some of the challenges faced in this project.

I CHOICE OF TERM, DEFINITION, AND SELECTION PRINCIPLE

The first two questions for this project were naming and defining the phenomenon.
Our hypothesis was that there is a distinct phenomenon in which certain judges,
especially in apex and constitutional courts, distinguish themselves from their peers.
We had some prototypes in mind, such as President Aharon Barak of Israel and
Chief Justice Bhagwati of India, who were singular figures in expanding the authority of their respective courts and developing fundamental rights jurisprudence. We
also hypothesized that this phenomenon is interesting and robust enough to warrant
a broad comparative study. But, how would we name it and what would be the
criteria for including judges within this category?

We considered several names. First, "Herculean judges," following Ronald
Dworkin's hypothetical judge, Hercules, who is all knowing and all capable.[1] This
term captured the amazing capabilities of these judges and their larger-than-life
status in the public eye. However, it was too demanding and connoted an infallibility
that was too far removed from complex (and flawed) individuals discussed in this
volume. We also considered "hero judges." This term captured the struggles that
many of these judges faced vis-à-vis powerful political forces, requiring courage and
resilience, especially in times of revolution or constitutional upheaval. However, not
all judges that distinguished themselves operated under such conditions. In addition, this concept carried with it a positive normative connotation – heroes are
always good – while we aimed at a neutral concept that does not necessarily connote
a positive assessment of the judge and their legacy.

We finally opted for towering judges, which we believe captures the essential
characteristics of the phenomenon while allowing enough variance not to exclude
too many important examples. At a minimum, a "towering judge" is in some respects
"taller" than other judges and is therefore *individually* distinguishable from them. Thus,
there is something individualistic about a towering judge that we think is essential to
the phenomenon. This means that the judiciary in which such a judge operates is no
longer impersonal and uniform. Rather, there is one (at times more than one) judge
that draws disproportionate attention and has some disproportionate influence.
Towering also connotes not just a little bit taller but taller in some important or
substantial way. But this still leaves, intentionally, a lot open: it does not say or

---

[1] Ronald Dworkin, *Law's Empire* (Belknap, 1986).

determine in what way the judge is taller than other judges. It also does not say whether taller is necessarily better – is he or she taller in a good or in a problematic way? Our conception also allows different degrees of toweringness. Towering judges could be those that completely reshape the judicial, legal, and even societal landscape, but their impact need not be so far-reaching as to be viewed as such.

While we decline to provide a single definition of towering judges – a precise definition would probably do more harm than good for a project such as ours – there are two key aspects to the phenomenon that we hold constant in our selection: individualism and influence. That is, the judges in this volume have to be individually distinguished from their colleagues and they should have a substantial influence on their constitutional systems. As we will discuss, a towering judge's influence can be met with backlash that can undo some of their achievements, and a judge's worldview can become outdated or obsolete over time. However, we also include such judges under the assumption that a substantial stamp on the history of ideas always leaves a trace, even by way of antithesis, making it influential even if undone over time. The same criterion would also usually rule out judges that "tower" on irrelevant or immoral grounds: judges that "tower," for example, in corruptness or ineptitude. Such judges generally do not leave a significant trace on the history of ideas of their society.

We added one more important qualification – we included only judges that towered mostly, or substantially, in the field of constitutional law. There are two reasons for this. One is practical, as we wish to make a contribution in the field of comparative constitutional law. The other is more substantive. Constitutional law is inherently more political than other areas of law and its stakes for the broader society are usually higher. Judges, particularly those who aim to influence the course of their societies, often do so through constitutional law. Thus, we might expect the phenomenon of towering judges to be particularly well represented in this area. As a result of this choice, most of the judges in the volume operated in the past half-century. The global rise in the power and influence of constitutional courts is a relatively recent phenomenon in most parts of the world, beginning in earnest only after World War II. Finally, we also aimed to include judges from a variety of legal systems and geographical areas, as well as from both the global North and the global South so as to provide a wide case selection for comparative analysis and to make the volume as inclusive as possible.

Following these guidelines, we explore in this volume the legacy of the following judges (ordered here alphabetically by jurisdiction and including tenures on their respective apex or constitutional courts): Australia (Chief Justice Sir Anthony Mason, 1972–95[2]); Chile (Judge Eugenio Valenzuela, 1981–9/1997–2006); Columbia (Justice Manuel Cepeda, 2001–9[3]); Hong Kong (Chief Justice Andrew Li, 1997–2010; and Justice Kemal Bokhary, 1997–2012); Hungary (President László

---

[2] 1987–95 as chief justice.
[3] 2005–6 as president.

Sólyom, 1990–8); India (Chief Justice PN Bhagwati, 1973–86[4]); Ireland (Chief Justice Hugh Kennedy, 1924–36); Israel (President Aharon Barak, 1978–2006[5]); Nepal (Chief Justice Kalyan Shrestha, 2005–16[6]); Singapore (Chief Justice Chan Sek Keong, 2006–12[7]); South Africa (Chief Justice Arthur Chaskalson, 1994–2005[8]); United Kingdom (Lady Hale, President of the Supreme Court, 2009–20[9]); United States (Chief Justice Earl Warren, 1953–69; Chief Justice Charles Evans Hughes, 1930–41[10]; Justice William Brennan, 1956–90; Justice Hugo Black, 1937–71; and Justice Owen Roberts, 1930–45); and Vietnam (Chief Justice Truong Hoa Binh, 2007–16).

II PREVIEW OF CHAPTERS

In Chapter 1, Iddo Porat discusses towering judges in the context of global constitutionalism. This chapter explains how a strong cosmopolitan and liberal turn in global politics in the 1990s, and the creation of a global community of judges, may have incentivized the emergence of towering judges and affected the liberal content of their judicial legacies. It uses this hypothesis to highlight some of the normative concerns stemming out of toweringness and its possible relationship to the current conservative backlash in many jurisdictions. In Chapter 2, Mark Tushnet examines the concept of toweringness in relative terms and across different eras in the US Supreme Court. He focuses, in particular, on Chief Justices Charles Evans Hughes and Earl Warren and their relationships to other towering and less-than-towering justices. Gabrielle Appleby and Andrew Lynch discuss the legacy of Sir Anthony Mason in Chapter 3. Mason, who served on the High Court of Australia for twenty-three years (eight years as chief justice), forged a new jurisprudential path for the Court. He exercised "jurisprudential leadership" to move the Court away from the legalism of Sir Owen Dixon (another towering judge candidate) toward "constitutional guardianship" in which he defended the Court's rights-protective case law in the media and against public criticism.[11] In Chapter 4, Rosemary Hunter and Erika Rackley discuss the most recently active judge in the volume: Lady Hale, President of the UK Supreme Court until 2020. They examine Hale's jurisprudential, administrative, and wider community leadership as a justice and as president of the Supreme Court, drawing on a large data set of cases, extrajudicial speeches,

---

[4] 1985–6 as chief justice.
[5] 1995–2006 as president.
[6] 2015–16 as chief justice.
[7] Chan also served as a judicial commissioner (1986–8) and as a puisne judge of the Supreme Court (1988–92).
[8] President of the Constitutional Court (1994–2001); chief justice of South Africa (2001–5). This is the same position, but the title changed in 2001.
[9] 2017–20 as president.
[10] Hughes also served as an associate justice of the US Supreme Court (1910–16).
[11] Appleby and Lynch, Chapter 3.

publications, and annual reports since the Supreme Court's inception in 2009. In addition to this statistical analysis, Hunter and Rackley explore a further distinctive aspect of Hale's judicial approach – her feminism – including her substantive contributions to the jurisprudence of equality, human rights, diversity, and social justice.

Moving beyond these "usual suspects,"[12] Tom Daly brings to light the intellectual brilliance and statesmanship of Ireland's Chief Justice Hugh Kennedy in Chapter 5. Kennedy was a central architect behind the 1922 Constitution of the Irish Free State, which ensured maximal autonomy for Ireland from the British Empire. Later, as Ireland's first chief justice, Kennedy bolstered the reputation and independence of the Court, including an assertion (in dissent) that repressive constitutional amendments could be held unconstitutional, four decades before the Indian Supreme Court first announced the basic structure doctrine. In Chapter 6, Chin Leng Lim discusses the legacies of two founding justices of the Hong Kong Court of Final Appeal: Chief Justice Andrew Li and Justice Kemal Bokhary. Lim argues that these two justices explained better than their colleagues the meaning of the unique "one country, two systems" model under which Hong Kong is governed. While Li's judgments reflect a perfectionist theory of the "civic virtues" underlying Hong Kong's Basic Law, Bokhary's jurisprudence reflects a stance of "rights perfectionism" that seeks to advance particular political outcomes.[13]

Chapter 7 explores the towering judge phenomenon in a country with some authoritarian elements in its regime. Jaclyn Neo and Kevin Tan explain the importance of Chief Justice Chan Sek Keong (2006–12), whose keen intellect, administrative efficiency, and prodigious output allowed him to be a towering figure in a constrained political context. In Chapter 8, Mara Malagodi discusses another Asian judge who towered despite difficult circumstances. Chief Justice Kalyan Shrestha of Nepal served on the Supreme Court from the end of that country's civil war and through its tumultuous transition to constitutional democracy. Despite bouts of emergency and autocratic rule, the dissolution of a constituent assembly, and violence surrounding the constitution-making process, Shrestha remained a steadfast champion of fundamental rights and judicial independence.

The next four chapters focus on judges who initiated or presided over constitutional revolutions in their countries. In Chapter 9, Alon Harel discusses President Aharon Barak of Israel, the quintessential towering judge, who is renowned globally for his jurisprudence and scholarship. Harel argues that Israel under Barak's tenure as president of the Supreme Court (1995–2006) underwent two revolutions: the judiciary-empowerment revolution and the liberal rights revolution. He notes that while much of the criticism directed against Barak's legacy is directed against the former (judiciary-empowerment) revolution, conservative forces in Israel have no

[12] Ran Hirschl, *Comparative Matters: The Renaissance of Comparative Constitutional Law* (Cambridge University Press, 2014) 192.
[13] Lim, Chapter 6.

urgent interest in overturning that revolution. Rather, this judiciary-empowerment revolution is currently being used by conservative groups in Israel to undo the liberal revolution. Along similar lines, Rehan Abeyratne argues in Chapter 10 that Chief Justice PN Bhagwati's legacy in India has been undermined since his retirement. While Bhagwati was the driving force behind public interest litigation (PIL) in the 1980s, his aversion to formalism and regular procedural and evidentiary rules imbued the Supreme Court and High Courts of India with tremendous flexibility and independent authority to dictate the terms of public policy – powers they have not always wielded with care. In addition, many of his landmark judgments lack firm doctrinal foundations, and entrenched a style of *ipse dixit* decision-making in the Indian higher judiciary. In Chapter 11, David Landau assesses the legacy of Justice Manuel Cepeda of Colombia, whose main contribution was an institutional one. Though he served on the Constitutional Court for only eight years, Cepeda skillfully navigated the fraught political environment in Colombia to develop the *tutela* mechanism and permit the Court to engage in "mega-interventions" on issues of internally displaced persons and health without significant political backlash.[14] Another institution-builder, albeit in a different sense, was post-apartheid South Africa's first president of the Constitutional Court: Arthur Chaskalson. Dennis Davis, who currently sits as a judge on the High Court of South Africa, recounts Chaskalson's many accomplishments in Chapter 12. Among other things, Chaskalson was a prominent public interest lawyer who challenged the validity of pernicious apartheid-era laws. He played a key role in drafting South Africa's 1996 Constitution, and carefully guided the Constitutional Court in its early years to develop a reputation for legal rigor and excellence – a model for the rest of the world.

The final three country-specific chapters deal with towering judges in transitional or authoritarian states. In Chapter 13, Gábor Attila Tóth discusses the legacy of László Sólyom, president of the Hungarian Constitutional Court between 1990 and 1998. Tóth notes that while there is widespread agreement that Sólyom is the most influential Hungarian jurist of the post-Soviet era, there is no consensus on the nature or effectiveness of his legacy. Tóth's chapter does not offer "simple or easy answers";[15] instead, it analyzes Sólyom's complex legacy with respect to his role in Hungary's democratic transition, his main judgments on the Court, and his change of stance on key constitutional issues when serving as the head of state from 2005 to 2010. In Chapter 14, Bui Ngoc Son presents a case study of a towering judge in a socialist state: Vietnam. Truong Hoa Binh was appointed as chief justice of the Supreme People's Court despite having no legal training or prior experience as a judge. In fact, he served in the police force before his elevation to the Court. But, as Bui notes, this lack of training can be explained contextually, as the Supreme People's Court in Vietnam serves an instrumental function to propagate support

---

[14] Landau, Chapter 11.
[15] Tóth, Chapter 13.

for the Communist Party. Truong, as a loyal member of the Party, was able to fulfill this function, while also using his role as chief justice to bring about significant institutional reforms to the Vietnamese judiciary. Chapter 15, too, focuses on a judge in an authoritarian regime but one who chose a different modus operandi vis-à-vis the ruling regime. Judge Eugenio Valenzuela of the Chilean Constitutional Court opted to stand up to General Pinochet's dictatorship in the 1980s. As Sergio Verdugo explains, Valenzuela was able to turn "the Pinochet Constitution against the interests of Pinochet," including by enforcing the rules of a 1988 plebiscite that led to the downfall of the Pinochet regime.[16]

Finally, in Chapter 16, Rosalind Dixon draws insights from the previous chapters to bring greater clarity to the concept of towering judges. Among other things, she discusses (a) the relevant notions of judicial influence involved; (b) its temporal aspects; and (c) the relative versus absolute nature of the concept.

III REVIEW OF EXISTING LITERATURE

There are two main bodies of literature that our study engages with and contributes to: (1) comparative constitutional law and (2) judicial leadership and behavior. The comparative constitutional law literature is seldom concerned with the role of individual judges and judicial leadership. It is largely concerned with the institutional role and adjudicative functions of judges and courts. Our volume, therefore, fills a void in the comparative constitutional literature by adding the personal judicial angle and placing it within the larger and impersonal phenomena analyzed by the field. Meanwhile, the judicial leadership and behavior literature lacks the global and comparative perspectives that our volume seeks to provide. In what follows, we survey the existing literature in these two bodies of research to show how our study fits within it.

The existing literature on judges and judiciaries in comparative constitutional law focuses mostly on institutional aspects of the role and function of judges. There is, firstly, a large body of literature on judicial review. This literature includes a normative debate on the desirability and legitimacy of judicial review both at a theoretical level and in specific contexts. Famous in this context is the debate, which is partly comparative, between Jeremy Waldron[17] and Richard Fallon.[18] There is also descriptive and explanatory comparative research on judicial review. Tom Ginsburg, for example, links the rise of constitutional judicial review with the spread of democracy. He argues that parties who fear election losses may opt for

---

[16] Verdugo, Chapter 15.

[17] Jeremy Waldron, "The Core of the Case Against Judicial Review" (2006) 115 *Yale Law Journal* 1346 (arguing that judicial review, under specific conditions, is not necessary as legislatures can protect rights equally, if not more, effectively).

[18] Richard H Fallon, "The Core of an Uneasy Case for Judicial Review" (2008) 121 *Harvard Law Review* 1693, 1699 (responding to Waldron with a limited defense of judicial review in which he contends that some rights might be worthy of "overprotection" from multiple institutions and that judicial review could promote "morally better outcomes").

judicial review as "a form of political insurance that mitigates the risk of electoral loss."[19] In a recent large-N study, using a data set of constitutional review for 204 countries from 1781 to 2011, Ginsburg and Versteeg find that such strategic, domestic political considerations drive the adoption of constitutional review, much more so than "ideational factors" or the diffusion of norms.[20] In authoritarian or illiberal states, too, judicial review has expanded significantly in recent decades as a means, inter alia, to legitimate ruling regimes, to delegate controversial policy questions, and to provide legal certainty on economic matters to encourage foreign investment.[21] There is also a well-developed comparative literature on different forms of judicial review, such as strong and weak-form judicial review,[22] and on constitutional dialogue between the judiciary and political branches.[23]

Secondly, there is a large comparative literature on the globalization of constitutional adjudication, the interactions and sharing of ideas among constitutional courts, and the global rise of judicial power. Global constitutionalism has seen extensive research in recent times,[24] as has the documentation of trends in constitutional design[25] and of the migration of constitutional rights and norms across jurisdictions.[26] Ran Hirschl has shown how the global trend toward "juristocracy" has been aided by political elites who use judicial review for "hegemonic preservation."[27]

While both these types of comparative constitutional study – relating to judicial review and to globalization – greatly illuminate and set the background for the workings of the judges in our volume, none directly addresses the role of individual judges in driving constitutional change, which is the particular contribution of this volume.

---

[19]   Tom Ginsburg, "The Global Spread of Constitutional Review" in Keith E Whittington, R Daniel Keleman, and Gregory A Caldeira (eds.), *The Oxford Handbook of Law and Politics* (Oxford University Press, 2008).

[20]   Tom Ginsburg and Mila Versteeg, "Why Do Countries Adopt Constitutional Review?" (2013) 30 *Journal of Law, Economics, and Organization* 587, 589.

[21]   Tom Ginsburg and Tamir Moustafa, "Introduction: The Functions of Courts in Authoritarian Politics" in Tom Ginsburg and Tamir Moustafa (eds.), *Rule by Law: The Politics of Courts in Authoritarian Regimes* (Cambridge University Press, 2008).

[22]   See, e.g., Mark Tushnet, *Weak Courts, Strong Rights* (Princeton University Press, 2008) ch 2.

[23]   Peter W Hogg and Allison A Bushell, "The Charter Dialogue Between Courts and Legislatures" (1997) 35 *Osgoode Hall Law Journal* 75; Po Jen Yap, *Constitutional Dialogue in Common Law Asia* (Oxford University Press, 2015); Rosalind Dixon, "The Supreme Court of Canada, Charter Dialogue and Deference" (2009) 47 *Osgoode Hall Law Journal* 235.

[24]   See, e.g., Michel Rosenfeld, "Is Global Constitutionalism Meaningful or Desirable?' (2014) 25 *European Journal of International Law* 177; David S Law and Mila Versteeg, "The Evolution and Ideology of Global Constitutionalism" (2011) 99 *California Law Review* 1163.

[25]   David S Law and Mila Versteeg, "The Declining Influence of the United States Constitution" (2012) 87 *New York University Law Review* 762; Kim Lane Scheppele, "Aspirational and Aversive Constitutionalism: The Case for Studying Cross-Constitutional Influence Through Negative Models" (2003) 1 *International Journal of Constitutional Law* 296.

[26]   See, e.g., Alec Stone Sweet, "Constitutional Courts" in Michel Rosenfeld and Andras Sajo (eds.), *The Oxford Handbook of Comparative Constitutional Law* (Oxford University Press, 2012); Sujit Choudhry (ed.), *The Migration of Constitutional Ideas* (Cambridge University Press, 2009).

[27]   Ran Hirschl, *Towards Juristocracy: The Origins and Consequences of the New Constitutionalism* (Harvard University Press, 2004).

Our study also draws on, and contributes to, a second set of studies: those that focus on individual judges but usually do not emphasize the comparative angle. These are several academic genres relating to judicial personality and leadership.[28] First, there is a long-standing tradition of biographies of great judges and groups of judges in important historical moments.[29] There have also been studies on the role and importance of chief justices and constitutional court presidents. The chief justice of the United States has been the subject of several studies that have examined the effects of their institutional position and the concomitant strategic opportunities on judicial behavior.[30] Specifically, scholars have highlighted the chief justice's ability to set the agenda for deliberations, preside over the justices' internal conference, and assign opinions to individual justices as mechanisms for judicial leadership.[31] Kim Scheppele, in a study of President Laszlo Sólyom of the Hungarian Constitutional Court and Valerii Zorkin of the Russian Constitutional Court, noted that these men became leading public figures in the post-socialist era of their respective countries, and often took political leaders to task for failing to uphold constitutional principles.[32]

There are also studies about judicial leadership generally. In their study of judicial leadership in the United Kingdom – which has been adapted into Chapter 4 for this volume – Hunter and Rackley conducted a quantitative study of judicial leadership along three dimensions: administrative, jurisprudential, and community leadership.[33] Meanwhile, Arguelhes and Ribeiro argue that Brazilian Supreme Court justices may influence legal developments and the behavior of external actors in three ways: "(i) *agenda setting* (deciding what the court will decide); (ii) *position taking* (speaking on behalf of the court, thus signalling a potential judicial decision in specific directions); and (iii) *decision making* (resolving cases, controversies, and matters of dispute brought to the court)."[34]

---

[28] See, e.g., Richard A Posner, "The Learned Hand Biography and the Question of Judicial Greatness" (1994) 104 *Yale Law Journal* 511; Allan C Hutchinson, *Laughing at the Gods: Great Judges and How They Made the Common Law* (Cambridge University Press, 2012); Omri Ben-Zvi, "Judicial Greatness and the Duties of a Judge" (2016) 35 *Law and Philosophy* 615.

[29] See, e.g., Noah Feldman, *Scorpions: The Battles and Triumphs of FDR's Great Supreme Court Justices* (Twelve Books, 2010).

[30] See, e.g., Drew Noble Lanier, "Acclimation Effects and the Chief Justice: The Influence of Tenure and the Role on the Decisional Behavior of the Court's Leader, 1888–2007" (2011) 39 *American Politics Research* 682.

[31] G Edward White, "The Internal Powers of the Chief Justice: The Nineteenth Century Legacy" (2006) 154 *University of Pennsylvania Law Review* 1464.

[32] Kim Lane Scheppele, "Guardians of the Constitution: Constitutional Court Presidents and the Struggle for the Rule of Law in Post-Soviet Europe" (2006) 154 *University of Pennsylvania Law Review* 1757, 1758.

[33] Rosemary Hunter and Erika Rackley, "Judicial Leadership on the UK Supreme Court" (2018) 38 *Legal Studies* 191, 192.

[34] Diego Werneck Arguelhes and Leandro Molhano Ribeiro, "'The Court, It Is I'? Individual Judicial Powers in the Brazilian Supreme Court and Their Implications for Constitutional Theory" (2018) 7 *Global Constitutionalism* 236, 240.

Finally, there is a vast political science literature, largely emanating from the United States, on how judges decide cases. This literature largely rejects the traditional, "legal" model of adjudication in which judges decide cases on the basis of the facts and the relevant legal materials before them.[35] Instead, the American literature favors the "attitudinal model," which posits that judges' personal attitudes, backgrounds, and political views shape their judgments.[36] While this approach has great appeal in the United States, particularly with respect to the deeply divided Supreme Court, it is inapposite in a comparative context, as institutional and cultural factors also appear to affect judicial decision-making. Benjamin Alarie and Andrew J Green recently published a detailed cross-country examination of the apex courts in the United States, the United Kingdom, Canada, India, and Australia. They show that judges exhibit varying degrees of commitment to their own ideals and cooperation with their colleagues based on institutional design. As such, they describe four types of courts: (1) an "attitudinal court" (US Supreme Court) in which judges are "both politicized and independent"; (2) a "positivist court" in which judges are "independent and ground their decisions in legal considerations" (Australian High Court); (3) a "strategic court" that comprises judges that are both politicized and collegial (Canadian Supreme Court); and (4) a "deliberative court" in which judges look for the best answer and enlist their colleagues in that search (UK Supreme Court).[37]

The chapters in this volume draw on these bodies of literature. They also seek to contribute to these bodies from a new perspective. By shifting the focus away from institutional questions about the role and legitimacy of courts, and from judicial decision-making at the domestic level or among a few jurisdictions, this volume aims to make an original contribution to the comparative constitutional literature.

IV DIMENSIONS OF TOWERINGNESS

As the following chapters will demonstrate, there are several ways in which judges leave towering legacies. We distinguish among three dimensions along which a judge may be towering – the political, the institutional, and the jurisprudential. We should note that this is not meant to be an exhaustive set of criteria and there is some overlap among these dimensions. Of course, judges could tower in more than one of these categories and most of the judges included in this volume do precisely that.

Political towering judges are those that promote a particular ideological, moral, and/ or political agenda of change. Examples include President Barak and Chief Justices

[35] Benjamin Alarie and Andrew J Green, *Commitment and Cooperation on High Courts: A Cross-Country Examination of Institutional Constraints on Judges* (Oxford University Press, 2017) 3.

[36] Ibid.; Jeffrey A Segal and Harold J Spaeth, *The Supreme Court and the Attitudinal Model Revisited* (Cambridge University Press, 2002).

[37] Alarie and Green (*supra* n 35) 6–8. The Indian and Israeli Supreme Courts are a mix of the strategic and deliberative models.

Bhagwati and Warren, who pushed for a liberal and rights-protecting ideological change. Other judges pursued agendas tied to particular circumstances, such as helping to oust an autocratic regime in the case of Judge Valenzuela in Chile, or to integrate their country into the European Union, as President Sólyom sought to do in Hungary.

Institutional towering judges leave a lasting legacy in terms of the legal institutions they create, enhance, and/or protect. Some of these judges, including Chief Justices Kennedy and Chaskalson, along with President Sólyom, helped draft the constitutions that they would then interpret on apex courts. As Rosalind Dixon argues, the involvement of Chief Justice Chaskalson, among others, in the drafting process increased political support for the Constitutional Court of South Africa, while President Sólyom engaged in political advocacy on behalf of the Court he helped to create.[38] Several of our judges were elevated to the bench immediately after a new constitution was adopted, including Chief Justice Li and Justice Bokhary in Hong Kong, Chief Justice Kennedy in Ireland, and Chief Justice Shrestha in Nepal, and they were instrumental in building institutional legitimacy for their respective courts and guiding those courts through turbulent political times. President Barak is unique in this regard, as he initiated a constitutional revolution, based on two new Basic Laws in Israel, and then entrenched it through his judgments. Some judges built new institutional mechanisms that expanded their court's jurisdiction. For instance, Justice Cepeda was instrumental in creating the *tutela* system in Colombia, while Chief Justice Bhagwati was the driving force behind public interest litigation in India. Finally, some of these towering judges, like Justice Cepeda in Colombia, used their stature to protect judicial independence in the face of political pressure.

The last category is the most familiar – judges who leave a *jurisprudential* or intellectual mark on the court, through the force, legal craft, and/or sheer number of their opinions, or by marshaling their colleagues to move the law significantly in a particular direction. As Mark Tushnet notes in Chapter 2, some towering judges are intellectual leaders, while others are social leaders. Thus, while Justice Brennan was the intellectual leader of the Warren Court, in terms of authoring landmark judgments and developing the most consequential doctrines, Chief Justice Warren was the social leader, making the court work cohesively and serving as a mentor for other justices. Chief Justices Chan and Bhagwati along with President Barak fall into the former category, while Chief Justice Chaskalson fits in the latter. Other justices, such as Sir Anthony Mason, provided both kinds of leadership in near equal measure.

V TOWERING JUDGES IN CONTEXT

This volume is comparative in scope. It examines a common phenomenon – towering judges – on a spectrum of very different settings. This can tell us much

---

[38] Rosalind Dixon, "Constitutional Design Two Ways: Constitutional Drafters As Judges" (2019) 57 *Virginia Journal of International Law* 1, 31–4.

about the phenomenon as well as the various settings. We discuss three main comparative, contextual factors that affect the phenomenon of towering judges: institutional, historical, and political.

V.A *Institutional Context*

The first institutional distinction we draw is between the two main legal families – common law and civil law. This distinction quite obviously favors common law over civil law as a conducive institutional background for toweringness. As a generalization, common law personalizes the judicial product while civil law does the opposite by anonymizing it. The chapters in this volume bring out this distinction clearly. Both Neo and Tan and Chin Leng Lim emphasize how the common law tradition made the personalization of judgments almost inevitable, and thus allowed for the formation of towering judges, even within systems – Singapore and post-1997 Hong Kong – that, in other respects, sharply limited the opportunities for judicial personalization. Nine out of the fourteen jurisdictions covered in this volume are common law or common law affiliated systems: Australia, India, Ireland, Israel, Hong Kong, Singapore, South Africa, the United Kingdom, and the United States.

We also note that Western European civil law jurisdictions are missing from this volume, including Germany, Italy, France, and Spain. This can be attributed partly to the civil law tradition according to which, in France, for example, dissenting opinions are not published; nor is the voting count of the judges. Thus, one cannot attribute a decision to a particular judge. In addition, civil law decisions are very short and built as logical syllogisms. There is no established tradition of precedents. This prevents the personalization of judgments and the building of a personal jurisprudence as is seen in the common law world. The German Federal Constitutional Court (GFCC) stands as an exception. It publishes relatively long and detailed decisions, with dissenting opinions. However, in Germany, too, the activism of the Court is tempered by a strong formalist tradition that shies away from the personalization of judgment and from the glorification of individual judges.[39]

That there are no Western European civil law judges in the volume can also be attributed to the Kelsenian model of constitutional courts that became the norm in Europe after World War II.[40] In this model, among other things, judicial tenures are limited and judges rotate. As Tushnet points out in Chapter 2, the long tenures of US Supreme Court justices were crucial for the development of towering judges, as

---

[39] The Federal Constitutional Court has, nonetheless, contributed to significant – even transformative – constitutionalism in Germany. See Michaela Hailbronner, *Traditions and Transformations: The Rise of German Constitutionalism* (Oxford University Press, 2015); Michaela Hailbronner, "Transformative Constitutionalism: Not Only in the Global South" (2017) 65 *American Journal of Comparative Law* 527.

[40] Stone Sweet (*supra* n 26).

justices are able to develop their jurisprudence and build influence over a long period. In the United States, there is no retirement age for Supreme Court justices and, therefore, judicial tenures of two or three decades are not uncommon. The judges included in this volume from Israel and Australia also served for very long periods – each served at least twenty years on their respective apex courts. In continental Europe, by comparison, most constitutional courts have fixed tenures of at most twelve years (Germany and Slovakia). Constitutional Court justices serve for a nine-year term in Spain and Italy and for ten years in the Czech Republic. A few countries, such as Belgium and Austria, however, permit Constitutional Court judges to serve until a mandatory retirement age of seventy. The rotation of judges, and the rotation of chief justices, makes it hard to personalize entire courts or to view them in distinct periods. Consider, for instance, the Warren Court in the United States, or the Barak Court in Israel, each named after the chief justice. Meanwhile, in Germany, the GFCC is divided into two senates, each of which has its own chief justice and handles different types of cases. This institutional design makes it difficult to identify a leading judge at any particular time or to associate the jurisprudence of the Court with a singular figure.

However, we include two civil law jurisdictions from South America (Chile and Columbia) and one from Eastern Europe (Hungary). In South America, the civil law tradition makes for a fascinating setting that shapes the towering judges who emerge. Justice Manuel Cepeda, as Landau shows in Chapter 11, was able to tower despite a rigid civil law tradition and short judicial tenures. This was due, in part, to his common law education at Harvard Law School and the very activist nature of the Colombian Constitutional Court. The second judge from South America, Eugenio Valenzuela, stands out as a towering judge who is largely unknown, both in his time and today. As Verdugo points out in Chapter 15, Valenzuela's lack of public stature can be attributed to the lack of both precedent and personalization of judicial decisions. This raises the interesting question of whether reputation is necessary for identifying towering judges.

A third type of legal system, the socialist system, is represented in our volume by Bui Ngoc Son in Chapter 14 on Chief Justice Truong Hoa Binh from the Supreme People's Court of Vietnam. According to Bui, under socialist systems there is an institutionalization of personal judicial power, so that the chief justice becomes towering thanks mostly to his position as a senior Communist Party member rather than in recognition of any personal traits or judicial skills.

V.B *Historical Context*

Another contextual aspect that can shape, even induce, the emergence of towering judges is the historical moment in which they operate. In some cases, the moment almost necessitates judicial leadership and special judicial capabilities. Such is the case when the judiciary faces external threats or in times of political transition or constitutional foundation. Chief Justice Chaskalson was handpicked by President Mandela to build a court within a new constitutional system as the first chief justice of the South African Constitutional Court. This placed him in a strong position to become a towering judge. Moments of constitutional transition or revolution – as was the case of President Sólyom in Hungary, Justice Cepeda in Colombia, Chief Justice Shrestha in Nepal, and Chief Justice Li and Justice Bokhary in Hong Kong – are conducive to towering judges.

Such conditions, however, are neither sufficient nor necessary to produce these judges. Poland went through a democratic revolution akin to that in Hungary, but there does not seem to be a clear candidate for a towering judge in Poland. In addition, several of the judges surveyed in the volume did not operate in times of exception. This is true for President Barak in Israel, Chief Justice Warren in the United States, and Sir Anthony Mason in Australia. While these countries all experienced some societal transitions, their constitutional orders remained relatively stable when these towering judges emerged.

V.C *Political Context*

A third contextual aspect concerns the relationship between the judiciary and the political system; in particular, the perceived or actual strength and effectiveness of the political system vis-à-vis the judiciary. Several of the towering judges in the volume operated at times when the political system was weak or ineffective, or at least perceived to be so. In these situations, courts, led by towering judges, filled the void. And, in the process, these courts increased their popular legitimacy. As Harel shows in Chapter 9, President Barak led the Israeli Supreme Court to become an activist institution against the backdrop of an ineffective and crippled parliamentary system that characterized Israel in the 1980s. Appleby and Lynch similarly tell us in Chapter 3 how Mason's promotion of human rights and aboriginal rights occurred, in part, because of his diminished faith in parliament to protect minorities. In other countries, governance breakdowns were more severe. For instance, the Colombian Constitutional Court, led by Justice Cepeda (see Chapter 11), expanded the *tutela* mechanism, which expanded the Court's extensive administrative and managerial capacities in the face of bureaucratic failures with respect to internally displaced persons (IDPs) and the healthcare system. Similarly, Justice Bhagwati's entrenchment of PIL in India (see Chapter 10) capitalized on severe governance failures and the public's loss of faith in political leaders.

On the other end of the spectrum, Chief Justice Chaskalson in South Africa (see Chapter 12) limited the scope of his interventions to allow for the full operation of the newly elected democratic institutions under the post-apartheid Constitution, which were trusted to move South Africa forward. His towering stature, then, grew out of leading the court, hand-in-hand with the government, through a difficult transition and giving life to a new Constitution.

VI PERSONAL TRAITS AND BACKGROUND

Personality traits and background factors also contribute to the formation of towering judges. Among the judges studied, there is a great variety of backgrounds and individual characteristics. Some of these judges, like Justice Cepeda who attended Harvard Law School, received education from elite institutions. Many also came from well-established families. Justice Bhagwati's father, for instance, preceded him as a justice on the Indian Supreme Court. Others emerged from more humble backgrounds, such as President Barak, who was a Holocaust survivor and grew up in a family of very limited means. In terms of career paths, several of the judges surveyed, including Sir Anthony Mason, President Barak, and Chief Justice Chan Sek Keong, served as Attorney General before ascending to the bench. This background appears to have been useful, giving these judges political skills to deploy while on the bench.

Some judges also had political careers before their judicial tenures. Justice Cepeda served as a political advisor prior to becoming a judge. President Sólyom was involved with the opposition party in Hungary, while Chief Justice Hugh Kennedy was elected to the Irish Parliament for a short period. Chief Justice Warren of the United States was probably the most prominent politician among the judges in the volume. He served as the governor of California prior to his appointment as chief justice. While these judges arrived at the bench with political skills, others such as Chief Justice Chaskalson were known for their organizational, managerial, and leadership skills. Prior to his ascension to the Constitutional Court bench, Chaskalson helped to establish the Legal Resources Centre, a leading civil rights firm in South Africa, and served as its director from 1978 to 1993.

Two of the most activist and dramatic towering judges, President Sólyom in Hungary and President Barak in Israel, had distinguished academic careers. These were also some of the more theoretically ambitious judges. Both attempted to leave behind a well-developed theory of constitutional interpretation.[41] Truong Hoa Binh, perhaps fittingly in a socialist state, was a police officer with no legal training prior to becoming chief justice of Vietnam.

As with background and education, the personalities of these judges vary greatly. This variety attests to the fact that toweringness is not a quality that can be easily predicted by personality type. Leadership generally cannot be easily conditioned or taught, and leaders with a range of personalities may emerge. Personality traits range from the reserved and minimalist Chief Justice Chan to the very self-assured Justice Bhagwati to the charismatic President Sólyom. In some cases, as Mark Tushnet explains in Chapter 2 with respect to Chief Justice Hughes, a towering judge's

---

[41] Rivka Weill shows how Barak was able to strategically instill his jurisprudential legacy through well-calculated incremental steps. Rivka Weill, "The Strategic Common Law Court of Aharon Barak and Its Aftermath: On Judicially-Led Constitutional Revolutions and Democratic Backsliding" (forthcoming 2020) Law and Ethics of Human Rights, https://ssrn.com/abstract=3296578.

intellect enables dominance over less capable colleagues. In addition, many of these judges distinguished themselves through hard work and productivity. Many of the judges, including Chief Justice Chan and President Barak, were extremely product-ive, writing many more decisions than their peers, juggling managerial duties and even academic writing in addition to their judicial tasks. Such output permitted these judges to build a substantial jurisprudence that would endure and bind future judges.

VII TOWERING JUDGES AND THE OTHER JUDGES ON THE COURT

The towering judges surveyed in this volume adopted different approaches toward their fellow judges. To some extent, these approaches derived from the institutional and cultural contexts in which they operated, though there appear to have been some strategic calculations on the judges' part as well.

As Rosalind Dixon notes in Chapter 15, there are two broad approaches toward their fellow judges: collegial and individualist. Collegial judges manifest their leadership and influence on the court by forming coalitions, by building a sense of common purpose, and by assuming leadership among equals in a collegial body. This approach is evident in the leadership styles of Sir Anthony Mason and Chief Justices Li and Chaskalson.

A sense of collegiality is strengthened when the Court is socially cohesive. Sir Anthony Mason's tenure in Australia comprised judges that respected one another, were all individually very capable, and served together for a long time. These factors enabled the High Court to move forward collectively and to be viewed as "the Mason Court." Chief Justice Chaskalson's Court operated in a similar spirit. Although the South African Constitutional Court in its early years comprised judges from very different backgrounds – whites, blacks, anti-apartheid activists, and judges from the apartheid era – the judges cohered in terms of ethos and shared purpose, allowing Chaskalson to lead them in collegial fashion.

Other judges in the volume exercised collegial leadership in a more limited sense. In Chapter 15, Sergio Verdugo shows how Justice Valenzuela led a faction of Chilean justices against the Pinochet regime. Mark Tushnet explains in Chapter 2 how Chief Justice Warren was able to get his colleagues on board for the landmark *Brown* v *Board of Education* judgment, even if they were otherwise divided. President Barak, meanwhile, as Alon Harel reveals in Chapter 9, entered the Israeli Supreme Court at a time when it was not cohesive, although it gradually became more aligned under his leadership (and influence over the nomination process).

Other judges were less effective at coalition-building and sought to bring about constitutional change single-handedly. Justice Bhagwati, for instance, was disliked by many of his colleagues and the members of the government, which limited his ability to get allies appointed to the Supreme Court (see Chapter 10). President Sólyom (Chapter 13) and President Barak (Chapter 9), while not necessarily at odds with their peers, were both clear intellectual leaders of their courts. They attained greater status than their peers, rather than ruling in the more collegial manner of first among equals.

A final question arises as to the other judges who serve with a towering judge. Must toweringness always be assessed in relation to the qualities of the other judges on the court? And, if so, what community of judges must the towering judge be compared to when their legacy is assessed? These questions do not have a single answer. The chapters in this volume will each canvass the relevant community in relation to which particular judges towered. Further, while "toweringess" is a relational concept, the distinctiveness of a judge's contribution does not necessarily depend on the lack of ability of other judges, as some judges towered among very able colleagues. For instance, as Mark Tushnet argues in Chapter 2, Chief Justice Earl Warren and Justice William Brennan were towering judges who served concurrently but evinced different styles of leadership and impacted the US Supreme Court in distinct ways.

VIII TOWERING JUDGES AND GLOBALIZATION

Towering judges are not just the product of their own societies and individual circumstances. They are also local manifestations of global trends. This aspect of towering judges is evident throughout the volume, as many of these judges emerged between the 1980s and 2000s. As Iddo Porat discusses in Chapter 1, this period is the high watermark of global constitutionalism, with the diffusion of constitutional norms to a third wave of democracies and the rise in the influence and number of constitutional courts.[42] It is also the apex period for international human rights and for judges to attain global prestige. Thus, the phenomenon of towering judges is to some extent the product of an era, which is evident in some of the career paths of the judges in this volume.

Globalization interacts with the phenomenon of towering judges in other ways, too. Many of these judges had significant experiences abroad. Cepeda, Barak, Sólyom, Bokhary, and Shrestha all pursued higher studies in Western Europe or the United States. In addition, most towering judges regularly cited foreign court decisions as well as international human rights instruments. The jurisprudence of the European Court of Human Rights was particularly influential on many of the towering judges surveyed, as were the Universal Declaration of Human Rights (UDHR) and the International Covenant on Civil and Political Rights (ICCPR). Finally, many of

---

[42] Hirschl (*supra* n 27); Ian Kershaw, *The Global Age: Europe 1950–2017* (Penguin, 2019); Tom Ginsburg, "The Global Spread of Constitutional Review" in Keith E Whittington, R Daniel Keleman, and Gregory A Caldeira (eds.), *The Oxford Handbook of Law and Politics* (Oxford University Press, 2008).

these judges were part of an international judicial network. President Barak, President Sólyom, and Justice Cepeda were all part of the Global Constitutionalism Seminar at Yale Law School.[43] Sir Anthony Mason, following his retirement from the High Court of Australia, served as a non-permanent judge on the Court of Final Appeal (CFA) in Hong Kong. Lady Hale followed suit, joining the CFA as a non-permanent judge in 2018. Justices Bhagwati and Cepeda had extensive assignments from the United Nations and other international bodies, while President Barak regularly teaches courses in Israel and abroad.

IX METHODOLOGICAL AND OTHER CHALLENGES

We conclude by exploring some of the methodological and other challenges we faced in this project. We stress three main challenges: (1) normative assessment, (2) historical contingency, and (3) selection.

Assessing a judge's normative legacy raises several concerns. First, as Mara Malagodi points out in Chapter 8, the author's personal view of the judge may influence their scholarship. Malagodi, who interviewed Chief Justice Shrestha extensively and knows him personally, makes a point of reminding herself of this danger. In Chapter 2, Mark Tushnet similarly questions whether we can dissociate our normative assessment of these judges from our conferring towering status on them. A possible critique against our volume, therefore, is that it confuses towering judges with those judges that we, or the authors, deem praiseworthy, and that our professed attempt to dissociate normative from descriptive is unsuccessful. We are well aware of this danger. We are also aware of the danger that some would read this book as a work of praise for activist judges and judicial empowerment. This is not how we conceived of the project. We believe that the careful reader will be able to find a variety of perspectives on the phenomenon of towering judges, including some very critical ones. The careful reader will also gain a nuanced view of the judges described in this volume, which acknowledges many of them for great achievements while also analyzing their limitations and mistakes.

Another challenge with normative assessment relates to historical contingency. In Chapter 2, Mark Tushnet points out, for instance, that a judge's reputation may change over time. This raises the question of whether judges should be assessed in their own time or today. Take, for instance, US Supreme Court Justice Felix Frankfurter. While he was regarded highly in his own time, Tushnet argues that

---

[43]   See Judith Resnik and Clare Ryan (eds.), *Global Reconfigurations, Constitutional Obligations, and Everyday Life* (Gruber Foundation, 2018) iii https://documents.law.yale.edu/sites/default/files/gcs2018 .pdf ("As we continue the process of intergenerational transitions, this Seminar is indebted to its founding and early participants: Yale Law School professors ... and constitutional court justices including Aharon Barak (Israel), Pedro Cruz Villalón (Spain), Lech Garlicki (Poland), Dieter Grimm (Germany), Frank Iacobucci (Canada), and László Sólyom (Hungary)"). Justice Cepeda also appears in the program. See ibid. 1.

he has since fallen out of favor. The opposite may also happen: a judge who was not fully appreciated in their era may gain greater recognition over time. This creates a challenge in identifying towering judges. Similarly, one may ask, to what degree should a judge's impact over time be considered in the assessment of their "toweringness"? Tom Daly, for example, in Chapter 5, stresses that the magnitude of Chief Justice Kennedy's impact is greater in retrospect. Appleby and Lynch, meanwhile, argue in Chapter 3 that, if looked at from today's perspective, Sir Anthony Mason's influence is greater than Sir Owen Dixon's – his main rival as a towering judge in Australia. Other judges, however, have seen their legacy dismantled over time. This is clearly the case in Hungary, where the Orban regime has undone much of President Sólyom's work (see Chapter 13). It may also be the case with President Barak in Israel, whose legacy is under attack through a political backlash, as noted by Alon Harel in Chapter 9.

With respect to these challenges, all the judges chosen for this volume were towering figures in their own time and, for the most part, retain that status today. In terms of their impact, all the judges we chose had a significant impact on the development and course of constitutional law in their own jurisdiction. Finally, we did not penalize judges whose legacy has been eroded over time. This is because the degree to which a judicial legacy endures is based on a number of factors, including the political course a country may take, that are beyond the judge's control. And, as mentioned above, a reaction to a judge, even if in terms of attempting to negate their legacy, may also attest to their influence and, hence, their toweringness.

The final methodological challenge, as discussed in Section I, was selection. There are four criticisms that might be leveled at our final choice of towering judges: first, that the judges chosen were not as towering as others from the same jurisdiction; second, that some jurisdictions with towering judges were excluded; third, that most of our selected judges are liberal; and fourth, that most of these judges are male. With respect to the first potential criticism, we tried our best to choose judges that we view as clearly towering within each jurisdiction, though we recognize that reasonable minds may disagree and that some jurisdictions may produce more than one towering judge even at the same time. Tushnet, for example, discusses towering judges from the same eras on the US Supreme Court. As to the second potential challenge, we concede that judges from countries we did not include may, in fact, be towering figures. Our aim, however, was to include judges that would be conducive to an interesting scholarly and comparative analysis. Discussing every potential towering judge from around the world would not be manageable in a single volume.

A third selection concern is that we did not include any conservative judges, at least not within the liberal democracies that we surveyed. This is regrettable, and we hope that future research fills that void. As mentioned, our definition of a towering judge aims to be normatively neutral and does not convey any specific ideological or political worldview, so there is nothing in principle to exclude a conservative judge from our collection. However, there may also be good reasons for this absence. Conservative judges often associate themselves with a formalist and nonpersonal judicial style, which seems antithetical to toweringness. Some have also resisted the global constitutionalism movement that partly accounts for the rise of towering judges in recent decades.[44] It may, therefore, be harder to find such towering judges, although not impossible.[45]

A fourth concern is that only one of the judges in the volume is a woman. As Rosalind Dixon explains in Chapter 16, there are many possible explanations for this. Female judges may not assert themselves as forcefully as their male counterparts such that few rise to the status of "towering judge." It may also be that when female judges stake a claim to be a towering judge, they trigger an adverse reaction in their colleagues, which thwarts their rise. The fact that most of our chosen judges were chief justices may also account for the gender disparity, as few female justices around the world have been appointed to this post. Whatever the reason, we wanted to highlight this as a concern with the concept and selection of towering judges.

With these observations in mind, we hope that you find interest and insight in the coming chapters and that this volume can become the first installment of further studies of judges as drivers of constitutional change in a comparative perspective.

---

[44] See Norman Dorsen, "The Relevance of Foreign Legal Materials in U.S. Constitutional Cases: A Conversation Between Justice Antonin Scalia and Justice Stephen Breyer" (2005) 3(4) *International Journal of Constitutional Law* 519.

[45] Many constitutional scholars, including those that disagree with his jurisprudence, have cited Antonin Scalia as a great – even towering – judge. See, e.g., Jamal Greene, "Liberal Love for Antonin Scalia" *NY Times*, February 14, 2016, www.nytimes.com/2016/02/15/opinion/what-liberals-learned-from-antonin-scalia.html.

Towering Judges and Global Constitutionalism

Iddo Porat

In 2016, judges from around the world met, for the twentieth time, at the Yale Law School Global Constitutional Seminar. Opening this meeting, Yale Law Professor Owen Fiss described the circumstances that led to the creation of this seminar in 1996: "This seminar was a product of its time – a triumphant moment in the history of democratic constitutionalism viewed on a world scale ... [It] might be seen as a tribute to the triumph of democratic constitutionalism in so many parts of the world in the early 1990s ....."[1] The purpose of this chapter is to situate the phenomenon of towering judges in the context of the historical and global moment described above, which I will term the height of global constitutionalism. I will argue that to fully understand the phenomenon of towering judges, we must view it not only as a compilation of discreet instances, each couched in its own particular local circumstances, but also as a global phenomenon set at a particular time in global history.

By global constitutionalism, I mean three things: (1) the idea of constitutionalism and constitutional rights as a shared universal project, based on the notion of liberal cosmopolitanism; (2) the reality of constitutional courts and judges interacting globally around this notion; and (3) the particular historical time when this concept, together with a related set of ideas, came to the fore and dominated global politics.[2] For several (although not all) of the judges included in this book, the fact that they

---

[1] Owen Fiss, "Remarks on the 20th Anniversary of the Global Constitutional Seminar 1996–2016" (September 21, 2016), https://law.yale.edu/centers-workshops/gruber-program-global-justice-and-womens-rights/global-constitutionalism-seminar/global-constitutionalism-20th-anniversary/remarks-20th-anniversary.

[2] Definitions of global constitutionalism vary. See, for example, Antje Wiener, Anthony Lang, James Tully, Miguel Maduro, and Mattias Kumm, "Global Constitutionalism: Human Rights, Democracy and the Rule of Law" (2012) 1 *Global Constitutionalism* 1. See also Alec Stone Sweet and Jud Mathews, "Proportionality Balancing and Global Constitutionalism" (2008) 47 *Columbia Journal of Transnational Law* 72; Michel Rosenfeld, "Is Global Constitutionalism Meaningful or Desirable?" (2014) 25(1) *European Journal of International Law* 177; David S Law and Mila Versteeg, "The Evolution and Ideology of Global Constitutionalism" (2011) 99 *California Law Review* 1163; Peer Zumbansen, "Comparative, Global and Transnational Constitutionalism: The Emergence of a Transnational Legal-Pluralist Order" (2012) 1 *Global Constitutionalism* 16.

became towering judges, the particular ways in which they were towering judges, and the ideas and values they promoted were due, at least in part, to the fact that they operated during the height of global constitutionalism between the early 1980s and the late 2000s. It is, therefore, no coincidence that out of the nineteen judges included in this book, all but six (Chief Justice Hugh Kennedy from Ireland, and the five American justices surveyed in Chapter 2) operated roughly within these relevant years.[3]

I will explore three main interrelated reasons for the connection between global constitutionalism and towering judges. First, global constitutionalism placed constitutional judges at the center of the moral and ideological revolution it presented. This revolution, which started as a reaction to World War II and reached its peak after the fall of the Soviet bloc, replaced the nationalism and populism of the Nazi and Fascist regimes with cosmopolitanism, elite institutions, and human rights protections of minorities. Constitutional judges shared all these attributes in the clearest way and thus became the personification of this new age. This, in turn, empowered constitutional judges and enhanced judicial personal agency, which sometimes manifested as "toweringness."

Second, and relatedly, global constitutionalism was also a project, a direction, and an ideal at which to strive. During the height of global constitutionalism, judges participated in a collaborative global effort to instill and protect a shared and objective set of universal rights and sought to bring their respective societies as close as possible to that ideal. I call this "the Platonic Conception" of constitutional rights. This collaborative effort, too, empowered judges and enhanced toweringness, as it required leadership and personal agency.

Finally, global constitutionalism consisted of interactions among courts and judges around the globe and created a *global community of judges*.[4] The Yale Law School Global Constitutional Seminar, mentioned at the start of this chapter, is a prime example of this community. Its participants over the years included several of the judges analyzed in this book.[5] To belong to this community, domestic judges

<hr/>

[3] Following is the list of judges covered in this volume that operated roughly within the relevant years, ordered by jurisdiction: Australia (Chief Justice Sir Anthony Mason, 1972–95); Chile (Judge Eugenio Valenzuela, 1981–9 and 1997–2006); Columbia (Justice Manuel Cepeda, 2001–9); Hong Kong (Chief Justice Andrew Li, 1997–2010; Justice Kemal Bokhary, 1997–2012); Hungary (President László Sólyom, 1990–8); India (Chief Justice PN Bhagwati, 1973–86; Israel (President Aharon Barak, 1978–2006); Nepal (Chief Justice Kalyan Shrestha, 2005–16); Singapore (Chief Justice Chan Sek Keong, 2006–12); South Africa (Chief Justice Arthur Chaskalson, 1994–2005); United Kingdom (Lady Hale, President of the Supreme Court, 2009–20); and Vietnam (Chief Justice Truong Hoa Binh, 2007–16).

[4] The term follows Anne-Marie Slaughter's similar term: "global community of courts." Anne-Marie Slaughter, "A Global Community of Courts" (2003) 41 *Harvard International Law Journal* 191. Although terming it a community of courts rather than judges, Slaughter stresses: "This community of courts is constituted above all by the self-awareness of the national and international judges who play a part" (ibid. 192).

[5] Presidents Barak and Sólyom are recognized as among the founding members of the seminar: "As we continue the process of intergenerational transitions, this Seminar is indebted to its founding and early

had to distinguish themselves from the other judges in their country and indeed to tower above them. If a judge wanted to be included in this prestigious club of international judges, it was not enough, to use Mark Tushnet's term, to be "merely competent."[6]

Global constitutionalism can, therefore, help to explain the phenomenon of towering judges. It can also help to elaborate the content of their judicial contributions and explain why many of the judges in this volume produced cosmopolitan, liberal, and activist jurisprudence, based on nontextualist and expansive interpretations of constitutional rights. Lastly, global constitutionalism can also help to provide a critical assessment of towering judges as it shows them to be global political actors, actively engaged in political and normative debates.

This chapter proceeds as follows. Section 1.1 outlines the historical background of global constitutionalism and how it gave constitutional judges moral and political authority in their jurisdictions. Section 1.2 describes the Platonic Conception of constitutional rights and how it led to a creative and goal-oriented interpretation of rights. Section 1.3 discusses the global community of judges and its incentives. Section 1.4 explores the normative implications of the towering judges phenomenon.

1.1 GLOBAL CONSTITUTIONALISM AND JUDICIAL EMPOWERMENT

1.1.1 *The Rise of Global Constitutionalism*

Global constitutionalism, with its liberal and cosmopolitan ideology, and the view of constitutionalism as a shared global project evolved after World War II and as a reaction to it. The countries of Western Europe – Germany in particular – tried to reformulate themselves as an antithesis to the two major forces that shaped the Fascist and Nazi regimes – populism and nationalism.[7]

First, as a reaction to populism, the new European ideology put an emphasis on the education and inculcation of the liberal ideals of human dignity, equality, and democracy.[8] Those ideals were to be promoted top-down by elite institutions rather

participants: ... constitutional court justices including Aharon Barak (Israel), ... and László Sólyom (Hungary)." See Judith Resnik and Clare Ryan (eds.), *Global Reconfigurations, Constitutional Obligations, and Everyday Life* (Gruber Foundation, 2018) iii, https://documents.law.yale.edu/sites/default/files/gcs2018.pdf. Justice Manuel Cepeda was also a participant at the 2018 seminar (ibid. i).

6   See Chapter 2 in this volume.

7   According to Hanna Arendt, Nazism and Fascism rose to power because the democratization process gave political weight to the opinions and preferences of the masses, in a period in which they were especially vulnerable to irrational arguments and manipulation by demagogues. See Hanna Arendt, *The Origins of Totalitarianism* (Schocken, 1951). See also the discussion in Tony Bennett, "Theories of the Media, Theories of Society" in Michael Gurevitch (ed.), *Culture, Society and the Media* (Routledge, 1982) 30.

8   See, for example, David Phillips, *Educating the Germans: People and Policy in the British Zone of Germany, 1945–1949* (Bloomsbury, 2018) (documenting the evolution and development of education

than being left to evolve bottom-up from the general populace. The general populace, after all, cheered for Hitler and Mussolini and brought them to power, and
"ordinary men" were swept by demagogical rhetoric and extreme ideology to
become "Hitler's willing executioners."[9] Western Europe had to get away from the
populist sentiments of the masses, through the empowerment of elite figures and
institutions, in order to find a new and safe vantage point from which it could
reinvent itself.[10] In addition, the lessons of World War II and the Holocaust were that
popular democracy could not be trusted to run its course. Majorities must be
controlled and limited, lest they attack minority groups. Again, elite, counter-
majoritarian institutions that are not dependent on popular support were needed
in order to control popular and populist passions and keep them under the rule of
reason and morality.[11] Law, judges, and especially constitutional judges were crucial
in this regard. Adjudicating based on reason, not subject to populist pressures,
promoting liberal and individual values, and able to check and restrict majoritarian
politics, constitutional judges personified such elite institutionalism.

   Second, as a reaction to the nationalism that had swept it into World War II,
Europe adopted a universalist, transnational, and cosmopolitan view of polity. This
new European identity emphasized individualism rather than collectivism, shared
values rather than unique national values, and cosmopolitanism based on a shared
responsibility for humanity and, later on, even the environment rather than the
protection of national interests per se.[12] This identity was manifested most powerfully in the (previously unimaginable) creation of the European Union.
Constitutional courts and judges fit within this cosmopolitan turn. Constitutional
courts protect individuals, sometimes even at the expense of national interests. They
are, thus, symbols of individualism rather than communitarianism or nationalism.
They are institutionally designed to reflect the ideals of reason, objectivity, and

policy in the British zone of Germany between 1945 and 1949 around three aims: denazification,
   reeducation, and democratization).

[9]   To use the titles of two seminal books on World War II and the Holocaust: Chris Browning, *Ordinary
     Men: Reserve Police Battalion 101 and the Final Solution in Poland* (HarperCollins, 1992) and
     Daniel Goldhagen, *Hitler's Willing Executioners: Ordinary Germans and the Holocaust* (Alfred
     A Knopf, 1996).

[10] An example of a very influential elitist democratic theory after World War II is Joseph Schumpeter,
     Capitalism, Socialism and Democracy, 2nd edition (Harper & Brothers, 1947). See also Geoff Eley,
     "Legacies of Antifascism: Constructing Democracy in Postwar Europe" (1996) 67 *New German
     Critique* 73.

[11] These ideas are best exemplified by the theory of Militant Democracy developed by the German
     scholar Karl Loewenstein already in the 1930s and adopted as a constitutional doctrine in post-World
     War II Germany and then in many other jurisdictions including the European Court of Human
     Rights. See Karl Loewenstein, "Militant Democracy and Fundamental Rights" (1937) 31 *American
     Political Science Review* 417; Jan-Werner Müller, "Militant Democracy" in Michel Rosenfeld and
     András Sajó (eds.), *The Oxford Handbook of Comparative Constitutional Law* (Oxford University
     Press, 2012) 1253.

[12] See, for example, Jed Rubenfeld, "Unilateralism and Constitutionalism" (2004) 79 *New York
     University Law Review* 1971 (documenting the creation of a universalist conception of human rights
     as a reaction to the nationalism of World War II).

impartiality that are universal rather than local; and they enshrine human rights and the values of human dignity, liberty, and equality, which are also universal.

It was only natural, therefore, that the liberal and cosmopolitan turn after World War II was accompanied by the creation of new constitutional courts all over Europe. Most of these courts were empowered to enforce entrenched bills of rights against legislatures – a rarity in Europe, before World War II – and experienced growing prestige and influence.[13] In addition, supranational instruments protecting human rights were created following World War II. These instruments often came with their own supranational, semiconstitutional courts. These included the UN Charter, the UN Universal Declaration of Human Rights, and the International Covenant on Civil and Political Rights. The European Union and the European Convention of Human Rights (ECHR) also had their own very influential supranational, semiconstitutional courts: the European Court of Justice (ECJ) and the European Court of Human Rights (ECtHR).

Constitutional courts, both local and transnational, were created in many other parts of the world following another post-World War II phenomenon – decolonization. The three decades following World War II saw the most dramatic process of state creation that the world has ever seen, as Europe withdrew from the rest of the world and the age of empires was over. Practically all of the newly created states (including those that became de facto authoritarian regimes) adopted constitutions with bills of rights and constitutional courts, which became the international standard.[14] Regional human rights provisions also extended beyond Europe and were created in Latin America, Africa, and Asia.[15]

Global constitutionalism reached the common law world as well, including in those countries that adopted the UK model of parliamentary sovereignty and "political constitutionalism" and were thus averse to constitutional courts and bills of rights: Canada, Australia, New Zealand, and the UK itself. Gradually, and incompletely but nevertheless substantially, all of these countries were affected by global constitutionalism.[16] Canada was the first to adopt a European-style Charter of Rights and Freedoms as part of its patriation and separation from the British Crown in 1982. This move influenced New Zealand to adopt its Bill of Rights Act in 1990, and the UK adopted its Human Rights Act in 1998. Australia, which did not adopt any such instrument at the federal level, adopted bills of rights at the subnational level and

---

[13]   See, generally, Víctor Ferreres Comella, *Constitutional Courts and Democratic Values: A European Perspective* (Yale University Press, 2009).

[14]   See, for example, Tom Ginsburg, "Constitutional Courts in New Democracies: Understanding Variation in East Asia" (2002) 2 *Global Jurist Advances*, ISSN (Online) 1535–661, https://doi.org/10.2202/1535-1661.1057.

[15]   See the American Convention on Human Rights (1978); the African Charter of Human and People's Rights (1981); the Cairo Declaration on Human Rights in Islam (1990); and the Asian Human Rights Charter (1986).

[16]   See Stephen Gardbaum, *The New Commonwealth Model of Constitutionalism: Theory and Practice* (Cambridge University Press, 2013).

saw its High Court interpret its Constitution as protecting some individual freedoms despite not having a bill of rights.[17] While only Canada adopted a full judicial review model, High Courts in all of these nations, once safely couched in UK-style parliamentarism, began engaging intensively with rights jurisprudence of the continental European style, adopting such concepts as proportionality and human dignity.[18]

These processes, which started after World War II, reached their peak after the fall of the Soviet bloc. In the same address that was quoted at the start of this chapter, Owen Fiss eloquently describes the chain of events that followed:

> The period began in November 1989, when the Berlin Wall collapsed and the Soviet empire began to disintegrate ... The newly freed nations of Central and Eastern Europe soon held elections and then rushed to consolidate these gains through the adoption of democratic constitutions. At the same time that these developments were occurring in Europe, the apartheid system in South Africa collapsed – another world historic event ... These newly won victories of democratic constitutionalism in Europe and Africa had their counterpart in Latin America ... [I]n 1993 and again in 1994, the United Nations established two international tribunals to punish those responsible for ... crimes against humanity ... [T]heir underlying ethos was the same as that of the constitutional courts of the era: to use the reason of the law to further liberal, democratic values.[19]

The rapid breakdown of authoritarian regimes all the way from the Eastern bloc to South Africa and South America and their replacement with constitutional democracies created a sense of a winning model destined to take a global hold and famously described by the historian Francis Fukuyama as the "end of history."[20] These new democracies generally adopted constitutional bills of rights with constitutional courts to enforce them. Meanwhile, additional supranational courts, such as the International Criminal Court, were also created in this period, making it the height of global constitutionalism.[21]

---

[17]   See David Erdos, *Delegating Rights Protection: The Rise of Bills of Rights in the Westminster World* (Oxford University Press, 2010); Scott Stephenson, *From Dialogue to Disagreement in Comparative Rights Constitutionalism* (The Federation Press, 2016).

[18]   See, for example, with regard to the UK, Alison L Young, Patrick Birkinshaw, Valsamis Mitsilegas, and Theodora A Christou, "Europe's Gift to the United Kingdom's Unwritten Constitution – Juridification" in Anneli Albi and Samo Bardutzky (eds.), *National Constitutions in European and Global Governance: Democracy, Rights, the Rule of Law* (Springer, 2019) 83. ("The report observes that membership of the EU and of the ECHR has helped to subject the UK constitution to juridification.").

[19]   Fiss (*supra* n 1).

[20]   Francis Fukuyama, *The End of History and the Last Man* (Free Press, 1992).

[21]   See, generally, Doreen Lustig and JHH Weiler, "Judicial Review in the Contemporary World: Retrospective and Prospective" (2018) 16 *International Journal of Constitutional Law* 315; and Mila Versteeg, "Understanding the Third Wave of Judicial Review: Afterword to the Foreword by Doreen Lustig and J. H. H. Weiler" (2019) 17 *International Journal of Constitutional Law* 10.

1.1.2 *The Empowerment of Judges*

The age of global constitutionalism has, thus, put judges – constitutional judges especially – in a very central position. Judges have always been prominent figures in Western societies, especially so in common law countries and most of all in the United States.[22] However, historically, they were not so clearly placed at the core of the moral and political ethos as they had become now, at the height of global constitutionalism.

Global constitutionalism has seen judges increase their standing and influence in a number of ways. First, rights jurisprudence and the role of judges as the guardians of human rights upscaled judicial authority from what was once mainly a professional and legal authority to a *moral authority*. Rozen Zvi has documented this process in Israel where judges separated themselves from lawyers by claiming that they, unlike lawyers, had moral authority and that "the judiciary has since the 1970s engaged in a collective social mobility project to transform its professional authority into a moral power."[23] He quoted a public survey from 1991 that placed the Supreme Court of Israel as the institution having the highest moral authority in Israel and another showing that "judgeship was the most prestigious profession of the 1990s, replacing physicians who occupied the head of the pyramid throughout the 1980s."[24]

Second, in Europe and elsewhere, global constitutionalism engaged constitutional courts and constitutional judges in questions of high political and moral visibility that previously were not their domain. Indeed, Alec Stone Sweet in 2000 described European democracies as "governing with judges"[25] and Ran Hirschl in 2004 described the global phenomenon of "juristocracy."[26]

Third, in transitional countries, including those countries that emerged from authoritarianism, judges were also involved in the act of state-building. The most prominent examples of judicial state-building during global constitutionalism surveyed in this volume are Chief Justice Chaskalson in South Africa, President Sólyom in Hungary, and Justice Cepeda in Columbia. These judges, using Ros Dixon's terminology, were "drafter-judges" – involved in both the drafting and the

---

[22] See Alexis de Tocqueville, *Democracy in America*, ed. and trans. by Harvey C Mansfield and Delba Winthrop (Chicago University Press, [two vols, 1835 and 1840] 2000), part 1, ch VI: Judicial Power in the United States.

[23] Issachar Rosen-Zvi, "Constructing Professionalism: The Professional Project of the Israeli Judiciary" (2001) 31 *Seton Hall Law Review* 760, 781.

[24] Ibid. 782 ("By the mid-1980s, the judiciary had managed to achieve formidable moral status and high prestige within the Israeli society ... In a survey of the Israeli Jewish population from 1991, more than 70% of the respondents answered that they considered the High Court of Justice (the Israeli Supreme Court) the institution with the highest moral authority in Israel.").

[25] Alec Stone Sweet, *Governing with Judges: Constitutional Politics in Europe* (Oxford University Press, 2000).

[26] Ran Hirschl, *Towards Juristocracy: The Origins and Consequences of the New Constitutionalism* (Harvard University Press, 2004).

initial implementation of new constitutions.[27] Drafter-judges, according to Dixon, are sometimes "agents of democratic constitutional change – i.e., judges who resemble a majority of democratic constitutional drafters by possessing both legal and political relationships, skills, and commitments."[28] Other judges featured in this volume, while not constitutional drafters, were among the first to interpret and apply new constitutions. As mentioned in the Introduction to this volume, this includes Chief Justice Li and Justice Bokhary in Hong Kong and Justice Shrestha in Nepal.[29] Judges operating in transitional periods were often viewed as the principal guardians of those transitions, acting as a bulwark against reactionary forces and regression into authoritarianism. Judges and the protection of democracy became synonymous.[30] Finally, as part of democratic constitution-building in the new nation-states that emerged in the 1990s, as well as in other states trying to strengthen their rule of law institutions, judges from some jurisdictions – the United States and Germany in particular – gained new prominence as sought-after advisors, mentors, and teachers.[31]

Does the increase in the stature, prominence, moral authority, and political influence of judges mean that there will be more towering judges? Not necessarily, but certainly the two are not antithetical, and we would expect a positive correlation between them. Towering judges would not evolve, even though judiciaries rise in moral authority and influence, in places and periods where the personalization of the judiciary is tempered by institutional, jurisprudential, and cultural boundaries. This, as described in the Introduction, is probably why we do not have prominent examples of towering judges in Western Europe. However, it is logical to assume that as judges move from professional authority to moral authority and from more technical and strictly legal engagement to more open-ended value- or policy-based engagement, their personalities would have a greater impact, and certain personalities would rise over others. To the extent that we associate courts themselves with leadership, it would be natural to see leadership of some judges within those courts.

---

[27] Rosalind Dixon, "Constitutional Design Two Ways: Constitutional Drafters as Judges" (2019) 57 *Virginia Journal of International Law* 1.
[28] Ibid.
[29] See Introduction to this volume.
[30] Bojan Bugaric criticizes the view held by many constitutional scholars "that the most significant bulwark against the return of repression is the presence of strong constitutional courts." See Bojan Bugaric, "Can Law Protect Democracy? Legal Institutions as 'Speed Bumps'" (2019) 11 *Hague Journal on the Rule of Law* 447. https://doi.org/10.1007/s40803-019-00127-w.
[31] See, for example, Bryant Garth, Hon. Lourdes Baird, Hon. Ronald Lew, Hon. Beverly Reid O'Connell, Hon. David Carter, and Hon. Barbara Rothstein, "Panel Discussion: Judges Teaching Rule of Law Abroad" (2016) 23(1) *Southwestern Journal of International Law* 73. On this panel, Judge Lourdes Baird of the US District Court for the Central District of California said: "From roughly 1989 to 1999, there were only about two years that I wasn't involved in this sort of judging ... But for a full eight years I was able to partake in this experience. We would provide numerous lectures and demonstrations." See also Louis Aucoin, "The Role of International Experts in Constitution-Making: Myth and Reality" (2004) 5(1) *Georgetown Journal of International Affairs* 89.

1.2 THE PLATONIC CONCEPTION OF RIGHTS: JUDGES AS MOVING SOCIETY TOWARD THE IDEAL

A second aspect of global constitutionalism that contributed, I would argue, to the phenomenon of towering judges is the particular conception of constitutional rights that emerged during this time: what I term, the Platonic Conception of constitutional rights.[32] According to this conception, there is a common, universal, and objective template of constitutional rights, so that the texts of the different bills of rights in the different constitutions of the world are imperfect reflections of it (they are its Platonic Object or Matter).[33] As they are human creations, subject to the failings of political interests, historical short-sightedness, and human error, the texts of the different constitutions are inherently incomplete and flawed. Constitutional judges, according to this idea, owe their allegiance to the objective Platonic Conception of rights, and not to the subjective and imperfect reflection of rights as represented in the legal text of their particular constitution. Their role is to bring their societies as close as possible to this Platonic Conception of constitutional rights, and to interpret their own constitutional text so that it resembles this Platonic Conception as much as possible.[34]

The Platonic Conception of rights is not new, and some version of it has been part of the idea of constitutional rights from its inception and is included in the idea of natural rights.[35] As against this Platonic or reason-based Conception of constitutional rights, there is a contractarian or will-based conception of constitutional rights, according to which rights are legal arrangements that are the result of a pact between the people and their sovereign (or between the people and themselves) to subject their political system to some limitations so as to protect the people from future tyranny and abuse.[36] At different times and in various places, one of these conceptions was more dominant than the other.[37] Global constitutionalism, following the processes described in Section 1.1, was a period in which the Platonic

---

[32] See Iddo Porat, "The Platonic Conception of the Israeli Constitution" in Rosalind Dixon and Adrienne Stone (eds.), *The Invisible Constitution in Comparative Perspective* (Cambridge University Press, 2018) 268.

[33] One of the most famous representations of the Platonic Theory of Ideas (or Forms) is the Allegory of the Cave in Plato's *Republic* (514a–520a). According to this allegory, the objects that we perceive through our senses are but reflections of the real Ideas which we cannot perceive directly, in the same way as prisoners put in a cave in front of a wall can see only the shadows of the real objects put in front of a fire behind them. See Stephen Watt, "Introduction: The Theory of Forms (Books 5–7)" in *Plato: Republic* (Wordsworth 1997) xiv–xvi.

[34] Porat (*supra* n 32) 288.

[35] Ibid. 290.

[36] See, generally, Anne Cudd and Selena Eftekhari, "Contractarianism" in Edward N Zalta (ed.) *The Stanford Encyclopedia of Philosophy* (Summer 2018 Edition), https://plato.stanford.edu/archives/sum2018/entries/contractarianism/.

[37] Thus, in nineteenth-century England, natural rights theory was seriously challenged by Bentham, who famously termed natural rights "nonsense upon stilts." See Jeremy Bentham, "Rights, Representation, and Reform: Nonsense upon Stilts and Other Writings on the French Revolution" in P Schofield, C Pease-Watkin, and C Blamires (eds.), *The Collected Works of Jeremy Bentham* (Oxford University Press, 2002) 317–401.

Conception was particularly strong. In addition, during global constitutionalism, as judges became the primary caretakers and protectors of constitutional rights, the practical implications of the Platonic Conception for the judicial role became clear.

In terms of the judicial role, the prominence of the Platonic Conception means two main things: first, that the role of the constitutional judge is creative and transformative; and second, that it is not strictly local, as the judge takes part in a global project that includes judges from around the world. Both these self-understandings of the judicial role, I argue, are conducive to the evolution of towering judges and are shared by key examples of towering judges in this volume. I will deal with the second of these self-understandings in Section 1.3.

As to the first aspect – of bringing society closer to an ideal understanding of human rights – it is far removed from a traditional conception of the judicial function as interpretative and backward-looking, in the sense of applying a preexisting set of norms put forth (in the case of constitutional law) by the drafters of the constitutional text. It is also not limited to a "living tree" role of adjusting the constitutional text to present conditions and norms. Rather, it has a direction, a purpose, and a goal. And judges are active and creative agents of bringing about social change toward that goal. Indeed, for several of the judges included in this volume, their interpretation of constitutional rights was very creative and expansive, and some expressly admitted their historic role in bringing their societies forward toward a human rights protection ideal that had an international consensus around it. Furthermore, for several of the judges, such expansionist interpretations clearly departed from the constitutional drafters' intentions. They viewed the democratic popular will behind the constitutional text as having limited importance for interpretation at best, and as being problematic or redundant at worst.

Thus, László Sólyom expressly asserted the historical task of change entrusted to the Court during Hungary's transition to democracy. Sólyom argued that "the Court must fulfill its task embedded in history. The Court is the repository of the paradox of 'revolution under the rule of law'"[38] and should develop "unwritten constitutional principles, substitute rules, and creative interpretations."[39] The judicial role, for Sólyom, was anything but static and backward-looking; it was creative and even revolutionary.

In addition, Sólyom did not view the public's involvement in the adoption of the constitutional text as key to judicial interpretation or to the validity of constitutional rights. As Tóth writes in his chapter, for Sólyom, "representative forms of democratic decision making were regarded with ambiguity" and he "degraded" Parliamentary involvement in constitutional drafting "by viewing it as being motivated by actual

---

[38] Judgment 11/1992 (III. 5.) HCC (Hungary).

[39] László Sólyom, "The Role of Constitutional Courts in the Transition to Democracy, with Special Reference to Hungary" in Saïd Amir Arjomand (ed.), *Constitutionalism and Political Reconstruction* (Brill, 2007) 305.

political interests." Therefore, the fact that the interim 1989 Hungarian Constitution did not originate from the people was not a major flaw for Sólyom. Moreover, its completion through a democratic adoption of a permanent constitution was not necessary, as "the Court as the highest-ranking constitutional body could replace the constitution-making authority by its principled judgments."[40] The creative and transformative task of the judge is, therefore, not limited to creative *interpretations* of a constitution but extends to the *creation* or at least completion of the constitution itself, amounting to what Tóth describes as "judicial constituent power."

President Aharon Barak of Israel had a similarly expansive view of the judicial role. He wrote:

> As judges we are not limited to interpreting and operating the existing laws. We are the spear's edge of the aspiration to a more desirable and better law ... We are the architects of social change. We have the abilities to build a better and a more just legal system. We do not see our role as limited to legal technocracy, but we perceive our role to include legal statesmanship.[41]

For Barak, too, the formal adoption of a bill of rights through the democratic process was not necessary, as the Supreme Court could fill in the gaps within an incomplete bill of rights, and even apply constitutional law directly without a constitution. As Harel shows in his chapter, even before constitutional rights were formally incorporated in two Israeli Basic Laws from 1992, Barak wrote: "Theoretically and as a matter of principle, there exists the possibility that a court in a democratic society declares the invalidity of a law that is contrary to the fundamental principles of the system even if those fundamental principles are not entrenched in a rigid constitution."[42] In addition, once these two Basic Laws were enacted, Barak was willing to read into them a long list of rights that were intentionally excluded from them as part of the political compromise that led to their enactment. Harel views this, together with other ambitious interpretative moves, such as acknowledging the superiority of these two Basic Laws as a quasi-constitution, as Barak's "liberal revolution."[43] Barak, therefore, was engaged in a revolutionary and transformative project of completing a full set of constitutional rights and moving Israel toward the global or universal model.

Justice Bhagwati of India also had a very expansive approach to constitutional interpretation. He wrote: "[A] constitutional provision must be construed, not in a narrow and constricted sense, but in a wide and liberal manner so as to anticipate and take account of changing conditions and purposes."[44] Abeyratne writes in Chapter 10 in this volume that Bhagwati had a "disdain for legal formalism and

---

[40] Chapter 13 in this volume.
[41] Aharon Barak, "The Rule of Law" in Shimon Shetreet (ed.), *Collection of Lectures Delivered at the Seminar for Judges 1976* (Sacker Institute, 1977).
[42] HCJ 142/89 *La'or Movement v Speaker of the Knesset* [1990] IsrSC 44(3) 529, 554.
[43] Chapter 9 in this volume.
[44] Chapter 10 in this volume.

desire to untether the Indian legal system from conservative precedents and doctrine." Abeyratne further notes that Bhagwati broadened the scope of the right to life
in the Indian Constitution to include the right to "live with human dignity,"[45]
which, according to Bhagwati, included also "the bare necessities of life such as
adequate nutrition, clothing and shelter."[46] The Indian Constitution includes these
provisions only as Directive Principles of State Policy, which were meant by the
founders to be nonjusticiable. Such interpretations show that, like Barak and
Sólyom, Bhagwati prioritized judicial allegiance to universal principles of rights
and justice, over allegiance to than the political will behind the constitutional text,
and was willing to go directly against the logic and intention of the constitutional
text. He even used the same apparatus as Justice Barak and Sólyom to expand rights –
reading new rights through the concept of human dignity.

Two other judges in this volume that broadly fit this pattern are, first, Sir Anthony
Mason of Australia. He led the High Court to read into the Australian Constitution,
which has no Bill of Rights, an implied freedom of political communication.[47] Secondly,
Lady Hale of the UK Supreme Court, who played an important role in incorporating
rights jurisprudence including the apparatus of proportionality, through the application
of the Human Rights Act, in a system that was averse to such jurisprudence.[48]

Such transformative, goal-oriented, and entrepreneurial jurisprudence, while,
again, not necessarily connected to the personalization of the judiciary and the
emergence of towering judges, can definitely be associated with these phenomena.
The bringing about of transformation, let alone revolution, usually requires personal
leadership. It is true that a collective body could be goal-oriented, but a transformative
and revolutionary function quite naturally incentivizes leadership and personal
agency. The idea of a collective and impersonal judiciary fits much better with
a passive, backward-looking, and strictly professional view of the judicial role, rather
than a transformative and revolutionary one. In addition, the kinds of latitude and
creativity in adjudication that accompany this type of transformative jurisprudence
allow for the personal characteristics and inclinations of judges to shine through,
which, in turn, leads some judges to distinguish themselves and tower over their peers.

Indeed, most judges included in this volume can be described as nonformalists, at
least within the spectrum of formalism within their own legal culture. It may be that
these two characteristics – aiming for change and transformation on the one hand,
and nonformalism on the other hand – are related. In the late twentieth century,
when a number of these judges operated, American legal realism was already internalized in the legal consciousness of many legal systems, and legal formalism was not
a very attractive legal theory.[49] However, it may well be that their nonformalism can be

[45] Ibid.
[46] Ibid.
[47] Chapter 3 in this volume.
[48] Chapter 4 in this volume.
[49] See, for example, the discussion of Sir Anthony Mason's "turn to realism" in Chapter 3 in this volume.

attributed as much to global constitutionalism; specifically, the kind of hope for change and progress that it included.

1.3 A GLOBAL COMMUNITY OF JUDGES

The third aspect of global constitutionalism that contributed to the phenomenon of towering judges is the emergence of a global community of judges. The emergence of this community both as an idea and as a reality relates to the two processes discussed earlier – the prominence and empowerment of judges in a liberal and cosmopolitan political atmosphere and the adoption of the Platonic Conception of rights that entrusts judges with the task of completing their constitutions according to a global ideal.

As to the first of these processes, as described in Section 1.1, constitutional judges came to prominence, in part, because they represented a set of liberal values and individual rights that transcended the borders of the state and, hence, were associated with transnationalism and cosmopolitanism. Those ideas were at the heart of the new Europe and what was thought to be the New World Order following the Cold War.[50] This self-conception of judges as promoting cosmopolitan liberal values allowed and fostered interaction among judges around these ideas and the creation of a sense of a global judicial community. Indeed, the idea of a global community of judges was part of what was described by some scholars as an eschatological cosmopolitan vision that became prominent during the 1990s.[51] It followed Kantian ideas of a "Universal History with a Cosmopolitan Purpose" and there being a "historical trajectory that would lead to the liberation of individuals enjoying human rights in a global federation under the rule of law."[52] Note, for example, the following description of the cosmopolitan spirit of the period and its relation to the rule of law: "[T]hen came 1989 and all the enthusiasm about a global rule of law – human rights, trade, environment, criminal law, sanctions and world police. The end of the Cold War was understood – especially in Europe – as a removal of obstacles on the way to history's natural progress towards a universal federation."[53]

As to the second and related process – the Platonic Conception of rights – this conception, as described in Section 1.2, came hand-in-hand with the idea that constitutional judges can transcend their particular constitutional texts to reach for the shared universal ideal of constitutional rights. Constitutional judges worldwide thus constituted a community that could engage in a similar project and along similar lines. The clearest manifestation of these trends can be seen in Anne-Marie

[50]   Anne-Marie Slaughter, *A New World Order* (Princeton University Press, 2004).
[51]   See, for example, Luca Pasquet, "Dialogue or Interaction? A Non-cosmopolitan Reading of Transjudicial Communication" in Andrei Muller (ed.), *Judicial Dialogue and Human Rights* (Cambridge University Press, 2017) 467.
[52]   Martii Koskenniemi, "The Fate of Public International Law: Between Technique and Politics" (2007) 70 *Modern Law Review* 1, 2–3.
[53]   Ibid. 3.

Slaughter's work in the 1990s and 2000s. Slaughter coined the terms "transjudicial communications"[54] and "global community of courts."[55] According to Slaughter, there emerged a phenomenon of "collective judicial deliberation"[56] under "the presumption of an integrated system."[57] These deliberations would have the effect of "spread[ing] ... [the] enhanced protection of universal human rights,"[58] considered "the core of judicial identity in many different courts."[59] All this may lead to the following: "Imagine a world of regular and interactive transjudicial communication ... [I]t is a vision of a global community of law."[60]

Thus, the global community of judges should be understood first as an ideal and a goal toward which to strive. The culmination of that goal is a global rule of law, where judges in each country are representative of the global regime and where there is integration and convergence around the same liberal ideas. It should also be understood as a way of achieving that goal. Judges in different places in the world share ideas, tactics, and doctrines in order to promote, each in his or her own jurisdiction, the ideas of a shared understanding of the rule of law and human rights. As Fiss wrote: "The aim was to create a forum for those judges engaged in the practice of democratic constitutionalism to learn from one another. We assumed that by sharing their knowledge and experience[,] the values then being applauded [the values of "liberal democracy, constitutionalism, and cosmopolitanism"] would be deepened and extended."[61]

Slaughter's writings as well as the passages from Fiss show a mix of description and normative aspirationalism. The extent of the actual convergence between legal systems and the emergence of a global community of law may be different from the picture they portray, and such accounts have been challenged.[62] But Slaughter's writings effectively document both the ethos of the period as it related to constitutional judges and a set of phenomena that did not previously exist to the same degree.

The global community of judges, even as a phenomenon less robust than what Slaughter portrayed, has several practical manifestations. First, there were a host of judicial practices, including judicial dialogue, constitutional transplants, the use of similar global doctrines, and the citation of foreign, transnational, and international law in court decisions.[63] These are all phenomena that were extensively

---

[54] Anne-Marie Slaughter "A Typology of Transjudicial Communication" (1994) 29 *University of Richmond Law Review* 99, 135.

[55] Anne-Marie Slaughter, "A Global Community of Courts" (2003) 44 *Harvard International Law Journal* 191.

[56] Slaughter (*supra* n 54) 119.

[57] Slaughter (*supra* n 55) 204.

[58] Slaughter (*supra* n 54) 122.

[59] Ibid. 134.

[60] See Anne-Marie Slaughter, "Judicial Globalization" (1999) 40 *Virginia Journal of International Law* 1103, 1114.

[61] Fiss (*supra* n 1).

[62] See, for example, David S Law and Wen-Chen Chang, "The Limits of Global Judicial Dialogue" (2011) 86 *Washington Law Review* 523.

[63] For a critical account of judicial dialogue, see Law and Chang (*supra* n 62).

documented in the literature on the use of foreign law in constitutional adjudication in the late 2000s,[64] and many of the judges included in this volume took part in these practices. For example, Sólyom, Hale, Barak, Chaskalson, Li, and Bokhary all adopted variants of the global doctrine of rights adjudication – proportionality. The spread of this doctrine, facilitated by some of the judges included in this volume, such as Barak and Sólyom, is one of the principal indicators of a global community of judges.[65] In addition, all the aforementioned judges, to varying degrees, cited foreign law in constitutional adjudication and even cited each other, as described in the Introduction to this volume.[66]

The other practical manifestation of this global community of judges was their interactions in meetings, conferences, and associations. In addition to the Yale Law School Global Constitutional Seminar, there were several other international meetings taking place in Europe, the United States, and elsewhere. There was also the international association of judges, which brought judges from different parts of the world together to formulate statements of purpose, model rules, and so on.[67] Such physical encounters might enhance mutual citation and the sharing of ideas.

A third manifestation of this global community or, more generally, of the globalization of the judiciary is a set of global post-judicial careers, such as foreign judicial positions, UN positions, or global teaching opportunities, which were mentioned in the Introduction and embarked upon by several of the judges included in this volume.[68]

The practices and ideas of the global community of judges, I would argue, incentivized toweringness mainly for the reason that, in order to be included in that community, it was very helpful to tower. This community was comprised of representatives from different legal systems. Those representatives usually included one or two judges from each system, as including whole courts in meetings or gatherings was impracticable. It is true that representatives could be randomly selected, such that each year a different judge attends a conference or that judges are selected according to judicial function (such as Chief Justice). However, more often than not, this was not the case. Rather, those judges that are the most distinct representatives of the system, the most eloquent, bright, knowledgeable, and influential, are the ones to become part of

---

[64] See, for example, Mark Tushnet, "When Is Knowing Less Better than Knowing More? Unpacking the Controversy Over Supreme Court Reference to Non-US Law" (2006) 90 *Minnesota Law Review* 1275; Vicki Jackson, "Constitutional Comparisons: Convergence, Resistance, Engagement" (2005) 119 *Harvard Law Review* 109; Richard Posner, "No Thanks, We Already Have Our Own Laws" (July–August 2004) *Legal Affairs* 40; Jeremy Waldron, "Foreign Law and the Modern Ius Gentium" (2005) 119 *Harvard Law Review* 129; Richard Alford, "Four Mistakes in the Debate on 'Outsourcing Authority'" (2006) 69 *Alberta Law Review* 653.

[65] See Stone Sweet and Mathews (*supra* n 2) 162; Aharon Barak, *Proportionality: Constitutional Rights and Their Limitations* (Cambridge University Press, 2012) 199–202; Moshe Cohen-Eliya and Iddo Porat, *Proportionality and Constitutional Culture* (Cambridge University Press, 2013) 10–14.

[66] See Introduction to this volume.

[67] See *supra* n 31.

[68] See Introduction to this volume.

the global community of judges. In addition, as will be discussed shortly, being included in the network of judges incentivizes toweringness of a particular type – of judges that excel in expanding conceptions of rights and in promoting liberal and human rights ideas.

Naturally, judges are moved by a host of reasons when they end up distinguishing themselves: the desires to promote justice, effectuate change, engage intellectually with ideas, and so on. But it is not unimaginable to assume that, in addition to these reasons, they also considered the advantages of belonging to the global community of judges. First, the meetings of this community are lucrative and involve travel and hospitality of a high level. Judges work hard and this would be a well-appreciated addition to their routine. Second, these meetings are likely to be intellectually enriching and informative, enabling judges to reinforce each other's jurisprudence and share experiences and difficulties. They may also provide networking opportunities. Finally, the kind of reputation that comes from being included in a global circle of judges can also be conducive to the lucrative post-judicial positions that some of these judges acquired around the world. Therefore, judges have good reasons to want to belong to this community. Towering above their peers may help them, or even be necessary, in order to achieve that. I should stress that I do not argue that any of the judges included in this volume acted intentionally out of the motivation to be included in a global community of judges. I highlight only those incentives that exist and that might contribute, perhaps unconsciously, to the emergence of towering judges.

In addition, the idea of a global community of judges may lead to towering judges since, as explored in Section 1.2, it is a goal-oriented community that has a direction and a shared project. This goal-oriented, entrepreneurial, and transformative conception of the judiciary can enhance the personal agency that brings about toweringness.

1.4 NORMATIVE IMPLICATIONS

Thus far, I have argued that the phenomenon of towering judges can be explained, at least in part, by global constitutionalism and that global constitutionalism may have fostered the creation of towering judges. But what does that mean in terms of our assessment of this phenomenon? What does it mean for the question of whether towering judges are beneficial for a constitutional system?

The answers to these questions will vary, to some degree, based on one's views of global constitutionalism and the ideas and values that it manifests. Certainly, some of the values promoted by global constitutionalism are shared across the entire moral and political spectrum within liberal democracies. These include the rule of law, personal autonomy, individual freedom, democracy, and nontyranny. To the extent that towering judges, as part of global constitutionalism, promote these values, we may have a very positive assessment of the phenomenon of towering judges.

However, this chapter also exposes some challenges or difficulties related to the phenomenon of towering judges. I will review here, briefly, four such challenges: (1) the creation of unwanted biases in adjudication; (2) a disconnect between some judges and their constituencies; (3) a democratic deficit; and (4) judges as politicians.

On the first challenge, one might think of a bias toward greater rights protection and the expansion of rights at the possible expense of other interests such as local or national interests. This follows especially from the incentive to belong to the global community of judges, as the currency of excellence and the ticket into that club run through an expansive and liberal conception of rights and a record of enlarging the scope of rights. Excelling in the protection of national interests or local values would not be helpful for getting into that club. A New Zealand survey found that the use of foreign law in interpreting the New Zealand Bill of Rights Act has been substantially biased in favor of expanding the scope of rights, rather than diminishing it, and termed this a "ratcheting up effect" in terms of the scope of rights.[69] David Law identified a similar phenomenon: a "race to the top" in terms of advanced "packages" of rights protections among countries, to attract foreign investments.[70] A similar type of bias may come from the incentives to tower in the context of global constitutionalism as it requires competing along the lines of expanding rights.

The second challenge is the possible disconnect between a judge and his or her constituency. This can happen as a result of the fact that the towering judge may speak to two audiences – the local audience and the international or global audience. As such, a judge may get assurances and positive reactions from the global community and lose track of the fact that the same ideas are met with less enthusiasm back home. In other words, it might create a false sense of consensus around (usually liberal) ideas. This also connotes a false sense of security and nonvulnerability that could later create backlash and resistance to the judicial legacy of a towering judge. Both Barak and Sólyom, as explored in Chapters 9 and 13 in this volume, respectively, are examples of judges whose ideas were met with great enthusiasm outside their country but raised much resistance and debate among the population of the country. This, in turn, resulted in a political backlash in Israel and Hungary after these judges stepped down.

Third, and connected to the previous challenge, is the relatively low importance that popular democracy played in the interpretative doctrines adopted by some of the towering judges who operated during global constitutionalism. As mentioned earlier, several of the judges included in this volume were willing not only to depart

---

[69] James Allan, Grant Huscroft, and Nessa Lynch, "The Citation of Overseas Authority in Rights Litigation in New Zealand: How Much Bark? How Much Bite?" (2007) 11 *Otago Law Review* 433, 445.
[70] David Law, "Globalization and the Future of Constitutional Rights" (2008) 102 *Northwestern University Law Review* 1277.

from the plain meaning of the text but also to interpret it in ways that conflicted with the political will behind it. In some cases, these judges created, in effect, a new text. This followed from the elitist and anti-populist lessons of World War II, as well as the Platonic Conception of constitutional rights. The outcome, however, for several of the towering judges in this volume was a democratic deficit and a lack of democratic accountability. As part of the liberal cosmopolitan project, some towering judges drew their legitimation not from their local constituency and the way it incorporated its ideas in its constitution but from general and ostensibly universal ideas of human rights and liberal democracy. When these eventually conflicted with the political currents in some jurisdictions – such as in Australia, Israel, and Hungary – the result was a backlash (varying considerably among these examples) and the wish to make the judiciary more democratically accountable.[71]

Finally, the idea of towering judges as social engineers, revolutionaries, and leaders who bring their countries toward global standards, and so on, departs from ideals of judicial neutrality and objectivity under the rule of law and portrays judges as political actors. Judicial legitimacy usually rests on the idea that judges apply the law objectively and fairly. When judges are also engaged in social and political change, this is in conflict with that type of legitimacy. When there is relative unanimity in society as to the direction it should take, such judicial entrepreneurship may be welcome. But once discord erupts, judges are taken as being political agents of one side of the political map (usually the liberal side) and the enemies of the other (usually the nationalist and conservative one).[72]

1.5 CONCLUSION (AND LIMITATIONS)

In this chapter, I attempted to situate the phenomenon of towering judges in the historical context of global constitutionalism. The thesis of this chapter is painted in broad strokes and is thus subject to the limitations of such types of explanations; mainly, the tendency toward generalization and simplification. For that reason, this chapter could not properly account for many of the differences between the various towering judges – some fit the model of global constitutionalism to a greater extent than others. This is, however, an inevitable limitation of such type of account, and hopefully the remaining chapters in this volume will make up for it.

Second, this chapter and the thesis it puts forward cannot, and does not intend to, provide a sole or full explanation of the phenomenon of towering judges. For sure, there were towering judges before the time frame discussed in this chapter, and there will be towering judges after this time frame. In addition, many aspects of

---

[71] See Chapters 3, 9, and 13 in this volume.
[72] Compare with Hirschl (*supra* n 26) (arguing that political elites that had lost their hold on power used judiciaries that were ideologically akin to them, to retain a power stronghold and outweigh their weakness in the political realm).

toweringness are not related to the aspects of cosmopolitanism, the Platonic Conception of rights, or a global community of judges that are discussed in this chapter.

That being said, this chapter attempted to show that the global and historical context of the phenomenon discussed in this volume matters and is crucial in its understanding. It also argued that unique and ideologically powerful circumstances accounted for the flourishing and the contours of the phenomenon of towering judges in the recent decades. This unique setting is now going through a dramatic transformation, as populism and nationalism are back in vogue. Time will tell whether this trend will also affect the phenomenon of towering judges, and how.

2

The Landscapes that Towering Judges Tower Over

Mark Tushnet

2.1 INTRODUCTION

According to Felix Frankfurter, US Supreme Court Justice Owen Roberts told him (after Roberts's retirement), "Who am I to revile the good God that he did not make me a Marshall, a Taney, a Bradley, a Holmes, a Brandeis or a Cardozo?"[1] The judges Roberts enumerated are candidates for towering justices of the US Supreme Court. Roberts's observation, though, reminds us that one cannot be a towering judge without there being other judges over whom one towers.

Toweringness is a *relational* concept. A judge towers over some sort of landscape. As Roberts's observation suggests, the landscape might be the judges' colleagues on the Court. It might be the Court's history. Scholars in the United States use and discuss the inadequacies of a "chief justice" synthesis that defines eras in the Supreme Court's history by the chief justice who happened to be in place during the era. The chief justice synthesis implicitly treats the sitting chief justice as the most significant figure during his tenure.[2] Or, the landscape might be the Court understood as a bureaucratic institution: A judge might become towering by working out ways in which the judge and his and her colleagues can wrestle an overwhelming caseload into manageable shape. This chapter uses examples from the United States to sketch these and other aspects of toweringness as a relational concept.

Roberts's statement also suggests that the US Supreme Court – the longest-lived constitutional court in the world – has had many judges who towered over others. Sometimes they towered over the judges with whom they served, sometimes they are towering figures in the Court's history – and sometimes they seemed to be towering shortly after they completed their service but now no longer seem quite as large as they did earlier. The long history of the US Supreme Court offers many examples of different kinds of toweringness, some of which I explore in this chapter: toweringness

[1] Felix Frankfurter, "Mr. Justice Roberts" (1955) 104 *University of Pennsylvania Law Review* 311, 312. Frankfurter prefaces this statement with "Roberts wrote" but does not identify where Roberts did so.
[2] For a discussion of the chief justice synthesis, see Mark Tushnet, "Writing Supreme Court Histories" (1993) *Journal of Supreme Court History* 11, 17–18.

as a relation between one judge and his or her colleagues (Section 2.2), as dependent upon the historical circumstances in which judges find themselves (Section 2.3), as an aspect of the Court's bureaucratic or institutional organization (Section 2.4), and as subject to reevaluation (Section 2.5). In each section, I offer case studies, some detailed, others less so, illustrating the concepts at play.

2.2 "TOWERINGNESS" AS A COLLEAGUE-DEPENDENT RELATION

Whether a judge towers over the judges with whom she or he sits obviously depends upon both who the judge is and who the other judges are. Here, toweringness is a *colleague-dependent* relation. My argument is this: Some judges tower over others because they are much better lawyers than the others.[3] My primary case study involves US Supreme Court Chief Justice Charles Evans Hughes and Justice Owen Roberts.

2.2.1 *Hughes and the New Deal Crisis*

The case study deals with two pairs of decisions by the US Supreme Court in the midst of Franklin Delano Roosevelt's first presidential term. The cases involved labor law – minimum wage statutes and statutes requiring that employers engage in bargaining with representatives chosen by their employees collectively. In the first case in each pair, the Court, with Roberts in the majority, held the statutes unconstitutional. And in the second case in each pair, the Court, again with Roberts in the majority, rejected constitutional challenges. Chief Justice Hughes dissented in the first minimum-wage case and concurred in the first collective-bargaining decision; he wrote the Court's opinions in the second cases in each pair. The question to be examined is why Justice Roberts changed sides in the second cases in each pair. And the most plausible answer, which Roberts himself gave, is that he was overcome by Hughes's persuasive legal advocacy. Here, Hughes towered over Roberts because of their relative legal abilities.[4]

---

3   I impose something like a "boundary condition" on my inquiry, though. Consider the saying "In the land of the blind, the one-eyed man is king." I will exclude from my purview that possibility – that is, I will not treat as "towering" a judge who stands out from his or her colleagues simply because they are (for example) incompetent or corrupt and he or she is merely competent or honest. That is not to say, however, that examining such judges is not a worthwhile endeavor. For example, we might learn a great deal by seeing what it is that makes a person stay honest when surrounded by corruption. The genre of "noir" detective novels is composed substantially of such case studies, as indicated by the classic line "Down these mean streets a man must go who is not himself mean ..." Raymond Chandler, "The Simple Art of Murder" in Frank McShane (ed.), *Later Novels and Other Writings* (Library of America [1944]1995) 977, 992.
4   For other purposes, Hughes's role as the median justice and as ultimately on "the right side of history" might be important in evaluating how he towered over other judges, but not for the purpose of understanding the specific relation between Hughes and Roberts.

In 1923, the US Supreme Court held unconstitutional a Washington, DC statute setting up a board to establish and enforce a minimum wage for women.[5] The statute directed the board to set the minimum using "the necessary cost of living" as its benchmark. A decade later, New York enacted its own minimum-wage statute. The New York statute directed the wage-setting board to take the "value of the service ... rendered" into account as well. New York's highest court had held the statute unconstitutional because it was no different from the District of Columbia's. Defending the statute against constitutional challenge, the state's lawyers argued that the inclusion of the additional criterion distinguished its statute from Washington, DC's statute. In *New York ex rel Morehead* v *Tipaldo*, a majority of the US Supreme Court disagreed and affirmed the state court's decision. That the board could consider the cost of living at all was sufficient to render the statute unconstitutional.[6]

Justice Roberts agreed with that argument – that is, in his view the District of Columbia and New York statutes were unconstitutional. Hughes's dissent asserted that the inclusion of the "value of the services" criterion was a material difference between the two statutes. His dissent did little to explain why it was material, though, and most of the dissent was a full-scale attack on the 1923 decision. Roberts agreed that the 1923 decision was mistaken and should be overruled, but he would not go along with a dissent that disingenuously, in his view, asserted that the statutes were distinguishable.[7]

Several months later, the Court received a petition to review a decision by the Washington state's supreme court upholding its state's minimum-wage statute, which was identical to New York's. Unsurprisingly, the petition for review relied upon the 1923 decision. Acting with only the petition for review before it, and so without any papers asking the Court to overrule the 1923 decision, the Court granted the petition for review. When the state later filed its response by means of its brief on the merits of the case, it tried, as New York had, to distinguish its statute from that in the District of Columbia.

The Court treated the case, *West Coast Hotel* v *Parrish*, as giving it the opportunity to overrule the 1923 decision, and it did so.[8] That outcome was consistent with Roberts's views on the merits as he later explained those views. Why, though, had Roberts gone along with Hughes's decision to overrule the 1923 decision when no one had actually asked the Court to do so? That is, if Roberts had refused to overrule the 1923 decision in *Morehead* v *Tipaldo* because no one had asked the Court to do so, why was he willing to overrule it in a case a few months later where, once again, no one had asked the Court to do so?

---

[5] *Adkins* v *Children's Hospital* [1923] 261 US 525.
[6] *New York ex rel Morehead* v *Tipaldo* [1936] 298 US 587. The statute is quoted at 605.
[7] Roberts's explanation came in a memorandum written in 1945 and reprinted in Frankfurter (*supra* n 1).
[8] *West Coast Hotel* v *Parrish* [1937] 300 US 379.

There is no documentary evidence explaining Roberts's decision. There is one hint, on which some historians have pegged a great deal. Hughes spent an unusually long time visiting Roberts at the latter's farm between the date of the New York decision and that of the Court's decision to grant review in *West Coast Hotel*.[9] Some historians have suggested that Hughes discussed the Court's recent decisions with Roberts and somehow persuaded him to change his mind.

Beyond this speculation, there is a more legalistic point. Under its practices, the US Supreme Court has discretion to affirm a lower court's decision on any ground sufficient to support the decision, whether or not that ground was argued by any party. In contrast, the Court's practices strongly counsel against reversing a lower court on a ground not urged upon the Court. Now, go back to the postures of the New York and Washington state cases. Overruling the 1923 decision in *Morehead v Tipaldo* would have meant reversing the lower court. In contrast, doing so in the Washington state case led to *affirming* the state court's decision. Overruling the 1923 decision in *West Coast Hotel* meant that the Court exercised its ordinary discretion with respect to grounds for affirming a lower court, whereas doing so in *Morehead* would have required it to exercise discretion in circumstances where doing so was possible but discouraged. Roberts may have thought – or, more likely, Hughes may have pointed out – that the circumstances triggering a discretionary decision to consider arguments not presented to the Court differed for *Morehead* and *West Coast Hotel*.[10]

The labor relations cases are more complicated. *Carter v Carter Coal Co.* the first, held unconstitutional a federal statute setting up a comprehensive system for regulating prices and labor practices in the bituminous coal industry.[11] The labor provisions required employers to engage in collective bargaining with unions desig-nated by their workers. Employers challenged the provisions on the ground that Congress lacked power under the Constitution to regulate those practices. Congress's power extended only to commerce "among the several States," and labor practices at mines were not "in" interstate commerce. Existing doctrine did allow Congress to regulate local practices that "affected" interstate commerce, but, the employers argued, labor relations did not do so in the sense that the term "affected" was used in that doctrine.

Writing for the Court, Justice George Sutherland agreed with the employers. The doctrine required that local activities – here, labor relations – *directly* affect interstate commerce. For Sutherland, that question reduced to whether there was some

---

9   I discuss the evidence about the visit, and historians' interpretations of it, in the historiographical essay in my forthcoming study of the Hughes Court. Mark Tushnet, The Oliver Wendell Holmes Devise History of the United States Supreme Court, vol 11, From Progressivism to Pluralism (Cambridge University Press, forthcoming 2021). My conclusion is that the visit probably happened as most historians describe but that it probably did not have any especially strong effects on Roberts's actions thereafter.

10 For a discussion of Roberts's view of Hughes, see the text accompanying n 17 later in this chapter.

11 [1936] 298 US 238.

"efficient intervening agency" between the local practice and consequences for interstate commerce.[12] And, as Sutherland read both the statute and the record, no one had shown that there was such an "agency." Instead, the government relied on the proposition that the accumulation of individual labor disputes and strikes had a large effect on interstate commerce. But, according to Sutherland, magnitude was irrelevant. Chief Justice Hughes appears to have accepted this argument, though his separate opinion on that precise question consists of a single conclusory sentence.

The National Labor Relations Act extended the collective-bargaining require-ment through the entire economy. Not surprisingly, employers argued that it was vulnerable to the same objections as the Bituminous Coal Conservation Act. The Court disagreed, with Hughes writing a majority opinion in which Roberts joined.[13] The case involved the application of the statute to the Jones & Laughlin Steel Company's operations in Aliquippa, Pennsylvania. Jones & Laughlin was one of the nation's largest steel companies, and its Aliquippa plant was the heart of its operations. Hughes's opinion is rhetorically quite effective, but to some degree the rhetoric obscures the underlying analytic point he made.

After describing the statute, Hughes turned to an extensive description of the company's operations at Aliquippa, the flow of raw material into the plant, the flow of manufactured steel from the plant to other states, and the like. The description made clear just how large the plant was and how central it was to Jones & Laughlin's business. Yet, these were observations about magnitude, which *Carter* v *Carter Coal* said were irrelevant. What was needed was a characterization of labor relations at the Aliquippa plant as "logically" related to disruptions of interstate commerce.

Hughes believed that he could supply that characterization. He argued that "the recognition of the right of employees to self-organization and to have representatives of their own choosing for the purpose of collective bargaining is often an essential condition of industrial peace." Denying that right had sometimes led to "industrial war," with "paralyzing consequences" for interstate commerce. At least in Hughes's eyes, the right to organize was logically connected to interstate commerce "when industries organize themselves on a national scale."[14] And so, he concluded, inter-fering with that right had the required direct effect on interstate commerce.

Much can be said about whether *Jones & Laughlin*'s analysis of "direct effect" is consistent with *Carter* v *Carter Coal*. In writing that the question of whether an effect was direct or indirect was "necessarily one of degree,"[15] Hughes might be taken to have imported ideas about magnitude – an interpretation supported by the extensive account he gave of how the Aliquippa plant operated. And Hughes did nothing to

---

[12] Sutherland emphasized that this was a logical rather than an empirical relationship. "The distinction between a direct and an indirect effect turns not upon the magnitude of either the cause or the effect, but entirely upon the manner in which the effect has been brought about" (298 US at 308).
[13] *National Labor Relations Board* v *Jones & Laughlin Steel Co* [1937] 301 US 1.
[14] 301 US at 41–2.
[15] 301 US at 37.

distinguish *Carter v Carter Coal*. Here is his complete discussion: "In the *Carter* case, the Court was of the opinion that the provisions of the statute relating to production were invalid upon several grounds [listing the grounds] . . . These cases are not controlling here."[16] That said, Hughes did provide a legal analysis different from the one expressly rejected in *Carter v Carter Coal*.

Having dissented in *Morehead*, Hughes did not change his position in *West Coast Hotel*. He did change his position in the collective-bargaining cases. Having been willing to overrule the 1923 decision in *Morehead*, Roberts did not really change his position in *West Coast Hotel*, but, like Hughes, he did change in *Jones & Laughlin*. My interest here lies with Roberts, not Hughes, and in particular in the relation between them.

Roberts told Hughes's biographer Merlo Pusey that he "felt . . . keenly" Hughes's "intellectual superiority."[17] According to Frankfurter, Roberts later said that he "wonder[ed] why the hell" he took a broad position in another New Deal case, and answered for himself, "just to please the Chief."[18] According to Roberts, Hughes "often came up with ingenious arguments which averted dissents."[19] The word "ingenious" suggests that Roberts saw a difference between Hughes's and his own capacity to come up with acceptable legal arguments. This view is, of course, not the only thing that Roberts had; wanting to "please the Chief" suggests that inter-collegial relations matter too. But, in Roberts's self-report, legal ability matters.

My suggestion, then, is that one thing that makes some judges tower over others is that they are simply better lawyers. What, though, does legal ability consist in? Here I rely on Duncan Kennedy's account. For Kennedy, the legal materials available to a judge are typically sufficiently rich to enable a judge, using widely accepted techniques of legal reasoning, to reach a result the judge believes to be just.[20] But, using those techniques – distinguishing one case from another, analogizing the case at hand to others, and more – requires what Kennedy calls "work." For Kennedy, the amount of work a judge is willing to do depends on the "stakes" of the case: When the stakes are high, a judge is willing to do more work than when they are low.[21] The stakes are measured by the chance that good or bad outcomes will occur. Kennedy's account can be supplemented by noting that the work he describes takes time, and

---

[16] 301 US at 41. Hughes used the plural "cases" because he was also dismissing another case on which *Carter v Carter Coal* had relied.

[17] Edward L Carter and Edward E Adams, "Justice Owen J. Roberts on 1937" (2012) 15 *Green Bag 2nd* 375, 384–5. The full quotation from Roberts is taken from Interview with Owen J Roberts, May 21, 1946, Box 13, Merlo J Pusey Papers, L Tom Perry Special Collections, Harold B Lee Library, Brigham Young University, Provo, Utah, pp 10–11.

[18] Frankfurter (*supra* n 1) 312. Frankfurter's attributions of specific words to Roberts probably should be taken with a grain of salt.

[19] Carter and Adams (*supra* n 17) 386.

[20] Kennedy's formulation is "how I want to come out." I prefer the weaker formulation, which leaves more room for an account of ability, "where it would be nice to come out if I can."

[21] Duncan Kennedy, *Critique of Adjudication: Fin de Siècle* (Harvard University Press, 1997).

sometimes time runs out before the judge is able to do all the work required to reach the result that the judge believes to be just.

For present purposes, another supplement is important. No matter how much work they do, some judges are simply not able enough to see their way through to the conclusion they seek. Sometimes they end up going the other way – that is, voting for a position they disagree with in some sense because they cannot see an adequate legal argument for the one they want. Sometimes they simply leap over the difficulty, accepting conclusions not supported by the arguments they are able to develop. The key here is that the towering judges of whom I write are not like that. They *always* can use the available legal materials to reach the conclusion they think most desirable. That is what Roberts was describing in his characterization of himself in relation not only to Hughes but also to Marshall, Taney, Bradley, Holmes, Brandeis, and Cardozo.

2.2.2 *The Possibility of Multiple Towering Judges Serving Together*

The US Supreme Court has had nine members since 1869. I think it would be difficult to use a colleague-dependent concept of toweringness and conclude that all nine – or even five or six – justices were towering judges.[22] The US experience suggests, though, that sometimes we can find two or perhaps three judges serving together for a reasonably long period of time, all of whom we describe as towering though not always along a single dimension. This section uses Justices Hugo L Black and William J Brennan as examples of two justices serving contemporaneously and each of whom towers above others in their consistent commitments to methods of constitutional interpretation that have enduring value and that produced attractive results.[23]

Justice Black famously carried a copy of the US Constitution in his pocket. He was a thorough-going textualist who believed that every constitutional question was resolved by simply reverting to the document's words and those words alone. In the First Amendment, the words "Congress shall make no law … abridging the freedom of speech" meant "no law" – period. For Black, the constitutional provision saying that members of the House of Representatives shall be chosen "by the People of the several States" meant that each person's vote for a member of Congress should have the same value as the vote of every other person in the state, implying that each congressional district within a state had to have exactly the same population, with only trivial deviations allowed.[24] The Fourteenth Amendment's statement that "No State shall … deprive any person of life, liberty, or property, without due process of

---

[22]   We might call such a court a "strong" court, and we might say that the court as a whole towered over its predecessors or successors, placing the court in a historical landscape.
[23]   On the importance of results, see the text accompanying n 52 later in this chapter.
[24]   *Wesberry v Sanders* [1964] 376 US 1.

law" meant that states were bound by the Bill of Rights exactly as was the national government.

As these examples suggest, Black's textualism was more than a little idiosyncratic. That "no law meant no law" required Black to distinguish, sometimes implausibly, between speech and conduct and to characterize as conduct activities such as picketing that many would think functionally identical to speech. One can get from "the People of the several States" to "one person, one vote," but the route almost certainly takes one through the forest of political philosophy; the Constitution's words are not enough.

Why then was Black a towering judge? For three reasons, in my view: his insistence on the text's importance, his persistence and general consistency, and the fact that his readings of the text led to results that many observers regarded as good ones. That the text is important should be obvious, but Black wrote against a background in which many judges and scholars had argued that cases could properly be decided by invoking unwritten principles of natural justice or by referring generically to American traditions. Black's persistence guaranteed that judges would always at least start with the text even if, unlike Black, they did not end there. Further, Black adhered to his textualism with no more than a handful of deviations, which was possible, of course, because he could almost always generate an idiosyncratic reading of the text sufficient to explain his position. And, finally, during his lifetime and for quite a while after his death in 1973, scholars were willing to cut him some slack because they agreed with the results he reached.

Black had been on the Court for almost two decades when Brennan joined him. Over time, Brennan developed his own understanding of the basis of constitutional interpretation. In a speech delivered in 1985 – more than a decade after Black died – Brennan insisted that interpretation had to begin with the text.[25] But, for Brennan, the Constitution's text reflected the value choices that its authors made. The implications of those choices for contemporary problems were frequently unclear or ambiguous. Brennan concluded that it was "the very purpose of a Constitution- and particularly of the Bill of Rights to declare certain values transcendent, beyond the reach of temporary political majorities." He summarized those values as "human dignity" and argued that constitutional controversies should be resolved by asking whether impugned statutes were inconsistent with human dignity.

Brennan distinguished his method of interpretation from a free-standing philo- sophical inquiry into human dignity and its implications for political theory; he was, he agreed, a judge and not a moral philosopher. He argued that judges had to treat the Constitution as value-based, as often ambiguous, and as an instrument for advancing human dignity in contemporary circumstances. In short, Brennan was an exemplar of what came to be known as living constitutionalism.

---

[25] Brennan's most extended articulation of his approach came in a speech at Georgetown University, summarized in Seth Stern and Stephen Wermiel, *Justice Brennan: Liberal Champion* (University Press of Kansas, 2013) 475–6.

Black's textualism stakes its claim at one of the poles of contemporary constitutional discourse, now more commonly presented as originalism rather than textualism. Brennan's living constitutionalism stakes its claim at the other pole. Together, Black and Brennan are towering judges because they set the terms of constitutional argument for several generations. Their time may pass sometime in the future, but in retrospect they will be seen as having dominated their era.

2.3 TOWERINGNESS AS HISTORICALLY CONTINGENT

The example of Hughes and Roberts raises additional questions beyond that of the role of relative legal ability: whether there can be towering judges (properly so-called) only during some periods of a nation's constitutional development, and the extent to which judgments about a judge's place relative to his or her colleagues are historically contingent.

How long and when a judge serves are important conditions on becoming towering. As to how long: One common, though not universal, feature of toweringness is that it is quite difficult for a judge to become towering if he or she does not serve on a court for a reasonably long period of time.[26]

As to when: Judges play roles in a nation's constitutional development, and that development typically takes place in stages: creation, crisis, resolution, routine operation, and the like. Sometimes judges become towering because they serve during founding eras and contribute decisively to setting the nation's constitutional course.[27] Sometimes they serve during periods of acute national crisis, as Hughes and Roberts did. And sometimes judges "tower" in a somewhat peculiar sense: Their work helps consolidate political developments in a more articulate way than legislative and executive leaders have done.

Chief Justice Earl Warren and, again, Justice Brennan offer US examples of this last form of toweringness. Warren served from 1953 to 1969, Brennan from 1956 to 1990. The period they served together was one in which a liberal synthesis about power and liberty coalesced into what we can call the New Deal-Great Society constitutional order.[28] In that order, legislatures, both state and national, had robust power to regulate the economy, and courts, sometimes collaborating with the national legislature, provided robust protection to civil rights and civil liberties.

---

[26] What counts as reasonably long probably has to be measured against the average tenure on the court on which the towering judge serves. In India, for example, strong norms about who is qualified to be appointed to the Supreme Court have meant that most justices serve quite short terms. There, a judge who serves ten years is long-serving, whereas in the United States such a judge would be seen as serving a relatively short term.

[27] See, e.g., Chapter 5 in this volume (on Hugh Kennedy) and Chapter 12 in this volume (on Arthur Chaskalson).

[28] For discussions of that order, see Bruce A Ackerman, *We the People: Volume 2: Transformations* (Harvard University Press, 1998) and Bruce A Ackerman, *We the People: Volume 3: The Civil Rights Revolution* (Harvard University Press, 2014).

The so-called Warren Court fit comfortably into the New Deal-Great Society order, which, as the label suggests, was primarily created by presidential leadership and congressional enactments.

In what sense, then, were Warren and Brennan towering judges? Of course, Warren gave his name to the Supreme Court period during which he was chief justice, but the Court itself was only one, and probably a secondary, player in the New Deal-Great Society constitutional order. I suggest that Warren was a towering *judge*, although not necessarily a towering figure in the constitutional order as a whole, for two reasons. He symbolized the Supreme Court's participation in the New Deal-Great Society order simply by being the nominal head of one of the three branches: Warren was to the Supreme Court what Franklin Roosevelt and Lyndon Johnson were to the presidency as an institution. In addition, Warren wrote *Brown v Board of Education*,[29] *Reynolds v Sims*,[30] and *Miranda v Arizona*,[31] opinions that came to symbolize the civil rights and civil liberties components of the constitutional order.[32]

Brennan's role was different. Elsewhere I have suggested that we should call the Court during the relevant period the "Brennan Court" rather than the "Warren Court."[33] This insider's perspective reflects the fact that the liberal thrust of constitutional jurisprudence persisted for a while after Warren's retirement: A periodization that reflected that would span 1954 through perhaps 1976. During the time they served together, Warren and Brennan divided leadership tasks within the Court between them and Brennan took on the entire set of tasks after Warren left.[34]

Those who lead the US Supreme Court, and perhaps other constitutional courts as well, must get enough of their colleagues to go along with them.[35] The job of "mustering a court" can be broken down into at least two components. First, the leader or leaders must convince colleagues that they want to go along with the leaders, and second, they must show them that they can do so in opinions that are compatible with the other judges' views about what the law requires or permits.

---

[29] [1954] 347 US 483 (holding unconstitutional the racial segregation of public schools).

[30] [1964] 377 US 533 (holding that the US Constitution requires that legislative districts in a state each have roughly the same number of people).

[31] [1966] 384 US 436 (holding unconstitutional the admission of a defendant's statements taken without the defendant having been notified that she or he has a right to a lawyer during questioning).

[32] On the term "wrote," see the discussion of law clerks in the text accompanying ns 42–5 later in this chapter.

[33] See, e.g., Mark Tushnet, "Foreword: Comment" (1991) 77(4) *Virginia Law Review* 631, 634.

[34] For a description of this division of labor, see, generally, Stern and Wermiel (*supra* n 25).

[35] My thinking here has been shaped by reflecting upon an early study by David J Danelski, "The Influence of the Chief Justice in the Decisional Process of the Supreme Court" in David J Danelski and Artemus Ward (eds.), *The Chief Justice: Appointment and Influence* (University of Michigan Press, 2016) (chapter originally written in 1960), but I use terms and concepts different from his. I note that my approach does not leave room for a towering judge who is a persistent dissenter. For a brief discussion of a related issue, see the text accompanying n 52 later in this chapter.

Ties of personal affection sometimes can tip the balance. One can find notes from one justice to another to this effect: "I continue to disagree, but it's a small matter, so let it go."[36] Appeals to institutional interests often matter. Take one episode in the deliberations over *Brown v Board of Education*. Justice Stanley Reed, an old New Dealer from segregated Kentucky who was generally skeptical about the exercise of broad judicial power, believed that racial segregation in education was constitutionally permissible. After Warren had received votes from all the other justices to support finding segregation unconstitutional, Warren appealed to Reed's institutional loyalties, telling Reed that it would be bad for the Court and the country were there to be a dissent from the majority's holding. Reed agreed, suppressed his qualms about the holding, and joined Warren's opinion.[37]

Warren and Brennan were both seasoned politicians who knew how to build and use their personalities to get colleagues to go along with them. Those qualities could get them only so far, though. Judges see themselves as men and women of the law, and the opinions they join must seem to them compatible with their views of what the law allows. Accounts of Warren's tenure on the Court suggest that he saw Brennan as his right-hand man in performing this task. Warren was not a great legal craftsman. In contrast, Brennan, like Hughes before him, was able to figure out how to formulate doctrine that supported the results he (and Warren) believed to be correct, in ways that fit into the doctrinal universes their colleagues inhabited.[38]

The development of Brennan's opinion for the Court in *Plyler v Doe* is an extreme example, but – like a good caricature – it captures the essentials of Brennan's ability. Texas had adopted a policy that excluded from public schools children of parents not lawfully present within the United States.[39] The Supreme Court divided five-to-four in holding the policy unconstitutional. Justice Lewis F Powell, a conservative who had been deeply involved in Virginia's efforts to resist the desegregation of the state's public schools, was the key vote. Having seen the terrible effects that had occurred when some Virginia schools closed their doors rather than desegregate, Powell was firmly convinced that Texas's policy was fundamentally unwise. However, moving from that judgment to an opinion that was consistent with his views about the Constitution and its interpretation proved difficult.

Warren Burger, then the chief justice, voted to uphold the Texas policy. That meant that Brennan, as the senior justice in the majority, had the power to designate the justice who would draft the initial opinion for the majority. He assigned the opinion to himself. His initial opinion had three analytical components, each

36   For example, see Robert Post, "The Supreme Court Opinion As Institutional Practice: Dissent, Legal Scholarship, and Decisionmaking in the Taft Court" (2001) 85 *Minnesota Law Review* 1267, 1340–4.
37   The story is laid out in Richard Kluger, *Simple Justice* (Alfred A Knopf, 1976) 698.
38   Having figured that out, Brennan typically left the precise formulations to his law clerks, who received substantial guidance but not word-for-word direction from him.
39   *Plyler v Doe* [1982] 457 US 202. The events recounted here are described in Stern and Wermiel (*supra* n 25) 504–5.

resting upon different aspects of existing doctrine dealing with differential (discriminatory) denials of public services. For present purposes, we can see the components in this way: (1) Policies that adversely affect "suspect classes" receive "strict scrutiny," that is, they can be justified only by the most pressing social interests and are justified by those interests only if the policies are extremely well designed to promote those interests with as small an adverse impact as possible. (2) Policies that adversely affect "fundamental interests" by burdening some people but not others also receive strict scrutiny. (3) All policies must satisfy a requirement of minimal rationality.

Brennan's draft opinion tracked these three components. Texas's policy affected the suspect class, "children of those unlawfully present in the United States." Strict scrutiny was justified because neither the members of the class nor, important to the analysis, their parents were able to defend their interests in ordinary politics (the parents, as noncitizens, being unable to vote in US elections). The policy also implicated the fundamental interest in receiving the basics of an education. And, finally, the policy was fundamentally irrational in relegating children to being on the streets rather than in schools.

Justice Powell was troubled by Brennan's initial draft. He had already written an opinion expressly stating that education was not a fundamental interest for these doctrinal purposes,[40] and he found Brennan's effort to distinguish the case unpersuasive. He was concerned, as well, about the identification of the children as a suspect class because he was unsure how far Brennan's doctrinal proposal would reach. When Brennan received Powell's letter noting these concerns, Brennan redrafted the opinion incrementally. First, he basically eliminated the doctrinal treatment of education as a fundamental interest and tinkered with the "suspect class" analysis. Powell responded by approving Brennan's changes on the first item but continuing to express concern about the second. Brennan responded with another draft, this one basically eliminating the "suspect class" argument as a doctrinal basis for the holding.

At the end of the drafting process, Brennan had an opinion treating the Texas policy as irrational. That version of the opinion was almost certainly weaker as an analytic matter than prior drafts. It had one great virtue, though: Justice Powell was willing to sign it, thereby giving Brennan the fifth vote he needed.

An important feature of this account must be emphasized: Brennan led the Court by using legal arguments – some less persuasive in the abstract than others, also in the abstract. Judges work in concrete settings, not abstract ones, though. And sometimes leadership requires adopting weaker arguments that one's colleagues find acceptable within the legal frameworks with which they are comfortable, rather than stronger arguments that the judge drafting the opinion could have devised. Or, put another way: Hughes used his legal ability to overpower objections from Roberts; Brennan used his legal ability to craft a weak opinion that gave in to Powell's concerns while getting to where both Brennan and Powell wanted to come out.

---

[40] *San Antonio School Dist v Rodriguez* [1973] 411 US 1.

2.4 TOWERINGNESS AS A CONCEPT IMPLICATING
BUREAUCRACY

Courts are – among other things, of course – bureaucratic organizations. Cases
arrive at a constitutional court and have to be processed according to the organization's rules, both formal and informal. Formal rules might spell out when a court
must give a case plenary consideration, for example. Those rules might be so lax that
the court finds itself overwhelmed with cases. Standard management theory would
suggest that the court as a bureaucracy will develop informal rules that allow it to
process the caseload. Some judges might become towering by devising workable
informal rules and persuading the other judges that such rules are legally permissible notwithstanding the formal rules about plenary consideration.[41]

The contemporary role of law clerks on the US Supreme Court suggests some
difficult-to-identify forms of toweringness when we look at constitutional courts as
bureaucracies. Many constitutional courts employ law clerks either as members of
a general staff or as aides to individual judges. In the United States, the growth of
justices' staffs was rather clearly associated with bureaucratization. Beginning as legal
secretaries and personal assistants, the law clerks gradually became assistants doing legal
research for the judges who employed them, then initial drafters of some opinions, then
drafters of substantial numbers of opinions.[42] The reasons for these developments
include increasing caseloads,[43] which required the justices to develop techniques that
allowed them to process cases within their offices better, and the consequences of the US
system of life tenure for judges, which means that many justices continue to serve on the
Supreme Court even as their capacity for some aspects of the work declines.

Changing norms about appropriate judicial behavior also matter. Sometimes the
law clerks play a substantial role in writing opinions that are published under the
name of one of the court's judges. That practice, which appears to be more
widespread in the United States than in most other nations,[44] raises questions
about whether we can use a judge's legal ability as a component in assessing whether
the judge is a towering figure. In the United States today (2020), an opinion that
works with the legal materials exceptionally well might be drafted almost entirely by

[41] Chief Justice William Howard Taft persuaded Congress and his colleagues to change the rules about
     access to the US Supreme Court from requiring that the Court give plenary consideration to nearly
     every case to allowing the Court complete discretion over doing so with respect to most of its docket.
     He was able to do so in part because he plausibly assured Congress that the justices were committed to
     an informal rule that the Court would give plenary consideration of any case where four justices –
     a minority – wished to do so. For the background, see Edward A Hartnett, "Questioning Certiorari:
     Some Reflections Seventy-Five Years After the Judges' Bill" (2000) 100 *Columbia Law Review* 1643.
[42] For discussions of the history of law clerk use in the US Supreme Court, see Todd C Peppers,
     Courtiers of the Marble Palace: The Rise and Influence of the Supreme Court Law Clerk (Stanford
     University Press, 2006); Artemus Ward and David L Weiden, *Sorcerers' Apprentices: 100 Years of Law
     Clerks at the United States Supreme Court* (New York University Press, 2006).
[43] Peppers (*supra* n 42) 15.
[44] My understanding is that staff members equivalent to law clerks do significant drafting in Mexico,
     Colombia, and many international human rights courts, and do relatively little in Canada and Israel.

a law clerk. Attributing the opinion to the judge and using it as part of our evaluation of the judge's legal ability would be a mistake.

Getting good information about the actual process of drafting opinions within the US Supreme Court is extremely difficult, mostly because law clerks are understandably protective of "their" justices' reputations. Sometimes one hears comments similar to this: "We thought that the opinion was pretty good when we sent it in to the justice, but it was even better when it came back." One does not know whether the improvement occurred in connection with the opinion's legal analysis or its rhetorical power. Another comment one runs across is similar to this: "We sent a draft opinion to the justice, and when it came back the justice had completely rewritten it and made it much better."

Such comments help isolate something else that can make a contemporary US justice a towering figure nonetheless. The judge had to have hired the law clerks in the first place – had to have identified people who could, in fact, perform legal analysis at an extremely high level. So, perhaps, today, the "ability" criterion is not that the judge has superior legal abilities but that he or she is much better than his or her colleagues at identifying legal talent in other people, and especially in young and relatively inexperienced people.

We might call this ability a certain kind of "judgment," and that term suggests another view of what makes a judge a towering figure. Towering judges might be judges who have exceptionally good judgment: They can see a case as a whole and understand what the best outcome should be. For them, "where it would be nice to come out" is very often where they *should* come out – even if they themselves cannot figure out exactly how to get there. Couple good judgment of that sort with good judgment in assessing the potential of subordinates like law clerks and we would restore "ability" as a criterion for identifying towering figures, having refined it to take into account the bureaucratic structure of judicial decision-making (where such a structure exists). Something along these lines might be essential if we are to treat William Brennan as a towering judge because, for most of his career on the Court, Justice Brennan relied heavily on his law clerks to draft the opinions that were published under his name.[45]

2.5 TOWERINGNESS AS A JUDGMENT SUBJECT TO REEVALUATION

I have argued that Charles Evans Hughes was a towering judge because of his legal ability, that Earl Warren and William Brennan were towering judges because of their relation to the dominant constitutional order of their time, and that Brennan was a towering judge for the additional reason that his judgments about how to

---

[45] See Stern and Wermiel (*supra* n 25) 525 (expressly referring only to the law clerks' role during Brennan's final years on the Court).

appeal to his colleagues and about how to organize his chambers were of high quality. How stable are these evaluations?

Consider the case of Felix Frankfurter. For perhaps twenty years before and then twenty years after Frankfurter's death in 1965, Frankfurter was (for some) *the* exemplary justice towering over his colleagues. Frankfurter's star has faded, though. Similarly for John Marshall Harlan – a judge's judge or a lawyer's lawyer then and for some still today, but not a figure of historical importance similar to Warren's.

Roberts's inclusion of Justice Joseph Bradley on the list of justices he believed "better" in some sense than he, and the example of Frankfurter, jointly raise another concern. Bradley, now, is known as the author of the Court's opinion in the *Civil Rights Cases*[46] – which, though still mostly good law, is not in the pantheon of great opinions – as well as being known as the author of a sexist concurrence in *Bradwell v Illinois*[47] and, to some, the author of a secondary dissent in the *Slaughterhouse Cases*.[48] Time has pushed Bradley aside. The same might be said of Frankfurter, whose acolytes in the legal academy made him a towering figure on the Court on which he served. Yet, in Noah Feldman's account of four great justices in the mid-twentieth century, Frankfurter comes off as too often missing the mark, too self-assured, and rather unlikeable.[49] Feldman's judgment is, I think, widely shared.[50] Supreme Court scholars today are, in my view, puzzled at the reputation Frankfurter had two or three scholarly generations ago.

These examples suggest that just as *being* a towering judge might be historically contingent, for example, on timing and circumstances, so too might the *reputation* for being a towering judge be historically contingent. The possibility of reputation's historical contingency points us to the possibility of doing an intellectual history of judicial reputation.[51] The case of Bradley, for example, suggests rather strongly that a judge will not qualify as towering during periods when the general social assessment of the results that he or she reached is that the judge was wrong too often. Putting it more affirmatively, to be regarded as a towering judge, the judge must have

[46] [1883] 109 US 3 (holding unconstitutional a federal statute banning racial discrimination in places of public accommodation, because such a statute was not authorized by the Fourteenth Amendment).

[47] [1873] 83 US 130 (finding no constitutional violation in the state's exclusion of women from the bar).

[48] [1873] 83 US 36 (upholding against a constitutional challenge a city ordinance requiring that all slaughtering be done by a state-approved monopoly).

[49] Noah Feldman, *Scorpions: The Battles and Triumphs of FDR's Great Supreme Court Justices* (Grand Central Publishing, 2010).

[50] See, e.g., Richard M Abrams, "Review: The Reputation of Felix Frankfurter" (1985) 10 *American Bar Foundation Research Journal* 639, 652 (Frankfurter "was incapable of giving appropriate weight to the principles of liberalism that applied more directly to the circumstances of the new American environment after the 1930s").

[51] For an express example of such an inquiry, though not in my view a terribly deep one, see Richard Posner, *Cardozo: A Study in Reputation* (University of Chicago Press, 1993). For a better example, though not as express in its concern for evaluating the sources of reputation, see G Edward White, *The American Judicial Tradition* (Oxford University Press, 1976).

reached what the people doing the ranking regard as the correct results most of the time.

We should consider the possibility, though, that a judge could be a towering judge *for his or her time* because, at that time, the judge reached results that were then generally regarded as correct. In time, those results – and the society that regarded them as correct – may come to be seen as bad or even evil. That seems to be the case for Chief Justice Roger Taney, included on Roberts's list with which we began. No one today would call Taney a towering judge, in large part because, whatever his other qualities, he wrote the lead opinion in the *Dred Scott* case, now regarded as one of the lowest points in US Supreme Court history. Perhaps we can situate a judge historically and treat him or her as towering over contemporaries but not towering over history.

Note, though, that, even here, the judgment of toweringness includes a component of correctness. Can we treat as towering a judge who reaches results that have always been regarded as mistaken overall? This collection does not include an example. Perhaps there are judges about whom we could say, "This judge has been persistently wrong overall, but the judge's opinions are always more interesting and thought-provoking than those of any of his or her colleagues." And, finally, perhaps we might treat that judge as a towering figure.[52]

2.6 CONCLUSION

The more-than two-hundred-year history of the US Supreme Court provides numerous opportunities to consider the ways in which toweringness is a relational concept. The judge is towering in relation to something else – colleagues, the court's history overall, the political scene in which the judge operates, and more. The conditions that allow for or support toweringness may vary depending upon which relation we are considering. Earl Warren was towering in some sense but not in others, for example. This and other examples in this chapter suggest how considering toweringness as a relational concept allows us to identify different dimensions and conditions that should be taken into account when we think about what judges are "towering" in what senses.

---

[52] One testing example for the United States is, for liberals, Justice Antonin Scalia. He is not a testing case for conservatives because they believe that he reached correct results most of the time. The equivalent testing case for conservatives might be William Brennan. My guess is that liberals would be quite reluctant to call Scalia a towering judge, and that conservatives would be equally or more reluctant to call Brennan one. If I am right, correctness in results would seem to be an important component of judgments about toweringness.

3

Sir Anthony Mason: Towering Over the High
Court of Australia

Gabrielle Appleby and Andrew Lynch

3.1 INTRODUCTION

Two judicial figures, both chief justices, tower over the history of the High Court of Australia: Sir Owen Dixon and Sir Anthony Mason. Dixon articulated a vision of a court constrained by the rigour of legalism, confirming the legitimacy of the Court's traditional conservative approach. Through Dixon's long tenure and giant reputation, 'Dixonian legalism' would hold the Australian High Court in its grip for more than half a century. But today it is Mason, not Dixon, who is the 'towering judge' of the Australian High Court. Mason's challenge to Dixon's orthodoxy has reset and sustained contemporary debates about the role of the Court in the Australian constitutional system.

In Section 3.2 of this chapter, we introduce Mason and provide a brief biography of his legal career. In Section 3.3, we briefly outline the High Court's embrace of legalism, most powerfully articulated by Dixon, so as to better understand the impact that Mason had in forging a new approach. We then turn to Mason's legacy. In Section 3.4, we address the direction of Mason's views and jurisprudence during his tenure as chief justice and the personal characteristics and experience that might have guided his 'jurisprudential leadership'.[1] Evident in Mason's jurisprudential legacy is what Richard Cornes has referred to as constitutional 'guardianship', providing and explaining to the nation a coherent and contemporary constitutional vision.[2]

As acknowledged in the introduction to this book, the particular manifestation of judicial leadership is inevitably a product of the broader legal, political and social setting in which the individual judge operates. Accordingly, in Section 3.5, we turn to the broader context of Mason's jurisprudential direction – particularly national

---

[1] See, particularly, Rosemary Hunter and Erika Rackley 'Judicial Leadership on the UK Supreme Court' (2018) 38(2) *Legal Studies* 191; Richard Cornes, 'A Point of Stability in the Life of the Nation: The Office of Chief Justice of New Zealand – Supreme Court Judge, Judicial Branch Leader, and Constitutional Guardian and Statesperson' [2013] *New Zealand Law Review* 549.

[2] Cornes (*supra* n 1).

developments during his tenure and his colleagues on the High Court – to understand his successes in their political and social setting.

Finally, in Section 3.6, we explain in greater depth Mason's relational leadership[3] through his extra-curial forays, dealing in particular with the executive and the media, defending judicial independence and integrity against government and public criticism, and promoting access to and efficiency of justice, while also furthering his reputation as constitutional guardian and statesperson. Through almost a quarter of a century's work since leaving the bench, Mason has cemented his legacy on the Court, and set the tone of the debate around the role of the Australian High Court to the present day and, we predict, for decades to come. Section 3.7 concludes.

3.2 ANTHONY FRANK MASON

After his admission to the New South Wales Bar in 1951, Anthony Mason's rise was rapid, his reputation glittering. Beginning as an advocate primarily in commercial and equity cases, he was increasingly briefed by the Commonwealth in constitutional matters. He would also tutor in equity at the University of Sydney in these early years of his career. Mason was very highly regarded by Sir Garfield Barwick, the leading King's Counsel at the Sydney Bar, and was one of his favourite juniors.[4]

Barwick was elected to the Australian parliament in 1958, with Mason assisting him on the hustings. Soon after, Barwick assumed the position of Commonwealth Attorney General in the Menzies conservative coalition government and, in 1964, he was appointed to the High Court as chief justice. Barwick's loss to the Bar allowed Mason's career to advance further. He was the first incumbent of the office of Commonwealth Solicitor General in its modern form under the *Law Officers Act 1964* (Cth) and at the same time was elevated to Queen's Counsel. As Solicitor General, Mason was the government's chief independent counsel, appointed under statute to be outside of politics and the public service.[5] From this vantage point, Mason acquired particular insight into the messy realities of policy development and governing.

Mason was appointed to the New South Wales Court of Appeal in 1969 by a conservative coalition government and, just three years later, the federal coalition appointed him to the High Court. Mason's arrival on the Court, at a mere forty-seven years old and soon after that of one of Barwick's other preferred juniors, Ninian Stephen, marked the start of a generational change in the institution.

---

3 See Gabrielle Appleby and Heather Roberts, 'The Chief Justice: Under relational and institutional pressure' in Gabrielle Appleby and Andrew Lynch (eds.), *The Judge, the Judiciary and the Court: Individual, collegial and institutional judicial dynamics in Australia* (forthcoming).

4 David Marr, *Barwick* (Allen & Unwin, 1980) 239.

5 See, further, Gabrielle Appleby, *The Role of the Solicitor-General: Negotiating Law, Politics and Public Interest* (Bloomsbury, 2016).

The general assessment of Mason, both upon his appointment to the High Court by a conservative government just weeks before its twenty-three-year hold on power ended and during his tenure as a puisne judge, was that he was an 'orthodox' legal figure[6] – 'extremely cautious',[7] 'relatively conservative' and 'not a particularly adventurous judge'.[8] In part, Barwick's irascible domination of his Court exerted a broadly constraining effect upon the younger members.[9] That does not mean that Barwick always got his own way – as Mason put it, 'Barwick had a dominating intellect but his thinking was not always shared by other members of the Court'.[10]

The Whitlam Labor government's Attorney General, Lionel Murphy, was appointed to the Court in 1975 and positioned himself squarely outside the orthodoxy. But Murphy's radicalism was generally unattractive to his colleagues and he was destined to be an isolated figure on the bench. Murphy's tenure ended in controversy after, in 1985, he was convicted of attempting to pervert the course of justice. While he would successfully appeal the conviction and be found not guilty in a retrial, he died in office before the conclusion of a parliamentary inquiry into whether his conduct amounted to misbehaviour within the meaning of the constitutional removal provisions.

Mason was appointed chief justice in 1987 by the Hawke Labor government, following the conservative Sir Harry Gibbs in the post. Consistent with the Hawke government's 'broader constitutional attitudes', the appointment was neither perceived nor intended as a transformative one.[11] Hawke was the first Labor prime minister elected after the reformist and controversial Whitlam government's tenure in the first half of the 1970s. Whitlam had been dismissed by the Commonwealth Governor General (the Queen's representative), Sir John Kerr, in November 1975, in a moment of acute constitutional crisis for Australia. Hawke sought an uncontroversial appointment in the known quantity of Mason.

Mason's elevation to the chief justiceship would not have been remotely likely had Hawke known of Mason's role in advising the Governor General ahead of the Dismissal of the Whitlam government. This later revelation would raise serious questions about Mason's judgement in relation to the fundamental principles of separation of powers and judicial independence. While Barwick's provision of advice to Kerr on how his powers might be exercised had been revealed by both

---

[6] Brendan Lim, *Australia's Constitution After Whitlam* (Cambridge University Press, 2017) 165.

[7] Michael Kirby, 'AF Mason: From *Trigwell* to *Teoh*' (1996) 20 *Melbourne University Law Review* 1087, 1088.

[8] Kristen Walker, 'Mason, Anthony Frank' in Tony Blackshield, Michael Coper and George Williams (eds.), *The Oxford Companion to the High Court of Australia* (Oxford University Press, 2001) 459, 459.

[9] Marr (*supra* n 4) 279–80.

[10] Anthony Mason, 'The Barwick Court' in Tony Blackshield, Michael Coper and George Williams (eds.), *The Oxford Companion to the High Court of Australia* (Oxford University Press, 2001) 59, 59. See, e.g., *Queensland v Commonwealth* (*Second Territory Senators Case*) (1977) 139 CLR 585.

[11] Lim (*supra* n 6) 167. See also Jason Pierce, *Inside the Mason Court Revolution: The High Court of Australia Transformed* (Carolina Academic Press, 2006) 205.

Kerr and Barwick at the time of the Dismissal, in his autobiography, Kerr wrote enigmatically of a 'third man' who provided him with counsel during the period.[12]

In 1994, Mason's identity as the 'third man' came to light when it was revealed that Barwick had sought his opinion on the advice he had prepared for Kerr. In 2012, an examination of Kerr's papers made clear the full extent of Mason's direct dealings with the Governor General, far outstripping in frequency those that Kerr had with Barwick.[13] A former minister in the Hawke government indicated that had this information been known earlier, it would have jeopardised Mason's appointment because of 'the extraordinary level of indifference to constitutional convention his behaviour revealed'.[14] While it has *ex ante* caused some disquieted reflection on Mason's integrity and commitment to constitutional values, it had little effect on his tenure: Mason retired as chief justice in 1995, upon reaching the constitutionally mandated retirement age of seventy years.

The significance of Mason's personal contribution and intellectual leadership of the Court between 1987 and 1995 is considered in Sections 3.4 and 3.5, with his substantial post-retirement career addressed in Section 3.6. But to appreciate Mason's impact, some brief description of the orthodoxy that he challenged is necessary.

3.3 THE HIGH COURT OF AUSTRALIA AND THE LEGACY OF DIXONIAN LEGALISM

For much of its history, the High Court's dominant constitutional method has been avowedly legalistic. Australia's Constitution is primarily concerned with the creation and regulation of a federal system of government. The Court has generally viewed traditional principles of statutory construction as offering a safer path in the resolution of federal disputes than the adoption of some more textured philosophical approach that has been favoured in systems with more rights-sympathetic constitutions. This course was set in the Court's landmark 1920 decision of *Amalgamated Society of Engineers* v *Adelaide Steamship Co Ltd* (*Engineers Case*),[15] which saw the abandonment of two constitutional implications limiting the powers of the Commonwealth in order to preserve the pre-Federation powers and position of the states. These implications, the majority claimed, had been based on principles and a conception of federalism held by the Court's first bench that were extraneous

---

12 John Kerr, *Matters for Judgment: An Autobiography* (Macmillan, 1978) 341.

13 Jenny Hocking, *The Dismissal Dossier: Everything You Were Never Meant to Know about November 1975* (Melbourne University Press, 2015); Paul Kelly and Troy Bramston, *The Dismissal: In the Queen's Name* (Penguin, 2015).

14 Troy Bramston, 'Role with Kerr "would have barred Mason as top judge"', *The Australian*, 1 September 2012, www.theaustralian.com.au/national-affairs/role-with-kerr-would-have-barred-mason-as-top-judge/news-story/144c138be5ba4a61b9f1cd2c4b004b52.

15 *Amalgamated Society of Engineers* v *Adelaide Steamship Co Ltd* (*Engineers Case*) (1920) 28 CLR 129.

from the text of the Constitution itself or 'vague, individual conception[s] of the spirit of the compact'.[16]

The legalism of *Engineers* was an affirmation of the positivist English legal tradition that was congenial to the professional disposition of Australian lawyers.[17] The appeal of that tradition was made plain by the insistence in *Engineers* that the Constitution should be interpreted by reference to the 'settled rules of construction ... distinctly enunciated by the highest tribunals of the Empire'.[18] So strong was this identification with Australia's Westminster inheritance that the Court emphatically turned its back on the constitutional jurisprudence of the United States – a federal system with a written constitution from which the Australian federal provisions had largely been influenced.

Australia's legalistic methodology was given its most famous articulation by Sir Owen Dixon, the Court's unrivalled intellectual leader since his appointment in 1929, on his swearing in as chief justice in 1952. He insisted that 'close adherence to legal reasoning is the only way to maintain the confidence of all parties in Federal conflicts ... There is no other safe guide to judicial decisions in great conflicts than a strict and complete legalism.'[19]

In 1935, Dixon highlighted the status of the Australian Constitution as an enactment of the Imperial parliament and so contrasted it to the position in the United States.[20] This recognition of the different sources of authority for the Constitutions of the two countries had fundamental significance for the High Court's conception of its role in the polity. Despite having assumed a power of judicial review on a par with that of the US Supreme Court, the High Court did not wield this power 'for the people' but in exercise of a more narrowly conceived institutional function. Relevantly, this sustained a positivistic legalism through which the Court was reticent about engaging with the policy implications or social consequences of the law. It was able to do so in the absence of any significant constitutional rights claims appearing before it. Reinforced by judicial principles designed to exert a conservative effect, such as the doctrine of precedent, legalism offered the Court a rhetorical defence from criticism of its decisions and also a scope within which its legitimacy to decide the predominantly federal diet of the Court was unassailable.

The danger of this approach was that it could result in constitutional positions that were almost ahistorical in nature.[21] Yet one of Dixon's legacies was his simultaneous

---

[16] Ibid. 145.
[17] Jeffrey Goldsworthy, 'Australia: Devotion to Legalism' in Jeffrey Goldsworthy, *Interpreting Constitutions: A Comparative Study* (Oxford University Press, 2006) 106, 155.
[18] *Engineers* (supra n 15) 129, 148.
[19] 'Swearing In of Sir Owen Dixon as Chief Justice' (1952) 85 CLR xi, xiii. For context, see William Gummow, 'Law and the Use of History' in JT Gleeson and RCA Higgins (eds.), *Constituting Law: Legal Argument and Social Values* (Federation Press, 2011), 74.
[20] Sir Owen Dixon, 'The Law and the Constitution' (1935) 51 *Law Quarterly Review* 590, 597.
[21] For example, the obiter of Latham CJ in *South Australia v Commonwealth (First Uniform Tax Case)* (1942) 65 CLR 373, 429.

affirmation of legalism as the only legitimate method while tempering the narrow excesses of an overly formalistic approach, carefully securing the acceptance of federal implications that, he opined, were nonetheless consistent with the orthodox methodology embraced in *Engineers*.[22] Despite Dixon's efforts, the persistence of legalism tended to trap the High Court in jurisprudential mazes without the necessary resources with which to secure its escape.

Legalism's predominance also had the effect of inhibiting the way in which decisions were explained to the Australian community. While pivotal to the Court maintaining the fiction that law-making was not a part of the judicial role and so protecting the Court and its judges from political attack, legalism chafed whenever the Court was confronted with a clear choice to make between competing legal resources both possibly applicable to the question before it. As in other common law jurisdictions, the declaratory theory of law proved difficult to sustain in the face of the profuse statute and case law of a modern society, never mind the theoretical and empirical examination of the realist movement from the early years of the twentieth century.

Yet when Mason was appointed to the High Court of Australia in 1972, it was still an institution in denial about these forces and perspectives, maintaining the language of legalism and a crabbed approach to constitutional interpretation. What it was that Mason himself brought to this setting, and how the times worked not to constrain him but to his advantage, is the key to appreciating his unique reputation.

3.4 THE THREE JURISPRUDENTIAL LEGACIES OF CHIEF JUSTICE MASON

Mason's judicial legacy is most closely related to his tenure after he ascended to the chief justiceship, with the general consensus being that there are two distinct intellectual periods in his High Court career.[23] His jurisprudence is best understood in three distinct dimensions, each of which has endured to such a degree as to cement Mason's position as the towering jurist of contemporary Australian law.

The three dimensions can be broadly categorised as, first, his rejection of the formalistic legalism that had dominated the Court, at least in its rhetoric, since the 1920 decision in the *Engineers* case and been famously defended by Dixon. By advocating for a more transparent examination of value judgments in judicial development of law, Mason launched Australia's first sustained conversation about the proper role of the judge as a law-maker. Indeed, this ongoing conversation continues to be defined by reference to the value-based reasoning

---

[22] *Melbourne Corporation* v *Commonwealth* (1947) 74 CLR 31 and, more controversially, *Commonwealth v Cigamatic Pty Ltd (in liq)* (1962) 108 CLR 372.

[23] See, especially, Kirby (*supra* n 7), but also Walker (*supra* n 8) and the views quoted in Pierce (*supra* n 11) ch 6.

introduced by Mason.[24] The second was his turn away from an unfaltering faith in parliament's role in securing the protection of the rights of individuals, and the concomitant rise in the role of the Court in securing these protections. The third was his articulation of a consistent set of constitutional values through which he would approach the resolution of constitutional issues, at the core of which was the protection of the individual and the promotion of their place in the democratic system.

3.4.1 *Mason's Turn to Realism*

During his period as puisne judge under the leadership of Chief Justices Barwick and Gibbs, Mason's intellectual repudiation of Dixon's 'strict and complete legalism' had not manifested explicitly; indeed, he appeared to defend it in both private and public law cases. In a negligence case, *State Government Insurance Commission v Trigwell*, Mason issued a stern warning against overzealous embrace by courts of their law-making role, warning that 'the court is neither a legislature nor a law reform agency'.[25] In constitutional law, Mason's early approach to the judge's interpretative role is often associated with his tart statement in *Miller* v *TCN Channel Nine*:

> There was an alternative argument put by the defendant, based on the judgment of Murphy J in *Buck* v *Bavone*, that there is to be implied in the Constitution a new set of freedoms which include a guarantee of freedom of communication. It is sufficient to say that I cannot find any basis for implying a new s 92A into the Constitution.[26]

Yet, in later cases after his ascension to the chief justiceship, both in the development of the law of negligence[27] and in drawing the now well-established implied freedom of political communication,[28] Mason exhibited far less consternation as to a more proactive role for the judge as law-maker.

The idea that Mason's career can be perfectly bifurcated is, however, too simplistic. As early as 1975, Mason extra-curially explored a view that courts should more 'actively develop the law by reference to political, social and economic considerations in the

---

[24] See, e.g., Rosalind Dixon, 'The Functional Constitution: Re-Reading the 2014 High Court Constitutional Term' (2015) 43(3) *Federal Law Review* 455; Rosalind Dixon (ed.), *Australian Constitutional Values* (Hart, 2018).

[25] *State Government Insurance Commission v Trigwell* (1979) 142 CLR 617, 633; see also *Dugan v Mirror Newspapers Ltd* (1978) 142 CLR 583; *Australian Conservation Foundation v Commonwealth* (1980) 146 CLR 493, 552.

[26] *Miller v TCN Channel Nine* (1986) 161 CLR 556, 579.

[27] See, e.g., *Trident General Insurance v McNiece* (1988) 165 CLR 107; *Burnie Port Authority v General Jones* (1994) 179 CLR 520; *Bryan v Maloney* (1995) 182 CLR 609.

[28] *ACTV v Commonwealth* (1992) 177 CLR 106; *Nationwide News v Wills* (1992) 177 CLR 1; *Stephens v West Australian Newspapers* (1994) 182 CLR 211; *Theophanous v Herald & Weekly Times* (1994) 182 CLR 104.

fashion of the United States courts'.[29] Consistent with his stance in *Trigwell*, Mason expressed hesitancy based on the institutional limitations of the courts. But he was dismayed that '[i]ncreasingly it seems that Parliaments are concerned with the politics of survival, and in this process regular law reform is not likely to receive its due measure of attention'.[30] In 1985, Mason delivered a lecture at the University of Virginia Law School titled 'The Role of a Constitutional Court in a Federation: A Comparison of the Australian and the United States Experience'.[31] The Virginia address is pivotal to understanding the development of Mason's thinking. He explained the relationship between the interpretative approach of the courts and constitutional amendment as follows: 'The need for constitutional reform is directly affected by the methods of constitutional interpretation adopted by courts, for if courts apply static rather than dynamic principles of interpretation, the case for reform will be so much the stronger.'[32] Mason then explained the High Court's adoption of legalism by reference to the prevailing belief in the supremacy of parliament and the primacy of parliament as law-maker.[33] But, despite the restraint of the Court, the Australian parliament and electorate had proven stubbornly resistant to formal change.[34]

Mason proceeded with a devastating critique of Dixonian legalism, saying that this orthodoxy has led to 'an unwillingness on the part of our courts to undertake an activist role' and to participate in the determination of political issues and even engage with policy.[35] Legalism was a fallacy: '[I]t is impossible to interpret any instrument, let alone a constitution, divorced from values.'[36] He then articulated his vision of interpretation, creating a framework in which judges should transparently reason out their conclusions, for the 'ever present danger is that "strict and complete legalism" will be a cloak for undisclosed and unidentified policy values'.[37] Those covert values were sustained by the doctrine of precedent, showing the inherent conservatism of legalism and its resistance to changes in community expectations. Mason was candid that a shift from the orthodoxy of 'strict and complete legalism' would affect not just the substantive decisions of the Court but also the engagement of Australian society with the Constitution and the Court's judgments. The criticism this would inevitably attract would be a 'small price to pay' if it were to contribute 'to a stronger sense of constitutional awareness on the part of the community and a more accurate appreciation of the issues arising for decision'.[38] He acknowledged

---

[29] Anthony Mason 'Where Now?' (1975) 49 *Australian Law Journal* 570, 572.
[30] Ibid. 573.
[31] Anthony Mason, 'The Role of a Constitutional Court in a Federation: A Comparison of the Australian and the United States Experience' (1986) 16 *Federal Law Review* 1.
[32] Ibid. 2.
[33] Ibid. 4.
[34] Ibid. 2.
[35] Ibid. 4.
[36] Ibid. 5.
[37] Ibid.
[38] Ibid. 12.

that this approach would require judges to explain their decisions, articulate the competing values in a case and how they balanced these values to arrive at the particular outcome. No longer would the Court be able to assert a single correct resolution; rather, it would place itself in a conversation about the foundational constitutional values of the modern Australian nation. He explained: 'We may then persuade the rational and intelligent reader that the Court's decision stems from a reasoned and balanced consideration of relevant factors, even if its correctness continues to be the subject of continuing debate.'[39] Mason's repudiation of legalism was not to be confused with the unshackled and subjective approach of the controversial Justice Lionel Murphy. Rather, he accepted the inherent and inevitable role of values in interpretation and the desirability of objectively articulating, elaborating and defending their choice and utility. When considered against his earlier views on the Court's role as a law-maker and the failure of the Australian parliament to engage in serious long-term reform, what emerges is not a picture of a judge turned activist but a carefully considered compromise. The transparency and rigour that Mason advocated in lieu of legalism are what explains the jurisprudential appeal and longevity of his vision.

That Mason would ultimately adopt such an approach in constitutional interpretation is perhaps no surprise. He had a long history in equity as both a practitioner and a teacher, in which the role of judicial discretion, informed by legal values such as justice and equality, was not just well accepted but foundational. Indeed, in his private law jurisprudence, Mason would also extend the reach of equitable remedies and discretion into the broader commercial sphere.[40]

Mason's jurisprudential vision augured an interpretative and therefore doctrinal change for the High Court of Australia that he would go on to lead. 'Activism' was a label that Mason himself used to describe a Court that embraced a more explicitly and transparently law-making role with responsibility for grappling with policy and value choice. During his tenure as chief justice, particularly after the Court's decisions in 1992 establishing the implied freedom of political communication,[41] and native title,[42] government and conservative political and legal commentators would deploy the label of 'activist' more negatively, with the undertone of a Court that had *inappropriately* overstepped its legitimate institutional role. 'Activism' evoked an affront to the orthodoxy born of a tradition of parliamentary supremacy and a belief that legal change based on changing social values was the exclusive province of the legislature.

Mason had foreseen, and appeared to embrace, the prospect of robust criticism of a more transparent and values-explicit judicial reasoning. He went on to engage as

---

[39]   Ibid. 28.
[40]   See, further, Anthony Mason, 'The Place of Equity and Equitable Remedies in the Contemporary Common Law World' (1994) 110 *Law Quarterly Review* 238.
[41]   *ACTV v Commonwealth* (1992) 177 CLR 106; *Nationwide News v Wills* (1992) 177 CLR 1.
[42]   *Mabo v Queensland [No 2]* (1992) 175 CLR 1.

a statesman, to defend extrajudicially, including in the media, his conception of the role of the Court and its interpretative approach and reasons. However, he had not, at least explicitly, anticipated the *institutional* response of the political branches. Mason's term as chief justice co-existed alongside an unbroken Labor government in Canberra. In 1996, a conservative government under then prime minister John Howard was elected. Howard's response to the Mason Court was to expressly engineer a return to the conservative values protected through legalism and respect for parliamentary decision-making through new judicial appointments.

In its midst, many commentators overestimated the political and legal conservative backlash against and retreat from Mason's interpretative legacy in the late 1990s and early 2000s. The contemporary High Court has been less antagonistic towards, and indeed has re-embraced, the explicit value-evaluated reasoning of the Mason era. Even Howard's supposed conservative appointments displayed a jurisprudence strongly reflective of Mason's realism and extended the Court's role in updating the Constitution to accord with contemporary community values. The perceived wisdom that the Court under Mason's successor, Murray Gleeson, was attempting to distance itself from open-values-based legal reasoning has been assessed by Leslie Zines as 'more a matter of tone and style than of substance'.[43] Most notably, the Gleeson Court extended the individual protections offered by the provisions that provide for Australia's parliament to be 'directly chosen by the people' to include an implied constitutional 'right to vote'.[44] Recently, under Chief Justice Susan Kiefel, a majority of the Court has adopted a European-style structured proportionality test under the implied freedom of political communication, requiring more transparent and explicit evaluation of competing constitutional values.[45]

3.4.2 *Displacing Parliament as the Protector of Rights*

Part of Mason's turn towards a more explicit value-balancing interpretative approach responded to his disillusionment with the modern parliament; accordingly, his denunciation of legalism included its perpetuation of parliament's role as rights protector. In the Virginia speech, he summarised the Australian orthodoxy: '[W]e have regarded the United Kingdom, where parliamentary supremacy is not qualified by any constitutional guarantees, as the shining illustration of a free and democratic society in which the rights of the individual are fully protected by law.'[46] But, through an American comparison, Mason reflected favourably on judicial decision-making as

---

[43] Leslie Zines, 'Gleeson Court' in Tony Blackshield, Michael Coper, and George Williams (eds.), *The Oxford Companion to the High Court of Australia* (Oxford University Press, 2001) 307, 308.
[44] *Roach v Australian Electoral Commission* (2007) 233 CLR 162.
[45] See *McCloy v New South Wales* (2015) 257 CLR 178; *Brown v Tasmania* (2017) 261 CLR 328; *Clubb v Edwards* [2019] HCA 11.
[46] Mason (*supra* n 31) 11.

'more likely to be principled and reasoned' than the political process for protection of rights.

Mason's shift was more nuanced than simply a diminished faith in parliament's capabilities. He reached for a more highly developed understanding of democracy, away from simple and exclusive emphasis on parliament's acts as an expression of majority will and towards 'a notion of responsible government which respect[ed] the fundamental rights and dignity of the individual'.[47] As he explained in 1989, legislative actions will often be distorted by unequal voting rights, political structures and practices, and, often, 'majority' will be 'no more than a selfish pursuit of the majority interest in disregard of the legitimate interests of the minority'.[48]

Mason's preference for judicial intervention to protect and promote the rights of individuals was evident in a multitude of legal areas and drew on a slew of constitutional values that we explore in Section 3.4.3. Most controversial were the 1992 decisions pertaining to native title and those relating to the implied freedom of political communication. In *Mabo v Queensland [No 2]*, the High Court, for the first time, accepted that Australia had not been 'terra nullius', as asserted by the British in their act of settlement, and that native title continued to be recognised under the common law. The leading judgment of Justice Brennan, with which Mason agreed, drew on changing international expectations and 'the contemporary values of the Australian people'.[49] The implied freedom of political communication cases drew on constitutional requirements of democratic participation to found an implied limit on legislative power.[50] In his reasoning, Mason looked to the foundational values of popular sovereignty and the protection of the integrity of the constitutionally prescribed democratic system. Other rights-related decisions of the Mason era included protecting the right to legal representation of an indigent accused charged with a serious offence[51] and affirmation of the rule of statutory construction known as the principle of legality, in which the Court will presume that parliament does not intend to override fundamental common law rights except by express words or necessary intendment.[52]

The legacy of Mason's faith in the judiciary to undertake a rights-protecting role has continued at both the legal and the political level in Australia. Despite later conservative appointments to the High Court, none of the Mason Court's doctrines were overturned. Although there was a period of abeyance in their use, to strike down legislation, more recently, Mason's concern with protecting the right to a fair trial has been extended in the Court's reinvigoration of its chapter III and

---

[47]   Anthony Mason, 'Future Directions in Australian Law' (1987) 13 *Monash Law Review* 149, 163.
[48]   Anthony Mason, 'A Bill of Rights for Australia?' (1989) *Australian Bar Review* 79, 81.
[49]   *Mabo v Queensland [No 2]* (1992) 175 CLR 1, 42.
[50]   *Nationwide News v Wills* (1992) 177 CLR 1 and *ACTV v Commonwealth* (1992) 177 CLR 106.
[51]   *Dietrich v The Queen* (1992) 177 CLR 292.
[52]   *Coco v The Queen* (1994) 179 CLR 427.

separation of powers jurisprudence.[53] The principle of legality has continued its ascendancy unabated to become one of the most important contemporary rules of statutory construction. Despite minority protestations by some judges, the High Court has extended the democratic foundations of the implied freedom of political communication to an implied protection of the franchise and has used the implication to strike down four legislative schemes.[54] Politically, Australia has seen the introduction of comprehensive legislative rights schemes in the Australian Capital Territory, Victoria and now Queensland, with ongoing debate as to whether a comprehensive national rights framework is needed.

3.4.3 *Articulating Australian Constitutional Values*

Mason's interpretative aspiration for the Constitution, to move towards a more transparent and rigorous articulation of the values that inform judicial decision-making in place of legalism's cloaking of a conservative value set, required him to identify, deploy and defend his own set of constitutional values. Those values can be examined at various levels of abstraction with different focal points. Here, we cleave them into three meta-values: popular sovereignty and the role of the individual in a democratic system; federally driven values, emphasizing the need for equality across the nation and a strong national government operating in a global system of governance; and the importance of judicial fair process.

Popular sovereignty: Mason's move away from the political protection of rights unsurprisingly led to a particular focus on the individual. Not simply following a global trend of elevating the protection of liberal rights values over others, Mason's approach was intimately connected to his understanding of the democratic foundations of the Australian constitutional system. This was evident in his embrace of popular sovereignty as the foundation of Australia's constitutional document, rather than its status merely as an act of the Imperial parliament. By reference to this foundation and the democratic platforms provided in the constitutional text, Mason drew the implied limitation on legislative power to protect communication about government and political matters. The foundation operates generally to protect the civil and political freedoms of the people of the Australian demos. As Brendan Lim has explained, Mason's claims to popular sovereignty would also buttress his vision of the Court as a law-maker, as it gave the Court 'its own power to speak for the sovereign people when legislative processes were perceived to have failed'.[55]

---

[53] See, e.g., Brendan Lim, 'Attributes and Attribution of State Courts: Federalism and the Kable Principle'(2012) 40 *Federal Law Review* 31; Gabrielle Appleby and John Williams, 'A New Coat of Paint: Law and Order and the Refurbishment of *Kable*' (2012) 40 *Federal Law Review* 1.

[54] *Unions NSW v New South Wales* (2013) 252 CLR 530; *Brown v Tasmania* [2017] HCA 43; *Roach v Electoral Commissioner* (2007) 233 CLR 162; *Rowe v Electoral Commissioner* (2010) 243 CLR 1.

[55] Lim (*supra* n 6) 163. This position, of course, raises the now familiar questions about the ability of courts to make decisions on behalf of the people, particularly when they are in opposition to the decisions taken by the democratically elected branches.

Federally driven values: Reflecting his experience as Commonwealth Solicitor General, Mason was always perceptive as to the place of the central government in the Federation and the interrelationships among the states across it. His federalism jurisprudence was distinctly centralist, which continued and extended the effect of the Court's methodology from the *Engineers* decision. But, in contrast to the legalistic explanation of *Engineers*, Mason provided a rationale for preferring a broader interpretative approach to federal power as part of Australia's broader social progress:

> [T]he complexity of modern life, the integration of commerce, technological advance, the rise of the welfare society, even the intrusive and expanding reach of international affairs into domestic affairs, require increasing action on the part of the national government, so that it seldom appears that a narrow interpretation would best give effect to the objects of the Constitution.[56]

Mason's sensitivity to the Commonwealth's place in the Federation was no doubt informed by his understanding, likely gleaned by his work with the United Nations Commission on International Trade Law (UNCITRAL) and other international bodies during his time as Solicitor General, of Australia's emergence as a nation independent from Britain and the increasingly rapid globalisation of all dimensions of governance. A strong central government, able to engage in the international sphere, drove, for instance, an interpretation of the external affairs power that allowed the Commonwealth to implement all of its international obligations, regardless of whether their subject matter concerned matters of purely domestic concern.[57]

Mason was also alive to the dangers of discriminatory treatment in the Federation for the nation's economic harmony and international competitiveness.[58] This was evident in many areas of the Court's jurisprudence, including the interpretation of protections granted to inter-state residents,[59] the protection of inter-state trade and commerce,[60] and in protecting the states from Commonwealth legislation that would undermine their capacity to operate as autonomous units in the Federation.[61] Yet, Mason was not inflexible: economic competitiveness was not always a trumping priority and must be placed in its wider social context. His judgments moulded exceptions that allowed regulatory and social welfare-based exceptions to his broadly drawn prohibitions.

Judicial fair process: Lastly, fairness was a key value over Mason's jurisprudence. While evident in his development of a doctrine of substantive equality in the

---

[56]   Mason (*supra* n 31) 23.

[57]   *Commonwealth v Tasmania (Tasmanian Dam Case)* (1983) 158 CLR 1.

[58]   Anthony Mason, 'Law and Economics' (1991) 17 *Monash University Law Review* 167.

[59]   Section 117: *Street v Queensland Bar Association* (1989) 168 CLR 461.

[60]   Section 92: *Cole v Whitfield* (1988) 165 CLR 360.

[61]   Under the *Melbourne Corporation* doctrine: *Queensland Electricity Commission v Commonwealth* (1985) 159 CLR 162, 217.

federalism sphere, and clear in his recognition of continuing native title in *Mabo*, it was most explicit in cases concerning judicial process. Chief examples are where the Court exercised its discretion to stay a trial to protect the right to legal representation of an indigent accused charged with a serious offence,[62] and in requiring jury warnings to be provided in relation to uncorroborated police confessions made in the absence of a lawyer.[63]

The clarity with which Mason revealed and articulated this value-set had no comparable precedent in Australian constitutional law. It is unquestionably a progress-minded set of values, each conceived to reflect the changing context in which Australia found itself. Such an avowed judicial commitment to moving the nation forward was absent in Australian constitutional history. The other seismic shift in Australian constitutional law, Chief Justice Isaac Isaacs's turning of the Court in 1920 in the *Engineers* decision, occurred through the prism of legalism and was explained only in progressive-value terms in much later hindsight.[64] This value-set was capable of attracting a majority of the Court. Remarkably, it has also endured, and indeed supported the further development of the implied right to vote by the Gleeson Court (1998–2008) and a more explicit articulation of requirements for fair process by the French Court (2008–2017) in its chapter III jurisprudence.

3.5 CHIEF JUSTICE MASON IN CONTEXT: HIS TIMES AND HIS COURT

Fortune features in Mason's claim to judicial greatness – he came to the chief justiceship at a propitious time in the life of both the nation and the High Court, which was intellectually, geographically and experientially diverse (in comparison, for instance, to the backgrounds of the judges on the Dixon Court) yet remarkably cohesive. Under these circumstances, Mason's personal strengths were not merely amplified but also afforded new and broader possibilities – which he grasped, when others may have demurred.

3.5.1 *Mason's Times*

Former High Court justice Michael Kirby identified various factors that might explain what he saw as Mason's 'judicial metamorphosis' from the orthodox judge who arrived at the High Court in 1972.[65] Among these is included the 1981 move of the High Court to a permanent home in the 'constitutional triangle' of parliament

---

[62] *Dietrich v The Queen* (*supra* n 51).

[63] *McKinney v The Queen* (1991) 171 CLR 468.

[64] Although note *Victoria v Commonwealth* (*Payroll Tax Case*) (1971) 122 CLR 353, 395–7 (Windeyer J).

[65] Kirby (*supra* n 7) 1091. For a more institutionally focused account, see Cheryl Saunders, 'The Mason Court in Context' in Cheryl Saunders, *Courts of Final Jurisdiction: The Mason Court in Australia* (Federation Press, 1996) 2.

and the executive offices in the national capital. Kirby speculated that this provided a symbolic impetus to 'a new national vision of the Court'.[66] This physical positioning of the Court within view of the two other branches of government was followed soon after by the formal affirmation of Australia's independence as well as a growing sense of distinctive national identity, through events such as that which celebrated the bicentenary of European settlement and a greater willingness to look outwards for its place in a rapidly globalising world.

In 1986, the year before Mason's elevation to the chief justiceship, Australia attained full legal independence from the United Kingdom through the enactment of the Australia Acts by the states, Commonwealth and the Imperial parliament at Westminster. The passage of these Acts severed all remaining institutional ties to the UK, including the presence of the Privy Council in the Australian courts system, and prompted reflection on what sustained the Constitution's authority and what this might mean for its interpretation.

Although contemporary commentary accepted that popular sovereignty may now provide 'an additional, although not necessarily alternative', explanation to the historical fact of the Constitution's legally binding character as an Imperial enactment, the impact of this change was forecast as unlikely to be major.[67] However, Mason was quick to signal the possible implications of the legal independence secured by the Australia Acts, which he likened in his Virginia speech to the patriation of the Canadian Constitution just a few years earlier.[68] Acknowledging the popular process of drafting and ratifying the Australian Constitution bill over the late 1890s before it was presented to the Imperial parliament for enactment, Mason concluded that the Constitution 'is as much a reflection of the will of the people as the United States Constitution and it should be interpreted accordingly'.[69] He then added that the Australia Acts now provide 'a firmer foundation for the view that the status of the Constitution as a fundamental law springs from the authority of the Australian people'.[70]

This was an unmistakeable shift from the prevailing orthodoxy that the Constitution did not derive its legal force from the inherent authority of the people to constitute their government.[71] Prior to the Australia Acts, only Murphy had challenged this understanding. While debate continues over Murphy's later influence on the decisions of the Mason Court,[72] Mason's view was that Murphy's 'judicial methodology and judicial style made it very difficult to agree with his

[66] Kirby (*supra* n 7) 1093.
[67] Geoffrey Lindell, 'Why Is Australia's Constitution Binding? The Reasons in 1900 and Now, and the Effect of Independence' (1986) 16 *Federal Law Review* 29, 37, 43–9.
[68] Mason (*supra* n 31) 4.
[69] Ibid. 24.
[70] Ibid.
[71] Sir Owen Dixon, 'The Law and the Constitution' (1935) 51 *Law Quarterly Review* 590, 597.
[72] Michael Coper and George Williams (eds.), *Justice Lionel Murphy: Influential or Merely Prescient?* (Federation Press, 1997); Michael Kirby, 'Lionel Murphy and the Power of Ideas' (1993) 18 *Alternative Law Journal* 253; and Lim (*supra* n 6).

judgments'.[73] But the passage of the Australia Acts decisively altered the constitutional landscape so as to make the question of popular sovereignty inescapable to some degree. The Constitution's provision of representative, as well as responsible, government acquired significant potential through the underlying authority of popular sovereignty to transform the High Court's role as a protector of individual freedoms. As described in Section 3.4.2, this was seized with alacrity by Mason and a majority of the Court he led in the implied rights cases of the early 1990s and has sustained other innovations since, notably regarding voting rights.

Just why the Mason Court moved on rights when it did prompt acknowledgement of an additional contextual factor – the failure of a major attempt at constitutional reform over the second half of the preceding decade. The Hawke Labor government had experimented with successively weaker drafts of human rights instruments in its first two terms – ultimately abandoning the exercise despite obtaining passage of a bill through the lower house.[74] In the alternative, the government established a Constitutional Commission in 1985, tasked with reporting on possible reform of the Australian Constitution, including for the protection of democratic rights, by mid-1988. In his Virginia speech, Mason noted this development but observed that 'if past history is a reliable guide[,] only a bold prophet would predict that the Commission's deliberations will result in wide-ranging constitutional reform'.[75]

His scepticism was vindicated. The work of the Commission and its five Advisory Committees fell victim to political expediency – the findings of its Interim Report being selectively used to support a rushed and poorly pitched referendum campaign for formal amendment of the Constitution that was decisively rejected by the people in 1988.[76] Unsurprisingly, there was no political appetite later for the Commission's two-volume Final Report containing a comprehensive set of recommendations for substantial change. Mason's views on the deficiencies of the political branches in carrying out law reform, voiced as early as 1975, have already been traced. It is not hard to imagine that, first, the timidity and, then, the incompetence of the Hawke government in securing better protection of rights spurred the Court to assume greater responsibility to do so, consistent with the significance of popular sovereignty in recasting its institutional role.

3.5.2 *Mason's Court*

As so much of the judicial leadership literature recognises, it is impossible to understand the work of any senior appellate judge in strict isolation from their

---

73 Anthony Mason, 'Personal Relations: A Personal Reflection' in Tony Blackshield, Michael Coper and George Williams (eds.), *The Oxford Companion to the High Court of Australia* (Oxford University Press, 2001) 531, 531.

74 George Williams and Daniel Reynolds, *A Charter of Rights for Australia*, 4th edition (University of New South Wales Press, 2017) 101–2.

75 Mason (*supra* n 31) 3.

76 George Williams and David Hume, *People Power: The History and Future of the Referendum in Australia* (University of New South Wales Press, 2010) 167–81.

colleagues. Mason's reputation depends as much on the decisions of the 'Mason Court' as it does on those he personally delivered. The fact that it was rare for the two to be at odds with each other is one reason why the familiar (but not unproblematic) practice of affixing a chief justice's name to demarcate eras in the institutional life of a court seems appropriate in his case. To speak of the 'Mason Court' means something – in the way that to speak of the 'Warren Court' does in respect of the US Supreme Court. But, as Mason was keen to point out: 'The High Court is not a monolithic institution. It is at any time a group of seven justices who are obliged to hear and determine, according to their individual judgment, particular cases.'[77]

Sir Gerard Brennan, who served with Mason for fourteen years and succeeded him as chief justice, acknowledged the utility of referring to the 'Mason Court' but emphasized that it did not accurately describe 'the dynamics of a Court constituted by Justices of robust independence of mind, willing and able to give cogent expression to their own views'.[78] In this regard, it is important that our nomination of Mason as a 'towering' judge is viewed through the lens of collegial leadership that is provided by Rosalind Dixon in Chapter 17 of this book. While the traditional norm in the High Court of Australia has been one of high individualism through the separate expression of opinions *in seriatim*,[79] the Mason Court tended more often to express its reasoning in unanimous and joint judgments when consensus could be reached – most famously in the s 92 thunderbolt of *Cole* v *Whitfield*.[80] Conversely, the number of cases decided through separate concurrences with no dissent was correspondingly low.[81] This was at least in part the result of Mason's fostering of a 'collegiate spirit' amongst the justices,[82] which stood in stark contrast to the High Court he had joined in 1972, whose abrasive chief justice, Sir Garfield Barwick, struggled in a misguided attempt to impose order.

While leading the Court in a 'more concerted effort' to achieve joint or majority judgments,[83] Mason was aware that 'diversity of opinion was ... one of the consequences of the movement away from traditional legal formalism to a concern with openness and substance rather than form'.[84] His aspiration, to draw the Court

---

[77] Sir Anthony Mason, 'Foreword' in Haig Patapan, *Judging Democracy: The New Politics of the High Court of Australia* (Cambridge University Press, 2000) viii–ix.
[78] Sir Gerard Brennan, 'A Tribute to Sir Anthony Mason' in Saunders (*supra* n 65) 10, 10. See also Sir Anthony Mason, 'A Reply' in Saunders (*supra* n 65) 113, 113.
[79] Paresh Narayan and Russell Smyth, 'The Consensual Norm of the High Court of Australia 1904–2001' (2005) 26 *International Political Science Review* 147.
[80] *Cole* v *Whitfield* (1988) 165 CLR 360.
[81] Matthew Groves and Russell Smyth, 'A Century of Judicial Style: Changing Patterns in Judgment Writing on the High Court 1903–2001' (2004) 32 *Federal Law Review* 255, 272–3; Andrew Lynch, 'Does the High Court Disagree More Often in Constitutional Cases? A Statistical Study of Judgment Delivery 1981–2003' (2005) 33 *Federal Law Review* 485, 497–500.
[82] Brennan (*supra* n 78), 13.
[83] Sir Anthony Mason, 'The Centenary of the High Court of Australia' (2003) 5 *Constitutional Law and Policy Review* 41, 42.
[84] Mason (*supra* n 83).

towards a more transparent, objective and rational articulation of the values that underlie judicial decision-making, was always likely to inhibit the delivery of more majority joint judgments of the Court. In his Virginia speech articulating his interpretative vision, he said that 'in some cases we reach a point where principles of the individual cannot be sacrificed to the expedient compromise' and that compromise 'blunts the points of principle'.[85]

As one judge among seven (with just one change between 1987 and 1995), Mason enjoyed a very low personal rate of dissent – just over 6 per cent. By contrast, all those who served with him had a dissent rate that was more than double that, and sometimes triple it.[86] Mason's uniquely low incidence of dissent on his own Court held in constitutional cases – unlike his immediate predecessor Chief Justice Gibbs, whose constitutional views were marginalised on his own Court. Yet, consistent with the institutional pattern described in Section 3.5.2, all members of the Mason Court had a high rate of participation in unanimous judgments, in the low 20 per cent range.

The overall picture is of a court operating at full strength, each individual's independence explaining the frequency of minority views across the bench, but-tressed by a clear capacity to work towards the common expression of agreement, and the chief justice sitting at the intellectual centre, creating the optimal conditions for his colleagues to carry out their institutional responsibilities. The Court under Dixon, whose members were highly regarded, might be described in similar terms, but the dynamic of that body was arguably unbalanced by his unquestioned domin-ance and its intellectual conformity. Further, it lacked the geographic and experi-ential diversity of the Mason Court, drawn not just from the two most populous states of New South Wales and Victoria but also from Queensland and Western Australia. A former Commonwealth Solicitor General, Mason was joined by three former state Solicitors General (Daryl Dawson, Mary Gaudron and Ronald Wilson), who each would have brought with them a keen understanding of the operations of govern-ment and an ease with the machinations of policy-making. Justice William Deane, who arrived at the High Court in 1982 and had, like Mason, been taught at the University of Sydney in the 1940s by influential Challis Professor of Jurisprudence and International Law Julius Stone,[87] was an especially important foil for Mason's intellect – unlike Murphy, Deane was able to articulate fresh ideas, particularly in respect of rights protection, in a way that was capable of attracting support and that demanded serious engagement.[88]

---

[85] Mason (*supra* n 31) 28.

[86] Lynch (*supra* n 81) 506–8.

[87] Michael Kirby, 'Julius Stone and the High Court of Australia' (1997) 20 *University of New South Wales Law Journal* 239, 245–6.

[88] George Williams, 'Lionel Murphy and Democracy and Rights' in Michael Coper and George Williams (eds.), *Justice Lionel Murphy: Influential or Merely Prescient?* (Federation Press, 1997) 63.

3.6 MASON BEYOND THE BENCH

Mason's call for transparency and candour in the decisions of the High Court was matched by a commitment to frank engagement with the profession, the media and the public about the Court's work and the shortcomings of Australia's constitutional system. He was aware that his ultimate vision for the High Court, in which the values that informed judicial law-making were articulated, contested and defended, would move it into a sphere of public and political controversy and criticism.[89] Judges would have to step into the public debate, explaining the role of the Court and, where necessary, individual decisions.

This need was made acute by a growing political disinclination to fulfil the traditional role of the Commonwealth Attorney General in defending the judiciary.[90] Although Mason rejected that stance,[91] he was already convinced of the need for a more active role for the judiciary:

> Attorneys-General do not and cannot always be expected to speak up for the judges. Even if they did, their remarks lack impact. These days people expect the actors themselves to speak so that they can form some picture of them as personalities. More than that, judges are in a better position than anyone else to give an account of what they are doing and enhance media and public understanding of the role of the courts. Greater communication by the judges will, I hope, lead to a better understanding of what the courts are doing and more informed debate about proposals for change which affect the Judiciary.[92]

Mason made himself publicly available to an unprecedented extent, including to defend the Court from what he saw as uninformed criticism of its decisions. Such criticisms included allegations of 'judicial radicalism' by conservative commentators,[93] 'naïve adventurism' by the head of a mining company[94] and descriptions by politicians of its engaging in 'political sophistry of the worst kind' and 'overstepp[ing] the line of the separation of powers and … [making] law'.[95] A former Attorney General and Supreme Court judge observed that there was 'something disquieting' about 'unelected judges making laws that are based on their assessments of what should be public policy',[96] and the dean of a leading Australian law school described the Mason Court as engaging in a 'judicial coup

[89] Mason (*supra* n 31); Anthony Mason 'The State of the Judicature' (1994) 68 *Australian Law Journal* 125, 134.
[90] First expressed when shadow attorney general; see Daryl Williams, 'Who Speaks for the Courts?' (1994) *AIJA* 183.
[91] Anthony Mason, 'No Place in a Modern Democratic Society for a Supine Judiciary' (1997) 35(11) *Law Society Journal* 51.
[92] Anthony Mason, 'The Australian Judiciary in the 1990s' (1994) 2 *Australian Law Librarian* 65, 71.
[93] Gerard Henderson, 'March of the High Court Murphyites', *Sydney Morning Herald*, 1 December 1992, 17.
[94] Margaret Easterbrook, 'Top Judge Backs Mabo', *The Age*, 2 July 1993, 1.
[95] Anne Davies and Peter Smark, 'High and Mighty', *Sydney Morning Herald*, 10 July 1993, 37.
[96] Attributed to Kep Enderby, ibid.

d'etat'.[97] In one of Mason's notable public interventions as chief justice, he provided a widely reported interview to the editor of the *Australian Lawyer* in which he responded to criticism of the Court's *Mabo* decision by explaining and defending the Court's reasoning.[98] While previous chief justices had made public speeches reported in the media, Mason's more strategic engagement was praised as 'a very important innovation' and, in the circumstances, a 'bold enterprise' that was nonetheless 'as successful as it was desirable'.[99] After his retirement, Mason justified his public explanations in these instances as important to correct 'erroneous criticisms' of the Court, including that it 'was wrong for judges to make law'.[100]

In the course of his chief justiceship, Mason delivered two 'State of the Judicature' addresses,[101] a practice inaugurated by Barwick in 1977 that provides an overview of the judicial systems across the Federation and an opportunity for the chief justice 'of Australia' to reflect on pressing issues facing the judiciary. In each of these addresses, while Mason covered a plethora of recent judicial developments, two themes dominated.[102] The first was the protection of judicial independence, with Mason particularly alive to institutional threats to the administrative independence of the courts: the adequate and independent funding of the courts and the payment of appropriate judicial salaries.[103] He also expressed concerns around the proper procedure for judicial removal and had earlier expressed disapproval of the new commission-based complaints scheme that had been introduced in New South Wales in 1987, advocating instead for a judge-led process.[104] But Mason also proved able to accommodate innovations within his conception of judicial independence, and saw virtue in, and defended, the advent of formalised systems for judicial education, at a time when these were still controversial.[105] He defended a judge-led system against concerns of indoctrination and inducement, and connected the importance of judicial education to his propounded theory of judicial interpretation, explaining that the 'need to maintain judicial independence is no argument against the desirability of judges becoming better informed about the interaction of law and society'.[106] The second key theme of Mason's State of the Judicature addresses was a deep and

---

97 Attributed to Professor Geoffrey Walker in Innis Wilcox, 'Judgment Was Most Divisive in History – Lawyer', *The Age*, 15 July 1993.
98 Barrie Virtue, 'The Chief Justice on Mabo', *The Age*, 2 July 1993. See also, e.g., Paul Chamberlin and Anne Davies, 'Top Judge Angers Miners', *Sydney Morning Herald*, 14 July 1993.
99 Leslie Zines, 'Sir Anthony Mason' (2000) 28 *Federal Law Review* 171, 175. See also Brennan (*supra* n 78) 13.
100 Anthony Mason, 'The Courts As Community Institutions' (1998) 9 *Public Law Review* 83, 87.
101 Anthony Mason 'The State of the Australian Judicature' (1989) 15 *Commonwealth Law Bulletin* 1533–40; Mason, 'The State of the Judicature' (*supra* n 89).
102 Mason, 'The State of the Judicature' (*supra* n 89) 131.
103 See, further, Margaret Easterbrook and Prue Innes, 'Duffy in Row with Top Judge on Pay', *The Age*, 4 April 1991.
104 Opening address to the Labor Lawyers Conference, 1987, reported in John Slee, 'The Ghost of Lionel Murphy', *Sydney Morning Herald*, 29 September 1987, 14.
105 Mason, 'The State of the Judicature' (*supra* n 89) 132–3.
106 Ibid. 133.

ongoing concern with the quality and accessibility of justice, including lengthy delays in criminal lists and the cost of justice in the form of prohibitive court fees and the provision of legal aid. Reflecting today on Mason's State of the Judicature addresses, we also find them worthy of mention because of what they *didn't* defend, most notably wariness around the value of diversity and representation in judicial appointment.[107]

A quarter of a century since he left the Court, Mason has continued to make influential extra-curial interventions responding to contemporary jurisprudence. His reflections on jurisdictional developments, in relation to exceptions to the separation of powers doctrines or the development of a structured proportionality test in the implied freedom of political communication debates,[108] have been significant in key doctrinal debates. He also continues to reflect on the institutional position and practice of the Court, for instance, offering an important intervention in the debate that erupted in 2013 relating to judicial collegiality and independence,[109] and observing the resilience of legalism.[110] Unsurprisingly, he has not shied from public debates about major constitutional law reform, including the move towards a republic[111] and the introduction of a national bill of rights.[112] His jurisprudential influence has also extended through his acceptance of institutional academic positions and, beyond these more formal roles, he continues to teach, supervise and mentor law students and young scholars in both a formal and an informal capacity.

Lastly, Mason's contribution to the law outside Australia, in particular through his post-High Court judicial appointments, must be acknowledged. Global constitutionalism is a theme of this book's examination of 'towering' judges and Mason's judicial career unambiguously displays this. He has been a foreign judge sitting on the final courts of appeal in Fiji, the Solomon Islands and Hong Kong, and has worked as a judge and lecturer at the Chinese National Judges College in Beijing. In these roles, Mason has once again been at the forefront in the development of a national constitutional jurisprudence for jurisdictions finding themselves at a point of fundamental systemic change – similar to the position of Australia when he became chief justice.

3.7 CONCLUSION

Australian jurisprudential debates today remain dominated by the tension between the old orthodoxy – the legalism that first triumphed in *Engineers* and would be

---

[107] Ibid. 131.
[108] Anthony Mason, 'The Use of Proportionality in Australian Constitutional Law' (2016) 27 *Public Law Review* 109.
[109] Anthony Mason, 'The High Court of Australia: Reflections on Judges and Judging' (2013) 16 *Southern Cross University Law Review* 1, 12.
[110] Anthony Mason, 'Foreword' in Rosalind Dixon and George Williams (eds.), *The High Court, the Constitution and Australian Politics* (Cambridge University Press, 2015) v.
[111] Anthony Mason, 'The Convention Model for the Republic' (1999) 10 *Public Law Review* 147.
[112] Anthony Mason, 'The Australian Judiciary in the 1990s' (1994) 2(2) *Australian Law Librarian* 65, and, post-retirement, Anthony Mason, 'Rights Bill a Matter for Judgement', *The Age*, 29 March 2006, 17.

cemented through the towering affirmation of Sir Owen Dixon – and the more explicitly values-driven reasoning that was introduced and developed under Sir Anthony Mason. Since he retired in 1995, it is against Mason's legacy that a new generation of legalists have had to define – and, indeed, defend – themselves. Yet, in the face of a conscious political attempt through the government's power of judicial appointments to push back against the innovations of Mason and his Court, his methods, values and doctrinal developments have proved remarkably resilient.

This resilience rests on a complex amalgam of factors. Mason and his Court managed to find the previously elusive middle ground between outright top-down, values-driven exercises of judicial power and the strictures and veneer of formalistic legalism. The constitutional values that he and his Court identified in the 1990s have continued to resonate, demonstrating that the Court was remarkably attuned to changing Australian social expectations as well as international ones. Mason was able to produce a coherent explanation of a forward-looking constitutional vision, institutionally locating the court as against the political branches and explaining the judiciary's appropriate role in law-making. And he was able to work collegially on this vision with the Court he led, creating strong precedents even in areas of new constitutional development. Finally, Mason brought the Court to the public: in extra-curial forays with the political branches and the media, he would defend the judiciary, fair process and access to justice in a way that no chief justice before him had. Today, almost three decades after Mason left the Court, he continues in these interventions, cementing a personal legacy as Australia's modern constitutional statesperson.

4

Lady Hale: A Feminist Towering Judge

Rosemary Hunter and Erika Rackley

4.1 INTRODUCTION

The choice of Lady Hale as the UK's representative towering judge in this collection will not be uncontroversial. Others might identify different contenders from amongst the senior UK judiciary of the twentieth and early twenty-first centuries, including Lord Diplock, Lord Reid, Lord Denning and Lord Bingham.[1] Some of these may indeed have had greater 'influence' from a strictly constitutional perspective, although the extent to which a strictly constitutional perspective is meaningful in the context of the UK's notoriously unwritten constitution is an open question. Our choice of Lady Hale is not intended to suggest that a number of her predecessors have not also towered in significant (although different) ways. Rather, we have chosen to write about Lady Hale because her judicial career and approach to judicial leadership have been consistently groundbreaking and, in the process, have challenged taken-for-granted notions of what it means to lead, and to tower, as a judge. The discussion of Lady Hale as a towering judge therefore provides an opportunity to explore the category of 'towering judge' more broadly.

There are many measures by which Lady Hale's status as a towering judge may be established. Her appointment as the first woman president of the UK Supreme Court (UKSC) in 2017 followed a lifetime of other firsts.[2] As an academic, she co-authored the first English textbook on women and law;[3] she subsequently became the first woman and the youngest person then appointed to the Law Commission,

---

[1] See, e.g., Mads Andenas and Duncan Fairgrieve (eds.), *Tom Bingham and the Transformation of the Law: A Liber Amicorum* (Oxford University Press, 2009); Richard Cornes, 'Gains (and Dangers of Losses) in Translation: The Leadership Function in the United Kingdom's Supreme Court, Parameters and Prospects' (2011) *Public Law* 509; Alan Paterson, *The Law Lords* (Hart Publishing, 1982) 116–19; Alan Paterson, *Final Judgment: The Last Law Lords and the Supreme Court* (Hart Publishing, 2013) 146.

[2] See, further, Erika Rackley, 'First Woman President of the UK Supreme Court, Brenda Hale, 2017' in Erika Rackley and Rosemary Auchmuty (eds.), *Women's Legal Landmarks: Celebrating the History of Women in Law in the UK and Ireland* (Hart Publishing, 2019) 645.

[3] Susan Atkins and Brenda Hoggett, *Women and the Law* (Blackwells, 1984; rprt Humanities Digital Library 2018).

and the first judge appointed to the High Court from an academic background rather than the practising Bar. She was the first and only woman ever appointed to the Appellate Committee of the House of Lords, the first woman appointed to the UKSC at its inception in 2009 and the Court's first woman deputy president and president. For twelve years from her appointment to the House of Lords in 2004 until Theresa May became prime minister in 2016, she was the most senior woman in the UK's constitutional structure after the Queen. Hale's catalogue of firsts is even more remarkable in that she was not a 'safe' appointment who closely resembled the traditional male incumbents of these offices; she was – and is – an avowed feminist who has consistently and strongly advocated for women's rights and greater judicial diversity.

She was also one of the UK's busiest and most accessible judges. By the time she retired in January 2020, she had written more UKSC judgments than any of her current or former judicial colleagues, and had also given more extrajudicial speeches and published more scholarly articles and books than any of those contemporaries. Long before her public profile reached its peak in late 2019, following her delivery of the *Miller* 2 decision declaring the prime minister's prorogation of Parliament to have been unlawful,[4] she regularly appeared on 'women in power' lists,[5] on the guest lecture circuit and on the Court's Instagram feed,[6] not to mention appearances in British *Vogue* and on the BBC's *MasterChef*, and being made the subject of a children's book.[7] Over the course of a career spanning more than fifty years, she influenced the development of UK law across a wide range of areas, having an impact on the lives of millions. She led the way on issues such as women's ownership of the family home, mental health and mental capacity, religious freedom, equality, children's rights, employment, housing and social welfare law, domestic abuse and sexual violence.

This chapter focuses particularly on the ways in which Lady Hale's feminism shaped and informed both how she was a judge and her 'towering' judicial status. First, in Section 4.2, we offer a brief overview of Lady Hale's life in law. We then go

---

[4] R *(on the application of Miller)* v *The Prime Minister; Cherry and others* v *Advocate General for Scotland (Scotland)* [2019] UKSC 41. For a tiny sample of the media coverage following this decision, see Lauren Cochrane and Martin Belam, 'Say It With a Brooch: What Message Was Lady Hale's Spider Sending?', *The Guardian*, 24 September 2019, www.theguardian.com/fashion/2019/sep/24/say-it-with-a-brooch-how-a-fashion-item-became-a-political-statement; Phoebe Cooke, 'Haleblazer: Who Is Lady Hale? Supreme Court Judge Whose Spider Broach Went Viral', *The Sun*, 25 September 2019, www.thesun.co.uk/news/9999888/lady-hale-supreme-court-judge-spider-brooch/; Sophie Gallagher, 'This Lady Hale Spider Brooch T-Shirt Sold Out in 24 Hours Raising £18k for Shelter', *Huffington Post*, 25 September 2019.

[5] Making it to number 4 on BBC Radio 4's Woman's Hour Power List in 2013, www.bbc.co.uk/programmes/profiles/2g5ZjCjovo2flw5qpCpkwHQ/baroness-hale-of-richmond.

[6] See, e.g., Katie King, 'Lady Hale Acknowledges "Beyoncé of the Legal Profession" Comparison', *Legal Cheek*, 25 October 2017, www.legalcheek.com/2017/10/lady-hale-acknowledges-beyonce-of-the-legal-profession-comparison/.

[7] Afua Hirsch, *Equal to Everything: Judge Brenda and the Supreme Court* (Legal Action Group, 2019).

on, in Section 4.3, to consider the various dimensions of her judicial leadership –
institutional, jurisprudential, political and beyond. In Section 4.4, we discuss
examples of her feminist judging and judgment-writing. We conclude, in Section
4.5, by arguing that as a *feminist* towering judge Lady Hale stood out but did not
stand in isolation from her judicial peers or the legal or wider community. In
contrast to the 'essential individualism' displayed by, and maybe expected of (at
least by some), other towering judges,[8] through her judgments as well as her
extrajudicial roles, Lady Hale created opportunities and spaces for others to flourish
and realise their own potential. Nor was she interested in 'tower[ing] over [her]
peers to distinguish [herself]'.[9] Rather, she used her institutional position to
redistribute power in several ways and to build ladders so that others, too, might
scale the walls.

4.2 A LIFE IN LAW

Most of Lady Hale's education and career took place within male-dominated
institutions. She lived in a boys' grammar school where her father was head,[10]
attended a boys' school for Latin lessons and was one of just six women reading
law in her year at Cambridge University, from which she graduated with a starred
first in 1966. After graduation, she joined the law school at Manchester University,
initially combining her academic post with study for, and later practice at, the
Manchester Bar. As an academic, she specialised in family law and was a pioneer
in the field of social welfare law, authoring one of the first textbooks on mental
health law[11] and becoming a founding editor of the *Journal of Social Welfare and
Family Law*. Her co-authored book on *Women and the Law* was also foundational
and demonstrated to generations of students[12] the value of bringing a feminist
perspective to the study of law. She joined the Law Commission in 1984 and, over
the next decade, was at the forefront of a number of law reform projects on children,
divorce and mental capacity, the fruits of which can still be seen today, most notably
in the Children Act 1989[13] and the Mental Capacity Act 2005. Both during her time
in academia and at the Law Commission, she consistently mentored and promoted
the careers of junior colleagues. In the words of one of her co-authors, she 'saw it as
a personal responsibility to advise, support and facilitate junior women [to] get

---

[8] Introduction to this volume.

[9] Ibid.

[10] Grammar schools were state-funded secondary schools that selected pupils on the basis of academic
    ability. Hale's background was middle class; her family was not part of the British social, political or
    economic elite.

[11] Brenda M Hoggett, *Mental Health*, 6th edition (Sweet & Maxwell, [1976]2017).

[12] Including the present authors.

[13] See, e.g., Lady Hale, '30 Years of the Children Act 1989', Scarman Lecture 2019 (Law Commission,
    London 13 November 2019), www.supremecourt.uk/docs/speech-191113.pdf.

published, especially in new and emerging disciplines' and set about 'doing something positive' to tackle covert barriers to women's careers 'quietly and effectively'.[14]

In 1994, she was appointed to the High Court, only the tenth woman ever to have received this accolade. Indeed, appointments of women to the Court were so few and far between that Hale inherited the judicial robes of Margaret Booth (the third woman appointee) who had in turn acquired them from Elizabeth Lane, the Court's first woman appointee.[15] Hale's promotion to the Court of Appeal in 1999 was relatively quick. While on the Court of Appeal, she proposed the foundation of the UK Association of Women Judges in 2003. She remains the Association's honorary president and, as attested by its website, 'has worked tirelessly with us and with the international association [of women judges] to promote the work of women judges in addressing women's issues'.[16]

In 2004, she was elevated to the Appellate Committee of the House of Lords. At this level, women were even more scarce. It would take almost fourteen years – and a further eighteen appointments – before another woman would join her.[17] In fact, Lady Hale's first duty as president of the UKSC in October 2017 was to swear in Lady Black, the second woman to be appointed to the Court.

Not everyone greeted Lady Hale's appointment to the UK's highest court with enthusiasm. By virtue of her previous work on the Law Commission, she was vilified by the conservative tabloid newspaper the *Daily Mail* as a 'hardline'[18] and 'radical'[19] feminist, a 'marriage wrecker'[20] with the potential to be 'trouble with a capital H',[21] whose 'elevation epitomises the moral vacuum within our judiciary'.[22] Her appointment made waves among her new judicial colleagues, too. Lord Hope, in his diaries,

---

[14] Susan Atkins, email to Rosemary Hunter, 16 September 2018.

[15] Paula Thompson interview with Brenda Hale for the National Life Story Collection (Hale, Brenda Marjorie, *National Life Story Collection: Legal Lives*, British Library Sounds, recorded 25 November 2008, 16 March 2010, 22 March 2010, 23 March 2010). The robes were later passed on to Dame Jill Black, now Lady Black, the second woman appointed to the UK Supreme Court. See, further, Royal Courts of Justice, 'Robes Event – Honouring Female Trailblazers in the Judiciary', 24 October 2019, www.judiciary.uk/announcements/robes-event-honouring-female-trailblazers-in-the -judiciary/.

[16] www.ukawj.org/who-we-are.

[17] The UK consistently languishes at the bottom of international league tables for judicial gender diversity. There is a voluminous academic literature on this issue, together with numerous reports and proposals for reform. A sample of recent publications includes: Graham Gee and Erika Rackley (eds.), *Debating Judicial Appointments in an Age of Diversity* (Routledge, 2017); JUSTICE, *Increasing Judicial Diversity* (2017) and *Increasing Judicial Diversity: An Update* (2020); Lord Chief Justice of England and Wales and Senior President of Tribunals, *Judicial Diversity Statistics 2019* (Judicial Office, 2019).

[18] Melanie Phillips, 'I Deplore His Actions but Actually His Cause Is Just', *Daily Mail*, 5 November 2003, www.dailymail.co.uk/columnists/article-229955/I-deplore-actions-actually-cause-just.html.

[19] Steve Doughty, 'The First Lady of the Law Lords (and She Wants to Abolish Marriage)', *Daily Mail*, 24 October 2003.

[20] Melanie Phillips, 'The Marriage Wrecker', *Daily Mail*, 13 November 2003, www.dailymail.co.uk /columnists/article-229952/THE-MARRIAGE-WRECKER.html.

[21] Ephraim Hardcastle, 'Editorial', *Daily Mail*, 13 January 2004.

[22] Phillips (*supra* n 18).

commented that 'Brenda will be a source of some anxiety until we adjust to the very different contribution that she will make'.[23] In this context, adverse commentary on the recent *Miller 2* case – accusing Hale of threatening parliamentary sovereignty[24] and of leading a 'cult' of 'girly swots' intent on dragging the law into politics[25] – combining criticism of her progressive views and perceived judicial activism with gender-based derision – was nothing new.[26] Nevertheless, it seems clear that she left the Court as one of the UK's most well-liked and respected[27] and certainly most well-known judges; a judge who – to paraphrase her final remarks at her valedictory ceremony – can 'retire content', having succeeded in her wish to inspire 'a younger generation to believe in the ideals of justice, fairness and equality and to think that they might put them into practice'.[28]

4.3 A RECORD OF JUDICIAL LEADERSHIP

As the editors of this volume note in their Introduction, one way in which to assess a judge's 'towering' credentials is through the lens of judicial leadership. While recognising that judicial leadership may be manifested in different ways, varying over time, by court and/or the personality of the judge, asking to what extent an

[23] Quoted in David Pannick, 'Judicial Gossip and Withering Verdicts: It's the Diary of a Law Lord', *The Times*, 14 March 2019, www.thetimes.co.uk/article/judicial-gossip-and-withering-verdicts-its-the-diary-of-a-law-lord-pbvr36rdz.

[24] Richard Ekins, *Protecting the Constitution: How and Why Parliament Should Limit Judicial Power* (Policy Exchange, 2020) 15.

[25] Ella Whelan, 'The Cult of Lady Hale', *Spiked*, 25 September 2019, www.spiked-online.com/2019/09/25/the-cult-of-lady-hale/. Cf. Richard Ekins and Graham Gee, 'Will the UK's New Senior Judge Change the Supreme Court?', *The Spectator*, 6 October 2017, www.spectator.co.uk/article/will-the-uk-s-new-senior-judge-change-the-supreme-court- who accuse Hale of being 'politically naïve'. 'Girly swot' is a term of abuse that encapsulates the cultural distaste for intelligent women and that can be applied as a put-down to both women and men. It was famously used by UK Prime Minister Boris Johnson in reference to former prime minister David Cameron, with regard to his introduction of the Fixed Term Parliaments Act 2011, which prevented Johnson from calling an election in late 2019, resulting in his attempt instead to prorogue Parliament for a lengthy period. See, e.g., Peter Walker, 'Boris Johnson Calls David Cameron "Girly Swot" in Leaked Note', *The Guardian*, 6 September 2019, www.theguardian.com/politics/2019/sep/06/boris-johnson-calls-david-cameron-girly-swot-in-leaked-note. The 'cult' of girly swots referred to in Whelan's article comprised Lady Hale, Gina Miller (the businesswoman who brought the prorogation case in England) and Joanna Cherry (the politician who brought the conjoined Scottish case).

[26] See, also, Rosemary Hunter, 'The High Price of Success: The Backlash Against Women Judges in Australia' in Elizabeth Sheehy and Sheila McIntyre (eds.), *Calling for Change: Women, Law and the Legal Profession* (Ottawa University Press, 2006) who argues that women judges are subjected to heightened legal and public scrutiny and have to be twice as good as men to achieve acceptance and legitimacy.

[27] See, e.g., remarks from Lord Reed, Richard Atkins QC, Christina Blacklaws and Dinah Rose QC at Lady Hale's valedictory ceremony (18 December 2019): www.supremecourt.uk/news/valedictory-ceremony-for-lady-hale.html. For an account of the public adoration of Lady Hale following the *Miller 2* decision (albeit a more jaundiced one), see Whelan (*supra* n 25).

[28] Lady Hale, Closing remarks at her valedictory ceremony (18 December 2019): www.supremecourt.uk/news/valedictory-ceremony-for-lady-hale.html.

individual judge might be considered a 'leader' nevertheless provides a useful framework through which to begin to consider their contribution to a particular court, as well as to a body of jurisprudence and the judiciary as a whole.

In our previous work, we have discussed judicial leadership in terms of four overlapping dimensions: administrative, social, community and jurisprudential leadership.[29] Administrative leadership is largely concerned with the running and governance of the judiciary and/or of a specific court. It includes managing and negotiating relationships with other branches of government as well as with institutions such as the court service and judicial appointment bodies. These tasks are usually (but not always) within the remit of a formal leadership position such as chief justice or court president. Social leadership, in contrast, focuses on the collegial and emotional needs of the court, how the court works as a team and remains socially cohesive. While social leadership looks inwards, community leadership looks outwards, beyond the judiciary as an institution. It encompasses the extrajudicial and 'outreach' work, what Richard Cornes describes as 'judicial statespersonship',[30] which helps to instil public and professional confidence in the court, reinforcing its accessibility and openness, and expressing a commitment to judicial institution-building at the broadest level. Finally, jurisprudential or 'thought' leadership refers to a judge's influence on the decisions or jurisprudence of the court, either in relation to a specific area of law or more generally, including the development of a line of thought that is at odds with the court's general position but that is nonetheless jurisprudentially important.

Of course, some forms of leadership are more readily observable than others. While jurisprudential and community leadership are publicly manifested and may be discerned from analysis of reported cases, legal databases, library catalogues, court websites, publications, annual reports and press releases, many of the tasks of administrative leadership are performed behind closed doors. Similarly, social leadership is likely to be known only to 'insiders' or to someone who has closely observed and/or interviewed members of the court.[31] At the same time, while all of the written judgments of apex courts are generally accessible, there is no ongoing centralised or systematic record of many of the activities that might be seen to reflect community leadership: public lectures, school visits, mentoring, network-building, academic publications and so on. What we have in this regard are snapshots of certain activities, for some judges more than others, and these are heavily skewed towards the last ten to fifteen years or so as courts and judicial offices have become more media and web savvy.

---

[29] See, further, Rosemary Hunter and Erika Rackley, 'Judicial Leadership on the UK Supreme Court' (2018) 38 *Legal Studies* 191.

[30] Cornes (*supra* n 1).

[31] See, e.g., Alan Paterson's famous 'coffee pot' example involving Lord Brown (*supra* n 1) 167–9.

4.3.1 *Lady Hale's Administrative, Community and Social Leadership*

While we do not, therefore, have a systematic record of Lady Hale's (or indeed any judge's) judicial leadership in its entirety, we do know that she was clearly evidencing her 'towering' leadership tendencies long before her appointment to the Supreme Court. We have already noted her foundation of the UK Association of Women Judges, and her mentoring, network-building and community leadership were also evident in her roles as president of the Association of Women Barristers (1998) and president of the International Association of Women Judges (2010–12).[32] Such leadership may also be seen in her thirteen-year period as chancellor of Bristol University (2004–16),[33] her ongoing role as visitor of Girton College Cambridge (since 2004)[34] and her significant role on the committee responsible for the operational establishment of the Supreme Court.[35]

As deputy president of the UKSC, she departed from the example of her predecessor, Lord Hope, when it came to the allocation of opportunities to write leading judgments. The Court's practice is for the presiding judge on any case – almost always either the president or the deputy president – to determine, after the post-hearing conference, who will write the leading judgment.[36] Lord Hope took it upon himself to write a very high proportion of the leading judgments in the cases in which he presided.[37] Lady Hale, by contrast, was more egalitarian, providing greater opportunities to other justices to write leading judgments and to develop their own jurisprudential leadership.[38]

As president of the UKSC in the highly controversial *Miller 2* litigation,[39] Lady Hale not only produced a powerful and decisive judgment but also persuaded all her colleagues to agree with it in its entirety, thereby cementing its power and decisiveness.

---

[32] Arline Pacht and Susan Glazebrook, *The IAWJ: Twenty Five Years of Judging for Equality* (International Association of Women Judges, 2016) 217–19, www.iawj.org/wp-content/uploads/2017/05/Jubilee-Book-2016-Final.pdf.

[33] University of Bristol, 'University of Bristol Chancellor to Step Down after 13 Years', press release, 30 November 2015, www.bristol.ac.uk/news/2015/november/chancellor-retirement.html.

[34] Cambridge University, 'The Governing Body of Girton College Has Elected the Rt. Hon Baroness Hale of Richmond to the Office of Visitor', press release, 2 April 2004, www.cam.ac.uk/news/visitor-to-girton-college.

[35] Lady Hale, 'Should the Law Lords Have Left the House of Lords?' Michael Ryle Lecture 2018 (London, 14 November 2018).

[36] Hunter and Rackley (*supra* n 29) 204.

[37] Ibid. 203.

[38] Ibid. 203, 206.

[39] This case was doubly controversial in that it concerned the respective constitutional roles of the executive and the judiciary, in the context of Brexit, a political topic that had divided the nation and produced parliamentary paralysis for the preceding three years. An earlier Supreme Court case, also initiated by Gina Miller, had decided that the executive could not notify Britain's intention to withdraw from the European Union without consulting and gaining the assent of Parliament: *R (on the application of Miller and another) v Secretary of State for Exiting the European Union* [2017] UKSC 5 (*Miller 1*). Lord Neuberger was then president of the Supreme Court, and the Court divided eight to three in the result. In *Miller 2*, the prime minister had advised the queen (as head of state) to prorogue Parliament for over a month, with the aim of curtailing debate on the proposed EU withdrawal agreement and obviating the

Her navigation of the Court through the *Miller 2* litigation was based on skills honed through many years of judicial leadership, including, as we found in our earlier study, her unsurpassed ability to engender unanimous decisions in the cases in which she presided.[40]

In our research on judicial leadership on the UKSC, Lady Hale emerged as the Court's pre-eminent community leader in terms of the sheer number of her speeches, overseas engagements and academic publications.[41] Between 2009 and 2019, for example, she published seventy-three speeches on the Court's website, accounting for almost a third of all speeches given by all of the justices during the Court's first decade and outstripping her nearest rival and predecessor as president, Lord Neuberger (sixty speeches), by a considerable margin. Unsurprisingly, the number of speeches she gave increased after she became president; she published thirty-two speeches in her final two years on the Court, amounting to more than half of the total number of speeches published in those two years.

Looking at the nature of Lady Hale's speeches, it is clear that she was invited to speak to a wide range of people and organisations, including university students, academics, professional bodies and associations (in the legal profession and beyond), Parliament, international courts and members of the public. She spoke most often on issues relating broadly to human rights and social justice, followed by the constitutional position and/or workings of the UKSC and family and child law. During 2019, she was much in demand at events celebrating the centenary year of women's formal entry into the legal profession in the UK.

4.3.2 *Lady Hale's Jurisprudential Leadership*

There are differing views on what amounts to jurisprudential or 'thought' leadership. While some seek to employ a narrow conception of jurisprudential leaders as the judges who 'bring others with them', who have dominant voices on the bench and who are able to persuade others to their point of view,[42] in our view, jurisprudential leadership is broader than this. It encompasses the development of a line of thought that may be at odds with the court's general position at the time but that is nonetheless jurisprudentially significant. Thus, as well as leading judgments, the writing of concurrences and dissents may involve a form of jurisprudential leadership, as the

---

risk of a successful no-confidence motion against his minority government. The questions before the Court were whether the prime minister's advice to the queen was justiciable and, if so, whether it was lawful. The Court unanimously held against the government on both questions.

[40] Hunter and Rackley (*supra* n 29) 203.

[41] Ibid. 213–17.

[42] See, e.g., Lady Hale's discussion of Lord Bingham's leadership style in Brenda Hale, 'A Supreme Judicial Leader' in Mads Andenas and Duncan Fairgrieve (eds.), *Tom Bingham and the Transformation of the Law: A Liber Amicorum* (Oxford University Press, 2009) 209; and also Cornes (*supra* n 1) 512.

judge articulates alternative reasoning that represents a marginalised point of view and/or that may later be taken up by others and so have influence over time. Further, in the UK context where the UKSC (unlike other apex courts in the common law world) does not sit *en banc*, the frequent presence of a justice on hearing panels, contributing to judicial conversations in a variety of areas, may constitute a form of jurisprudential leadership.

Lady Hale provided early evidence of her jurisprudential leadership through her many academic publications, including authorship of leading textbooks on family as well as mental health law[43] and her Hamlyn lecture series in 1996.[44] She became a jurisprudential leader of the UKSC in a number of respects. At the time of her retirement, she was not only the longest serving justice[45] but had sat on more UKSC cases than any of her colleagues by a very wide margin.[46] During the Court's first six years, she participated in 54 per cent of the decisions issued by the Court, while the average for all justices was around 44 per cent.[47] During her period as deputy president and president, the average number of cases she sat on each year increased from thirty-six to forty-two.[48]

Lady Hale also wrote a substantive judgment (as opposed to simply agreeing with another justice or justices) in a higher proportion of her cases than most.[49] She wrote relatively high rates of both concurring and dissenting judgments,[50] as well as more leading judgments than any of her colleagues during her time on the Court (eighty-four).[51] Crucially, her leading judgments were not only in cases in which she was seen as a specialist (for example, in family law) and in which the rest of the Court might have been expected to defer to her expertise. In our study of the Court's first six years, Lady Hale wrote leading judgments in eighteen different subject areas. She was more likely to write leading judgments, and indeed to sit, on civil cases involving individual rights and interests (what we have termed 'human' cases) than on

---

[43] Hoggett (*supra* n 11); Brenda Hale, *Parents and Children: The Law of Parental Responsibility*, 4th edition (Sweet & Maxwell, [1977]1993); Brenda Hale, David Pearl, Elizabeth Cooke and Daniel Monk, *Family, Law and Society: Cases and Materials*, 6th edition (Oxford University Press, [1983] 2008).

[44] Brenda Hale, *From the Test Tube to the Coffin: Choice and Regulation in Private Life* (Sweet & Maxwell, 1996). The lecture series was established in 1949; Hale was the second woman to give the lectures (after Claire Palley in 1990).

[45] Lady Hale sat on the House of Lords and then the UKSC for sixteen years. Lord Kerr, who retired in September 2020, was the last UKSC justice who served on the House of Lords, but he was appointed in 2009, just before the establishment of the UKSC.

[46] Aishah Hussain, 'Cambridge Uni Law Student Shares His Geeky – But "Mostly Useless" – Supreme Court Facts', *Legal Cheek*, 2 October 2019, www.legalcheek.com/2019/10/cambridge-law-student-shares-his-geeky-but-mostly-useless-supreme-court-facts/, reporting on Lewis Graham's finding that Lady Hale 'sat on the greatest number of cases (385) representing over 56% of all Supreme Court cases'. Next in the ranking was Lord Kerr who sat on 269 cases.

[47] Hunter and Rackley (*supra* n 29) 205–6.

[48] Hussain (*supra* n 46).

[49] Hunter and Rackley (*supra* n 29) 209–10.

[50] Ibid. 206–10.

[51] Hussain (*supra* n 46).

criminal, commercial or public law cases. But these comprised a wide range of cases covering discrimination law, employment law, family law, habeas corpus, housing law, human rights, immigration/asylum law, medical law, occupational health and safety, privacy, probate, professional regulation, tort law and welfare law, and they constituted the largest proportion (over half) of the UKSC's caseload.[52]

This statistical picture adds substantially to the most widely discussed aspect of Lady Hale's jurisprudential leadership – her introduction of a feminist perspective in a number of high-profile cases.[53] It is possible that these well-known feminist judgments may have obscured the wider dimensions of her jurisprudential leadership. Nevertheless, there is no doubt that a very significant and unique element of Hale's jurisprudential contribution to the UKSC was her representation and inclusion of the marginalised experiences of women in decision-making and judicial law-making. In this way, her jurisprudence – sometimes in dissent or concurrence but often in leading judgments – has been transformative. It is to this feature of her 'toweringness' that we now turn.

4.4 SITTING IN (FEMINIST) JUDGMENT

Lady Hale is a prominent and self-identified feminist judge.[54] Being a feminist judge in a male-dominated institution inevitably means challenging and seeking to change doctrines derived from exclusively masculine experience in order to render them more gender inclusive, while at the same time seeking to expand the application of progressive laws and conventions to promote substantive equality.[55] Early, paradigm-shifting feminist judgments before she reached the House of Lords included *Re D* in the Family Division of the High Court,[56] in which she rejected the stereotyping of mothers in family disputes as 'implacably hostile' to contact and highlighted the importance of understanding the reasons for a mother's opposition to her child having contact with the father, which might be entirely justified in the context of domestic violence. In *Parkinson v St James and Seacroft University Hospital NHS Trust* in the Court of Appeal,[57] she reframed the 'harm' of wrongful birth in terms of the woman's loss of autonomy. In the House of Lords in *R v J*,[58] she

---

[52] In our study to 2015, 'human' cases constituted 57 per cent of the total cases decided by the court, with 'public law' being the second largest broad category at 32 per cent: Hunter and Rackley (*supra* n 29) 210–11. Note that these were overlapping rather than mutually exclusive categories.

[53] See, e.g., Erika Rackley, 'Difference in the House of Lords' (2006) 15 *Social and Legal Studies* 163; Erika Rackley, 'What a Difference Difference Makes: Gendered Harms and Judicial Diversity' (2008) 15 *International Journal of the Legal Profession* 37; Erika Rackley, *Women, Judging and the Judiciary: From Difference to Diversity* (Routledge, 2013) 180–5.

[54] See, e.g., Brenda Hale, 'A Minority Opinion?' (2008) 154 *Proceedings of the British Academy* 319.

[55] For an extended discussion of feminist approaches to judging, see Rosemary Hunter, 'Feminist Judging in the "Real World"' (2018) 8(9) *Onati Socio-Legal Series* 1275.

[56] *Re D (Contact: Reasons for Refusal)* [1997] 2 FLR 48.

[57] *Parkinson v St James and Seacroft University Hospital NHS Trust* [2001] QB 266.

[58] *R v J* [2005] 1 All ER 1.

dissented from her colleagues' focus on procedural over substantive justice in the case of a young girl who had been sexually abused by an older man. But she led the court in *K v Secretary of State for the Home Department; Fornah v Secretary of State for the Home Department*[59] in adopting a gender-sensitive, gender-inclusive interpretation of the 1951 Refugee Convention, and in *Stack v Dowden*,[60] her holistic approach to quantifying a cohabitant's beneficial interest in the family home was so persuasive that Lord Neuberger's initial majority evaporated and he found himself in lone dissent.[61]

In the UKSC, Lady Hale wrote two prominent feminist dissents in *Radmacher v Granatino*[62] and *R (on the application of McDonald) v Royal Borough of Kensington and Chelsea*.[63] The former concerned the legal recognition of prenuptial agreements, with the all-male majority deciding that prenuptial contracts should be recognised and given effect in English law, on classic liberal grounds of liberty and autonomy,[64] and by analogy with any other kind of contract. Only Lady Hale observed the salient differences between prenuptial contracts and arm's length commercial contracts, and the typical effects of such contracts on the equality interests of the economically weaker spouse, who was usually (though not invariably) the woman.[65] In doing so, she commented that 'there is a gender dimension to the issue which some may think ill-suited to decision by a court consisting of eight men and one woman'.[66] *McDonald* concerned the question of whether a local government care package for an elderly lady could include the provision of incontinence pads at night rather than assistance to go to the toilet. The majority thought that this decision was not unreasonable, while Hale found it to be irrational because it did not respond to the applicant's actual needs (help to get to the toilet rather than management of incontinence). In seeking to highlight the affront to dignity created by the local authority's decision, Hale pointed out that it could apply equally to someone being left lying in their own faeces,[67] an observation that appeared to bring the issue uncomfortably home to her male colleagues, provoking unusually sharp responses from them in their own judgments.[68]

By contrast, in her leading judgment in *Yemshaw v London Borough of Hounslow*,[69] Lady Hale persuaded the other members of the Court to join her in

---

[59] *K v Secretary of State for the Home Department; Fornah v Secretary of State for the Home Department* [2006] UKHL 46.

[60] *Stack v Dowden* [2007] UKHL 17.

[61] Paterson (*supra* n 1) 129.

[62] *Radmacher v Granatino* [2010] UKSC 42.

[63] *R (on the application of McDonald) v Royal Borough of Kensington and Chelsea* [2011] UKSC 33.

[64] *Radmacher v Granatino* [2010] UKSC 42 per Lords Phillips, Hope, Rodger, Walker, Brown, Collins and Kerr at [78].

[65] Ibid. per Lady Hale at [132], [135], [137].

[66] Ibid. at [137].

[67] *McDonald* (*supra* n 63) at [77].

[68] Ibid. per Lord Brown at [27], Lord Walker at [32].

[69] *Yemshaw v London Borough of Hounslow* [2011] UKSC 3.

extended the meaning of the term 'domestic violence' in the Housing Act 1996 to encompass forms of behaviour beyond physical violence, such as threats and intimidation, and psychological, emotional and financial abuse, in accordance with developing national and international understandings of domestic violence. While this decision was welcomed by domestic abuse charities, it provoked another backlash from the tabloid press,[70] with one journalist exclaiming:

> Thank goodness Lady Hale has never set foot in our home, or I'd be sleeping under Blackfriars Bridge tonight. I am, you see, guilty of domestic violence: I shout at my husband on a regular basis, with everything from accusations ('You slob!') to threats ('I'm going to throw that BlackBerry out of the window!') ... This judge is an ass! (And I'm not afraid to shout it, at the top of my lungs!)[71]

However, it would be wrong to assume that these notorious examples were Lady Hale's only feminist judgments. In a systematic study of UKSC judgments, we identified 114 cases between October 2009 and October 2017 that raised feminist or gender issues, and that therefore might have provided an opportunity for a feminist judgment.[72] These made up around 20 per cent of the Court's caseload over the period. Lady Hale sat on ninety-eight of these cases – a clear indication of her acknowledged expertise in this area – and wrote a substantive judgment in nearly two-thirds of them (sixty-two): a higher proportion than her overall 'writing rate' noted in Section 4.3. In more than half of the cases in which she wrote, she provided the leading judgment (thirty-four) – in a few cases jointly with other justices but most often alone – as well as writing sixteen concurrences and twelve dissents.

Not all of Lady Hale's judgments in these cases included feminist reasoning, but we identified such reasoning in forty-five of her opinions in these cases – almost three-quarters of those in which she wrote a judgment.[73] These included a number

---

[70] See, e.g., Anon, 'Shout at Your Spouse and Risk Losing Your Home: It's Just the Same as Domestic Violence, Warns Woman Judge', *Daily Mail*, 27 January 2011, www.dailymail.co.uk/news/article-1350761/Women-entitled-council-house-partner-shouts.html; Tom Utley, 'Like Every Weedy Husband, I Don't Shout – I Sulk. But How Long Before a Judge Says That's Domestic Violence?' *Daily Mail*, 28 January 2011, www.dailymail.co.uk/debate/article-1351282/Like-weedy-husband-I-dont-shout-I-sulk-But-long-judge-says-thats-domestic-violence.html.

[71] Christina Odone, 'I'm Always Shouting at My Husband but No, Lady Hale, I Don't Think I Ought to Lose My Home Because of It', *The Telegraph*, 24 November 2011.

[72] For a description of our methodology in identifying 'feminist/gender' cases, see Rosemary Hunter and Erika Rackley, 'Feminist Judgments on the UK Supreme Court' (2020) 32 *Canadian Journal of Women and Law* 85, 91–7.

[73] In identifying 'feminist' reasoning, we took a broad view based on the literature on feminist judging. Our approach is described in Hunter and Rackley, ibid. Briefly, substantive feminist reasoning is reasoning that seeks to achieve gender justice and/or to implement feminist theoretical or ethical commitments, such as substantive equality, relationality, the ethic of care, reproductive justice, women's rights and the elimination of gender bias. Feminist reasoning may also be found in observed methods and techniques of feminist judging, including 'asking the woman question' (noting the differential impacts of apparently neutral rules on women and men or on different social groups), 'telling the story' (recounting the facts in a way that brings previously marginalised experiences to the fore), 'contextualisation' (placing the legal issues in their wider social and/or policy context),

of less-high-profile leading, dissenting and concurring judgments in relation to housing and welfare benefits, matrimonial property and reproductive justice, as well as in cases concerning discrimination law, employment law (particularly on part-time workers and equal pay), parents and children, the right to family life, positive duties of the state under the Human Rights Act, and access to justice.[74] While some of these judgments dealt with private law or disputes between individual and/or corporate parties, in the public law context, Lady Hale's feminist judgments were particularly focused on two main (and sometimes overlapping) themes – ensuring that the particular situations of women and other vulnerable groups were not excluded from state provision and protection; and valuing and protecting relationality and family life.

The *Yemshaw* and *McDonald* decisions clearly fall within the former theme. But, in addition to *Yemshaw*, two other of Lady Hale's feminist judgments dealt with local authorities' interpretations of their duties to provide housing for people who would otherwise be homeless. *Nzolameso* v *City of Westminster*[75] concerned the lawfulness of a local authority offering housing to a homeless single mother that was located a long distance from the authority's own area where she had previously lived. In her leading judgment allowing the appeal, Lady Hale held that the authority had failed to discharge its statutory duty to the appellant and failed to take into account all relevant considerations, including the needs of her children. In the subsequent case of *Hotak* v *London Borough of Southwark*,[76] which concerned the local authority's duty towards 'vulnerable' homeless people, Lady Hale dissented from the majority's interpretation of 'vulnerable', arguing that the local authority should not be able to rely on the availability of family support to escape its duty to provide housing, and, conversely, that the vulnerability of a dependant should be a basis for giving housing priority to a homeless carer. In a slightly different housing context, Lady Hale gave the leading judgment in *R (on the application of Coll)* v *Secretary of State for Justice*,[77] holding that the severely limited availability of bail hostels for women released from prison on licence, which meant that women ex-prisoners were more likely than men to be located at some distance from their homes, families and communities, constituted unlawful sex discrimination by the Department of Justice.

understanding the specificities of women's lives, paying attention to particularities and avoiding abstraction, believing women's accounts and affirming their experiences of violence and abuse, and citing feminist scholarship or feminist 'common knowledge'. See Rosemary Hunter, 'Can *Feminist Judges Make a Difference?*' (2008) 15 *International Journal of the Legal Profession* 3; Rosemary Hunter, 'An Account of Feminist Judging' in Rosemary Hunter, Clare McGlynn and Erika Rackley (eds.), *Feminist Judgments: From Theory to Practice* (Hart Publishing, 2010) 30–43; Hunter (*supra* n 55).
74   Hunter and Rackley (*supra* n 72) 99–108.
75   *Nzolameso* v *City of Westminster* [2015] UKSC 22.
76   *Hotak* v *London Borough of Southwark* [2015] UKSC 30.
77   *R (on the application of Coll)* v *Secretary of State for Justice* [2017] UKSC 40.

While the *McDonald* case involved local authority provision of adult social care, A v *Essex County Council*[78] concerned local authority provision for children who have special educational needs. In this case, the child A had severe disabilities and challenging behaviour and for an eighteen-month period had not been provided with adequate schooling by the local authority. He sought damages for infringement of his right to education under article 2, protocol 1 of the European Convention on Human Rights, and the court was required to determine the extent of the obligations imposed by the article. The majority held that it does not confer a right to education that meets a child's special needs regardless of resource implications, hence the trial judge had been right to strike out the claim as having no reasonable prospects of success, and to refuse to extend the limitation period. Lady Hale dissented, arguing that there was a triable case as to whether A had been unjustifiably denied access to the kind of education provided by the local authority for children like him, and, although it was accepted that the local authority had not intended any harm, that '[w]e have to protect people from well-meaning interferences with their human rights by public authorities as much as from those who mean them ill'.[79] Further, in disagreeing on the limitation point, she expressed the view that 'the judge erred in principle by approaching this as if it was a judicial review case and by minimising the importance of vindicating the human rights of the individual claimant and setting standards for others in a position similar to this'.[80]

Two further cases concerned national welfare benefits. In R *(on the application of Carmichael and Rourke) v Secretary of State for Work and Pensions*,[81] Lady Hale used her concurring judgment to draw attention to the specific adverse impact that housing benefit cuts introduced by the 2010–15 Coalition government would have on women living in sanctuary housing.[82] Under the cuts, people judged to be living in houses with more bedrooms than they needed for the size of their family had their housing benefits reduced to reflect the number of bedrooms deemed necessary. This was widely dubbed the 'bedroom tax'. Sanctuary housing schemes are arrangements offered to high-risk victims of domestic violence to increase the safety of their homes, often including a reinforced 'safe room' into which they can retreat in case of intrusion by their ex-partner. Such safe rooms were caught by the 'bedroom tax', resulting in survivors of violence having their benefits cut, meaning, in many cases, that they could no longer afford to pay the rent or mortgage on their sanctuary house. A safety-net accompanying the cuts allowed local authorities to provide additional funding to some benefit recipients in cases of hardship, on a discretionary basis.

---

[78]   A v *Essex County Council* [2010] UKSC 33.
[79]   Ibid. at [110].
[80]   Ibid. at [119].
[81]   R *(on the application of Carmichael and Rourke) v Secretary of State for Work and Pensions* [2016] UKSC 58.
[82]   Ibid. at [72]–[80].

However, as Lady Hale noted, access to this funding was far less secure and more onerous to apply for than the previous benefit provisions.

R (on the application of SG and others) v *Secretary of State for Work and Pensions*[83] concerned another aspect of the Coalition government's welfare cuts, the 'benefit cap', which imposed a limit on the benefits payable to any welfare recipient equivalent to the net average weekly earnings of a working household, regardless of the number of dependants, housing costs or other circumstances of the benefit recipient. This had an adverse impact on women since women (single mothers) were the majority of welfare beneficiaries; however, the majority of the Court held that the discrimination was justified. In her dissenting judgment, Lady Hale was the only one of the justices to acknowledge the circumstances of the appellants, their reasons for being unable to work and the reasons why they could not be expected to move to live in a cheaper area.[84] She explained in detail the serious effects of the benefit cap in general and its particular effects on victims of domestic violence.[85] In determining the question of justification, she referred to the Convention on the Elimination of All Forms of Discrimination Against Women (CEDAW) and the Convention on the Rights of the Child,[86] concluding that the Secretary of State had failed to justify the discrimination.

In two decisions concerning publicly funded abortion services, Lady Hale sought to maximise women's access to services. In *R (on the application of A and B)* v *Secretary of State for Health*,[87] she dissented from the majority's decision that it was not unlawful for the Secretary of State not to make provision for women resident in Northern Ireland (where abortion services were severely restricted) to be able to obtain abortions in England free of charge. In *Greater Glasgow Health Board* v *Doogan*,[88] on the other hand, she led the Court in narrowly interpreting the conscientious objection provision in the Abortion Act 1967, in the process noting the policy of the Act to provide women with lawful, safe and accessible services.[89] Similarly, in *Michael* v *Chief Constable of South Wales Police*,[90] she took an expansive view of another public service. Ms Michael had been murdered by her violent ex-partner, but her death could have been prevented if police had responded promptly to her 999 call. Her parents and children brought actions against the police in negligence and under article 2 (right to life) of the European Convention on Human Rights. While the majority of the Court upheld the established position that the police do not owe a duty of care to members of the public with regard to operational decisions, Lady Hale, with Lord Kerr, dissented. Far from making the

[83]   *R (on the application of SG and others)* v *Secretary of State for Work and Pensions* [2015] UKSC 16.
[84]   Ibid. at [169]–[177].
[85]   Ibid. at [178]–[187].
[86]   Ibid. at [211]–[224].
[87]   *R (on the application of A and B)* v *Secretary of State for Health* [2017] UKSC 41.
[88]   *Greater Glasgow Health Board* v *Doogan* [2014] UKSC 68.
[89]   Ibid. at [27].
[90]   *Michael and others* v *Chief Constable of South Wales and another* [2015] UKSC 2.

task of policing more difficult, she considered that the imposition of a duty of care 'might conceivably . . . lead to some much-needed improvements in their response to threats of serious domestic abuse'.[91]

The relational/family life theme in Lady Hale's feminist judgments may be illustrated by two cases concerning immigration regulations and extradition. In *HH v Deputy Prosecutor of the Italian Republic, Genoa*,[92] European arrest warrants had been issued against a couple (HH and PH) and a single mother (FK), and the question for the Court was whether extradition would be incompatible with the rights of their children to respect for their private and family life under article 8 of the European Convention on Human Rights. Lady Hale gave the leading judgment, and upheld the appeal of FK on the basis of expert evidence that her youngest children would suffer serious harm if she were extradited. But she was in the minority in also upholding the appeal of PH, who was the primary carer of their children, accepting that these children would also suffer significant harm if he were extradited. *R (on the application of Ali) and R (on the application of Bibi) v Secretary of State for the Home Department*[93] concerned a challenge to new immigration rules that required the foreign spouses or partners of British nationals to pass an English language test in order to be allowed to enter the UK. The rules were challenged under article 8 of the European Convention on Human Rights by two British women whose Pakistani and Yemeni husbands did not speak English and had no practical ability to learn English to the required standard. While Lady Hale in her leading judgment accepted that there was some justification for the rules, she held that, in individual cases such as this, they interfered with family life to such a substantial degree that they failed to strike a fair balance, and there was a need for the wider operation of discretion in such cases.

Finally, *The Christian Institute and others v The Lord Advocate (Scotland)*[94] concerned a challenge to Scottish legislation on the basis that it both exceeded the powers of the Scottish Parliament and constituted an interference with article 8 rights. The legislation proposed that all children and young people in Scotland should have a 'named person' responsible for oversight of their well-being, with powers and duties including sharing information about children and their families with various services. Lady Hale gave the leading judgment jointly with Lord Reed and Lodge Hodge. Although the Court found the ultra vires challenge not to be made out, it did find an unjustified interference with rights to private and family life, highlighting the importance of parent–child relationships and the role of the family

---

91 Ibid. at [198].
92 *HH v Deputy Prosecutor of the Italian Republic, Genoa; PH v Deputy Prosecutor of the Italian Republic, Genoa; FK (FC) v Polish Judicial Authority* [2012] UKSC 25.
93 *R (on the application of Ali) v Secretary of State for the Home Department; R (on the application of Bibi) v Secretary of State for the Home Department* [2016] UKSC 68.
94 *The Christian Institute and others v The Lord Advocate (Scotland)* [2016] UKSC 51.

in protecting individual freedoms in a liberal democracy, and also recognising the importance of protecting children's privacy.

This analysis shows that far from appearing in isolated cases, Lady Hale's feminist judgments were not only numerous but also consistent and significant in developing lines of jurisprudence designed to make UK law and state actors more responsive to and inclusive of women's lives and experiences and more respectful of family life and the value of family relationships.

4.5　CONCLUSION: A *FEMINIST* TOWERING JUDGE

The editors of this volume in their Introduction suggest that there are two key characteristics of a towering judge: influence and individualism.[95] Leaving aside for the moment the question of whether these are qualities we might want judges to have (independence? yes; dominance, self-centredness or egotism? perhaps not), influence and individualism certainly have gendered associations: they are qualities (usually) identified and celebrated in men, and not identified or celebrated in women. Where women demonstrate influence and individualism, such qualities may instead be characterised – and denigrated – as 'ambition' or 'aggression'. The qualities women – including women judges – are expected to display are different from those of men.[96] Take, for example, this comment by one of Lady Hale's former colleagues: 'She is a totally fascinating woman, but I found it difficult to work with her … You have to be obstreperous as a woman to get there, to break that glass ceiling. It's painful, it leaves you with cuts.'[97] To her credit, when asked whether she recognised that description, Lady Hale said that she did. But, she continued, 'I also think certain people find women "obstreperous" when they would not find the same behaviour from a man obstreperous. They'd just call them determined or authoritative. It wouldn't be a criticism.'[98] Indeed, they may even be called 'towering'.

This is not to suggest that women judges can never meet the requirements of influence and individuality, to be distinguishable from the crowd or to be unconventional. Indeed, it is easy to show that Lady Hale – woman, state-educated, academic, mother, feminist, so many times a first – was one of the UK's most individual judges. And, without doubt, she is one of the UK's most influential contemporary legal thinkers, law reformers and judges. She has left an indelible mark on the first decade

---

[95]　Introduction to this volume.

[96]　See, for example, ibid. at 20: '[F]emale judges may not assert themselves as forcefully as their male counterparts such that few rise to the status of "towering judge".'

[97]　Afua Hirsch, 'Lady Justice: Is the Judiciary Ready for Brenda Hale?' *Prospect*, 14 November 2017, www .prospectmagazine.co.uk/magazine/lady-justice-is-the-judiciary-ready-for-brenda-hale. This is not an isolated view: see also Joshua Rozenberg, 'An Insider's Account of the "Brenda Agenda"', *Law Society Gazette*, 3 February 2020, www.lawgazette.co.uk/commentary-and-opinion/an-insiders-account-of-the-brenda-agenda/5102903.article.

[98]　Simon Hattenstone, 'Lady Hale: "My Desert Island Judgments? Number One Would Probably Be the Prorogation Case"' *The Guardian*, 11 January 2020, www.theguardian.com/law/2020/jan/11/lady-hale-desert-island-judgments-prorogation-case-simon-hattenstone.

of the UK Supreme Court. She has played a key role not only in shaping the law impacting on the lives of millions in the UK and beyond[99] but also in creating and leading the institution – and indeed the physical architecture – of the Court.[100]

It is necessary, however, to sound two notes of caution. First, the use of influence and individuality as key metrics of judicial toweringness may tend to perpetuate gender-based blind spots and inequalities and to discriminate indirectly against women. As Rosalind Dixon suggests, we may find our list of towering judges both limited and slanted because we are looking for qualities that are much easier for some to demonstrate than others.[101] Second, there are dark sides to influence (to exert power in the interests of the privileged) and individuality (to be more interested in individual people than society as a whole) to which we might hope no judge aspires, and which Lady Hale has certainly eschewed.

In fact, what Lady Hale demonstrates is the importance of a judge who is part of and values and supports community, connections, collegiality and inclusivity. This is not a new understanding of a judge; it is well established in the feminist judicial literature.[102] Lady Hale is an exemplar of such a judge – a towering *feminist* judge as well as a feminist towering judge. In contrast to the isolated individualism of judges able – and willing – to dominate or 'tower over' others, Lady Hale, through her judgments, judicial leadership and extrajudicial activities, sought to bring people together and to create conditions in which others were enabled and empowered. This is not to suggest that she did not 'shine',[103] but rather that she did not do so at the expense of others. Having reached the top, she did not pull up the ladder; rather, she created many new ladders so that others might also climb. Consequently, she has become an inspiration and a role model for countless girls and women (and no doubt a good number of men as well).[104] This, too, might be seen as an index of toweringness.

Thus, a towering judge may also be highly collegial – these two categories of judges are not mutually exclusive.[105] Rather, Lady Hale's example prompts us to rethink what we mean by towering and what qualities should be valued in a (towering) judge. She reminds us of the importance of not uncritically accepting understandings of judging and judge-craft derived from centuries of male institutional domination. We can – and should – demand more.

---

[99] As a member of the Privy Council and (from 2018) a non-permanent judge of the Hong Kong Court of Final Appeal.

[100] Thompson (*supra* n 15).

[101] Rosalind Dixon, 'Towering v Collegial Judges', IACL-AIDC Blog, 6 March 2019, https://blog-iacl-aidc.org/towering-judges/2019/3/6/towering-v-collegial-judges, and see chapter 16 of this volume.

[102] Patricia Cain 'Good and Bad Bias: A Comment on Feminist Theory and Judging' (1988) 61 *Southern California Law Review* 1945; Robin West, *Caring for Justice* (New York University Press, 1997); Elizabeth Sheehy (ed.), *Adding Feminism to Law: The Contributions of Justice Claire L'Heureux-Dubé* (Irwin Law, 2004); Hunter, 'Can *Feminist* Judges Make a Difference?' (*supra* n 73).

[103] Introduction to this volume.

[104] See, further, Lord Reed, Richard Atkins, Christina Blacklaws and Dinah Rose (*supra* n 27).

[105] Cf. Dixon (*supra* n 101).

5

Hugh Kennedy: Ireland's (Quietly) Towering
Nation-Maker

Tom Gerald Daly

5.1 INTRODUCTION: AN OVERLOOKED LEGACY

Independence. Decolonisation. Democratic transition. Conflict. Creative and comparative constitution-drafting. Constitutions as peace settlements. The development of a national constitutional identity. Constitutional unamendability in the face of rule-of-law threats. The challenge of leaving the past behind. The story of Hugh Kennedy, independent Ireland's first Chief Justice, has it all. In a way, Kennedy's story connects many of the other chapters in this collection, forming a bridge between stable democratic states and unstable, post-independence or post-conflict democratising states, and between the early twentieth century – when 'towering judges' were rare creatures – and the rather court-centric present day, when they are more common.

Kennedy came to prominence at a crucial moment in Irish constitutional history and his impact on the Irish legal system was profound, across the political, institutional and jurisprudential dimensions of 'toweringness' identified in the editors' Introduction to this collection. In under fifteen years, Kennedy was a central architect of the Irish constitutional order. As the Attorney General of the provisional Irish government, he was the dominant force in drafting the 1922 Constitution produced for the new Irish Free State created after the War of Independence, ensuring maximal autonomy for the new state within the British Empire by tying it to Canadian law and practice. He created a new court system capable of holding the confidence of the people. As the first chief justice of the Irish Free State for twelve years (1924–36) he crafted a uniquely Irish jurisprudence of popular sovereignty unlike anything found in the existing British tradition. His robust defence of rights and the rule of law in the 1930s set the scene for a dramatic expansion of the Supreme Court's power in the 1960s and 1970s, and lingers still. His work was central to Ireland's trajectory towards declaration of an unambiguously independent republic in 1948. In short, although he was evidently not perfect and his legacy remains contested, he was so central to the design, interpretation and development of the Irish constitutional and judicial orders that he can be called not only Ireland's answer to England's Lord Coke, Israel's Aharon Barak, India's Chief Justice Bhagwati or the United States's Chief Justice John Marshall but also, perhaps, Ireland's Hamilton, Jefferson or Madison.

Yet, he remains somewhat overlooked. Ask a hundred constitutional lawyers worldwide to name a 'towering judge' and there is little chance that you will hear Kennedy's name. Despite his remarkable role in shaping Ireland's post-imperial constitutional system, and clear recognition across the domestic judiciary and academia,[1] Kennedy's full legacy also remains under-appreciated among the Irish public: he is certainly not a cultural icon. Indeed, when I first began working in the Supreme Court of Ireland in 2005, he was little more to me than a portly figure in a portrait right outside the chief justice's chamber complex; a man who, the sitting chief justice told me, was still remembered in the joke that barristers upon seeing him striding to court would say: 'There he goes, pregnant with judgments.'[2] This lack of recognition is, in many ways, an unsatisfactory state of affairs.

This chapter seeks to make the case to an international audience that Kennedy, as equal parts founding father and father of a distinctly Irish jurisprudence, deserves a place in the top tier of the global pantheon of towering judges. It does this by examining his impact according to the various criteria set out by the editors in the Introduction to this collection, two of which he clearly meets: individual singularity and substantial influence on the constitutional system. An account of his work also provides an illuminating case study of the background conditions that can spur the rise of a towering judge. The context in which Kennedy worked – a time of overwhelming change, potential and danger for the newly minted Irish polity, including a wholesale but ambiguous constitutional re-founding – permitted him to make his mark in a way that would be inconceivable in today's Ireland but that was also predicated on his own blend of professional and social background, alongside personal traits such as intellect and political nous. Importantly, Kennedy's story also underscores that although towering judges have become more common in what Iddo Porat calls the 'high watermark of global constitutionalism' between the 1980s and 2000s,[3] this phenomenon has a long historical pedigree and the imperial and post-imperial contexts of the earlier twentieth century provide a different crucible for transnational constitutionalism and the 'global' judge.

The chapter proceeds in six parts, which build the case for Kennedy clearly counting as a towering judge within the meaning of this volume, especially as a founder judge and one ahead of his time in linking his national context to

---

[1] See, in particular, T Towey, 'Hugh Kennedy and the Constitutional Development of the Irish Free State, 1922–1923' (1977) 12(2) *Irish Jurist* 355; and R Keane, 'The Voice of the Gael: Chief Justice Kennedy and the Emergence of the New Irish Court System 1921–1936' (1996) 31 *Irish Jurist* 205.

[2] I first heard this from The Hon. Mr Justice John L Murray, Chief Justice of Ireland (2004–11), for whom I clerked from 2005 to 2011.

[3] Introduction to this volume.

a much wider transnational context. Section 5.2 briefly sketches the overall context in which Kennedy operated; one of recent conflict, ambiguous independence, democratic transition, lingering socio-political strife and strong tensions between a clean break with the past and continuity with Empire. Section 5.3 discusses Kennedy's role in crafting Ireland's first Constitution of 1922. Section 5.4 briefly recounts Kennedy's redesign of the highly politicised imperial-era court system. Section 5.5 focuses on Kennedy's principled, learned and innovative (if, at times, unsuccessful) jurisprudence. Finally, Sections 5.6 and 5.7 examine Kennedy's jurisprudential and constitutional legacy, both in Ireland and transnationally. Section 5.8 concludes.

5.2 PROFOUND CHANGE, DANGER AND HOPE: THE CONTEXT IN WHICH KENNEDY OPERATED

The context in which Kennedy rose to prominence was not only one of Ireland's transition from core imperial territory to nascent nation-state; it was also one of transition from war to peace and – given the undemocratic manner in which Ireland was governed under the Empire – from undemocratic to democratic rule.

At the time of Kennedy's birth in 1879, Ireland had been conjoined to Great Britain in a political union for almost eighty years (the United Kingdom of Great Britain and Ireland).[4] This was the culmination of foreign domination of the island of Ireland, with roots reaching back to the Norman invasion of 1169, defeat of Ireland's top-tier nobility by the forces of Queen Elizabeth I in 1602, and centuries of misrule, including: legal and political repression of the Catholic majority; marginalisation of Catholic leaders; exacerbation of religious cleavages between the Catholic majority and the Protestant minority; manipulation of judicial mechanisms to achieve political objectives (e.g. through the 'packing' of juries in trials against anti-British defendants[5]); an exploitative economic approach that benefited Britain's growing industrial economy while leaving Ireland an underdeveloped agrarian economy; and a starkly inadequate response to the devastating Great Famine of 1845–9, which reduced Ireland's population of eight million to under six million through death and emigration. Despite formally being part of a united kingdom with Great Britain, Ireland was governed in a manner akin to colonies within the Empire, from Kenya to India: as a subjugated territory under highly centralised and unresponsive administration. The perceived glories of liberal democracy in Britain – adherence to the rule of law, clear channels for meaningful political representation, independent judges, strongly protected civil and political

---

[4]   Scotland and England had entered a political union to become the United Kingdom of Great Britain in 1707.

[5]   See, e.g., K Quinn 'Jury Trial in Republic of Ireland' (2001) 72(1) *Revue internationale de droit pénal* 197, 199.

liberties, and growing prosperity – were simply not present in Ireland or were subverted to serve undemocratic ends.[6]

Successive attempts to achieve greater autonomy through re-establishment of a parliament in Dublin ('Home Rule') were frustrated, particularly by the postponement in 1914 of the Home Rule Act, which had been passed by the British parliament, due to the outbreak of World War I.[7] Despairing of political solutions, and continuing a long tradition of intermittent Irish insurrections against foreign rule, a band of revolutionaries in 1916 staged a bloody revolt on Easter Monday in 1916. The 1916 Rising set Ireland on an entirely new constitutional and political trajectory. It set the scene for the War of Independence in 1919–21, which led to an international treaty establishing an Irish Free State within the British Empire (the Anglo-Irish Treaty of 1921[8]), but only through the trauma of partitioning the island of Ireland into two separate political entities: the Irish Free State formed from twenty-six of the island's thirty-two counties; and six counties in the north and northeast remaining within the UK as the separate jurisdiction of Northern Ireland. The Treaty itself led to a schism within pro-independence forces and civil war from June 1922 to May 1923, between those who supported the settlement it enshrined and those who viewed it and the twenty-six-county state it created as invalid. The validity of the state was contested for decades (and remains contested by some political forces today), and insurgency and state legitimacy remained live issues for the rest of Hugh Kennedy's life, until his death in 1936.

From today's vantage point of a stable democratic Ireland, it is easy to overlook how much change Kennedy experienced in his short life of fifty-seven years. He entered his thirties as Ireland was still fully ensconced within the Empire and the main option for greater autonomy was the limited autonomy of Home Rule. By his early forties, Ireland was taking its first steps towards independence and Kennedy was himself transitioning: from member of the old Establishment – a successful barrister educated in the British tradition – to one of the midwives of the new dispensation, which had been won through violent rebellion rather than incremental constitutional reform. Kennedy occupied central positions from the early 1920s onwards, as the Law Officer (Attorney General) in the provisional government that negotiated a new constitution after the War of Independence, first Attorney General of the new Irish Free State and finally chief justice of the new state until his death in 1936.

5.3 CRAFTING AN INDEPENDENCE CONSTITUTION

It was in this context of profound change and tension between constitutional nationalism and physical-force nationalism (the former seeking autonomy exclusively through constitutional change; the latter viewing violent struggle as

---

[6] See, generally, K Kenny, *Ireland and the British Empire* (Oxford University Press, 2004).

[7] See, e.g., A O'Day, *Irish Home Rule, 1867–1921* (Manchester University Press, 1998).

[8] The formal name is the Articles of Agreement for a Treaty Between Great Britain and Ireland.

legitimate) that Kennedy's impact was first keenly felt. The Anglo-Irish Treaty of 1921, which set the terms for the cessation of the War of Independence, envisaged a new constitution for Ireland as a dominion state within the British Empire. Firmly rooted in the constitutionalist tradition, Kennedy's most profound impact on the Irish State was his central role in crafting the new Constitution for the newly minted entity, as Law Officer (Attorney General) to the provisional Irish government. He is a very early example of what Ros Dixon has shown is a growing global phenomenon of drafters-turned-judges (although Kennedy is not mentioned in her analysis), which comes through in other chapters in this book, such as Mara Malagodi's analysis of the Honourable Kalyan Shrestha of Nepal.[9]

The drafting process, involving negotiations between Irish and British representatives, presented both danger and opportunity. Tackled poorly, Ireland could receive an operating dominion status akin to other existing dominions (e.g. New Zealand, Newfoundland), with very limited autonomy from the seat of imperial power in London, further exacerbated by Ireland's geographic proximity – an outcome that would render the War of Independence a hollow victory. Tackled adroitly, the negotiations had the potential to achieve a measure of genuine, tangible and expansive autonomy that would honour the struggle for independence – and, as Kennedy saw it, might even placate those strongly opposed to the Treaty establishing the new Irish state.

Kennedy was not the sole negotiator on the Irish side in the process of drafting the 1922 Constitution: a drafting committee had been appointed by the provisional government in January 1922, including the president and the chairman of the provisional government as well as seven assorted prominent political figures and constitutional experts.[10] Yet, Kennedy had a decisive impact, playing 'the major role in the preliminary drafting, general discussion and final legal phrasing of the Committee's work'.[11] His impact was felt in three key ways. First, he marshalled his capacious historical and comparative legal knowledge to achieve expansive autonomy for the new state. Canny negotiation by Kennedy secured the greatest possible degree of autonomy by pursuing the same dominion status for the Free State as Canada and by expressly inscribing in the new Constitution the 'law, practice and constitutional usage' pertaining in Canada. As Towey has observed:

> The theoretically unfettered powers and prerogatives of the Crown found in other dominion constitutions were, through Kennedy's efforts, circumscribed at every turn by expressing or clearly implying the reality behind the Canadian Constitution. As he explained to the Provisional Government, 'what we have

---

[9]   R Dixon, 'Constitutional Design Two Ways: Constitutional Drafters as Judges' (2017) 57(1) *Virginia Journal of International Law* 1; Chapter 8 in this volume.

[10] For a fuller account of the process, see Towey (*supra* n 1); and B Farrell, 'The Drafting of the Irish Free State Constitution' (1970) 5(1) *Irish Jurist* 115.

[11] Farrell (*supra* n 10) 118.

done is to take the full length and breadth of the Canadian position in the widest terms'.[12]

Where the Canadian position tended to limit Irish autonomy, Kennedy drew on other comparative examples to push forward the Irish position. In particular, the Canadian constitutional structure permitted a theoretically unlimited right of appeal from the Canadian superior courts to the Privy Council in London. Perceiving how such a situation could operate to continue undue interference in Ireland's domestic affairs, Kennedy circumvented this perceived trap by focusing on the South African position, which permitted only a restricted avenue for such appeals where special conditions pertained to the case.[13] The first full drafts of the constitution, omitting any reference to the Privy Council – and, for that matter, Anglo-Irish treaty requirements that it include reference to the role of the king and the oath of allegiance – were met with consternation, UK Prime Minister Lloyd George calling it 'a complete evasion of the Treaty and a setting up of a republic with a thin veneer'.[14] Rowing back somewhat still meant that the Irish State would enjoy much greater freedom than any other dominion.

More broadly, Kennedy ranged far beyond the common-law world in seeking inspiration for the 1922 Constitution. In 1932, ten years after enactment of the Constitution, in his preface to a book presenting systematic analysis of the 1922 text, he referred to a wide range of sources including the Swiss and the US constitutions and, in particular, indicated his admiration for the Weimar Constitution of 1919, describing it as 'a political *tour de force* framed to work in contemporary conditions'.[15] Kennedy was, in this sense, a true global comparativist and was instrumental in the creation of a genuinely innovative constitution that sought to learn from as many states as possible.

Second was Kennedy's tactical abilities. His skills as a jurist were married with significant political nous, honed during his days as a student politician (where he once won an election victory over a contemporary, James Joyce) and his continued involvement in the leading political movements of the day such as the Gaelic League, a movement dedicated to reviving a distinctly Irish cultural identity and the Irish language. After the constitution-drafting negotiations, Kennedy even won election as a member of parliament in 1923, although his tenure was swiftly cut short by appointment as the first chief justice in 1924. These political skills appeared to allow him to perform two simultaneous roles: pushing the Irish position to its greatest possible extent in the negotiations with the British government, while

---

[12]   Towey (*supra* n 1) 360.

[13]   Towey (*supra* n 1) 362.

[14]   See T Mohr, 'Law Without Loyalty: The Abolition of the Irish Appeal to the Privy Council' (2002) 37 *Irish Jurist* 187, 189.

[15]   See Kennedy's preface to L Kohn, *The Constitution of the Irish Free State* (George Allen & Unwin, 1932).

placating political leaders on the Irish side where there was concern that still too much ground had been conceded to British power.

Third, in his endeavours, Kennedy appeared to recognise the dual role of the new Constitution itself as not only the product of a peace treaty but also an integral part of an enduring peace settlement in itself – a recognition that presages the increasing view of constitutions as forming a core part of peace agreements since the end of the twentieth century, in countries and territories from Bosnia-Herzegovina to Bougainville.[16] Kennedy's hope was that the achievement of maximal autonomy might be enough to take the air out of much of the anti-Treaty movement. As Towey puts it: 'Along with everyone else who supported the Treaty settlement, Kennedy was aware of the substantial minority who denied the legitimacy of the state. Therefore, the institutions of the state would have to appear Irish to defuse the accusation that the Free State and its Government were nothing more than a British puppet.'[17] Although this was not to be fully borne out, in the sense that strong anti-Treaty sentiment persisted after enactment of the 1922 Constitution, it was sufficient to bring the main anti-Treaty political forces within the structures of the new state. The Constitution was adopted by an Act of Dáil Éireann (the house of deputies) sitting as a constituent assembly on 25 October 1922, with a corresponding Irish Free State Constitution Act 1922 of the British parliament – unlike the later 1937 Constitution, it was not put to the people in a popular referendum. While the final constitutional text was highly imperfect, it is evident that Kennedy's skills were central, as a pragmatist who was capable of both exacting judgment and (from a British perspective) constitutional sleight of hand aimed at diminishing British power in Ireland to an extent unseen in other dominions, including reducing the Governor-General to scarcely more than a ceremonial position. In less capable hands, or uncompromising hands, the negotiations could have ground into an unhappy stalemate or produced a constitution that left little real autonomy for the new state, thus derailing the new statehood project or even sparking renewed civil war.

The 1922 Constitution, although inevitably still the product of compromise between the two sides, departed in striking ways from the unentrenched British Constitution. While it retained a parliamentary form of government (with a bicameral legislature comprising the *Dáil* (house of deputies) and *Seanad* (senate)), it was a highly innovative document. In the most fundamental departure from the British monarchical tradition, the text emphasised popular sovereignty as its core value.[18] It reflected key elements of contemporary constitutional thought and practice by enshrining a tripartite separation of state powers and setting out an express bill of rights guaranteeing core civil and political rights, including rights to freedom of

[16]   See C Bell, *On the Law of Peace: Peace Agreements and the Lex Pacificatoria* (Oxford University Press, 2008) 150.

[17]   Towey (*supra* n 1) 355.

[18]   See L Cahillane, 'The Influence of the Post-War European Constitutions on the Constitution of the Irish Free State' (2011) 15(1) *Electronic Journal of Comparative Law* 1, 5.

expression, association, assembly, liberty and equality before the law. The text also included substantial additional innovations, such as the possibility for legislation permitting proposals for laws or constitutional amendments by popular initiative (article 48).

Perhaps of most practical importance – representing another significant departure from British models of parliamentary supremacy and representative democracy (and one that would come to strongly shape future constitutional development) – the 1922 Constitution empowered the superior courts to invalidate legislation incompatible with the constitutional text. This, at a time when no other common-law constitution contained such an express power (including in the United States) and the notion of judicial review was still a novelty in Europe (in Weimar Germany, Austria and Czechoslovakia). Felix Frankfurter described it as 'the most arresting provision' of the new Constitution.[19] However, the potential of this power was significantly circumscribed by the power granted to the new parliament to amend the Constitution through ordinary legislation for the first eight years after enactment of the Constitution; thereafter, amendment would be limited to a full popular referendum (article 50). As discussed in Section 5.5, the serious tension between these two dimensions of the new Constitution would come to a head before the Supreme Court in 1934, prompting Kennedy to issue his most famous judgment on the rule of law.

5.4 REDESIGNING IRELAND'S POLITICISED JUDICIAL SYSTEM

Before turning to Kennedy's impact as first chief justice of the new state, it is important to note that he not only shaped the new Constitution but also oversaw and designed the complete overhaul of the Irish court system after enactment of the Constitution – which resonates, to some extent, with the impact of other judges on their court systems (e.g. in quite a different context, Chief Justice Truong Hoa Binh in Vietnam). The Constitution had expressly mandated the creation of a new Supreme Court and a new High Court; thus, one of Kennedy's first tasks as the Attorney General of the Free State was assignment to a committee advising the executive council (the cabinet) on the structure of the new system. It is said that he played 'a prominent part in the committee's deliberations'.[20] The Courts of Justice Act 1924 swept away the old system of lay magistrature, county courts and superior courts, replacing it with a four-tier system comprising the District Court (now run by professional judges), Circuit Court, High Court and Supreme Court.

This move, in Kennedy's view, was crucial. First, in practical and political terms, the judiciary under British rule in Ireland had been highly politicised and represented merely an arm of the administration. Judges would routinely sign orders suppressing

---

[19] Cahillane (*supra* n 18) 9.
[20] See a speech by former chief justice Ronan Keane, 'Kennedy, Hugh', produced for the University College Dublin Decade of Centenaries, available at http://centenaries.ucd.ie/wp-content/uploads/2015/04/Kennedy-Hugh.pdf, p. 2.

political and even literary organisations of a nationalist or anti-imperial hue.[21] This presented a central obstacle to the development of a functioning rule of law, which has been seen throughout the twentieth century in states worldwide, in democratic transitions from military rule in Latin America, from fascist dictatorship and Communist rule in Europe and from other forms of undemocratic rule (e.g. apartheid in South Africa), and which continues to feature in contemporary democratic transitions in states such as Tunisia and Gambia.[22] Kennedy described the compromised nature of the imperial-era judiciary as follows: 'A Judge might drop into [Dublin Castle, the seat of British power in Ireland] in the morning on his way to Court and as part of the Executive make an Order in Council, and then go on to the Bench and try an issue between the Executive and the people.'[23] More broadly, the transformation of the court system reflected Kennedy's view that, in order to win lasting legitimacy in the eyes of the Irish people, the new Irish State and its emanations must reflect the people and a unique Irish identity. For this reason – and further demoting imperial institutions – the 1924 Act made no reference to the king, the Governor-General, appointment of judges by the Governor-General or appeal to the king in council, at variance with the constitutional text itself.[24] This lack of fidelity to the express text of the 1922 Constitution appears entirely objectionable until one considers Ruti Teitel's argument that, in unstable contexts of democratic transition and wholesale constitutional transformation, the notion of the rule of law is contingent and, by operating both to maintain order and to facilitate political transformation, requires a lesser fidelity to ordinarily cardinal precepts such as consistency and predictability in the law.[25] Yet, as Brice Dickson has observed, although considerable attention was paid to reform of the lower courts, little thought was expended on the role of the apex courts:

> It does not seem to have occurred to the politicians, or to their legal advisers, that the Supreme Court would be acquiring powers which could make it at least as significant a player in the building of the new nation as the government and the legislature. The spirit of the times, steeped as it was in the Diceyan glorification of the sovereignty of Parliament, simply did not envisage a Supreme Court which would actively develop a peculiarly Irish approach to constitutional review. It is interesting, too, that no mention was made in the parliamentary debates of the role which the Judicial Committee of the Privy Council would continue to play in Ireland's legal system.[26]

---

[21] Towey (*supra* n 1) 366.
[22] See, e.g., TG Daly, *The Alchemists: Questioning Our Faith in Courts as Democracy-Builders* (Cambridge University Press, 2017) chs 2 and 4.
[23] See Towey (*supra* n 1) 366.
[24] See Patrick C Kennedy, *Hugh Kennedy: The Great but Neglected Chief Justice* (Ireland Print Doctor Ltd, 2015) 31.
[25] R Teitel, 'Transitional Jurisprudence: The Role of Law in Political Transformation' (1997) 106 *Yale Law Journal* 2035.
[26] B Dickson, *The Irish Supreme Court: Historical and Comparative Perspectives* (Oxford University Press, 2019) 20.

Kennedy seemed to be both a creature of the times and capable of envisioning a different approach. One need only consider his unsuccessful dreams to jettison the English common law and to completely re-found a new Irish legal system based on some modernised version of the Brehon law (the system of autochthonous island-wide law that was supplanted by the English common law), blended with aspects of European civil codes and even Roman law. They were, arguably, far too transformative to be achievable or practical without provoking crisis within the legal system. More modest plans to replace the magpie black-and-white British judicial robes with vividly coloured costumes based on Brehon robes (with rank denoted by colour) were also stymied by fierce resistance from the political and judicial communities.[27] The face of justice in the new Ireland would remain British in character. Yet, while seemingly not in favour of a dominant role for the judiciary, he would have considerable success in crafting a distinct Irish approach to constitutional review.

5.5 PRINCIPLED, PROFOUND AND INNOVATIVE JURISPRUDENCE

As might be expected, given his wider role as a founder judge, Kennedy's brand of constitutional nationalism also extended to the bench, where he sought to craft a principled jurisprudence that made the most of the new Constitution and that strongly vindicated key principles such as the separation of powers and the sovereignty of the people – as opposed to the sovereignty of the British Crown.

As reflected by his defeats on issues such as judicial attire, Kennedy at times found himself at odds with his colleagues (the Court then comprising merely three judges). As mentioned in Section 5.3, the 1922 Constitution marked a radical departure from the British insistence on the supremacy of parliament by conferring on the superior courts the authority to set aside legislation deemed incompatible with the Constitution.[28] However, Irish judges initially made relatively little use of the power, and there was no marked 'judicialisation of politics' for the first four decades post-1922. It has long been orthodoxy in Ireland that for the first decades of the new state, a 'British' judicial mentality persisted, hidebound by tradition and the settled way of doing things, which cut across assertive exercise of the review powers in the 1922 Constitution. However, more recent research contests this view, observing that it would be a mistake to say that the courts were uniformly deferential[29] and arguing that many judges simply cleaved to a different view of the judicial role, which had

---

[27] See, in particular, Keane (*supra* n 1) 221–2.

[28] The constitutionality of legislation could be challenged through concrete review, before the High Court at first instance and the Supreme Court on appeal.

[29] See D Coffey, 'The Judiciary of the Irish Free State' (2011) 33 *Dublin University Law Journal* 61.

less to do with British tradition than a firmly held conceptualisation of judicial power within the confines of the new Constitution, taken on its own merits.[30]

Spatial constraints prevent a full review of Kennedy's jurisprudence in his twelve years as chief justice. This analysis canvasses four cases that give a sense of how Kennedy put in place the very fundamentals of a distinctively Irish rule-of-law state in his strong vindication of the separation of powers, judicial independence and the very nature of the autonomous constitutional order established by the 1922 Constitution.

In *Lynham v Butler (No.2)*[31] in 1933, Kennedy set out what is still considered the definitive statement on the tripartite separation of powers and the contours and nature of judicial power under the new constitutional settlement, in a case challenging the powers of the Irish land commission (governing state appropriation of land) on the basis that it was purporting to engage in the administration of justice. In *O'Foghludha v McClean*[32] in 1933, Kennedy emphasised that the recognition of the Irish language as the national language of the Irish Free State in article 4 of the Constitution was neither mere symbolism nor a retreat from reality given that English had become the dominant language across Irish society. Rather, it placed a clear obligation on the state 'to do everything within its sphere of action (as for instance in State-provided education) to establish and maintain it in its status as the National language'.[33] In *Moore v Attorney General*[34] in 1934, Kennedy delivered a landmark judgment, in a case concerning a claim of ancient Crown-granted lucrative fishery rights against local claims for open fishing backed by the Attorney General, as to whether the indigenous Brehon law had been superseded by the enactment of the Magna Carta Hiberniae in 1216 (enacted by Henry III for Anglo-Norman magnates in Ireland and modelled on the English Magna Carta of 1215) – a fact on which the claim hinged. The judgment is a showcase of Kennedy's expansive historical and comparative legal knowledge, and it rewards a full read.

Perhaps the keystone to understanding Kennedy is his blistering, principled and learned dissent against the majority of the Supreme Court in *The State (Ryan) v Lennon*[35] in 1934. The case concerned a wide-ranging amendment to the 1922 Constitution[36] introducing draconian measures against armed subversives, which granted the state sweeping powers of arrest, detention and military trial of defendants without the protection of established rules of evidence: the amendment would establish a standing military tribunal comprising army officers chosen by the

---

[30] See, e.g., T Hickey, 'Judges and the idea of 'principle' in constitutional adjudication' in L Cahillane, J Gallen and T Hickey (eds.), *Judges, Politics and the Irish Constitution* (Manchester University Press, 2017) 64–7; and D O'Donnell, 'The Sleep of Reason' (2019) 40(2) *Dublin University Law Journal* 191.

[31] *Lynham v Butler (No.2)* [1933] IR 74 410.

[32] *O'Foghludha v McClean* [1934] IR 469.

[33] Ibid. at 483.

[34] *Moore v Attorney General* [1934] IR 44 (the Erne Fishery case).

[35] *The State (Ryan) v Lennon* [1935] 1 IR 170.

[36] Article 2A (Emergency Powers).

executive, empowered to try any offence referred to it by the executive and to impose any penalty (including death) even contrary to existing legislation – and from which there might be no right of appeal. Kennedy's two colleagues on the Court, in a majority judgment adopting an entirely positivist approach, reluctantly upheld the validity of the amendment on the basis of formalist arguments that the amendment had been adopted according to the correct constitutional procedure and that substantive review of the validity of constitutional amendments was beyond the purview of the Court.[37]

The case did not merely concern an isolated amendment of highly dubious nature in any purportedly democratic state; rather, it constituted the latest instance in a pattern of amendments by ordinary law that had seen the 1922 Constitution reduced to a mere plaything of partisan politics. Most egregiously, the statutory amendment power was used to extend the eight-year life of the amendment power to sixteen years on the eve of its expiry, thus raising the potential for the power to become a permanent feature. As a contemporary critic observed, this practice had imperilled the entire constitutional project, with a tendency towards amendments against both the 'spirit and [the] letter of the constitution' (including amendments ensuring that innovations such as the popular initiative powers to trigger legislation were never brought into effect).[38] It closely resembles what today is called 'abusive constitutionalism' – namely, the use of mechanisms of constitutional change to erode the democratic order (although it would be unfair to say that this was the intention of Irish governments in the 1930s).[39]

Against this background, and departing decisively from the majority, Chief Justice Hugh Kennedy appeared to see the need to assert a greater level of judicial control. Decrying the permanence and expansive nature of the new measures of arrest, detention and military trial, and the lack of adequate safeguards,[40] he insisted that they effected a radical alteration of the constitutional scheme, stating: 'In general it may be said that some of the provisions to which I have been referring are the antithesis of the rule of law, and are, within their scope, the rule of anarchy.'[41] For Kennedy, the extent of the amendment power had to be limited:

> The Constituent Assembly declared in the forefront of the Constitution Act . . . that all lawful authority comes from God to the people, and it is declared by Article 2 of the Constitution that 'all powers of government and all authority, legislative, executive, and judicial, in Ireland are derived from the people of Ireland'. It follows that every Act whether legislative, executive or judicial, in order to be lawful under the Constitution, must be capable of being justified under the authority thereby

---

[37] See the judgments of Fitzgibbon and Murnaghan JJ.
[38] See Coffey (*supra* n 29) 62; and DG Morgan, 'The Indian Essential Features Case' (1981) 30 *International and Comparative Law Quarterly* 307, 312.
[39] D Landau, 'Abusive Constitutionalism' (2013) 47 *UC Davis Law Review* 189.
[40] See Kennedy's judgment (*supra* n 35) at 189ff.
[41] Ibid. 198.

declared to be derived from God. From this it seems clear that, if any legislation of the Oireachtas (including any purported amendment of the Constitution) were to offend against that acknowledged ultimate Source from which the legislative authority has come through the people to the Oireachtas, as, for example, if it were repugnant to the Natural Law, such legislation would be necessarily unconstitutional and invalid, and it would be, therefore, absolutely null and void and inoperative.[42]

History has tended to place central emphasis on the natural-law and religious dimensions of Kennedy's dissent, which can make him seem a distant figure from a very different era and obscure the relevance of his thinking to contemporary constitutional law. Certainly, passages such as that just cited, with its explicit reference to God, are jarring to contemporary sensibilities. However, the dissent has a much broader rationale. As Donal Coffey has observed, Kennedy's dissent raised four grounds for limiting the amendment power: an overarching limitation on the basis of natural law; limitation of amendments inconsistent with the Anglo-Irish Treaty of 1921; a limitation based on the fundamental principles that the Constituent Assembly enshrined in the Constitution, including the right to liberty; and the clear principle, from the face of the constitutional text, that, after a period of eight years, constitutional amendments must be effected by popular referendum. The latter meant not only that the amendment challenged in the case was invalid; so, too, was the early amendment extending the power of statutory amendment.

Ciarán Burke has similarly observed that the judgment is better understood as resting on three legs: natural law, popular sovereignty and fundamental rights. Kennedy's pleas to natural law were made in defence of individual rights, presaging in this respect the post-war embrace of human rights and human dignity (and, latterly, democracy) as overarching constraints on positive law, including constitutional law.[43] In a sense, while natural-law thinking remains central to the dissent, the overall principle and normative thrust of the judgment can be quite easily transposed to the contemporary setting, where a concern for rights, dignity, democracy and the core integrity of a constitution have provided the basis for many courts to assert the power to adjudicate on the constitutionality of constitutional amendments.[44]

It is also important to emphasise here that Kennedy did not appear to embrace anything as open-ended as President Sólyom's 'invisible constitution' in 1990s Hungary, discussed in Gábor Atilla Tóth's chapter.[45] As Kim Scheppele has recounted, Sólyom in a 1990 Constitutional Court judgment (issued shortly after enactment of the 1989 Constitution[46]) set out this notion due to a worry that the new

---

[42]   Ibid. 204–5.

[43]   C Burke, *An Equitable Framework for Humanitarian Intervention* (Bloomsbury Publishing, 2013).

[44]   See, in particular, Y Roznai, *Unconstitutional Constitutional Amendments: The Limits of Amendment Powers* (Oxford University Press, 2017).

[45]   Chapter 13 in this volume.

[46]   Technically, the 1989 Constitution was a wholesale amendment of the 1949 Constitution, passed by the outgoing Communist parliament.

parliament would repeatedly amend the Constitution 'to the point where it lost its core principles', which appears to echo the context in which Kennedy's *Lennon* dissent was issued (and which has been borne out in Hungary by the dismantling of the democratic order under the sitting Fidesz government).[47] While Kennedy's judgment pushed the very notion of constitutional review far beyond anything found in the common-law world (including the United States) and Europe, his approach was not as free-wheeling as Sólyom's, who famously expressed, in his 1990 judgment on the death penalty, his only limiting framework to be 'the concept of constitutionality' itself, and whose rhetorical reference to the invisible constitution attracted considerable controversy from parliamentarians and the media.[48] As discussed earlier in this section, Kennedy's approach was rather more carefully tethered to the domestic constitutional text. It was also well grounded in existing strains of thought. Notably, his judgment references a key passage from Alexander Hamilton in *The Federalist*, No. LXXXIV, which states: 'The creation of crimes after the commission of the fact or, in other words, the subjecting of men to punishment for things which, when they were done, were breaches of no law, and the practice of arbitrary imprisonments, have been, in all ages, the favorite and most formidable instruments of tyranny.'[49] Overall, Kennedy appeared to evince more caution in how transcendent principles might be invoked to strike down government measures. *Lennon*, after all, concerned a constitutional amendment clearly antithetical to any notion of liberty, while Sólyom's invisible constitution was invoked to strike down all manner of legislation whose compatibility with constitutionalism and the rule of law was far more open to debate, ranging from welfare cuts to statutes of limitations.[50] As Gábor Tóth observes in his contribution to this collection (Chapter 13), while Sólyom was lauded by some for his robust defence of constitutionalism, others – not least András Sajó, former vice-president of the European Court of Human Rights – criticised his tendency to disregard the text of the Constitution as tending to undermine the rule of law.[51]

Finally, while Kennedy was unable to convince his colleagues to stand with him in this case, his dissent was to become one of the most important judgments in Irish history, as discussed in Section 6.6. Moreover, it is important to emphasise that on other fundamental matters, Kennedy and his colleagues found common ground. Most importantly, Kennedy and Fitzgibbon JJ were in clear agreement that the powers of the Irish Free State were derived solely from the Act of *Dáil Éireann* (the house of deputies) passed on 25 October 1922, sitting as a constituent assembly and

---

[47] See KL Scheppele, 'Guardians of the Constitution: Constitutional Court Presidents and the Struggle for the Rule of Law in Post-Soviet Europe' (2006) 154 *University of Pennsylvania Law Review* 1757, 1777ff.

[48] Ibid. 1777.

[49] *The State (Ryan)* v *Lennon (supra* n 35) 197.

[50] Scheppele (*supra* n 47).

[51] Chapter 14 in this volume.

representing the people of Ireland. This position roundly rejected the conventional position of the judicial committee of the Privy Council in London, insisting that the founding of the Irish Free State was based on the statutes passed by the imperial parliament in Westminster. While that was the settled view of dominions' status in the imperial constitutional order, the Irish judicial position was that Ireland had largely freed herself from the imperial system. The dispute underscores the contested and ambiguous nature of Ireland's independence after 1922.

5.6 KENNEDY'S LEGACY AND LINGERING INFLUENCE IN IRELAND

What is Kennedy's legacy, both at home and abroad? On the one hand, his legacy is clear. First is his contribution to the overall constitutional nature and trajectory of the Irish Free State. Without the maximal autonomy he was critical to winning for the new state and inscribing in the 1922 Constitution, it is hard to imagine how Ireland could have developed further autonomy over time. Ireland's constitutional story for the quarter-century after 1922 focused on the removal of the remaining elements of British sovereignty over Ireland, which included institutions such as the Governor-General. Landmarks in this process were the adoption of the 1937 Constitution and, eleven years later, the declaration of an independent republic and Ireland's departure from the British Commonwealth of Nations through enactment of the Republic of Ireland Act 1948. This evolutionary progress towards full independence may have been much more difficult without the practical foundations laid by Kennedy.

As regards the judicial system, the court system designed by Kennedy has stood the test of time. The overall structure has remained in place largely unaltered since 1924 – with the major exception that a Court of Appeal was inserted between the High Court and the Supreme Court in 2012 (through popular referendum, the only mechanism for constitutional amendment under the 1937 Constitution).

Kennedy continues to be cited as the source of the most foundational principles of Irish constitutional, criminal and administrative law, including the very nature of the state and constitutional order founded in 1922,[52] the jurisdiction of the courts,[53] the powers of the Attorney General,[54] the constitutional status of the Irish language[55] and the corroboration of evidence in criminal cases,[56] to provide just a few examples.

---

[52] See the judgments of Keane CJ and Denham J in *Maguire v Ardagh* [2002] IESC 21, citing Kennedy's dissent in *Lennon* and his extrajudicial writings.

[53] See Fennelly J's judgment in *Creavan v Criminal Assets Bureau; Creavan v Minister for Justice Equality and Law Reform* [2004] IESC 92, citing Kennedy's judgment in *R (Moore) v O'Hanrahan* [1927] IR 406.

[54] See the judgment of Fennelly, McKechnie and MacMenamin JJ in *Walsh & another v Sligo County Council* [2013] IESC 48 para 172.

[55] See, e.g., *Ó Murchú v An Taoiseach* [2010] IESC 26 and multiple judgments in *Ó Maicín v Ireland* [2014] IESC 12.

[56] See, e.g., Charleton J in *Director of Public Prosecutions v Fitzgerald* [2018] IESC 58 para 16.

More importantly, Kennedy's influence set the scene for a much more assertive judiciary. The 1960s and 1970s saw the Supreme Court adopt a dramatically activist approach: a 'judicial revolution', which was strongly coloured by Kennedian thought, especially as regards his emphasis on popular sovereignty and the core principles of the rule of law and rights protection, but which departed from his rather more cautious approach to the wielding of judicial power.[57] Chief Justice Cearbhall Ó Dálaigh and Justice Brian Walsh, both appointed in 1961 by a prime minister seeking a more active Court, formed a new axis of judicial energy, revitalising the Constitution through a more expansive reading of its text. The Ó Dálaigh Court was often inspired by US Supreme Court jurisprudence, which has continued to be one of the Court's main lodestars for decades.[58] In some ways, Irish case law was ahead of its time, epitomised in the Court's use of an 'unenumerated rights' doctrine in the 1960s to expand rights protection (which prefigured the full emergence of the similar doctrine in US jurisprudence in the 1960s[59]), recognising rights to bodily integrity, work, freedom of movement, and privacy in marital relations, among others. In just over ten years, the Court addressed as many cases as it had dealt with in the twenty-four years from 1937 to 1961.[60] As a recent account of the Court's history observes:

> At the height of the expansionist era, in the mid-1960s, one ground-breaking judgment followed another as the court embarked on a drive to expand citizens' individual rights, enhance the protections for defendants in criminal law and rethink fundamental legal principles such as judicial review and the separation of powers. In the process the court became a more powerful institution, and exerted greater influence over the lives of citizens, than ever before.[61]

Again – and reflecting a long-standing debate in Irish constitutional law about the place of natural-law thought – Irish constitutional lawyers and judges have tended to place inordinate emphasis on the natural-law dimensions to this revolution, which has done a disservice to the sophistication of Kennedy's thinking, discussed already. Certainly, we see in this line of jurisprudence repeated references to God, natural law, the 'Christian and democratic nature of the State' and even citation of papal encyclicals.[62] However, the emphasis on natural law and Catholicism need not necessarily be ascribed to Kennedy. After all, while natural-law thought was still common at the time of Kennedy's dissent in *Lennon*, by the 1960s natural-law thinking was decidedly passé (at least from an international perspective) and it

---

[57] See, e.g., A Kavanagh, 'The Irish Constitution at 75 Years: Natural Law, Christian Values and the Ideal of Justice' (2012) 48 *Irish Jurist* 71, 74.

[58] See, e.g., C Fasone, 'The Supreme Court of Ireland and the Use of Foreign Precedents: The Value of Constitutional History' in T Groppi and MC Ponthereau (eds.), *The Use of Foreign Precedents by Constitutional Judges* (Hart Publishing, 2013) 113–20.

[59] See R Keane, 'Judges as Lawmakers: The Irish Experience' (2004) 2 *Judicial Studies Institute Journal* 1, 11.

[60] R Mac Cormaic, *The Irish Constitution* (Penguin UK, 2016) 78.

[61] Ibid. 78.

[62] See Kavanagh (*supra* n 57) 74–5.

would surely have been possible for the courts to have founded their activism on
a different basis, including on the emphasis on the rule of law, popular sovereignty
and fundamental rights in Kennedy's judgments. Indeed, as leading Irish scholars
have recently observed, already in 1939, in a judgment holding expansive intern-
ment powers to violate the individual right to liberty, Gavan Duffy J in the High
Court (reversed on appeal) suggested that higher principles lay behind the
Constitution but did not make any reference to natural law:

> In my opinion, the right to personal liberty and the other principles which we are
> accustomed to summarise as the rule of law were most deliberately enshrined in
> a national Constitution, drawn up with the utmost care for a free people, and the
> power to intern on suspicion or without trial is fundamentally inconsistent with the
> rule of law and with the rule of law as expressed in the terms of our Constitution.[63]

In addition, to observe that Kennedy's thinking in his *Lennon* dissent in particular
set Ireland on a path of an extraordinary expansion of judicial power is not to
uncritically laud this trajectory as entirely positive. As a sitting judge of the
Supreme Court recently observed:

> [I]f the dissent in *State (Ryan) v Lennon* is to be treated as the genesis of indigenous
> constitutionalism, then it was also bound up with what I think commentators
> following Jeremy Waldron would identify as a particularly strong form of judicial
> supremacy. I am a little wary of that label, probably for the same reason as some
> writers are enthusiastic about it: it is both attention-grabbing and controversial. But
> there is no doubt that Kennedy's judgment puts the courts, and therefore the
> judiciary, front and centre.[64]

In fact, it is hard to say whether Kennedy himself would have approved of the
wholesale expansion of judicial power after his death. His dissent in *Lennon* appears
as a judgment *in extremis* to guard the very core of the constitutional and democratic
order, not the adoption of a general position that the proper role of the courts in
Ireland's democratic system was to engage in expansive adjudication. It is important to
highlight that, in other judgments, Kennedy remained a strict textualist and would not
contravene the letter of the law even where it might produce negative results. For
instance, in a case concerning tax legislation, decided shortly before *Lennon*, he cited
with approval English precedent holding that a liability for tax would apply if it came
within the letter of the imposing provision, 'however great the hardship may appear to
be to the judicial mind', but that, where it fell outside the wording of the provision, it
would not, 'however apparently within the spirit of the law the case might be'.[65]
Kennedy did not appear to view the judge's role as towering over the political branches.

---

[63] *State (Burke) v Lennon* [1940] IR 136 at 154, discussed in G Hogan, G Whyte and D Kenny, *Kelly: The Irish Constitution* (Bloomsbury Publishing, 2018) 1459.
[64] O'Donnell (*supra* n 30).
[65] *Revenue Commissioners v Doorley* [1933] IR 750; citing *Partington v Attorney General* LR 4 HL 100.

Recent decades have seen a significant retrenchment of the Supreme Court's expansive role. In particular, a sometimes rather slavish devotion to following US Supreme Court jurisprudence has, in some areas, led the Supreme Court of Ireland down a path of incrementally reducing rights protections painstakingly developed over decades. For instance, a 2015 judgment of the Court (by a bare four-three majority) further cut down previously wide protections against unconstitutionally obtained evidence by discarding a rule established in 1990 against the admissibility of any evidence obtained in breach of constitutional rights, whether knowingly or unknowingly. The move provoked strong dissents from three judges on the Court, decrying the decision's negative impact on individual liberties; an echo of *Lennon* eighty years after Kennedy's dissent.[66]

Although, like other judges in this volume such as Chile's Eugenio Valenzuela (Chapter 15), Kennedy remains little known by the public, it might be said that his influence is hard-wired across the fundamentals of the Irish democratic order. While he was eulogised after his death in 1936 as having made a profound contribution to the country and judiciary, as 'a judge of profound learning and of great impartiality',[67] his legacy is now 'part of the scenery' and is not personalised in a way that accords him cultural significance. This emphasises how toweringness can change over time, and that toweringness can rest on multiple and shifting criteria.

That is not to say that his legacy is uncontested. Discussions with a variety of Irish scholars and judges in the preparation of this chapter have raised key criticisms and questions, especially as to whether he was truly an intellectual and a social leader on the Supreme Court (using the framework from Tushnet's Chapter 2 in this collection). Was Kennedy's dissent in *Lennon* entirely principled or merely an expression of pique at 'his' constitution being incrementally dismantled by the political branches? Is it, as one sitting Supreme Court judge has recently offered, easier to laud his dissent in *Lennon* precisely because it was a dissent and did not bear the weight of implementation and enhanced scrutiny of a majority judgment?[68] If Kennedy had not partly grounded his *Lennon* dissent in an appeal to natural law, could it have convinced his colleagues on the bench to find common cause with him? Can we blame Kennedy for the fact that the 1922 Constitution allowed for statutory amendment in the first place? Was his influence entirely contingent on his historical circumstances? There are no easy answers to these questions. Donal Coffey argues that the sharpest mind of the era was in fact Judge William Johnston of the High Court, who he views as having outshone all members of the Supreme Court, including Kennedy, on the occasions when he sat on the Supreme

---

66 *Director of Public Prosecutions* v *JC* [2015] IESC 31. See in particular the dissent by Judge Adrian Hardiman.

67 G Horan, 'Chief Justice Kennedy: An Appreciation' (1937) 3 *Irish Jurist* 6, 6–7.

68 Remarks at launch of O Doyle, *The Constitution of Ireland: A Contextual Analysis* (Hart, 2018), Trinity College Dublin, 17 January 2019.

Court with them, including *Lynham* v *Butler (No.2)*, discussed in Section 5.5.[69]
From a longer historical perspective, for Gerard Hogan (former judge of the High
Court and currently Advocate General at the European Court of Justice), Seamus
Henchy – a formidable former Supreme Court judge whose rulings from the 1960s
to the 1980s markedly shaped Irish constitutional law – is Ireland's most towering
judge.[70] In that sense, and recalling the focus on the relational nature of 'toweringness' in this volume, Kennedy did not indisputably tower over his fellow judges
(whether contemporaries or otherwise). Even his negotiating abilities regarding
the 1922 Constitution have been questioned by Thomas Mohr.[71] While such
viewpoints are important, no other judge in Ireland can match Kennedy's impact
on the constitutional system, when the totality of his achievements is taken into
account.

Writing this chapter has also prompted me to reflect on another central question
for this collection: do we gravitate towards male 'towering judges' because female
judges are (historically speaking) a new phenomenon or because male judges fit
more neatly with our cultural lenses of what 'towering' means; of notions of leadership that value a masculinist concept of dominance, of power, of superiority? Why
did I not even think to pick our first female chief justice – Chief Justice Susan
Denham (2011–18) – for example? Partly, perhaps, it is simple: Kennedy was already
a presence in my mind, and the latter-day Supreme Court since the 1980s has long
been more a safe pair of hands than a site of genuine constitutional interest or
intellectual ferment. If it is constitutional innovation you want, that happens outside
the courts – with Ireland's Citizens' Assembly a prime example.

5.7 KENNEDY'S TRANSNATIONAL IMPACT

As regards Kennedy's transnational influence and recognition abroad, it is clear that,
while alive, he was active internationally: he was a member of the Canadian and US
bar associations and delivered lectures to both associations on a tour in 1928,
explaining the nature of the 1922 Constitution and the Canadian and US influences
on its drafting, which were later published.[72] His scholarship and constitution were
also admired in Europe and, interestingly, one of the first full treatises on the 1922
Constitution was published in the German language. Kennedy would later write the

---

[69]   D Coffey, 'Comparative and Institutional Perspectives on the Exercise of Judicial Power in the Irish
       Free State' in E Carolan (ed.), *Judicial Power in Ireland* (Institute of Public Administration, 2018)
       39–40.
[70]   Letter dated 4 February 2019 concerning an earlier draft of this chapter.
[71]   T Mohr, *Guardian of the Treaty: The Privy Council Appeal and Irish Sovereignty* (Four Courts Press,
       2016).
[72]   H Kennedy, 'Character and Sources of Constitution of the Irish Free State' (1928) 14 *American Bar
       Association Journal* 437; and 'The Association of Canada with the Constitution of the Irish Free State'
       (1928) 6 *The Canadian Bar Review* 747.

preface to the English translation of that work, published in 1932.[73] He appears, in this respect, as a precursor of today's globe-trotting towering judges, highly active outside the courtroom.

After his death, his dissent in *Lennon* was considered in depth by the justices of the Indian Supreme Court in the *Kesavananda* judgments in 1973, in which they asserted the power to review the constitutionality of dubious constitutional amendments under the authoritarian rule of Indira Ghandi. While Chief Justice Sikri, in particular, said that he would have concurred with Kennedy's dissent, the Court as a whole rejected Kennedy's reasoning.[74] The dissent today continues to be recognised as a landmark judgment in leading work on the idea of unconstitutional constitutional amendments.[75] However, the judgment's influence has been blunted by a central focus on its outmoded natural-law dimensions, which is somewhat alienating to modern audiences. Had his reasoning been based exclusively on the requirements of democratic governance or the rule of law, it is possible that his dissent would be much more widely known and cited today.

5.8 CONCLUSION: TIME TO GIVE IRELAND'S JUDICIAL NATION-MAKER HIS DUES?

In sum, Kennedy's profound legacy, although contested and frayed in places, remains remarkable and has shaped the very warp and weft of the Irish polity for almost a hundred years. Kennedy had a very clear vision of what a new, democratic and rule-of-law-based Irish state and judicial system could be, and he brought much of that vision to life. More broadly, Kennedy's work in negotiating, drafting and developing a strikingly innovative constitution for Ireland in 1922 deserves much wider recognition for its contributions to constitutional theory and practice, global comparative law and our understanding of effective transition from empire to nation, war to peace and undemocratic to democratic rule. At a time of ascendant narrow and authoritarian nationalism, especially in the 1930s, Kennedy managed to blend an outward-looking and intellectual approach with fidelity to a form of constitutional patriotism that drew on the very best traditions of the common law, Irish society and history. Decades before the post-war rise of the now-dominant constitutionalism centred on rights, democratic governance and judicial review, Kennedy pioneered a very particular form of this system in Ireland.

It is important to highlight here that Kennedy achieved this extremely diverse and far-reaching legacy in the extraordinarily short span of fifteen years. He passed away in 1936 at the young age of fifty-seven. It is tempting to contemplate an alternative

---

[73] L Kohn, *Die Verfassung des Irischen Freistaats* (Neue Folge, 1928). The English translation is *The Constitution of the Irish Free State* (George Allen & Unwin, 1932).

[74] See *Kesavananda Bharati v State of Kerala* (1973) 4 SCC 225, 358–89; and Coffey (*supra* n 69) 41 note 79.

[75] See Roznai (*supra* n 44) 77–8.

history where Kennedy lived, and remained on the Supreme Court, for another fifteen to twenty years. Surely, he would have left an even fuller suite of jurisprudence and may have even seen his dissents written into majority judgments. However, to dwell on this would miss the point: Kennedy's importance and legacy are profoundly significant as they stand. It is the full recognition of that legacy that remains lacking, both at home and abroad. Before the global rise in the late twentieth century of the judge-as-former-constitution-drafter, the fuller understanding of constitutions as peace settlements, the focus on constitutional identity, the rise of comparative law as both adjudicative technique and source of shared transnational democratic values, the spread of the notion of constitutional unamendability, and the idea of decolonisation through law (and decolonisation of law), there was Hugh Kennedy. He was, in so many ways, a judge before his time. He was, of course, also a judge *of* his time – as evidenced in the religious and natural-law overtones to his judgments. The latter should not diminish his standing or obscure his deserved place among the most important, impactful and powerful intellectual forces across the world's judiciary.

6

Judicial Rhetoric of a Liberal Polity:
Hong Kong, 1997–2012

CL Lim

6.1 INTRODUCTION

This chapter discusses two prominent voices – those of the former chief justice
Andrew Li and Justice Kemal Bokhary – as they were heard on Hong Kong's Court of
Final Appeal (CFA) during the period following the resumption of Chinese sover-
eignty over Hong Kong.

My claim is not that Li and Bokhary were towering judges because their judgments were necessarily analytically superior to those of their judicial brethren.[1] Li
was an undeniable force as chief justice during that founding era. As for Bokhary, he
made his voice heard even when concurring. Together, theirs were judgments that
drew together the basic threads of Hong Kong's Basic Law to form a tapestry,
especially as they concerned our freedoms, during a critical and agitated period.
Often, they discussed the moral-political justifications for those freedoms. They
tower, first, because their judgments were prominent; second, because the events
surrounding their work were equally prominent; and third, perhaps most important
of all, because constitutions neither reveal themselves nor can be followed simply.
As Cass Sunstein once observed, they have first to be explained.[2] Or, if it were to be
put starkly:

> [C]onstitutional theory would eventually drop the pretense of working from one
> taken-for-granted conception of democracy. It would ... bring into the open the
> contest among connotations of democratic politics that inevitably structures and
> animates the law. These would ... be more or less imprecise images, taken from and
> fit for use in constitutional argument. [3]

So here I present two visions culled from the judgments of two foundational
judges from Hong Kong as a democratic polity. They are contestable

---

[1] They may have been, but that would be for a separate paper.
[2] Cass R Sunstein, "Of Snakes and Butterflies" (2006) 106 *Columbia Law Review* 2234.
[3] Richard D Parker, "Democratic Honor: Liberal and Populist" (2004) 39 *Harvard Civil Rights-Civil Liberties Law Review* 291, 291.

conceptions.[4] That is the point of our understanding of constitutional law as a contest between competing visions rather than involving the discovery of some intrinsic meaning. Contests of this kind depend upon, and constitutional argument also becomes, a form of rhetoric.

Of Li's judicial pronouncements, these reflected a perfectionist theory of the Hong Kong Basic Law – a mini-constitution for Hong Kong that, at the same time, is PRC legislation.[5] He saw the Basic Law as an instrument for the inculcation of civic virtues in the absence of a fully democratized system of government.[6] In contrast, Bokhary's pronouncements tended to focus on preferred political outcomes founded upon our rights. I see the difference as civic versus rights perfectionism.[7] So let me, first, be clear about "perfectionism" in the sense used here.

Rather than being, for example, judges who were constitutional fundamentalists who could have sought original intent or majoritarians who would have tended to defer to the executive branch on the basis of a presumed representational legitimacy or indeed minimalists who decided cases on narrow grounds,[8] Li and Bokhary pressed fully articulated views about how the Basic Law seeks to make Hong Kong more perfect. I mean, simply, that there was an attempt to perfect the Hong Kong SAR by using the Basic Law as a hook or a frame and by fleshing out the purpose, nature, and contents of that Law in order that its purported ideals may be realized in practical terms.

Between them, they have approached the matter differently. Li sought to perfect our civic virtues, assuming ours to be a deliberative, democratic society,[9] while

---

[4] Or essentially contested concepts; see WB Gallie, "Essentially Contested Concepts," LVI *Proceedings of the Aristotelian Society*, 1956, New Series, 167.

[5] Adopted in 1990 by the National People's Congress, entering into force on July 1, 1997. It was to replace a constitutional order comprising the Letters Patent of April 5, 1843, the Hong Kong Royal Instructions to the Governor and Hong Kong's Bill of Rights. See, further, JMM Chan and CL Lim (eds.), *Law of the Hong Kong Constitution*, 2nd edition (Sweet & Maxwell, 2015), paras 1.011, 17.005–17.008; Kemal Bokhary, "The Rule of Law in Hong Kong Fifteen Years After the Handover" (2013) 51 *Columbia Journal of Transnational Law* 287, 289. The enactment as pursuant to the 1982 PRC Constitution, article 31 authorizing the creation of special administrative regions. See Lawrence YK Ma, *Hong Kong Basic Law: Principles and Controversies* (HK Legal Exchange, 2017), para 2-2.

[6] One in which not all seats in the legislature are returned by the exercise of universal, equal suffrage. On such perfectionism, see, e.g., James E Fleming, "The Incredible Shrinking Constitutional Theory: From the Partial Constitution to the Minimal Constitution" (2007) 47 *Fordham Law Review* 2885, 2887 discussing Rawlsian perfectionist liberalism.

[7] I borrow Fleming's typology of perfectionist constitutional theories in American constitutional thought. Ibid. 2886 et seq.

[8] This is a growing movement at present to repatriate Hong Kong's constitution in exile – one that comports more closely with what Beijing is presumed always to have intended. For "fundamentalism," "perfectionism" (as I believe was the preferred approach taken by Li and Bokhary), "majoritarianism," and "minimalism," see Cass Sunstein, *Radicals in Robes: Why Extreme Right-Wing Courts Are Wrong for America* (Basic Books, 2005).

[9] One derives the sense that he was less focused on self-determination and self-realization, except perhaps when it came to free speech, and that he had a less denuded conception of the moral subject. Li tended to emphasize the individual's participation in community. See, e.g., C Edwin Baker, "Sandel on Rawls" (1985) 133 *University of Pennsylvania Law Review* 895.

Bokhary sought continually to perfect the machinery of our democratic structure by holding the Basic Law to its promise of rights.

6.2 HONG KONG'S NEW CONSTITUTIONAL BEGINNING, 1997–2012

The resumption of Chinese sovereignty in 1997, commonly referred to as "the Handover," was treaty-governed; namely, by the 1984 Sino–British Joint Declaration. That treaty's implementation was, however, to be by way of the enactment of Hong Kong's Basic Law by China's National People's Congress (NPC). Under the Basic Law, Hong Kong retains a high degree of autonomy, the common law continues to operate, and Hong Kong will have its own distinct judicial system, at least until 2047,[10] after which the system could continue by and large or it may not; the debate having to do with when the matter of Hong Kong's post-2047 arrangements will have to be discussed.[11] Thus, the health of Hong Kong's own internal constitutional order remains a matter of continued, heightened interest.

For Hong Kong's highest court, the CFA, it was to be from the start a baptism by fire. The question faced from the beginning was this: Who interprets the Basic Law? The Basic Law says that Beijing's Standing Committee of the National People's Congress (the NPCSC) has that ultimate authority,[12] but there was perhaps an assumption initially that, barring certain exceptional cases, a referral to Beijing will be made only *if* the CFA considers it warranted. But as we shall go on to discuss, in the right of abode controversy (centered on the *Ng Ka Ling* case, discussed in a moment) the executive branch – rather than the courts – had referred the constitutional issue that arose to the NPCSC. The CFA's acknowledgment since – in another right of abode case, *Lau Kong Yung* – that Beijing possesses a plenary power of interpretation has now, probably, put paid to any idea of *acte claire*.[13] In other words, whether or not an interpretation is required is now itself a question for the NPCSC, sitting in Beijing, rather than for the judges in Hong Kong.[14]

The entire affair had exposed, early on, the complexity of that interface which the United Kingdom and China had sought to create between the preexisting Anglo-Hong Kong common law system and the new regime of Chinese socialist legality. Just two years after the Handover, the CFA – still testing its powers of

[10] See, e.g., Chan and Lim (*supra* n 5), paras 2.001–2.019; Yash Ghai, *Hong Kong's New Constitutional Order*, 2nd edition (Hong Kong University Press, 1999), generally.
[11] Chan and Lim (*supra* n 5) preface.
[12] Basic Law [hereinafter, BL], article 158.
[13] *Lau Kong Yung v Director of Immigration* (1999) 2 HKCFAR 300. Chan and Lim (*supra* n 5) paras 2.084–2.085.
[14] If for no other reason than that it will concern the relationship between the Central People's Government and the HKSAR, thereby amounting to an "excluded" provision, as will be discussed in a moment. See Chan and Lim (*supra* n 5) para 2.080, citing Trevor M Morris, PhD thesis (Cambridge University, 1992).

judicial review in the new climate – had been confronted with the question of whether Hong Kong should admit an estimated 300,000 people from the Chinese Mainland. At issue was the status of Mainland children born of Hong Kong permanent residents. There were a number of such cases, but the most famous was *Ng Ka Ling*, the 1999 case referred to just now. It concerned a Chinese Mainland requirement that a Mainland person would still require a "one-way permit" (i.e., an exit approval) from the Chinese authorities to come to Hong Kong. The decision of the Court, construing the right of abode under the Basic Law generously and admitting that such persons possess a right to abode thereunder, was to spark a grave social controversy.

It was the Court's reasons that, in particular, gave rise to constitutional doubt and no small measure of agitation. The CFA had considered that it wielded the power of referral, more importantly the power not to refer a question to the NPCSC at all. The Court would ask itself if the Basic Law provision to be interpreted were one that is excluded from the purview of the Hong Kong courts in the first place. For example, because it concerns the Central People's Government's affairs or the relationship Between the Central Authorities and the HKSAR, but if it were not an "excluded provision," would it then be necessary to refer it to the NPCSC at all? In such a case, constitutional provisions would need to be read together, and the Court answered by proceeding to ask which of more than one provision was predominant. If that which is the "predominant provision" were not itself an "excluded provision" then it would follow that no referral would be necessary.[15] One passage drew particular concern: "It is therefore for the courts of the Region to determine whether an act of the National People's Congress or its Standing Committee is inconsistent with the Basic Law, subject of course to the provisions of the Basic Law itself."[16] This was, then, a species of *acte claire*.[17]

The Tung Chee-hwa administration, relying upon article 158 of the Basic Law, proceeded to seek to overturn the Court's reading by referring the whole question about this approach to Beijing.[18] It naturally led to concerns about an encroachment upon the independent powers of the Court. Following the NPCSC's interpretation,[19] the CFA was widely seen to have backed down. In any case, it saw fit to issue an unprecedented "clarification" in *Ng Ka Ling (No. 2)*, purporting as

---

[15] Chan and Lim (*supra* n 5) paras 2.053–2.059, 2.081–2.083.

[16] *Ng Ka Ling v Director of Immigration* (1999) 2 HKCFAR 4, 25–6.

[17] Cf. *Srl CILFIT v Ministry of Health* (1982) Case 283/81.

[18] It was at that point at least unclear whether the government – rather than the judiciary – possessed this power of referral, but the government's ultimately successful argument was that, having been entrusted with enforcing the law, it too possessed the power of referral to Beijing. In fact, the referral concerned two cases, *Ng Ka Ling*, which concerned the constitutionality of the exit approval requirement, and a second case, *Chan Kam Nga v Dir. of Immigration* (1999) 2 HKCFAR 82, in which the question involved the child's right of abode despite being born before the fact of its parent's status as permanent resident.

[19] Which considered that children born outside the Hong Kong SAR must at the time of birth have at least one parent who was permanently resident.

it were to "clarify" its own earlier judgment.[20] A conflict between two systems – the Chinese and the common law systems – had emerged. Under the former, the final power of interpretation (or, if we use Justice Bokhary's terminology, of judicial resistance – "reinterpretation") lies with the NPCSC. However, from a common law viewpoint, this power vests in the courts. Hence the second judgment in *Ng Ka Ling (No.2)*, "clarifying" the CFA's judgment in *Ng Ka Ling (No. 1)*.[21] But, arguably, it had clarified nothing. Johannes Chan, whose distinguished reputation in the field does not usually invite challenge in Hong Kong, has written, rather, that the purported clarification succeeded perhaps only in assuring us of the fact that the Court had nothing to clarify but that it may have been more important to hear the Court acknowledge the fact. It was at any rate sufficient admission of Beijing's authority. Such was the difficulty that the Hong Kong CFA found itself in, practically from the beginning of the new constitutional era.[22]

Constitutional watchers soon realized that, in practical terms, where the line lies between socialist legality and the common law is precarious.[23] Still, *Ng Ka Ling (No. 1)* showed that Hong Kong's CFA cannot be faulted for want of trying and the Court subsequently construed the scope of that NPCSC interpretation narrowly.[24] Thus, even today, it is still asked which part of *Ng Ka Ling (No. 1)* remains, if any. On this subject, Bokhary at least has no doubt:

> Article 158 of the Basic Law vests the power of interpretation in the Standing Committee of the National People's Congress. But then – and vitally to the "one country, two systems" principle – the Standing Committee, by the same article, authorizes the Hong Kong courts to interpret on their own the provisions of the Basic Law which are within Hong Kong's autonomy. That means the whole of the Basic Law excluding only a limited category of provisions: those that concern affairs that are the Mainland Government's responsibility or that concern the relationship between the Mainland authorities and Hong Kong. Also according to Article 158, the Hong Kong courts are required to seek an interpretation from the Standing Committee if they need to interpret any excluded provision. That requirement, it is to be stressed, applies only to excluded provisions. And the Court of Final Appeal did not consider any such

---

[20] *Ng Ka Ling v Director of Immigration (No 2)* (1999) 2 HKCFAR 141, 142. See, further Johannes Chan, "What the Court of Final Appeal Has Not Clarified in Its Clarification: Jurisdiction and the Amicus Intervention" in JMM Chan, HL Fu, and Yash Ghai (eds.), *Hong Kong's Constitutional Debate: Conflict over Interpretation* (Hong Kong University Press, 2001) 171.

[21] See Chan and Lim (*supra* n 5) para 2.058; Chan (*supra* n 20) 180–1.

[22] Chan (*supra* n 20) 180–1.

[23] At the time, the most important textbook, by Yash Ghai, had already pointed out the difficulty of cocooning a common law system within a socialist legal order, but that was at best a theoretical concern that may have only occupied the imagination of teachers at the University of Hong Kong where Ghai and his colleagues struggled with such issues.

[24] Bokhary (*supra* n 5) 292, discussing *Lau Kong Yung* and *Chong Fung Yuen v Dir. of Immigration* (2001) 4 HKCFAR 211. See, further, Chan and Lim (*supra* n 5) paras 2.080–2.091.

provision to be involved in either of the two cases out of which the Reinterpretation arose. [25]

As I have mentioned, in a related case, the CFA had gone on, at the same time, to accept the NPCSC's power to be plenary – that is, to be absolute and unqualified.[26] But as to whether the Court had debased itself, a string of formative cases followed.

6.3 COMPARING HONG KONG'S TOWERING JUDGES

Particularly at a time when we hear dissatisfaction with Hong Kong's self-understanding of its mini-constitution, Andrew Li CJ and Justice Bokhary (sitting as a permanent justice of the Hong Kong CFA) found themselves placed upon Hong Kong's highest court during an extraordinary time in that extraordinary place. Together, they explained – perhaps more elaborately than most have – what, in essence, "one country, two systems" should mean.

Li focused on our capacity for self-government and the Basic Law's character-building role,[27] its role in other words in the inculcation of the attributes of an active citizenry;[28] whereas Bokhary emphasized the exercise of rights necessary for the development of democratic government.[29] I shall discuss the matter in that order: Li, then Bokhary.

6.3.1 *Civic Virtue and Democratic Society*

Following the resumption of China's sovereignty in 1997, the Li Court (1997–2010) faced events that soon laid the foundations of the newly established Hong Kong SAR's constitutional jurisprudence. Such foundations included acceptance that Beijing has ultimate and plenary authority to interpret Hong Kong's Basic Law.[30] Yet their task, as they saw it, was to interpret the mini-constitution of a modern constitutional democracy. Justice Bokhary once quoted Jeffrey Jowell, and it is telling: "[T]he general notions of fairness that may reside in the common law may prove helpful, but it is more helpful still to engage openly with the necessary

---

[25]   Bokhary (*supra* n 5) 291.

[26]   *Lau Kong Yung v Director of Immigration.*

[27]   Compare, for example, Stanley Ingber, "Liberty and Authority: Two Facets of the Inculcation of Virtue" (1994) 69 *St John's University Law Review* 421, 433 (discussing the argument for a federal bill of rights to supplement a constitution that was inadequate for its character-building role from the perspective of civic republicanism).

[28]   See, further, Linda C McClain, "The Domain of Civic Virtue in a Good Society: Families, Schools and Sex Equality" (2001) 69 *Fordham Law Review* 1617.

[29]   And, by extension, rights necessary for the enjoyment of all other rights including such economic rights as the right to affordable housing and to equal welfare benefits.

[30]   *Ng Ka Ling v Director of Immigration (No. 2)* (1999) 2 HKCFAR 141. See, further, Chan and Lim (*supra* n 5) paras 2.047–2.059; Chan, Fu, and Ghai (*supra* n 20).

qualities of a modern constitutional democracy." [31] The dispute itself – *Lau Kong Yung* – had involved seventeen applicants claiming the right of abode in Hong Kong by descent. It had concerned the proper construction of Beijing's NPCSC's unprecedented earlier interpretation of the Basic Law.[32] But while it was Bokhary who quoted Jowell, it is Li to whom that passage fits more neatly, and we turn to Andrew Li first.

In *Leung Kwok Hung*, a 2005 freedom of assembly case involving the Public Order Ordinance, Li CJ's majority judgment had referred to the freedoms of speech and assembly as freedoms that "lie at the foundation of a democratic society."[33] That judgment recalled an earlier 1999 flag desecration case where free speech had been extolled in lyric form just as quickly as the Court had refused the application to strike down a law protecting the Hong Kong and national flags and emblems for allegedly being too constrictive of the right to free speech and expression. Yet lyric tends to survive the particular constitutional outcome.

In that flag case, *Ng Kung Siu*, Li CJ had spoken of a "democratic" society in our legal imagination. He had considered "[f]reedom of expression ... a fundamental freedom in a democratic society" and that "[i]t lies at the heart of a civil society and of Hong Kong's system and way of life. The Courts must give a generous interpretation to its constitutional guarantee. This freedom includes the freedom to express ideas which the majority may find disagreeable or offensive and the freedom to criticise governmental institutions and the conduct of public officials." [34] In the 2005 peaceful assembly case, Li was to add, in a similar vein, that "[t]he freedom of peaceful assembly is a fundamental right. It is closely associated with the fundamental right of the freedom of speech. The freedom of speech and the freedom of peaceful assembly are precious and lie at the foundation of a democratic society." [35] How do such freedoms lie at the foundation of a democratic society? According to Li, it is because "[t]olerance is the hallmark of a pluralistic society."[36] This was to become perhaps the key motif in Li's most notable constitutional judgments. But what was his aim? His purpose? Would this improve our ideas about governance by ensuring the "vigor" of democratic debate? Or is it aimed instead at allowing minorities to be heard where otherwise they might not? According to Li:

> These freedoms are of cardinal importance for the stability and progress of society for a number of inter-related reasons. The resolution of conflicts, tensions and problems through open dialogue and debate is of the essence of a democratic

[31] *Lau Kong Yung v Director of Immigration* (1999) 2 HKCFAR 300, paras 38–9 (per Bokhary PJ).
[32] *Ng Ka Ling v Director of Immigration (No. 1)* (1999) 2 HKCFAR 4. Here was a line of cases that formed part of a whole string of immigration disputes about the entitlement of Mainland Chinese persons to the right of Hong Kong abode; they are known collectively as the "right of abode" cases; Chan and Lim (*supra* n 5) paras 2.047–2.057.
[33] *Leung Kwok Hung v HKSAR* (2005) 8 HKCFAR 229, at [1] (Li CJ, Chan PJ, Ribeiro PJ, Mason NPJ).
[34] *HKSAR v Ng Kung Siu* (1999) 2 HKCFAR 422 (per Li CJ).
[35] *Leung Kwok Hung*, at [1]–[2].
[36] Ibid.

society. These freedoms enable such dialogue and debate to take place and ensure their vigour. A democratic society is one where the market place of ideas must thrive. These freedoms enable citizens to voice criticisms, air grievances and seek redress. This is relevant not only to institutions exercising powers of government but also to organisations outside the public sector which in modern times have tremendous influence over the lives of citizens. Minority views may be disagreeable, unpopular, distasteful or even offensive to others. But tolerance is a hallmark of a pluralistic society. Through the exercise of these freedoms[,] minority views can be properly ventilated. [37]

Still, the Court was again to reject the constitutional challenge. The convictions were upheld.

But this time Bokhary broke judicial ranks, uttering dissent. In the earlier flag case, Bokhary had gone along – or perhaps had been persuaded to go along – with the chief justice and the majority, adding, however:

In the course of her powerful address, counsel for the 2nd respondent posed a rhetorical question. If these restrictions are permissible, where does it stop? It is a perfectly legitimate question. And the answer, as I see it, is that it stops where these restrictions are located. For they lie just within the outer limits of constitutionality. Beneath the national and regional flags and emblems, all persons in Hong Kong are – and can be confident that they will remain – equally free under our law to express their views on all matters whether political or non-political: saying what they like, how they like. [38]

It seems true to say that some of the Li Court's most notably elegiac moments were when those who had pressed their rights failed before the Court. Outcomes aside, Li's message was constant – that a democratic society is a society tolerant of diverse opinions, their articulation and their expression. The protection of minority groups and opinion became a noticeable preoccupation. At times, the whole lesson was but a pithy phrase that leapt at the reader from the law reports – homosexuals "constitute a minority in the community."[39] Such readers of the Hong Kong Law Reports understood his concerns about our civic health and his use of Hong Kong's mini-constitution as a true teacher of our own conscience.

6.3.2 A Political Rights Thesis in Comparison

In contrast, Bokhary's views went beyond liberal tolerance and the inculcation of civic virtues. Outcomes matter when construing and applying constitutional rights. I mean that he seemed to dislike paying homage to principle when outcome risked being orphaned. To some, he might simply appear to be a natural rights lawyer,[40]

[37] Ibid.
[38] Ng Kung Siu, at [98] (Bokhary PJ, concurring).
[39] Secretary for Justice v Yau Yuk Lung (2007) 10 HKCFAR 335, para 29.
[40] Kemal Bokhary, Croc of Final Appeal (Sweet & Maxwell, 2017).

but that would speak only to his creed, not to his views on the specific constitutional issues of the day.

Bokhary spoke directly to the preservation of Hong Kongers' freedoms and their fears of tyranny. In the flag case, he said:

> I am of the view that it is possible – even if by no means easy – for a society to protect its flags and emblems while at the same time maintaining its freedom of expression ... This is possible if its flag and emblem protection laws are specific, do not affect the substance of expression, and touch upon the mode of expression only to the extent of keeping flags and emblems impartially beyond politics and strife. In my view, our laws protecting the national and regional flags and emblems from public and willful desecration meet such criteria. They place no restriction at all on what people may express. Even in regard to how people may express themselves, the only restriction placed is against the desecration of objects which hardly anyone would dream of desecrating even if there was no law against it. No idea would be suppressed by the restriction. Neither political outspokenness nor any other form of outspokenness would be inhibited. [41]

He singled out "political outspokenness" before adding the words "nor any other form of outspokenness." Why single out – if indeed that is what he did – political outspokenness? Is he a Brandeisian, one who grades the relative value of different forms of speech and expression before singling out political speech as deserving of the highest protection? If so, he is unlike Andrew Li who, in American constitutional terms, is less Brandeis, more Holmes.[42] Yet all this is to be done only under the flags and emblems – the very symbols of "one country, two systems." After all, without the flags and emblems there is no Hong Kong SAR.

The end result is the same, but there are perceptible clues to different entire philosophies. While Bokhary's voice reflects closely Hong Kong's fear of tyranny, Li spoke often, indeed consistently, to our democratic nature and the abjuration of our own tyrannous sentiments. What is the significance of these two judges? What might we say, if anything, of their legacy today? Following, most notably, Bokhary's parting shot when, upon leaving the bench as a permanent justice, he warned of "clouds heralding a 'storm of unprecedented ferocity' gathering over the rule of law in Hong Kong."[43]

6.4 A DEMOCRATIC POLITY AND THE LAW'S COERCIVE POWERS

Li, as we have seen, wielded the Basic Law as an educational tool, preparing a polity for its democratic mission. Bokhary focused instead on the architecture of coercive state powers that might stifle our ever achieving a fully fledged democratic structure.

---

[41] *Ng Kung Siu*, at [96]–[97] (per Bokhary PJ).
[42] *Leung Kwok Hung*, at [2].
[43] Austin Chiu, "Retiring Court of Final Appeal Judge Warns of Legal Turmoil," *South China Morning Post*, October 25, 2012.

The right of abode affair had concerned the courts' power of judicial review, which, while it had always existed, lay dormant from 1843 when the Letters Patent were created until the enactment of Hong Kong's Bill of Rights Ordinance (BORO) in 1991.[44] In 1991, Justice Silke VP, in a case involving reverse burden of proof provisions under the Dangerous Drugs Ordinance, had held, regarding Hong Kong's new Bill of Rights, itself constituting an important prelude to the Handover, that

> the glass through which we view the interpretation of the Hong Kong Bill is a glass provided by the [International Covenant on Civil and Political Rights]. We are no longer guided by the ordinary canons of construction of statutes nor with the dicta of the common law inherent in our training. We must look, in our interpretation of the Hong Kong Bill, at the aims of the Covenant and give "full recognition and effect" to the statement which commences that Covenant. From this stems the entirely new jurisprudential approach to which I have already referred. [45]

Thus, the Li Court did not have to begin anew. BORO had sought to incorporate the Covenant and had been entrenched by way of an amendment to the Letters Patent.[46] After the Handover, the Letters Patent ceased to apply, but the Basic Law itself entrenched the rights contained in the Covenant.[47] At the same time, but for cosmetic repeal of a few provisions, the Bill was itself to remain a part of Hong Kong law.[48] The Basic Law requires the Covenant as it applied in Hong Kong previously to continue to be enforced and to be applied through Hong Kong law, creating a "tripartite framework" – one whereby rights under Hong Kong law are protected by the Basic Law itself, the provisions of the Covenant, and BORO.[49]

Recall the peaceful assembly case *Leung Kwok Hung* in which the CFA, after some uncertainty during the pre-Handover period, had also restored Justice Silke's view and reaffirmed the generous and purposive approach to be taken toward the interpretation of constitutional rights.[50] But it was also in that case that Bokhary had dissented. In *Leung*, Li CJ, writing for the majority, declared freedom of speech and

---

[44] Bokhary (*supra* n 5) 290; Chan and Lim (*supra* n 5) para 17.016.
[45] *R v Sin Yau Ming* [1992] 1 HKCLR 127, 139.
[46] Chan and Lim (*supra* n 5) paras 16.026–16.029.
[47] BL, article 39; Chan and Lim (*supra* n 5) para 16.035. As for the judicial power of substantive review, see BL, article 11, also article 18. See Chan and Lim (*supra* n 5) paras 17.015–17.016.
[48] Chan and Lim (*supra* n 5) paras 17.005–17.008.
[49] Ibid. paras 16.030–16.035.
[50] *R v Sin Yau Ming* (1991) 1 HKPLR 88, 107 (Silke VP). In *Leung Kwok Hung v HKSAR*, the CFA considered:

> It is well established in our jurisprudence that the courts must give such a fundamental right [to freedom of peaceful assembly] a generous interpretation so as to give individuals its full measure. On the other hand, restrictions on such a fundamental right must be narrowly interpreted. Plainly, the burden is on the Government to justify any restriction ... Needless to say, in a society governed by the rule of law, the courts must be vigilant in the protection of fundamental rights and must rigorously examine any restriction that may be placed on them.

assembly to be freedoms that "lie at the foundation of a democratic society."[51] The majority had considered that the notification requirement as a prerequisite to lawful assembly was constitutional but that the police commissioner's discretion to object was too vague if based on the notion of *ordre public*.[52] However, any vagueness could be cured by confining the basis of that discretion to the need to maintain law and order. Since the appellants challenged only the basis of the commissioner's discretion for being overbroad, their convictions should stand once such overbreadth was cured. Bokhary dissented on two grounds. First, while the imposition of a notification requirement was constitutionally sound, it suffered overbreadth in restricting spontaneous demonstration. Second, the various statutory grounds of restriction – national security, public order (*ordre public*), and public safety – were similarly overbroad and Bokhary would have allowed the appeal.

The freedoms of speech and of peaceful assembly go to the heart of Bokhary's philosophy – one that has a firm eye fixed upon the law's forcible constraints upon democratic development. In his extrajudicial writings, he has considered that

> [t]he rule of law is, as Lord Steyn said, "closely linked with the values of a liberal democracy." Absent full democracy, can the rule of law prevail? Yes, on certain conditions. First, there has to be independent judicial stewardship of an entrenched constitution. Second, powers must be properly separated. Third, human rights must be protected conformably with international norms. Fourth and finally, the existence of the rule of law must not be treated as justification for delay in democratic development.[53]

Absent full democracy, and it is absent in Hong Kong, certain preconditions must be met if the rule of law is to prevail. Bokhary would have had no reason to doubt judicial independence. No doubt, too, that he believed that there had been at least some attempt at recovery from the right of abode crisis. Still, the protection of human rights "conformably with international norms" is a precondition and, finally, the rule of law itself is no excuse for slowing democratic development.

We can all draw the line variously, but – if we assume that his views are reasonably coherent at different times in different places and even in different contexts, in this case when he speaks both judicially and extrajudicially – drawing the line where the majority did in *Leung Kwok Hung* did not conform with the international standard of rights protection. Unduly restricting the right to peaceful assembly cripples democratic development.

---

[51] *Leung Kwok Hung* v *HKSAR*.

[52] In other words, there is a constitutional requirement of clear and accessible laws. The statute granted such power on the commissioner's part to object "if he reasonably considers that the objection is necessary in the interests of national security or public safety, public order (ordre public) or the protection of the rights and freedom of others." Under the statute, the Commissioner is also obliged not to object if he reasonably considers that the statutory grounds just referred to could be met instead through the imposition of conditions.

[53] Bokhary (*supra* n 5) 295.

What then of Bokhary's concurrence in the flag desecration case? There are various theories. One popular notion is that the Court, having emerged from the right of abode affair, would have wished not to question what, in effect, was Mainland legislation extended to Hong Kong. I would argue against such broad skepticism in reading the Court's reasonings. We do not usually treat judgments as lies. Rather, it would appear that the Court had merely applied a well-known distinction drawn between restrictions on the content of speech and on its modes, the former being presumptively more restrictive. Bokhary, however, took a different tack, drawing the line at the flag as a symbol of the beginning of a new polity under "one country, two systems": "Beneath the national and regional flags and emblems, all persons in Hong Kong are – and can be confident that they will remain – equally free under our law to express their views on all matters whether political or non-political: saying what they like, how they like."[54]

The flags and emblems were themselves the symbols of Hong Kong's democratic promise.

6.5 ONE LEAVES; THE OTHER REMAINS

There is a sense in which this picture is monochromatic. One needs to ask more. Was not the chief justice's greatest contribution his ability to manage the direction of the Court and to achieve the necessary compromises in steering his brethren through choppy waters? Yet this chapter has focused on doctrine, while at the same time it would not be correct to leave an exaggerated impression of Bokhary as merely a steward of the Basic Law's democratic promise. He remained on the bench following Li's departure at the end of August 2010. Subsequently, the CFA, led by His Lordship Geoffrey Ma CJ, was to go on to address a broadening range of controversies over rights. Those related in particular to equality and economic, social, and cultural rights, the last category having always been a poor cousin of civil and political rights.[55] In Hong Kong, economic, social, and cultural rights had not enjoyed incorporation through specific legislation unlike civil and political rights under BORO. However, the Basic Law incorporates both civil and political rights as well as economic, social, and cultural rights. In viewing these cases, albeit doctrinally, we have a broader picture of Bokhary at least.

Bokhary previously had occasion to state, *obiter*, in a rent variation case:

> If it were necessary to do so in order to establish that the Authority is duty-bound to provide affordable housing, it might well be possible to pray the ICESCR powerfully in aid of construing the Housing Ordinance to impose that duty. As it happens, however, I have arrived at that construction even without taking the ICESCR into account.[56]

---

[54] *Ng Kung Siu*, at [98] (Bokhary PJ, concurring).
[55] See, e.g., Charles Fried, *Right and Wrong* (Harvard University Press, 1978), discussing "positive" versus "negative" rights.
[56] *Ho Choi Wan v Housing Authority* (2005) 8 HKCFAR 628, 653.

That did not prevent second-generation rights from coming to the fore in two cases, the second occurring after Bokhary had ceased to be a permanent justice of the Court upon reaching the age of retirement, becoming as he is today a non-permanent justice. The first case was *Catholic Diocese of Hong Kong v Secretary for Justice*.[57] It was a case in which the Catholic Church had argued that a newly introduced school management system would dilute Church control of Church-run schools. The Basic Law, for its part, protects the role of community organizations in providing education.[58] It protects even more specifically the right of religious organizations to provide education and welfare.[59] This is to be distinguished from the broader – and thus less specific – right to freedom of religious belief.[60] At its heart, the appellant's case was that its authority to appoint all of a school's management committee, as well as the supervisor and principal according to previous practice, deserved constitutional safeguarding. Unanimously, the CFA rejected such a right. Bokhary, in a separate concurrence, wrote:

> The challenge fails because the challenged legislation leaves religious organizations free to nominate a majority of the persons serving on the incorporated management committees of aided schools which they sponsor ... Plainly the core right or freedom on which the Catholic Diocese's constitutional challenge rests ... is the right or freedom of religious organizations to continue to run schools "according to their previous practice" ... The challenged legislation makes no direct attack on religious activities at schools. And as long as religious organizations are free to nominate the majority of the persons on the incorporated management committees of schools which they sponsor, religious activities at such schools are acceptably safe from indirect attack and from erosion. [61]

At bottom, the difference lay in the fact that Bokhary would employ the previous practices of Church-run schools as a benchmark,[62] although not going so far as to accept counsel Martin Lee SC's argument that all previous practices had been grandfathered. There is here an acute sensitivity not only toward questions of principle, of values, but also toward the need for judgments of fact and degree.

When it came to principle, Bokhary's approach to rights tended toward their indivisibility, as this second case shows. In *Kong Yun Ming v The Director of Social Welfare*, Justice Ribeiro PJ delivered the principal judgment of a unanimous court.[63] Bokhary, however, wrote a separate concurrence. Justice Ribeiro considered it

---

[57] (2011) 14 HKCFAR 754 (Chief Justice Ma, Justice Bokhary PJ, Justice Ribeiro PJ, Justice Tang NPJ, and Justice Gleeson NPJ).

[58] BL, article 132.

[59] BL, article 141(3).

[60] BL, articles 32, 141(1).

[61] *Kong Yun Ming*, [98]–[102] (Bokhary NPJ).

[62] Contra [67]–[70] (Ma CJ, Ribeiro PJ, with whom Tang and Gleeson NPJJ concurred).

[63] (2013) 16 HKCFAR 950 (Chief Justice Ma, Justice Ribeiro PJ, Justice Tang PJ, Justice Bokhary NPJ, and Lord Phillips of Worth Matravers NPJ).

unnecessary to treat counsel's argument that what a new seven-year residence requirement imposed on access to welfare entitlement – by precluding nonpermanent residents – violated the right to equality; at least once, the Court upheld the right to social welfare.[64] True, a right to social welfare cannot be reduced to a right to nondiscrimination,[65] but Bokhary found a violation of both the right to equal treatment and the right to welfare, in that order.[66] Regarding the latter, Bokhary considered:

> This case is about social welfare. Policy matters thereon are for the political branches of government. But there is in Hong Kong a constitutional right to social welfare. And the responsibility for enforcing constitutional rights, socio-economic ones no less than other ones, rests with the courts. In discharging this responsibility, it has to be recognized that courts are not ideally equipped to undertake resource allocation. At the same time, the courts cannot decline to intervene if the legislative (or administrative) scheme in question fails to accord people the basic necessities to which they are constitutionally entitled. The approach formed by those two propositions is one at which I arrive on principle. [67]

This was in stark contrast to the approach taken by the courts below.[68] In order to appreciate Bokhary's contribution, a comparison should also be drawn with an earlier case that had addressed the right to health care differently. Bokhary did not sit in that case, which concerned the constitutional permissibility of higher fees for obstetrics services supplied to nonresident Mainland Chinese women. Attempts to defend the decision in that case have concentrated on a suggestion that nonresidents are not entitled to equal treatment.[69] I would like to think that Bokhary's judgment in *Kong Yun Ming* was an attack on that view.

6.6 TO THE PRESENT

There is the assertion today that Hong Kong's constitutional discourse during that initial phase – spanning around the first fifteen years of the Hong Kong SAR – hinges upon some mistake. Crudely put, the criticism is that the Hong Kong constitutional order is conceived as if it were, in large part, insulated from Mainland laws. Public constitutional controversy in recent times has concerned a range of issues: (1) a 2014 State Council White Paper, (2) the emergence of fringe but worrying separatist sentiment, (3) the disqualification of political candidates, and (4) the application of

---

[64] Ibid. [21]–[22], [33], [137] (Ribeiro PJ); BL, article 36 read with article 145.
[65] Ibid. [32].
[66] Ibid. esp. [170], [173] (Bokhary NPJ).
[67] Ibid. [147].
[68] See, further, Chan and Lim (*supra* n 5) paras 17.074–17.078, 17.086 (on the use of the rational nexus and proportionality tests of constitutional scrutiny, and on the employment of strict scrutiny despite the margin of appreciation to be accorded to the government).
[69] See the chapter by Karen Kong in Chan and Lim (*supra* n 5) para 26.089.

Mainland law in the newly constructed West Kowloon terminus for the Guangzhou-Shenzhen-Hong Kong Express Rail Link (the "XRL"), which brought constitutional fears to the fore.

Regarding the first, a passage in Beijing's White Paper had been taken in certain quarters to suggest that patriotism – by which loyalty to the Central People's Government is an essential component – had become a prerequisite of judicial office, and this was seen as a threat to judicial independence. As for the second and third, these to a certain extent have overlapped, although not always. Separatist sentiments in recent years have been seen to question not only the notion of "one country, two systems" in the Basic Law but also the leadership of the Communist Party. Certain disqualifications from electoral office were related to this aspect. At the same time, an overall sense of Hong Kong's autonomy shrinking was compounded – at least in the public imagination – by the fact that Mainland law, in its entirety, would now apply, even if only to a small area of the West Kowloon terminus that the government claims to be necessary for the proper functioning of immigration controls.

Fresh concerns have therefore arisen about the continued functioning of the institutions that would make constitutional choice possible. Yet public controversy is not a sure guide to the otherwise quiet state of constitutional development,[70] even if it is the quiet of a storm center.[71] Jurisprudentially, the largest shift has been in how the Court approaches constitutional reasoning. Namely, there is now a full-blown doctrine of margin of appreciation when matters of state or community policies are assessed,[72] as an addendum to the four-part proportionality test.[73] Thus, where governmental social or economic choices are being assessed, there has emerged the question: Is the policy "manifestly without reasonable foundation"? I have mentioned the case on access to obstetrics services – *Fok Chun Wa* v *Hospital Authority*.[74] Here, then, is a margin of appreciation doctrine in operation, one that suggests heightened deference to the government's view. However, there is an important caveat, according to the current Court, where "core values" are involved – that is, where fundamental rights related to personal or human characteristics (such as race, color, gender, sexual orientation, religion, politics, or social origin) are implicated. Thus, where

> unequal treatment strikes at the heart of core-values relating to personal or human characteristics (such as race, colour, gender, sexual orientation, religion, politics, or social origin), the courts would extremely rarely (if at all) find this acceptable. These

---

[70] For an opposing view, see Johannes Chan, "A Storm of Unprecedented Ferocity: The Shrinking Space of the Right to Political Participation, Peaceful Demonstration, and Judicial Independence in Hong Kong" (2018) 16 *International Journal of Constitutional Law* 373.

[71] Oliver Wendell Holmes, Jr., Speech to the Harvard Law School Association of New York, February 15, 1913, quoted in Anthony Lewis, "Quiet of a Storm Centre" (1999) 40 *Texas Law Review* 933.

[72] Chan and Lim (*supra* n 5) para 17.073.

[73] *HKSAR* v *Lam Kwong Wai* (2006) 9 HKCFAR 574, paras 36–44; *Leung Kwok Hung* v *HKSAR*, para 253.

[74] (2012) 15 HKCFAR 409.

characteristics involve the respect and dignity that society accords to a human being. They are fundamental societal values. On the other hand, where other characteristics or status which do not relate to such notions or values are involved, and here I would include residence status, the courts will hesitate much more before interfering; in other words, more leeway is given to the Executive, Legislature or other authorities. [75]

Subsequently, in *Kong Yun-ming*, Ribeiro PJ did not consider the Church schools case to have implicated any core value. Yet, outcome-wise, the constitutional challenge prevailed. Might it have been the Bokhary factor? Might it be suggested, too, that, in these cases, tolerance of diversity – of new residents[76] or of educational diversity – may also have had a role to play as core values, albeit implicitly?

6.7 CONCLUSION

Such concerns were far away when two philosophical strands emerged during post-Handover Hong Kong's formative period; a period during which two perfectionist visions of the Basic Law were articulated. During that period, the Hong Kong's Basic Law was conceived as an instrument of liberal legality. The first strand, characterized by the chief justice's pronouncements in particular, had emphasized a "democratic" tolerance of diversity. The second, which Justice Kemal Bokhary stood for, brought the Basic Law's guarantees of political rights and freedoms to the fore. While it might be asked whether some of the Court's judgments would have been so forcefully liberal without Bokhary's influence, the two strands may at times have seemed indistinguishable. My argument is that they are. Our constitutional imagination is only a construct. It was, in a significant sense, a product of the Court on which Andrew Li presided. Much had occurred in the preceding years – the Sino-British talks that led to the Sino-British Joint Declaration, the drafting of the Basic Law, the enactment by the colonial authorities of BORO. However, treaties and legislation do not themselves create the constitutional imagination of a society. Judicial voices matter, their tone, their timbre, their persuasiveness, or otherwise.

Call it judicial rhetoric, if one must, but in recalling the contribution of these two judges from that early bench today, especially following Bokhary's parting shot when, upon his retirement, he warned of a storm of unprecedented ferocity, what is their judicial legacy? Have they enabled us to better understand Hong Kong's constitutional arrangements? In one sense, the boundaries have been tested, or at least that was the significance of that first phase of constitutional jurisprudence. We might say that attention turned inward – to fundamental questions about the nature of Hong Kong's society and way of life. This was not a matter simply of differences from the way of life on the Chinese Mainland. An optimistic appraisal might suggest

[75] Ibid. [77]–[78].
[76] See the remarks in the chapter by Karen Kong in Chan and Lim (*supra* n 5) para 26.081.

that this is all as it should be. That constitutional discourse in Hong Kong grew to maturity by attending to Hong Kong's own immediate domestic concerns. A cynic might suggest that this is all that the Hong Kong courts could do.

I suggest a different view. The Li Court's instincts were of a perfectionist sort. Both Li and Bokhary sought to construct at times competing, at other times overlapping, views about how the Basic Law makes Hong Kong society and the Hong Kong polity more perfect. The Li Court restored an approach to rights interpretation that aims to give a generous and purposive interpretation to rights. One judge placed great weight on the virtue of tolerance in a democratic, cosmopolitan, and multicultural modern society; the other on the architectural design of a democratic polity defined by rights. Whatever public fears may now lurk, we have a better appreciation of Hong Kong as a place that enjoys a high degree of autonomy.

The view that this or any other constitutional document can simply be followed ignores the fact that, in the common law mind, constitutional documents need first to be explained.[77] Not least if a generous and purposive approach is to be taken in interpreting constitutional rights – in other words, when a constitution is taken to be living. None can accuse Andrew Li or Kemal Bokhary of shying away from this task of explaining how a liberal-democratic, rights-based constitutional arrangement eman-ating from a socialist legislative act should function. Their perfectionism exhorts anyone who suggests that all of this is but a misunderstanding to offer a more attractive explanation. These judges have, for their part, made the best sense they can of the Basic Law.[78] Against this is the growing view today that we must recover the true meaning of the Basic Law as a piece of socialist legality, as it was presumed to have originally been intended.[79] The alternative, however, to some measurable degree of judicial explanation of Hong Kong's mini-constitution is to render the common law judge virtually incapable of adjudicating any Basic Law dispute.

---

[77] Sunstein (*supra* n 2) 2234.

[78] Ronald Dworkin, *Law's Empire* (Belknap Press, 1986).

[79] The criticism that Hong Kong judges have been "activist" is related for it is said that they have the power merely to adjudicate, not to interpret. The final power of interpretation lies elsewhere. This is not necessarily all that the Basic Law says, however – see article 158 – and therefore one needs to look further in saying that judges have no role in interpretation at all. Ideally, we would look to the PRC Constitution, but that leads to an untenable position for the common law judge. This is so because common lawyers understand that adjudication involves elements of interpretation; see, e.g., Dworkin (*supra* n 80). The best-known opposing view in the common law milieu is even more radical: that judges would simply have to fill in any gaps by way of 'judicial legislation' rather than by engaging in acts of interpretation; see HLA Hart, *The Concept of Law*, 3rd edition (Clarendon Press, 2012). Ultimately, the criticism that Hong Kong judges have been activist is an exaggeration of the propos-ition – which is entirely correct – that Hong Kong judges cannot interpret matters that fall outside Hong Kong's autonomy. For that proposition, see also Shigong Jiang, *China's Hong Kong* (Springer, 2017) 142–3; Zhenmin Wang, *Relationship Between the Chinese Central Authorities and Regional Governments of Hong Kong and Macao: A Legal Perspective* (Springer, 2019), 96.

7

Judicial Minimalism as Towering: Singapore's Chief Justice Chan Sek Keong

Jaclyn L Neo and Kevin YL Tan

7.1 INTRODUCTION

Towering judges don't always look the part. Those who do are much better known than others, but there really are not many judges who have achieved the significance and recognition we associate with judicial giants. When thinking of judicial giants or heroes, we tend to think of judges like Hale, Coke, Mansfield, Denning or Bingham (in England); or Marshall, Story, Holmes, Brandeis or Brennan (in America); or Duff, Laskin, Dickson or McLachlin (in Canada); or Evatt, Dixon or Mason (in Australia). They are towering figures because they have significantly shaped the law and/or played a key part in the shaping of their country's constitutional conversation. But for heroism to manifest, appropriate opportunities must first be present. For that reason, judicial greatness is more likely to flourish in countries with either large populations or long histories, preferably with both. Just as one is likely to find a highly skilled surgeon in a large metropolitan hospital with a large patient catchment than in a small provincial hospital, great judges are able to tower over others only when their operating environments allow them to do so. Towering judges are also more likely to emerge in common law jurisdictions since the common law tradition – of developing (or 'discovering') the law on a case-by-case basis – focuses its spotlight on judges who have a great talent for consolidating past precedents and expounding on general rules.

That said, towering judges do in fact exist in smaller and younger jurisdictions; they just do not 'tower' in the same way. Singapore is both a small and a young jurisdiction, with a population of 5.5 million and a political history as an independent state that stretches back only to 1963, when it became independent from Britain as a constituent state of the Federation of Malaysia. While it adopted the British Westminster system of parliamentary government, it also has a written constitution that declares itself to be the supreme law of the land. Thus, formally, Singapore adheres to the doctrine of constitutional supremacy, rather than parliamentary supremacy. The written constitution not only sets out the framework for government but also entrenches a range of fundamental liberties as constitutional rights. Judicial review has long been affirmed as an available avenue to 'enforce' the constitution, to ensure the constitutionality of laws and to guard against executive overreach.

However, the scope and reach of judicial review had been rather limited during the first thirty years or so of the Singapore Constitution. There are several factors for this. The first is that as a young nation, economic and political survival was foremost on the agenda of the accidental small state, and not constitutional legalities. This was the case for the ruling elite as well as for the citizens. Second, the political conditions were such that there was little policy space for judicial activism as the government has been dominated by the same political party (the People's Action Party or PAP) since the first Legislative Assembly elections under the self-governing constitution of British colony was held in 1959. Third, some critics have argued that, at least in the first few decades, judges appointed to the bench shared the same aspirations and concerns as the government and were willing to uphold governmental decisions because they were similarly minded.[1] Fourth, the common law tradition of judging through the use of analogy and incremental development of the law tended to discourage judicial activism and valorise judicial modesty. This milieu is probably a poor spawning ground for judicial giants.

We nonetheless argue that these conditions have thrown up a judicial giant in Chan Sek Keong, Singapore's third chief justice, who was in office from 2006 to 2012. Chief Justice Chan's ('Chan') tenure did not result in any radical overruling of legislation. Indeed, even though the constitution declares that any law inconsistent with the constitution shall be void to the extent of the inconsistency,[2] the record remains that only one law has ever been struck down by the courts in Singapore for being unconstitutional, and even then it was a High Court decision that was later overruled by the Court of Appeal.[3] It bears clarifying, however, that the courts have struck down certain executive and administrative decisions on constitutional and common law administrative law grounds.

In this chapter, we examine Chan's legacy and jurisprudence over the years and show his crucial contributions to the development of public law in Singapore both in substance and in attitude. In presenting Chan as a towering judge, we conceptualise 'towering' as a *relative* and *contextualised* idea. He towers because he is cleverer than most; he towers because he has a stronger commitment to the administration of justice than some he towers because his jurisprudence shifted the way the constitution is understood; and, lastly, Chan towers because he gave courage to others in what was often considered a challenging political context, where no judge has done before.

[1] Michael YM Hor, 'The Independence of the Criminal Justice System in Singapore' (2002) 2 *Singapore Journal of Legal Studies* 497.
[2] Constitution of the Republic of Singapore, article 4.
[3] *Taw Cheng Kong v Public Prosecutor* [1988] 1 SLR 943 (High Court); *Public Prosecutor v Taw Cheng Kong* [1998] 2 SLR(R) 489 (Court of Appeal).

7.2 PERSONAL AND INTELLECTUAL BACKGROUND

7.2.1 *An Unlikely Start*

In Chapter 2 of this volume, Mark Tushnet argues that judges may tower over others simply because they 'are much better lawyers than the others'.[4] On this measure, Justice Chan clearly fits the bill even though he does not look anything like a towering judge. He is not known for his eloquence, flamboyance or wit. Instead, he is shy and quiet to the point of reticence. An extremely private man, Chan looks more like an erudite scholar than the towering judge that he was. To have a better idea of how much he has achieved, it is important to have a glimpse into his journey to become the third chief justice of Singapore. Born in a modest household on 5 November 1937 in the town of Ipoh, in Perak, Malaya, he was the third of five children. His father was a bank clerk and his mother a housewife. His intellectual prowess was evident from a young age. In 1955, Chan scored eight distinctions in his Senior Cambridge School Certificate examinations and emerged one of the top students in all of Malaya. He continued his studies into the Sixth Form and was offered a government teaching scholarship but turned it down as he had decided that he did not want to be a teacher. Unsure of what to do after completing his studies, he took the advice of his English literature teacher, Dr Etherton, to study law because he 'had the sort of mind for the subject'.[5] Chan recalled:

> I should say that I hadn't the faintest idea what a degree in law meant in terms of a career. But since he was one of the best teachers I had ever had ... I thought I should inform my father. My father also had no idea what the study of law entailed or what the career prospects were. He however agreed to whatever I wanted. I was interviewed by Professor Sheridan and accepted as a student in the first batch of students admitted to the Law Faculty.[6]

At the University of Malaya – then located in Singapore – Chan took to the study of law like a duck to water. He found the law fascinating and intriguing, and enjoyed working out the logic of legal rules. A conscientious student, he read voraciously and in no time was acknowledged by his peers as being one of the most learned among them. Indeed, his classmate TPB Menon recalled that whenever they staggered out of a property or trust lecture not having understood anything the lecturer tried to convey, it was to Chan that they all turned for 'enlightenment'. He did well enough to win a University Book Prize at the end of his second year; at the end of his

---

[4] Mark Tushnet, 'The Judges Towering Judges Tower Over', *IACL-AIDC Blog*, 15 March 2019, https://blog-iacl-aidc.org/towering-judges/2019/3/15/the-judges-towering-judges-tower-over.

[5] ' In Conversation: An Interview with the Honourable Attorney-General, Mr Chan Sek Keong' (1993) 14 *Singapore Law Review* 1, 3.

[6] Ibid. 3–4. Professor Lionel A Sheridan was appointed professor of law by the University of Malaya in 1956 to establish the first local law faculty. The first students – which included Chan – entered the university in 1957 and graduated in 1961.

final year, Chan ended up as one of the top three students and won the BA Mallal Gold Medal for Advanced Property Law.

After his graduation, Chan, by his own admission, had no idea what to do and decided to return to Ipoh to try his luck. However, his family had no connections there and he could not find a job. Luckily, he had met John Skrine – who was then a partner in the Kuala Lumpur firm of Bannon & Bailey and external examiner for insurance law – who asked Chan to call on him in Kuala Lumpur if he ever needed a job. Skrine was as good as his word and Chan began his pupillage at Bannon & Bailey under Peter Mooney, as pupil master.

By this time, Chan had acquired a bit of a reputation within the profession for two reasons. First, he made headlines when he went before the Malaysian High Court to successfully plead his own case on why an abridgment of time should be allowed so that he should be called to the Bar. The Chairman of the Bar Council, resisting the application, had argued that the legislation required 'grounds', that is, more than one ground. The court ruled in Chan's favour.[7] Second, he had published the leading study and analysis of the much-vexed section 5 of the Civil Law Ordinance that had created much confusion on the question of the continuing reception of English law into Singapore.[8] After a year in Kuala Lumpur, Chan was invited by Punch Coomaraswamy, a partner in the venerable Singapore firm of Braddell Brothers, to join their ranks. His performance was exceptional and he was, within a space of three years, admitted as a partner in of the firm. In 1969, Chan joined the Singapore branch of the Kuala Lumpur firm of Shook Lin & Bok as junior partner. Over the next two decades, Chan established himself as Singapore's leading banking and corporate lawyer. His reputation as a lawyer rested on his piercing intellect and encyclopaedic knowledge of the law. At Shook Lin & Bok, other than being 'the Boss', he was also known as 'the Brain'. In 1984, Chan became the firm's managing partner.

7.2.2 *First Judicial Tenure*

In 1986, Chan was appointed Singapore's very first judicial commissioner. He served as a judicial commissioner and a puisne judge for six years and as Attorney General for fourteen years prior to being made chief justice. The judicial commissioner scheme had been introduced in 1979 to deal with the problem of shortage of High Court judges.[9] It allowed for senior practitioners to be appointed to serve in the capacity of a High Court judge for a fixed term and then to return to practice after that. Chan had been approached several times in the past to accept an appointment

---

[7] *Re Chan Sek Keong* [1962] MLJ 88 (High Court).
[8] Chan Sek Keong, 'The Civil Law Ordinance, Section 5(1): A Re-Appraisal' (1961) *Malayan Law Journal* lviii.
[9] Kevin YL Tan, 'A Short Legal and Constitutional History of Singapore' in Kevin YL Tan (ed.), *Essays in Singapore Legal History* (Marshall-Cavendish, 2005) 56.

to the bench, but he had each time demurred. He finally accepted the judicial commissioner appointment with the understanding that he would return to legal practice after two years. However, he was persuaded to remain on the bench and was elevated as a puisne judge in 1988.

From the start, Chan was clearly a judge with a mission. He felt strongly that it was important for judges to determine issues clearly and to clarify contested legal issues as best they could, and he worked hard to do this. Writing judgments was one way to develop Singapore law and this he did. Chan was an extremely productive judge, probably the most productive ever. In the six years that he was on the bench during his first stint in the court, Chan penned some 253 judgments – an average of 42 judgments a year or 1 judgment every 9 days (with no vacation between). What was even more remarkable was that he did all his own research and wrote all his own judgments without any help from the judicial law clerks in the court. Of these 253 judgments, 210 were reported in Singapore's official law report, the *Singapore Law Reports*. Chan also sat regularly as a member of the Court of Appeal during this time. Up till 1994, Singapore did not have a permanent coram in its Court of Appeal and, typically, the chief justice would sit with two other judges of the High Court. And when the appeal is against the decision of the chief justice, all three members of the Court of Appeal would be drawn from among the High Court judges. As chief justice, Chan was even more prodigious, writing 279 judgments over a six-year period. In all, Chan wrote a total of 546 judgments, 489 of which were reported.

It is not just the quantity but the quality of the judgments that sets Chan apart from all the other judges. More significantly, Chan sat in judgment in some of the most important constitutional cases of the period. Of these, the most important is *Chng Suan Tze v Minister for Home Affairs & Ors and Other Appeals*,[10] a case involving the legality of detention under the Internal Security Act. In this case, the Court of Appeal outlawed the subjective test in respect of ministerial discretion, applying an objective test instead. In so doing, the Court (including Chan) articulated the following principle of legality:

> There is one other reason for rejecting the subjective test. In our view, the notion of a subjective or unfettered discretion is contrary to the rule of law. All power has legal limits and the rule of law demands that the courts should be able to examine the exercise of discretionary power. If therefore the Executive in exercising its discretion under an Act of Parliament has exceeded the four corners within which Parliament has decided it can exercise its discretion, such an exercise of discretion would be ultra vires the Act and a court of law must be able to hold it to be so.[11]

[10]   *Chng Suan Tze v Minister for Home Affairs & Ors and Other Appeals* [1988] 2 SLR(R) 525 (Court of Appeal).

[11]   Ibid. 553.

This passage has since been repeated, quoted and reaffirmed in numerous leading public law judgments in the ensuing years.[12] Although the judgment is attributed to then chief justice Wee Chong Jin, Chan contributed to the most important parts of this judgment. In addition to the landmark *Chng* decision, Chan was also involved in the determination of other key public law cases of that period: *Cheong Seok Leng v Public Prosecutor*[13] (effect of subsidiary legislation); *Dow Jones Publishing Co (Asia) v Attorney General*[14] (foreign publication 'interfering in local politics'); *Peck Constance Emily v Calvary Charismatic Centre Ltd*[15] (application of natural justice principles in corporations); and *Jeyaretnam Joshua Benjamin v Attorney General*[16] (abuse of parliamentary privilege).

Chan's towering intellect was widely recognised. When he retired, the minister of law gave a rousing tribute in parliament calling Chan 'one of our greatest jurists and legal minds'.[17] His fellow judge in the Court of Appeal, VK Rajah, called him the 'finest legal mind Singapore has known'.[18] And the late Peter Birks, Regius Professor of civil law at Oxford University, praised Chan as 'the Master of the whole law'.[19]

7.3 COMMITMENT TO THE INTEGRITY OF THE ADMINISTRATION OF JUSTICE

That a judge should be committed to the integrity of the administration of justice should not be surprising. But Chan's single-minded commitment to ensuring fair and just outcomes was perhaps greater than most. One could see this even in how he conducted himself as Attorney General, a post he held for 14 years from 1992 before being made chief justice. It is not our purpose to discuss Chan's role as Attorney General during this long interregnum from the bench, but we wish to highlight a couple of matters that reflect his commitment to the integrity of the administration of justice in Singapore.

The first is an unfinished story from 1962 – section 5 of the Civil Law Act. Despite much talk about its amendment or repeal, nothing was done to address the problem of the continuing reception of English law to fill possible lacunae in Singapore's

---

[12] On the significance of this principle of legality, see Jaclyn L Neo, '"All Power Has Legal Limits": The Principle of Legality as a Constitutional Principle of Judicial Review' [2017] 29 *Singapore Academy of Law Journal* 667.

[13] [1988] 1 SLR(R) 530 (High Court).

[14] [1989] 1 SLR(R) 637 (Court of Appeal).

[15] [1991] 1 SLR(R) 57 (High Court).

[16] [1988] 2 SLR(R) 571 (Court of Appeal).

[17] 'Tribute to retired Chief Justice Chan Sek Keong by Minister for Law, Mr K Shanmugam, in Parliament', *Ministry of Law Singapore*, November 2012, www.mlaw.gov.sg/news/parliamentary-speeches/tribute-to-retired-chief-justice-chan-sek-keong-by-minister-for-.

[18] Janice Tai, 'Be Wise People, Not Just Smart Lawyers: Former Attorney-General V. K. Rajah Tells NUS Law Graduates', *The Straits Times*, 8 July 2017, www.straitstimes.com/singapore/courts-crime /be-wise-people-not-just-smart-lawyers-former-attorney-general-v-k-rajah-tells.

[19] Document on file with the author.

commercial law. Not content to return to the academic fray, Chan decided that as Attorney General, he now had an opportunity to set things right. It was one of the first things he attended to after taking office. He marshalled his arguments, canvassed the views of academics and practitioners, and convinced the politicians that the law was highly problematic and had to be changed. He then drafted the Application of English Law Act, which was passed in Parliament in November 1993.[20]

Another law reform that weighed heavily on Chan's mind concerned the common law offence of contempt by scandalising the court. Up till 2016, this was the only common law criminal offence in Singapore. Chan thought it improper to have an offence whose ambit and punishment was to be completely determined by the Court who would be placed in a conflict situation, given that the offence was directed at the Court itself. To this end, Chan initiated the first draft of the Administration of Justice (Protection) Act which spelt out the offence statutorily for the first time. He had completed the draft some time before his appointment as Chief Justice though the Act that was eventually passed was significantly different from Chan's draft.[21] It was Chan's unease with uncertainty in the law and the possibility that such arbitrariness might invite abuse, even by the Court, that led him to work towards this legislation.

His commitment to the integrity of the administration of justice was further brought to the fore in his treatment of a criminal prosecution that resulted in what he considered to be a manifestly harsh sentence. In this case, one Gilbert Louis Pius, in a fit of rage during divorce hearings, punched the woman lawyer representing his wife and fractured her nose. Pius was charged with voluntarily causing grievous hurt under section 322 of the Penal Code and was sentenced to six years' imprisonment by the district judge. This was one year less than the maximum sentence of seven years prescribed by section 11(3) of the Criminal Procedure Code. Pius appealed against his sentence. There was no cross appeal as the prosecution felt that the punishment was adequate. Then Chief Justice Yong Pung How, utilising a proviso of the same sentencing section, increased Pius's sentence to the maximum of ten years under section 325 of the Penal Code.[22] Chan felt that Yong CJ's sentence was overly harsh especially since the typical sentence for persons guilty of culpable homicide not amounting to murder was only six to seven years' imprisonment. Furthermore, he was certain that the chief justice had exceeded his jurisdiction in making the order. Justice demanded that something be done. As Attorney General and Public Prosecutor, he could not appeal against the sentence, and Pius, who had run out of money, decided not to appeal. Chan then applied for a motion for a criminal revision to the Court of Appeal, prepared all arguments himself and assigned Pang Khang Chau,

---

[20]   See Chan Sek Keong, 'Application of English Law Act 1993: A New Charter of Justice' in Goh Yihan and Paul Tan (eds.), *Singapore Law: 50 Years in the Making* (Academy Publishing, 2015) 69.

[21]   Administration of Justice (Protection) Act 2016.

[22]   See *Public Prosecutor v Louis Pius Gilbert* [2003] SGHC 33 (High Court); and *Public Prosecutor v Pius Gilbert Louis* [2003] 3 SLR(R) 418 (Court of Appeal).

a deputy public prosecutor (now a High Court judge), to argue the case. The problem was that, under ordinary circumstances, the proper authority to oppose the motion should have been the Public Prosecutor. To solve the problem, Chan requested the registrar of the Supreme Court to appoint Davinder Singh SC, widely regarded as the best litigator in Singapore, to act as *amicus curiae* (or 'friend of the court') to oppose the motion.[23] The Court of Appeal agreed with Chan's arguments, set aside the Chief Justice's judgment and affirmed the sentence of the district judge.

The last matter that concerned Chan as Attorney General was the matter of access to justice in respect of matters of public interest. He felt that it was the job of the Attorney General, as guardian of the public interest, to ensure that controversial but important matters of public interest – whether they be matters concerning constitutional rights or statutory interpretation – be properly argued before the Court. In this respect, he made it a policy not to ask for costs in such cases unless the litigant had mounted a frivolous or vexatious action.[24]

7.4 JURISPRUDENTIAL SHIFTS: DEVELOPING A SUPREME CONSTITUTION

7.4.1 *Epochal Shifts*

During his tenure as chief justice, there was a discernible and significant change in the way in which the Singapore judiciary engaged with public law as well as public international law. Thio and Chong observed in 2012 that 'the judicial trajectory under the Chan Court has been oriented towards greater and more nuanced engagement with academic ideas, foreign cases and international law, accompanied by more elaborated reason-giving by way of appeal to text, original intent, local particularities, with attention to foreign and international developments and first principles'.[25] Further, as Tan and Thio noted when discussing the various judicial epochs in Singapore:

> While Chan's tenure as Chief Justice was brief, his impact on the bench was tremendous. Universally regarded as one of the most learned and erudite judges to grace the Singapore bench, Chief Justice Chan demonstrated a deep understanding of constitutional and administrative law and appreciated the work of academics, habitually citing helpful articles by local scholars in his judgments.
>
> The quality of judgments – on the whole – improved dramatically during this period. In constitutional and administrative law, there was much greater focus on

---

[23] Interview with Chan Sek Keong, 27 August 2018.
[24] Personal communication with the authors.
[25] Thio Li-ann and David Chong, 'The Chan Court and Constitutional Adjudication: A Sea Change into Something Rich and Strange?' in Hick Tin Chao, Andrew Phang, VK Rajah and Tiong Min Yeo (eds.), *The Law in His Hands: A Tribute to Chief Justice Chan Sek Keong* (Academy Publishing, 2012) 118.

the intrinsic values of the law, such as matters of procedural fairness, and the procedural aspects of the Rule of Law and the Separation of Powers. Judgments were much longer, expository in nature and offered serious and nuanced reasoning justifying the verdicts. Unlike the Yong Court, the Chan Court took rights seriously and took pains to explain why constitutional rights are important and sought to balance individual rights against public interest . . .[26]

This increased engagement with public law is crucial. As Neo observes, this deeper engagement in constitutional interpretation is part of a crucial reason-giving exercise that demonstrates an absence of arbitrariness and enhances judicial legitimacy.[27] Indeed, CJ Chan himself stated in his 2008 Opening of the Legal Year Speech that the judiciary has an important role in developing quality jurisprudence for the following reason:

> Judicial outcomes are expressed in the decisions, rulings and orders of the courts, and their legitimacy and validity are measured by the quality of their fact finding and legal reasoning . . . Consequently, we are also taking more time to examine legal issues in greater depth, and this has resulted in longer and more comprehensive judgments. We also wish to raise the stature of our decisions in the common law world, and hope that this will be a positive factor in promoting Singapore as a legal services hub.[28]

There have also been quantitative changes – as the number of public law cases heard during his tenure increased. A count of reported cases in the *Singapore Law Reports* shows that while the average number of cases in which constitutional issues arise was 1.92 during the time of the Wee Chong Jin Court (1965–90), this number went up to 2.13 during the time of Yong Pung How's chief justiceship (1990–2006) and more than doubled to 4.83 during Chan's leadership of the Court.[29]

It was also during Chan's tenure as chief justice that the courts began to engage more with foreign law, eschewing the earlier 'four walls approach' advocated by his predecessor. This increased engagement has been noted by several authors. For instance, Tan and Thio observed in 2015 that:

> While the Chan Court also consciously worked towards development great auto-chthony in its own jurisprudence, it also abandoned the 'four walls' approach of the Yong Court and demonstrated its willingness to consider legal arguments and cases

---

[26] Kevin YL Tan and Thio Li-ann, *Fifty Constitutional Moments that Defined a Nation* (Marshall-Cavendish, 2015) 27–8.

[27] Jaclyn L Neo, 'Introduction: Judging the Singapore Constitution' in Jaclyn L Neo (ed.), *Constitutional Interpretation in Singapore: Theory and Practice* (Routledge, 2017) 5–6.

[28] Chan Sek Keong, 'Opening of Legal Year 2008: Response by the Honourable Chief Justice', *Supreme Court Singapore*, 5 January 2008, www.supremecourt.gov.sg/news/speeches/opening-of-legal-year-2008–response-by-the-honourable-the-chief-justice.

[29] Kevin YL Tan, 'Costs in Constitutional Adjudication: Patterns and Problems', paper presented at the Contemporary Issues in Public Law Litigation Conference, Centre for Asian Legal Studies, Faculty of Law, National University of Singapore, 6 January 2019.

from all jurisdictions, even cases emanating from the European Court of Human Rights. The Chan Court was willing to study and borrow foreign ideas, but to modify them to suit local circumstances.[30]

One example is in the case of *Review Publishing Co Ltd and another v Lee Hsien Loong and another appeal* (discussed in greater detail below),[31] where the Court of Appeal, helmed by Chan, rejected the argument that foreign judgments on defamation are of no relevance to Singapore. Instead, the Court examined the cases in great detail, taking the view that these judgments could be of relevance to Singapore as they raised freedom of speech to a higher (constitutional) order than statutory or common law rights. Accordingly, Lee observes that, unlike earlier courts, the Chan Court typically advanced substantive reasons for rejecting foreign law. Even then, Lee notes that the Chan Court 'remain[ed] cautious about applying foreign [cases] on the basis of differently worded bills of right'.[32] Thiruvengadam takes a similarly circumspect position with regards to Justice Chan's legacy; he argues that while there is marked departure from earlier approaches, these changes were 'ultimately, more superficial than substantial'.[33]

7.4.2 *Expanding Space: Strategic Disagreement and Judicial Minimalism*

Chan's style of decision-making coheres with what has been described by American constitutional scholars like Sunstein as 'judicial minimalism',[34] where judges base their decisions on the most limited grounds available.[35] Judicial minimalism has been described as a 'decisional strategy'[36] and a 'methodology', and it has been defended, inter alia, on the basis that it reduces the potential costs of wrong decisions.[37] Minimalism is achieved either procedurally or substantively. Courts may rely on procedural grounds to avoid making a decision; for example, by deciding that there is no standing/locus standi or by denying certiorari (in the

---

[30] Tan and Thio (*supra* n 26).

[31] *Review Publishing Co Ltd and another v Lee Hsien Loong and another appeal* [2010] 1 SLR 52 (Court of Appeal).

[32] Jack Lee, 'Foreign Precedents in Constitutional Adjudication by the Supreme Court of Singapore, 1963–2013' (2015) 24(2) *Washington International Law Journal* 253, 283.

[33] Arun Thiruvengadam, 'The Continuing Resistance to Foreign Law in Constitutional Adjudication in Singapore' in Jaclyn L Neo (ed.), *Constitutional Interpretation in Singapore: Theory and Practice* (Routledge, 2017) 318. See also Eugene KB Tan, 'Much Ado About Nothing? The Enigma of Engagement of Foreign Constitutional Law in Singapore' in Jaclyn L Neo (ed.), *Constitutional Interpretation in Singapore: Theory and Practice* (Routledge, 2017) 289.

[34] See the following works of Cass R Sunstein: 'The Supreme Court, 1995 Term-Foreword. Leaving Things Undecided' (1996) 110 *Harvard Law Review* 4; *One Case at a Time: Judicial Minimalism on the Supreme Court* (Harvard University Press, 2001); and 'Burkean Minimalism' (2006) 1055 *Michigan Law Review* 353.

[35] See, e.g., Cass R Sunstein, *One Case at a Time: Judicial Minimalism on the Supreme Court* (Harvard University Press, 2001).

[36] Owen Fiss, 'The Perils of Minimalism' (2008) 9 *Theoretical Inquiries in Law* 643.

[37] Ibid. 646.

context of the US Supreme Court).[38] Alternatively, even where courts must decide
on the merits of the case, it may adopt the substantively narrowest decision or
narrowest grounds. Judicial minimalism has been justified on many grounds.
These justifications may take the internal perspective, that is, that minimalism
best preserves the legitimacy of the courts within the constitutional framework,[39]
and/or the external perspective, which is that the political processes are better suited
to address broader policy issues.[40] Minimalism is thus an approach to judicial
decision-making that sees the court as interdependent with the political branches.

   Supporters of judicial minimalism argue that it is necessary for constructive
constitutional dialogues between the court and the elected government.[41] Indeed,
those who have been called 'New Minimalists'[42] have argued for a division of labour
between the court and the political branches; the court, it is said, should articulate
abstract and/or fundamental values and leave the implementation of those values
mainly to the political process.[43] Sunstein, however, sees a more active role for the
court, arguing that the court should actively facilitate or catalyse the democratic
process and not pre-empt democratic deliberation.[44] Minimalist judicial decisions
therefore would 'promote the democratic ideals of participation, deliberation, and
responsiveness', as well as allow for 'continued space for democratic reflection'
among the political branches and from the electorate.[45] In this regard, minimalism
is seen as democracy-enhancing, particularly in its deliberative variant. In fact,
Sunstein argues that the court should restrict 'maximalist' opinions to situations
where the decision would cement a pre-existing societal consensus.[46]

   Judicial minimalism may appear to contradict the idea of a towering judge. Indeed,
the minimalist judge has been described in counter-opposition[47] to the 'heroic vision
of judging', where judges see the role of the judiciary as 'large and potentially
transformative'.[48] Heroic judges are willing to invoke 'an ambitious understanding

---

[38] See, e.g., Alexander Bickel, *The Least Dangerous Branch: The Supreme Court at the Bar of Politics*,
      2nd edition (Yale University Press, 1986).
[39] Ibid.
[40] Ibid.
[41] Sunstein (*supra* n 35) 26 and Po Jen Yap, *Constitutional Dialogues in Common Law Asia* (Oxford
      University Press, 2015).
[42] Christopher J Peters, 'Assessing the New Judicial Minimalism' (2000) 100 *Columbia Law Review* 1454.
[43] Michael C Dorf and Charles F Sabel, 'A Constitution of Democratic Experimentalism' (1998) 98
      Columbia Law Review 267, 388–404, 444–69.
[44] Sunstein (*supra* n 35) xiv.
[45] Ibid.
[46] Ibid. 26.
[47] Neal Devins, 'Rethinking Judicial Minimalism: Abortion Politics, Party Polarization, and the
      Consequences of Returning the Constitution to Elected Government' (2016) 69(4) *Vanderbilt Law
      Review* 935.
[48] Cass R Sunstein, *Constitutional Personae: Heroes, Soldiers, Minimalists, and Mutes* (Oxford
      University Press, 2015) 5; see, further, Erwin Chemerinsky, *The Case Against the Supreme Court*
      (Viking Books, 2014) 10.

of the Constitution to invalidate the decisions of the government'.[49] In a fascinating article[50] – now expanded into a book[51] – Sunstein divides judges into four categories – heroes, soldiers, Burkeans (or minimalists)[52] and mutes, which clearly separates minimalists from heroism: 'Broadly speaking, Heroes are willing to invoke the Constitution to invalidate state and federal legislation; Soldiers defer to the actions of the political branches; Burkeans favour only incremental change; and Mutes prefer not to decide difficult questions.'[53] One could therefore imagine that the towering judge must similarly take on ambitious and heroic positions vis-à-vis the political branches. However, contrary to that first intuition, we argue that a judge may well become a 'towering' figure exactly because he or she understands the limits of his or her role and is able to strategically expand democratic and constitutional space by taking on a minimalist approach. This strategy of minimalism may be particularly necessary where the legal-political context is such that the scope for expansive judicial decision-making is limited. In this regard, the minimalist judge who focuses on the articulation of broad but abstract principles while concurrently adopting narrow *ratios* may be acting in way that causes them to tower over other judges.

There is little doubt that Justice Chan has expanded the scope and depth of public law jurisprudence in Singapore, thus opening up pathways for future developments in the law. His 'toweringness' manifests itself primarily through his jurisprudential contributions. As Abeyratne and Porat point out in their Introduction, this form of jurisprudential towering can take place through a variety of ways, whether through legal craft or sheer number of opinions, and/or by marshalling their colleagues to move the law significantly in a particular direction. This was clearly the case for Chief Justice Chan on all fronts. While previous chief justices have tended to take on a more formalistic approach to constitutional interpretation, Justice Chan's jurisprudence was analytical, with greater attention paid to normative foundations of the constitution. Thus, while his jurisprudence may be seen as minimalist in comparison with other 'towering' judges showcased in this volume and beyond, he towers in Singapore because of the sheer quality, volume and importance of his contributions to public law jurisprudence. His minimalism is aimed not at enhancing democracy per se but at expanding the judiciary's interpretive and decision-making space while preserving its legitimacy within a dominant party system. He does this by reasserting the legitimate place of the judiciary as the primary interpreter of the constitution and thereby as the primary upholder of the constitution within the scheme of separation of powers, through strategic disagreement and the articulation of foundational norms.

---

[49]   Sunstein (*supra* n 48) 5.
[50]   Cass R Sunstein, 'Constitutional Personae' (2013) 1 *Supreme Court Review* 433.
[51]   Sunstein (*supra* n 48).
[52]   In his 2013 article, Sunstein uses the term 'Burkean' to describe judges who 'favor small, cautious steps, building incrementally on the decisions and practices of the past'. These same judges are described as 'Minimalists' in his 2015 book.
[53]   Sunstein (*supra* n 50) 433.

7.4.2.1 Strategic Disagreement: Reasserting the Judicial Role

One of Chan's major contributions was to reassert the role of the court and of judges through articulation of the meaning of 'judicial power' under article 93 of the Constitution, which vests 'judicial power' in the High Court. Hitherto, no judge paid much attention to this provision, but it was Chan who articulated its foundational character and established it as a key pillar of the separation of powers doctrine and thus as part of the basic structure of Singapore's Constitution. The occasion for its articulation was Chan's final case as chief justice – *Mohammed Faizal bin Sabtu v Public Prosecutor*[54] – a special reference to the High Court on the constitutionality of certain provisions of the Misuse of Drugs Act. Chan, sitting alone, had occasion to consider whether the prescription of a mandatory penalty for a repeat offender amounted to an attack on the Court's judicial power. Drawing his arguments from history and constitutional structure, Chan held that '[a]ll Constitutions based on the Westminster model incorporate the principle of separation of powers as part of their constitutional structure in order to diffuse state power among different organs of state'[55] and was thus part of the 'basic structure' of the Constitution.[56] This requires, Chan held, that

> in so far as the judicial branch is concerned, that the legislative and executive branches of the State may not interfere with the exercise of judicial power by the judicial branch. This total separation between the exercise of the judicial power on the one hand and the exercise of the legislative and the executive powers on the other hand is based on the rule of law.[57]

Another significant case in which he reasserted the judiciary's rightful role over constitutional interpretation was the case of *Review Publishing Co Ltd and another v Lee Hsien Loong and another appeal* (mentioned above).[58] To be sure, this case is notable for its reasoning rather than for its outcome. It concerned a defamation suit by Singapore's prime minister Lee Hsien Loong and his late father, Lee Kuan Yew, then a senior cabinet minister in the government. They sued the *Far Eastern Economic Review*, its editor and the author (collectively 'FEER') for an allegedly defamatory article by an opposition politician. The plaintiffs argued that, in their natural and ordinary meaning, the offending words in the article bore the defamatory meaning that they were unfit for office because they were corrupt and had set out to sue and suppress those who questioned them for fear that such questioning would expose their corruption. The High Court gave summary judgment in favour

---

[54] *Mohammed Faizal bin Sabtu v Public Prosecutor* [2012] 4 SLR 947 (High Court).
[55] Ibid. 957.
[56] Ibid. On the basic structure argument, see Kevin YL Tan, 'Into the Matrix: Interpreting the Westminster Model Constitution' in Jaclyn L Neo (ed.), *Constitutional Interpretation in Singapore: Theory and Practice* (Routledge, 2017) 50–74.
[57] Ibid. 960.
[58] *Review Publishing* (*supra* n 31).

of the plaintiffs. On appeal, the Court of Appeal had to consider whether FEER could raise the defence of qualified privilege based on the test of responsible journalism. This specific defence had then only recently been developed by the English courts in the case of *Reynolds* v *Times Newspapers Ltd*.[59] While Singapore adopted the English common law on defamation, this new development in the law had yet to be applied in Singapore. The Court of Appeal was thus asked to consider – for the first time – if this specific defence of qualified privilege should be adopted in Singapore.

In the course of their judgment, the Court of Appeal had to address the broader question of whether Singapore should develop its law on defamation to provide greater protection for the freedom of speech in the Constitution. In earlier cases, the Court of Appeal, helmed by Chief Justice Yong Pung How, declined to follow American and European Court of Human Rights case law, which afforded greater protection to freedom of speech as a constitutional and convention right respectively. For example, in the 1992 case of *Jeyaretnam Joshua Benjamin* v *Lee Kuan Yew*,[60] the court took a strict textualist approach, holding that foreign jurisprudence was not relevant simply because the Singapore Constitution guaranteeing that 'every citizen of Singapore has the right to freedom of speech and expression' was drafted differently. Specifically, the Singapore Constitution explicitly subjected freedom of speech to laws on defamation in that:

> Parliament may by law impose on the rights conferred by clause (1)(a), such restrictions as it considers necessary or expedient in the interest of the security of Singapore or any part thereof, friendly relations with other countries, public order or morality and restrictions designed to protect the privileges of Parliament or to provide against contempt of court, defamation or incitement to any offence.

Thus, the Court of Appeal held that the words in the Constitution were sufficient to justify the use of defamation laws as a limitation on freedom of speech. That case is part of a line of cases adopting a strictly textualist approach eschewing developments in the common law that appear to respond to, or have been influenced by, European jurisprudence. Another instance of this judicial philosophy is in the courts' rejection of English common law jurisprudence on proportionality as a 'continental European jurisprudential concept imported into English law by virtue of the UK's treaty obligations'.[61]

---

[59] *Reynolds* v *Times Newspapers Ltd* [2001] 2 AC 127 (HL).
[60] *Jeyaretnam Joshua Benjamin* v *Lee Kuan Yew* [1992] 1 SLR(R) 791 (Court of Appeal).
[61] *Chee Siok Chin and others* v *Minister for Home Affairs and another* [2006] 1 SLR(R) 582 (High Court) [87] (Rajah J): 'Proportionality is a more exacting requirement than reasonableness and requires, in some cases, the court to substitute its own judgment for that of the proper authority. Needless to say, the notion of proportionality has never been part of the common law in relation to the judicial review of the exercise of a legislative and/or an administrative power or discretion. Nor has it ever been part of Singapore law.'

An understanding of this earlier judicial thinking is necessary to appreciate the significance of *Review Publishing*. Three points should be emphasized here. First, in delivering the judgment of the court, Chan did not merely adopt a textualist approach to justify all and sundry in defamation law as permissible limits to freedom of speech. Neither did the Court reject the test of responsible journalism simply on the basis of its ECHR influence. While accepting that the test arose from the United Kingdom's common law response to its ECHR obligations, the Court took the position that this was not sufficient to dispose of the matter. Instead, it asserted its right to exercise independent judgment as to whether the test could be adopted in Singapore. In other words, the Court could and should evaluate the suitability of the test on its merits.

Second, the Court affirmed that freedom of speech had the status of a constitutional right and therefore was of a higher order status than common law rights. This is important because the common law, which is the primary source of defamation laws in Singapore, treated freedom of speech as another common law right, co-equal with the right to reputation as protected by the law of defamation.[62] Thus, the question to be addressed – which had been avoided in earlier cases – was whether the common law rules on defamation should indeed be modified and narrowed in acknowledgement of freedom of speech as a higher order constitutional right. While the constitution specifically refers to defamation, it does not set out in detail what the law on defamation entailed.

Third, following the affirmation of freedom of speech as a higher order constitutional right, it was for the Court to decide how the balance between constitutional free speech and protection of reputation should be struck in Singapore.[63] The Court contemplated whether courts should 'shift the existing balance between constitutional free speech and protection of reputation in favour of the former where the publication of matters of public interest is concerned'.[64] According to the Court, applying the *Reynolds* rationale would mean that 'constitutional free speech would become the rule and restrictions on this right become the exception'.[65] Thus, unlike in the earlier generation of cases, the Court now did more than merely assert that the balance had already been struck by the legislature and that the Court's role is merely limited to applying existing laws on defamation.

These affirmative statements by the Court show an openness to greater protection of freedom of speech, but they were unfortunately only dicta. While the Court did not reject outright the test of responsible journalism as a possible form of qualified

---

[62]   Interestingly, the Court considered four possible ways to conceptualise rights as 'preferential', as 'fundamental', as 'co-equal' or as 'subsidiary'. The idea of a subsidiary right was discussed as reflecting a dominant interpretation of article 14 as subjecting free speech rights to the expressly permitted restrictions under article 14(2)(a) of the Constitution. *Review Publishing* (*supra* n 30) [260] and [286]–[289].

[63]   *Review Publishing* (*supra* n 30) [268]–[271].

[64]   Ibid. [267].

[65]   Ibid. [266].

privilege, it also did not adopt it in *Review Publishing*. The Court held that since freedom of speech is only a constitutionally guaranteed right available to *citizens*, this was not the appropriate case to consider if the balance between freedom of speech and defamation should be shifted since the defendants were not citizens.[66] Furthermore, various statements towards the end of the *Review Publishing* judgment reveal a cautious approach that appears to be directed at assuring parliament that the judiciary would not overreach. Indeed, the Court acknowledged that the Constitution 'expressly provides that it is Parliament which has the *final say* on how the balance between constitutional free speech and protection of reputation should be struck'.[67]

While this appears to contradict the earlier contemplation as to whether the judiciary should reconsider the balance between free speech and reputational rights, this could be understood as the court placing itself in dialogue with the legislature and acknowledging that the Constitution envisages legislative responses. The judgment suggests openness towards reconsideration, while also cautioning that any reconsideration would require a preponderance of evidence that change is appropriate. While more anxious observers may criticise the case for not going far enough in decisively adopting the test of responsible journalism to vindicate the constitutional status of freedom of speech, a more generous interpretation is that the Court is signalling not only to the legislature but also to potential litigants the various possible routes for change in the future. Chan's jurisprudence reflects a cautious laying down of foundations for the possibility of future changes in the law.

7.4.2.2 Articulating Fundamental Constitutional Norms

Justice Chan has also been responsible for reviving and entrenching important foundational constitutional doctrines and principles to 'normativise' the Singapore Constitution. Here, we are concerned with two key constitutional principles: (a) the principle of legality and (b) the basic structure doctrine.

We have already briefly discussed the 1988 landmark case of *Chng Suan Tze v Minister of Home Affairs*.[68] *Chng* was a landmark case because the Court overturned established precedents to hold that the ministerial discretion over ISA detentions is justiciable and subject to an objective (rather than a subjective) standard of review.[69] The old subjective standard gave the government almost absolute discretion over detention orders – all that was required was evidence that the detaining authority was subjectively satisfied that there were grounds for

---

[66] Ibid. [266]–[267].
[67] Ibid. [270].
[68] *Chng* (*supra* n 10).
[69] Ibid. [88]–[92]. Note, however, that the Court cautioned that where national security is implicated, the courts will subject the decision to less intense scrutiny.

detention.[70] While the specific ratio of *Chng* concerning the standard of review was legislatively overruled, the normative proclamations in *Chng* have endured and influenced the development of constitutional law in Singapore.[71] Indeed, Chan affirmatively stated – in *Yong Vui Kong* v *Attorney-General* (hereafter, '*Yong (Clemency)*')[72] – that Parliament 'left untouched the full amplitude of the *Chng Suan Tze* principle' and thereby 'implicitly endorsed' it.[73] Notably, Chan invoked the principle of legality in this case to justify subjecting the President's power of clemency to judicial review. According to him, the President's power of clemency is a legal power of an extraordinary character but it is not an 'extra-legal' power beyond legal constraints or restraints.[74] It is a constitutional power vested in the executive and is therefore subject to legal limits.

The key contribution of the principle of legality is in expanding the ambit of judicial review. Significantly, Chan stated – in *Yong (Clemency)* – that in countries with a written constitution, 'there will (or should) be few, if any, legal disputes between the State and the people from which the judicial power is excluded'.[75] This is noteworthy for its strong assertion of judicial review as part of Singapore's constitutional system. The power of judicial review to ensure legality or constitutionality of governmental action is not explicitly provided for under the Singapore Constitution, but it has always been implied as a function of judicial power vested in the courts (article 93), read in conjunction with the supremacy clause (article 4). While judicial review has been part of the common law adopted by Singapore, this was limited to the review on administrative law principles of administrative agencies and, to some extent, the executive powers of the government. To assert the reviewability of powers that are usually regarded as part of the 'high powers' of government raises the status of judicial review to a higher, that is, constitutional, order. In comparison, there is prior case law in Singapore suggesting that certain governmental decisions involving polycentric considerations may well be non-justiciable or at least that the courts should refrain from reviewing them.[76] Nonetheless, it bears noting that thus far, the principle of legality has been used only to ensure that the exercise of discretion can be reviewed. There is no evidence that the principle itself has resulted in an expansion of the scope of review.[77] Thus, in *Yong (Clemency)*, the scope of

[70] See *Lee Mau Seng* v *Minister for Home Affairs* [1971–3] SLR(R) 135 (High Court).
[71] Neo (*supra* n 12); Jaclyn L Neo, 'Unwritten Constitutional Norms: Finding the Singapore Constitution', *Singapore Law Gazette*, May 2019, https://lawgazette.com.sg/feature/unwritten-constitutional-norms-finding-the-singapore-constitution/.
[72] *Yong Vui Kong* v *Attorney-General* [2011] 1 SLR 1189 (Court of Appeal).
[73] Ibid. [79]. See also *Lim Meng Suang and another* v *Attorney-General* [2013] 3 SLR 118 (High Court) [112].
[74] *Yong Vui Kong* (*supra* n 72) [74] and [76].
[75] Ibid. [31].
[76] *Lee Hsien Loong* v *Review Publishing Co Ltd and another and another suit* [2007] 2 SLR(R) 453 (High Court).
[77] See Neo (*supra* n 12).

review remained rather narrow, that is, limited to bad faith for extraneous purpose and on other constitutional grounds. The principle itself has not produced a more stringent standard for review.[78]

A second foundational doctrine that Chan revived during his chiefship is the basic structure doctrine. He initiated this jurisprudence in the 2012 case of *Mohammad Faizal bin Sabtu v Public Prosecutor* (hereafter, '*Mohammad Faizal*').[79] Chan (sitting in the High Court) affirmatively stated that 'the principle of separation of powers . . . is part of the basic structure of the Singapore Constitution'.[80] The case addressed the question of whether section 33A of the Misuse of Drugs Act was an impermissible legislative intrusion into judicial power and a violation of the separation of powers.

Again, to fully appreciate the significance of Chan's contributions, one has to consider the state of the law prior to his pronouncements. The basic structure doctrine had long been rejected by the Singapore courts, although not entirely or conclusively. Nonetheless, when it first came up for consideration in the 1989 case of *Teo Soh Lung v Minister for Home Affairs*, the High Court declined to adopt the doctrine, holding that it was inappropriate considering Singapore's constitutional drafting history.[81] This is presumably because the Indian constitution was drafted by a constituent assembly while the Singapore Constitution is a mishmash of provisions derived from different 'constitutional' documents. It was not the product of 'We, the People'. This treatment of the basic structure doctrine was further affirmed in *Vincent Cheng v Minister for Home Affairs*.[82] It is important to note this initial aversion to the basic structure doctrine to understand how significant its current acceptance is.

After the basic structure doctrine was revived by Chief Justice Chan, it began to be referred to and adopted by the Court, although the doctrinal implications remain unclear. For instance, in the 2015 case of *Yong Vui Kong v PP*,[83] which was decided after Chief Justice Chan had retired, the Court of Appeal discussed *Mohammad Faizal* with apparent approval and even suggested that the right to vote could be part of the Basic Structure of the Constitution. The Court of Appeal nonetheless questioned whether Singapore should adopt the full measure of the Basic Structure Doctrine, as was held in the case of *Kesavananda*. While it did not reject this possibility outright, the Court of Appeal deferred the matter as it was not necessary to decide the matter at hand.[84] That said, the Court of Appeal appeared to accept some measure of the doctrine, even articulating a 'test' for determining

---

[78]   A similar approach was articulated in *Law Society of Singapore v Tan Guat Neo Phyllis* [2008] 2 SLR(R) 239 (Court of Appeal) and *Ramalingam Ravinthran v AG* [2012] 2 SLR 49 (Court of Appeal) [53], and was further affirmed in *Yong Vui Kong v Public Prosecutor* [2012] 2 SLR 872 (Court of Appeal).

[79]   *Mohammad Faizal* (*supra* n 54).

[80]   Ibid. [11].

[81]   *Teo Soh Lung v Minister for Home Affairs* [1989] 1 SLR(R) 461 (High Court).

[82]   *Vincent Cheng v Minister for Home Affairs* [1990] 1 SLR(R) 38 (High Court).

[83]   *Yong Vui Kong v PP* [2015] 2 SLR 1129 (Court of Appeal).

[84]   Ibid. [72].

whether a feature is to be included as part of the basic structure of the Singapore Constitution. It stated that such features must be 'fundamental and essential to the political system that is established thereunder'.[85] It remains to be seen what doctrinal implications the basic structure would give rise to. However, what seems clear is that the 'legal fact' of a basic structure, as was expounded upon and revived by Chief Justice Chan, is now firmly part of the jurisprudence in Singapore. Future cases will have to grapple with the possible legal doctrines arising from the recognition that the Singapore Constitution has a basic structure, including whether this would entail limiting the power of Parliament to amend the Constitution.[86]

7.5 GIVING COURAGE: PUBLIC LAW FROM THE MARGINS TO THE MAINSTREAM

While there may be several factors to account for the rise in constitutional jurisprudence, both qualitatively and quantitatively, one could potentially attribute this increase to a growing sense of acceptability among the judiciary of judicial review applications. Chan was instrumental in creating this greater sense of assurance. Just as his commitment to the integrity of the administration of justice led to his unusual intervention in the *Pius* case, he made it a point to publicly assure lawyers and litigants that the system would treat them fairly. In his 2010 extra-judicial lecture titled 'Judicial Review – From Angst to Empathy', Chan lamented the 'sense of unease about the dormant state of judicial review in Singapore' and 'the notion that the courts might have something to do with it'.[87] In a striking lecture, the chief justice clarified the legitimate role of the courts and affirmed the rightful place of judicial review. According to him, 'the rule of law requires the court to determine whether any public authority has crossed the line of legality'[88] and '[j]udicial review is the means by which legal rights are protected and good governance enforced'.[89]

This is a remarkable intervention by a sitting chief justice. It essentially signalled to the profession that the courts would regard constitutional law (as well as administrative law) cases in a professional light. In his speech, he even endorsed an earlier exhortation by Michael Hwang SC (then President of the Law Society) to the Singapore Bar to be 'more proactive in taking on judicial review cases to overcome

---

[85]   Ibid. [71].

[86]   The High Court had to grapple with this question in *Ravi s/o Madasamy v Attorney-General and other matters* [2017] SGHC 163, but it did not conclusively determine the matter.

[87]   Chan Sek Keong, 'Judicial Review – From Angst to Empathy: A Lecture to Singapore Management University Second Year Law Students' (2010) 22 *Singapore Academy of Law Journal* 469 [2].

[88]   Chan (supra n 87) [6]. On impact, see VK Rajah, 'Speech of the Attorney-General VK Rajah S.C. at the Opening of the Legal Year 2015', *Attorney-General's Chambers Singapore*, 7 January 2015, www .agc.gov.sg/docs/default-source/speeches/2015/opening-of-legal-year-2015_attorney-general-v-k-ra jah's-speech_5-jan_checked-against-delivery.pdf.

[89]   Chan (*supra* n 87) [7].

the perceived apathy of the Bar'.[90] The Chief Justice called this 'admirable', and argued that the fact that the President of the Law Society had sent this message to the Bar to commence judicial review proceedings 'must mean that he has faith in the courts and that judicial review proceedings are a good sign that the legal system and the operation of the rule of law remain functional'.[91]

Indeed, constitutional law has moved from the margins to the mainstream of litigation subject-matters in recent years. There has been a mindset shift in judicial and lawyerly attitudes, perhaps even governmental attitudes, towards judicial review. Rather than being seen as an 'illegitimate', even insolent challenge of governmental action, judicial review was seen as one of the many ways of ensuring good governance. Indeed, five years after CJ Chan's extra-judicial speech, in 2015, the then Attorney General VK Rajah, who had been on the bench with CJ Chan, gave a speech at the annual Opening of the Legal Year, noting that recent increase in civil litigation between the public and the state in administrative and constitutional law issues in recent years should not be seen as a 'negative' development but instead as reflecting a maturing citizenry. Furthermore, Rajah emphasized that 'judicial review is the hallmark of the judicial enforcement of the rule of law, in relations between the state and its people'.[92] Chief Justice Chan has no doubt been crucial in reforming public law litigation as a professional and legitimate endeavour, and not simply a political and politicised activity. In his insistence that judging is to be undertaken in a professional, impersonal and impartial manner, he gave courage to all who saw the law as a means to ensure fair and just outcomes.

7.6 CONCLUSION

It is perhaps a rare combination to find a person of such towering stature who remains humble and modest about his own achievements. Speaking to the *Singapore Law Review* shortly after being appointed Attorney General, Chan said:

> I am not sure what my contributions were while on the Bench. I have written a large number of judgments of variable quality. My wife says too many and too long. I don't know whether they have contributed anything to the development of the law in Singapore. This can only be judged by the profession and the academics. But I doubt that in the long run it would make any difference at all. Because we have a fused profession, it would take a Singaporean of unusual talent to reach the stature of Lord Atkin, Lord Denning or Chief Justice Dixon in the common law world. We are all generalists, trying our best to apply or develop a body of law appropriate to our own society and culture, and in a language which did not originate in the history and cultures of our peoples.[93]

[90] Chan (*supra* n 87) [7].
[91] Chan (*supra* n 87) [11].
[92] Rajah (*supra* n 88) [16].
[93] 'In Conversation' (*supra* n 5) 13.

Chan could be criticised by some for being an overly conservative judge. We have argued that his approach is a minimalistic one that was appropriate for the context in which he operated, but it is necessary to concede that, even by his own accounts, Chan was a highly principled but not necessarily an adventurous judge. He did not believe that the court had any role in constitutional *politics* but took very seriously the need to protect the court's judicial power and its independence. It was the role of the court to interpret the law and not to make it, and many of the judgments that emanated from the Chan Court reflected this careful but robust approach to constitutional interpretation. As Tan and Thio observed, Chan never felt that courts should be 'the first line of defence against administrative abuses of power'. Instead, 'control can and should come internally from Parliament and the Executive itself in upholding high standards of public administration and policy'. In this respect, Chan saw courts as playing 'a supporting role by articulating clear rules and principles by which the Government may abide by and conform to the rule of law'.[94]

A fascinating question for consideration in this volume has to be the relationship between the different dimensions of toweringness. As judges tower jurisprudentially, how does it affect their institutional and political legacies? Indeed, in relation to Chief Justice Chan in Singapore, one may suggest that his jurisprudential mark on the court has enhanced the reputation and esteem of the judicial institution. He has also decidedly and repeatedly affirmed the view that the court is a legal institution, not a political one.[95] The sheer force of his personal and intellectual reputation has lent great credence to his refutations of politics in the courts. In this regard, one might see the different dimensions of toweringness as not just overlapping, as Abeyratne and Porat point out in the Introduction, but also as interrelated.

In conclusion, we presented a claim at the start of this chapter that 'toweringness' should be seen as a 'relative and contextualised' concept. This relativisation and contextualisation allows us to see toweringness as an ability to work within the system, while rising above that system. Thus, while typologies like Sunstein's could provide useful insights into the personalities and predilections of judges, they often suffer from oversimplification and may not respond to the realities of judging or fully describe any particular real-life judge. Using Sunstein's typology again, the same judge could be a hero in one case, a Burkean in another and a mute in a third. In this account of Chan Sek Keong, we have cast him as a minimalist, a judge who prefers 'small, cautious steps, building incrementally on the decisions and practices of the past ... and narrow rulings, focused on the facts of particular cases'.[96] Although his ability to cleverly but quietly navigate the law may not seem heroic to some, it is our view that this is precisely what makes him to tower as a judge.

---

[94]   Tan and Thio (*supra* n 26) 29.
[95]   Chan (*supra* n 87).
[96]   Ibid. 443.

8

Nepal's Most Towering Judge: The Honourable Kalyan Shrestha

Mara Malagodi

A judge should not be 'towering' – that reminds me of the ivory tower. A judge should meet the expectations of the commoners. The tower is a way of separating the judge from living realities.

As a judge, I wanted to be in the foundations, not in the tower.

Kalyan Shrestha, Nepal's former chief justice[1]

8.1 INTRODUCTION

The present chapter aims to assess the influence of Nepal's former chief justice Kalyan Shrestha on the country's democracy-building and constitutional change at a key juncture in Nepali history. In particular, it seeks to reflect on the manner in which the relationship between sociopolitical contextual factors and the individual agency of this formidable, fearless judicial figure shaped the legacy of his eleven-year Supreme Court tenure (2005–16). Significantly, the time that Kalyan Shrestha served on the bench corresponded to one of the most turbulent decades of Nepali history. He was elevated to the Supreme Court in 2005 at the twilight of Nepal's ten-year-long civil war (1996–2006) and his tenure overlapped with the country's post-conflict transition to democracy and constitution-building process (2008–15). Justice Shrestha's time on the bench encompassed the second bout of emergency and autocratic rule by King Gyanendra in 2005; the beginning of the peace process in 2006; the election of two Constituent Assemblies respectively in 2008 and 2013; the embattled dissolution of the first Constituent Assembly in 2012; the formation of an interim government headed by the Supreme Court's Chief Justice Khil Raj Regmi (only on temporary leave from his post) in 2013; the beleaguered attempts to secure a transitional justice process; the emergence of embattled forms of identity politics also in the legal domain; two devastating earthquakes in the spring of 2015; and the

---

[1] Kalyan Shrestha, personal communication, Kathmandu, 22 December 2018.

febrile final negotiations over the drafting of the constitution eventually promulgated in 2015 along with the violent protests that accompanied the last phase of the constitution-making process.

This case study addresses two specific issues and makes two sets of claims. First, why do we tend to find towering judges in moments of constitutional and democratic change in some countries and not in others? Nepal, as a new and developing democracy, offers important insights into this issue. The dramatic set of events that surrounded Kalyan Shrestha's Supreme Court tenure posed an existential threat to the Nepali judiciary and most clearly to its apex institution, the Supreme Court. The re-democratisation of 1990 and the constitution that came with it had given a much greater role to Nepal's Supreme Court as a constitutional actor. Empowered by the constitution to review the constitutionality of laws and to hear public interest litigation (PIL) petitions on the basis of the Indian model, from the early 1990s the Supreme Court became more assertive and, as a result, progressively acquired a much greater constitutional role and enormous political salience. Thus, at the time when Kalyan Shrestha was elevated to the bench in 2005, the institutional preconditions for an enduring central role of the apex court in Nepal's constitutional politics were already present. However, the explosive political climate and the authoritarian turn since the beginning of the civil war had the potential to marginalise the Supreme Court to the point of obliterating its constitutional function as a crucial counter-majoritarian check on Nepal's powerful executive.

Second, and counterintuitively, this chapter argues that a certain type of towering judge is likely to emerge from dramatic contextual circumstances that potentially trigger a sort of 'fight or flight' stress response. Under this particular set of circumstances, such as in civil-war-era and post-conflict Nepal, towering judges demonstrate the resilience, confidence and moral integrity to stand their ground amidst cataclysmic events and political storms. In these cases, towering judges make the conscious choice to fight and resist. They fight to uphold the constitutional role of their respective institutions, preserve their professional integrity and protect their core identity as dispensers of justice. In doing so, towering judges in dramatic contexts charter a course for other judges to follow, marking what could be described as a 'judicial True North'. The modalities of 'judicial resistance' in the midst of political upheaval vary enormously depending on the personality of individual judges and the constitutional culture in which they operate. What appears to be the True North of towering judges in the midst of political maelstrom, however, is a commitment to upholding the values of constitutionalism.

Second, what kind of legacies do towering judges leave behind? The case study of Nepal's former chief justice Kalyan Shrestha offers limited insights in terms of his long-term legacy, as he retired in 2016 and his tenure was very recent. However, a modest claim can be made with regard to the political backlash produced by a fearless, activist judge impervious to political pressures, who had at his disposal the constitutional tools to hold the executive to account and strengthen the Supreme

Court's institutional position. In the case of Nepal, Kalyan Shrestha's tenure corresponded to the country's seventh constitution-making moment. Therefore, Nepali politicians had the perfect opportunity to rethink and redesign the institutional configuration of the judiciary, and in particular the Supreme Court. Their goal was to reduce the reach and powers of the Supreme Court. Thus, Nepal's 2015 Constitution weakens the position of the apex court in three ways: (a) the creation of the constitutional bench within the Supreme Court as the only organ empowered to review the constitutionality of laws has already led to a significant backlog in constitutional adjudication; (b) the easing of the impeachment procedure for judges has allowed for two (failed) attempts at impeaching Supreme Court justices in 2016 and 2017; and (c) the preservation of the procedure introduced by the 2007 Interim Constitution that requires the approval of the Parliamentary Hearings Committee (PHC) to confirm the nomination of the chief justice by the Constitutional Council and those of Supreme Court justices by the Judicial Council respectively, whereby both constitutional bodies are already dominated by members of the executive, has led to the unprecedented rejection by the PHC of the candidate to the office of chief justice in 2018.

In the last few years, Nepal's Supreme Court has come under increased scrutiny – and at times under fire – by the elected branches, the media and civil society. It remains to be seen whether Kalyan Shrestha's example will inspire today's Supreme Court justices in following in the footsteps of his 'judicial True North' and fighting to protect the constitutional role of the Court and its independence. This would be Kalyan Shrestha's greatest success and most enduring legacy.

8.2 METHODOLOGY AND CHALLENGES

This chapter adopts a sociolegal approach to the study of Kalyan Shrestha as a towering judicial figure, together with a doctrinal reading of his key judgments and analysis of the media reports on his cases and the Supreme Court's various Five Year Plan reports. This methodology reflects the fact that Kalyan Shrestha's tenure has been very recent, that he is alive and that he has been willing to discuss with me informally in person – and at length – his work at Nepal's Supreme Court. While this study does not squarely fit within the genre of legal biography as its focus is not the life of former chief justice Shrestha per se, it shares many assumptions and broad claims of legal life writing, which 'at its best ... illuminates the shifting interplay between agency, circumstance, and the material conditions prompting behaviour'.[2] Thus, the study of the web of interrelations between structure and agency may assist in devising a comparative framework with which to advance our understanding of the phenomenon of towering judges in the global judicial landscape.

---

[2]   David Sugarman, 'From Legal Biography to Legal Life Writing: Broadening Conceptions of Legal History and Socio-Legal Scholarship' (2015) 42(1) *Journal of Law and Society* 8.

At the same time, the case study of Nepal's former chief justice can be understood as a chapter of 'legal history in the making' given the close temporal proximity between Kalyan Shrestha's Supreme Court tenure and this piece of writing. On top of the difficulty of assessing his legacy given how recent these events are, an interdisciplinary approach to this case study – one that straddles law, politics and culture – also manifests itself in a 'messy, eclectic, impure narrative form'.[3] However, such a non-linear narrative can offer a compelling assessment of the role of Justice Shrestha as a towering judge.

> Great life writing is unsettling, challenging the way we look at the world, and inspiring us to develop new ways of knowing. It humanizes. It goes to the heart of our individual and shared existence. The dramas that comprise biography and autobiography are histories that speak to the state of our souls and the state of our world.[4]

The focus on the subjective experience of an individual judge at a discrete historical moment enhances the understanding of legal actors and institutions by inductively identifying sociopolitical contextual factors crucial for comparative analysis. Moreover, the extensive personal communications that I held with Justice Shrestha and the analysis of ancillary non-legal material have allowed me to present a 'thick' analysis of law in context, and to unearth otherwise covert ideological assumptions and values that inform and underpin judicial decision-making and conduct. In doing so, I discovered a crucial component of my hypothesis: the personality, integrity and resilience of the individual judge play a key role in determining the transformation of a judge into a towering figure in the midst of political upheaval. This approach presented me with the difficult challenge that David Sugarman originally identified with respect to Niki Lacey's pioneering biography of HLA Hart, given the author's close association with the Hart family, that of 'balancing engagement with detachment'.[5] Finally, the temporal proximity between the events of the case study and the writing of this chapter also makes it difficult to assess the legacy of former chief justice Kalyan Shrestha. In this respect, my conclusions can be only tentative; they reflect, to a great extent, the many challenges that Nepal's Supreme Court is now facing.

8.3 THE INDIVIDUAL: KALYAN SHRESTHA'S UNDERPINNING VALUES AND JUDICIAL COMPASS

Nepal's former chief justice Kalyan Shrestha remains an influential public figure both in Nepal and internationally. A well-liked and respected judge, at the time of his appointment as chief justice, a media article referred to Kalyan Shrestha as

---

[3]   Ibid. 15.
[4]   Ibid. 8.
[5]   Ibid. 20.

'a bold judge with a clean image',[6] while, in March 2016, a Nepali newspaper described him as 'known for his integrity and professionalism'.[7] Nepali politicians, civil servants and international organisations continue to call upon him frequently for advice, while Nepali media often reach out to him for comments. Thus, this section sets out to sketch the basis for his enduring towering reputation in Nepal. It does so by offering a brief biographical note of Justice Shrestha's life aimed at teasing out the underpinning values in his decision-making during his time on the Supreme Court and identifying his 'judicial compass', that is, the guiding light and direction-ality of his judicial work.

At our first meeting, I asked Kalyan Shrestha how he became involved in the practice of law. He told me how he chose a career in law and how it chimed with his personality.

> When I was sitting my School Leaving Certificate (SLC) examinations in the 10th grade, we had an unseen exam that consisted of an essay. The question was: 'what is your aim in life?' It suddenly came to me in the examination hall: I wanted to be a lawyer! When I was in school, one of the extra-curricular activities I was involved in was the school's debating society. I was the Leader of the Opposition. I was always on the other side of an argument; I was a contrarian who always wanted to do things differently, in my own way. I also always rooted for the underdog. I was critical; I was resilient, and maybe at times even aggressive. I was also never quite satisfied, and I worked very hard. I was to discover later in life that discipline matters a great deal when you are a judge. But since a young age I also had an inquisitive mind, and I was fiercely independent.[8]

The personal traits of independence of mind, resilience and firmness emerged throughout my conversations with Kalyan Shrestha; they became key themes that explained much of his ability to face Nepal's political maelstrom while on the bench.

A brief biographical overview of the start of Kalyan Shrestha's career also sheds light on the trajectory of his judicial work. He was born in 1951 to a Newar family in the mid-Western District of Baglung. After passing the Public Service Examination, he became a civil servant in 1972 and began his career as a district development officer in Nepalgunj.[9] He explained that the start of his career influenced him profoundly as he acquired a grassroots perspective. The poverty of people and the lack of services and resources that he witnessed first-hand at the local level in the first two years of his job pointed to the inadequacy of many development initiatives, the squandering of resources and widespread corruption. The benefits of development were not trickling down and there was no accountability. It was then that he decided to apply for transfer to the judicial track and became a career judge. In 1976, Kalyan

---

[6] www.spotlightnepal.com/2015/07/10/appointment-of-judges-priority-chief-justice-shrestha/.
[7] http://archive.nepalitimes.com/regular-columns/Legalese/judicial-match-fixing-Nepal, 674.
[8] Kalyan Shrestha, personal communication, Kathmandu, 7 August 2018.
[9] www.supremecourt.gov.np/pages/cv_justices/cv_kalyansh.html.

Shrestha was awarded a diploma in law by Tribhuvan University in Kathmandu and
between 1979 and 1983 he was a district judge in various district courts across the
country. At this time, the relationship between law and development began to take
shape in his mind: 'law cannot be empty development, and development cannot be
empty law'.[10] To him, the law has a markedly public function and its scope is to be at
the service of the people. Between 1983 and 1985, he worked briefly as under-
secretary at the ministry of law and justice and successfully pursued an MA in
political science at Tribhuvan University (1983) and a postgraduate diploma in
international law and development at the Institute of Social Studies in The Hague
(1984).

In 1990, he became an appellate court judge and worked in various courts until
2005. Justice Shrestha's extensive experience in many different parts of the country
made it clear for him that law is not simply legal; the social context in which it is to
be implemented is of paramount importance.

> As a judge I am not simply a technician, I am an architect. Processes can be
> reinvented and remedies redefined in order to right a wrong. The law is an enabling
> mechanism; it ought to act like a shield. As I said – I like to do things differently.
> Moreover, in South Asia we have a tradition of judges making the law, of judicial
> activism. I'm not just an adversarial judge, a neutral umpire. For instance, in
> environmental law cases I have a vested interest in environmental protection –
> I cannot dissociate myself.[11]

His tenure in the various Courts of Appeal across Nepal allowed him ample room to
experiment with public law remedies and to solidify his experience.

In 2005, when Kalyan Shrestha's Supreme Court tenure began, Nepal's apex
court had enjoyed fifteen years of extensive powers under the 1990 Constitution and
had progressively become bolder and more assertive in its decisions and role. The re-
democratisation of 1990 also entailed a significant shift towards the legal protection
of rights in Nepal. From a domestic perspective, the new constitution contained an
extensive fundamental rights section and mechanisms for judicial review of legislation and the enforcement of rights. From an international perspective, in the early
1990s Nepal ratified an array of international human rights instruments, which
became enforceable domestically. The promulgation of the 1990 Constitution also
brought substantial changes in the position and organisation of the Nepali judiciary,
expanding the powers and remit of the courts – particularly the Supreme Court.[12]
The new constitution directly linked judicial independence to the protection of
democratic constitutionalism.[13] Moreover, the Supreme Court became the only
institution authorised to provide the final and binding interpretation of the

---

[10] Kalyan Shrestha, personal communication, Kathmandu, 7 August 2018.
[11] Ibid.
[12] Const. of Kingdom of Nepal 1990, Part 11 The Judiciary, articles 84–96.
[13] Ibid. article 84.

Constitution. This was reflected in the Court's extensive powers to review the constitutionality of primary legislation and to void it.[14] In Nepal, the Supreme Court's power of judicial review explicitly featured in the Constitution, emulating jurisprudential developments in independent India.

Thus, the 1990 Constitution departed from the Westminster model by formally establishing limits on parliamentary sovereignty and institutionalising 'strong-form institutions of judicial review'.[15] In fact, the right to constitutional remedy directly linked the protection and enforcement of fundamental rights to judicial intervention.[16] It is also through the understanding of the concomitants, successes and popularity of PIL in India that it is possible to evaluate the scope and goal of Nepal's constitution-makers in 1990 in empowering the Supreme Court to issue prerogative writs and employ the mechanism of PIL.[17] The relaxation of the rule of *locus standi* led to a great number of litigants approaching the Court. Thus, the Supreme Court sought to streamline PIL petitions and identified the following key principles: the dispute ought to be based on existing laws and not be hypothetical; the petitioner must demonstrate a reasonable connection with and a substantial interest in the dispute; and all other remedies must have been exhausted.[18] The Supreme Court's powers of judicial review and PIL under the 2007 Constitution remained virtually unchanged from 1990 and allowed the Court to reinforce its position.[19]

The institutional preconditions were in place for a towering judicial figure to emerge when Justice Shrestha was elevated to the Supreme Court at the twilight of the civil war. I asked him at the outset whether he was ever afraid given the political climate in 2005. He said, 'No, I am not afraid of anything. And I was just doing my job.'[20] At our second meeting, I pressed him further about what he thought the job of the judge entails:

> "The job of the judge is to secure rights protection. Without rights there is no justice. Law can be local, but justice is universal. Justice is at the heart of humanity. If developments abroad have been conducive to justice, then judges ought to translate them into the Nepali context. Judges have to be judges, keen to broaden the spectrum of justice. A judge's temperament should not be overly national and local. A judge ought to be like a bridge and remain in constant dialogue with national and international developments. Ultimately Nepali law should not be a surprise to the rest of the world; our justice system should be up to international standards."[21]

[14] Ibid. article 88(1).
[15] Mark Tushnet, *Weak Courts, Strong Rights, Judicial Review and Social Welfare Rights in Comparative Constitutional Law* (Princeton University Press, 2007) 15.
[16] Const. of Kingdom of Nepal 1990, article 23.
[17] Ibid. article 88(2).
[18] *Radheshyam Adhikari v Council of Ministers*, 2048, 33(12) NKP 810 (1991).
[19] Interim Const. of Nepal 2007, article 107.
[20] Kalyan Shrestha, personal communication, Kathmandu, 7 August 2018.
[21] Kalyan Shrestha, personal communication, Kathmandu, 22 December 2018.

The substantive aims of Kalyan Shrestha's work as a judge illuminate the True North of his judicial compass. Influenced by globalisation and committed to a foundational judicial function, Justice Shrestha actively promoted compliance with international norms.

In terms of his judicial style and relationship with the other judges, in the majority of cases he decided that he was sitting either alone or on a division bench with another judge. He explained that there is not a particularly collegiate tradition within the Supreme Court and that the judges do not often discuss cases beyond the bench to which the case has come. Moreover, there is not a great tradition of dissenting judgments in Nepal. Usually, the most senior judge on the bench would draft the judgment, but, from the beginning of his tenure, in the majority of his cases he got into the habit of writing the judgments himself, and the other judge(s) would simply concur and undersign his judgment.[22]

In line with this attitude, he also sought to foster the process of institution-building of the Supreme Court from the beginning of his tenure and to create a vibrant and efficient judicial institution fit for contemporary work and modern times by introducing three Five-Year Strategic Plans, securing a sizeable budget from the government and setting up the National Judicial Academy. In this respect, he also fought fiercely to preserve judicial independence during Nepal's constitution-making process, ferociously countered the proposals for the creation of a separate constitutional court and then unhappily resigned himself to the compromise that was the eventual creation of a constitutional bench within the Supreme Court under the 2015 Constitution.

8.4 THE CONTEXT: NAVIGATING NEPAL'S MAELSTROM

The turbulent years of Nepali constitutional and political developments that correspond to Kalyan Shrestha's Supreme Court tenure are crucial to explaining his transformation into a towering judge. Justice Shrestha faced up to the democratic challenges of the times, categorically refused to bow down to various political pressures and indefatigably followed his judicial True North centred on the respect and promotion of constitutional rights and international law. Kalyan Shrestha deployed a three-pronged strategy during his Supreme Court tenure: he fought to defend judicial independence at all costs – even at the peril of making political enemies in high-profile cases and institutional decisions; he prioritised the protection of fundamental rights over political expediency; and he worked to strengthen the institutional capacity of the Supreme Court in terms of both structures and personnel. A perusal of his key judgments and institutional planning reveals an astonishing level of both ideological coherence and imperviousness to undue political influence.

---

[22] Ibid.

8.4.1 *Defending Judicial Independence Amidst Political Controversy*

Kalyan Shrestha has a long history of cases during his Supreme Court tenure in which he antagonised the executive. This section discusses two sets of decisions in which Justice Shrestha was involved, respectively the cases in which the Supreme Court had to act as the arbiter of a series of disputes between the government and the Nepal Army, and the cases over the dissolution of Nepal's first Constituent Assembly.[23]

First, on 24 March 2009, a single bench composed of Justice Kalyan Shrestha ruled in favour of eight Army brigadier generals seeking a stay order on the Maoist government's decision to force their retirement against the recommendation of the chief of Army staff. He argued that the law was clear and that the prime minister had acted outside of his powers. The Maoist cadres took to the streets and, in a series of violent protests in Kathmandu, they publicly burnt effigies of Justice Shrestha who had issued the stay order. When Kalyan Shrestha recounted the episode, he was somehow bemused. He found out about the protests at a dinner party from a German constitutional court judge who had just driven by the protests: 'I saw your picture being burnt on the streets while I was driving to the dinner venue, what are you doing here!' As a result, Justice Shrestha was placed under police protection.[24] On 31 March 2009, in a statement to the media, the Attorney General criticised the Maoist cadres for taking to the streets against the stay order and burning Shrestha's effigy.[25] In defence of Kalyan Shrestha and judicial independence, on 30 April 2009, the Supreme Court initiated contempt of court proceedings against Prime Minister Dahal and Finance Minister Bhattarai. Both politicians were summoned to the Court. They stated that they had no involvement in the protests, nor any role in instigating them, and the matter was eventually dropped.[26] The message that the Supreme Court sent was crystal clear: judges will not be cowered by thuggish behaviour. After an unsuccessful attempt by Maoist Prime Minister Dahal to sack the chief of Army staff, General Katawal,[27] on 11 May 2009, a division bench of the Supreme Court composed of Justices Anup Raj Sharma and Prem Sharma upheld the earlier interim order issued by Kalyan Shrestha in the generals' retirement case.[28]

Second, after the third extension of the Constituent Assembly, on 26 November 2011, a full bench of the Supreme Court comprising then chief justice Khil Raj Regmi and Justices Damodar Prasad Sharma, Rajkumar Prasad Shah,

[23] Mara Malagodi, 'Constituent Assembly Failure in Pakistan and Nepal' in Jon Elster, Roberto Gargarella, Vatsal Naresh and Bjørn Erik Rasch (eds.), *Constituent Assemblies* (Cambridge University Press, 2018) 104–6.
[24] Kalyan Shrestha, personal communication, Kathmandu, 7 August 2018.
[25] https://ekantepur.blogspot.com/2009/03/ag-vaidhya-condemns-demonstrations.html.
[26] https://thehimalayantimes.com/kathmandu/pm-fm-come-clean-before-apex-court/.
[27] http://archive.nepalitimes.com/article/nation/rookmangud-katawal-memoir,1567.
[28] https://thehimalayantimes.com/news-archives/latest/sc-upholds-reprieve-for-brigadiers/.

Kalyan Shrestha and Prem Sharma ruled on the writ petition filed by advocates Bharat Jungam and Balkrishna Neupane on 21 September arguing that it was a violation of article 64 of the Interim Constitution to extend again the Assembly's term. The bench ordered the Constituent Assembly to complete the drafting of the new constitution before the expiry of the six-month extension, that is, before May 2012. The Court issued an order stating that 'if the Constituent Assembly fails to promulgate the new constitution within the next six months, its term will automatically expire after six months'.[29] The decision caused outrage. The Supreme Court was accused by many politicians (especially Maoists) of overreaching and overstepping its constitutional role as the question of constitution-making was essentially political and outside of the Court's jurisdiction. Kalyan Shrestha reflected on the case and stood by the decision that the Supreme Court had reached in 2011. He said that the Supreme Court at that time was greatly concerned about interfering with constitutional amendments but that the Constituent Assembly was not making any progress with the drafting. Effectively, the order that the Supreme Court issued in that judgment was a sort of constructive notice forbidding further extensions of the Assembly's term. Justice Shrestha argued that constitution-making is not an exercise that can continue indefinitely without a fresh electoral mandate and that the Court had to resort to the doctrine of necessity under those circumstances.[30]

The Constituent Assembly was unable to complete the new dispensation within the extended time frame. Thus, on 22 May 2012, the government tabled the Constitution (13th Amendment) Bill supported by the main four political parties to extend the term of the Constituent Assembly by a further three months. Immediately, two petitions were filed in the Supreme Court. In the first case, advocates Rajkumar Rana, Kanchan Krishna Neupane and Bharat Mani Jangam sought a stay order on the 13th Amendment Bill tabled in the Assembly. The single bench of Chief Justice Khil Raj Regmi found for the petitioners and issued a stay order on the Amendment Bill, effectively disallowing any further extensions of the Assembly's term. The chief justice found the government to be in violation of the Supreme Court order issued in November 2011 and to be in breach of its duty to complete the drafting of the new constitution by May 2012.[31]

In the second case, on 24 May 2012, a single bench composed of Justice Kalyan Shrestha entertained a contempt of court petition filed by advocate Kamal Prasad Itani against Maoist Prime Minister Baburam Bhattarai and Nepali Congress

---

[29] *Adv. Bharat Mani Jangam and Adv. Bal Krishna Neupane v Prime Minister and Cabinet Office et al.* Writ n. 068-WS-0014. The petition was filed on 21 September 2011 and the decision was handed down on 21 November 2011.

[30] Kalyan Shrestha, personal communication, Kathmandu, 7 August 2018.

[31] *Adv. Rajkumar Rana, Adv. Kanchan Krishna Neupane and Adv. Bharat Mani Jangam v Prime Minister and Cabinet Office et al.* Writ n. 068-WS-1085, 1086, 1087. The petition was filed on 21 September 2011 and the decision was handed down on 21 November 2011.

Minister for Law and Justice Krishna Prasad Sitaula, claiming that the government's decision to seek the Constituent Assembly's term extension was against the constitution and violated the Supreme Court's November 2011 decision. Kalyan Shrestha responded to the petition by issuing an order demanding that the defendants furnished written replies before the Supreme Court.[32] Justice Kalyan Shrestha went as far as telling these two very senior politicians and party leaders that they could not send their representatives in such a case and that they would have to attend the hearing in person.[33] The backlash against this bold decision was immediate. Kalyan Shrestha recounted that, a few days after his decision in the contempt case, his father telephoned to tell him that he had heard on the radio that the Maoists were preparing an impeachment motion against him and the chief justice; it was a plan that they eventually dropped.[34]

Last-minute negotiations took place amongst the main political party leaders outside the Assembly, but to no avail. When the leaders failed to reach a compromise on federalism on 27 May, Prime Minister Bhattarai advised the president to dissolve the Constituent Assembly and called for new elections. The dissolution of the Assembly left Nepal with neither a legislature nor a constitution-drafting body in place for more than a year. It also led to a major constitutional crisis.

Shockingly, in February 2013, negotiations to form a government began amongst the main political parties, and the name of the Supreme Court chief justice, Khil Raj Regmi, was put forward as the next prime minister. Ironically, the prospective government was named 'Nepal Interim Election Council' to obscure the fact that Nepal's key executive institution was to be led by the head of Nepal's judiciary – a blatant violation of the doctrine of separation of powers. Regmi was also the adjudicator on the two key constitutional cases that had led to the dissolution of the first Constituent Assembly. The International Commission of Jurists, amongst other organisations, called for Regmi to step down from his judicial appointment as he was only on temporary leave from his post. In fact, the agreement amongst the four main political parties provided that Regmi would refrain from participating in his duties as chief justice of the Supreme Court while exercising the powers of the prime minister, but that, after the elections had taken place, he would resume his position and regular duties as chief justice.[35] Thus, on 26 February 2013, advocates Gyawali and Om Prakash Aryal filed a writ petition in the Supreme Court demanding that the appointment of Khil Raj Regmi as prime minister made by Nepal's president, Ram Baran Yadav, be withdrawn. The Supreme Court, however, kept the petition pending and refused to entertain it. In an effort to close ranks and present a unified front, the deafening silence of the Supreme Court dented the image of the Court even further.

---

[32] www.himalini.com/5539/22/24/05/.

[33] Ibid.

[34] Kalyan Shrestha, personal communication, Kathmandu, 7 August 2018.

[35] www.icj.org/icj-calls-on-nepali-chief-justice-to-step-down-as-judge-after-appointment-as-prime-minis ter/.

On 14 March 2013, a new consensus government was constituted. It was composed of ministers appointed by the political parties and headed by Chief Justice Regmi. Moreover, the new government remained unburdened by any form of parliamentary accountability since no legislature was in place, a particularly pernicious situation for a parliamentary democracy. Unsurprisingly, this interim period undermined the constitutionality of the political process by implicating the Supreme Court in executive politics and further eroded public trust in state institutions and political actors, both perceived as caught up in partisan politics and incapable of delivering institutional reform. Officially, such a manipulation was justified as an exceptional measure for exceptional circumstances, but Nepal's constitutional moment became irremediably lost. Kalyan Shrestha recalls this period as being a very difficult one for the Supreme Court: the decision of Chief Justice Regmi to accept the position at the helm of the executive would indeed produce long-term negative repercussions for the Supreme Court.[36]

Eventually, on 19 November 2013, the elections of the second Constituent Assembly took place and, on 22 January 2014, the new body held its first meeting. In February 2014, Chief Justice Regmi stepped down from his executive post and was replaced by the Nepali Congress president, Sushil Koirala. Finally, on 28 March 2016, the Supreme Court entertained the petition filed in 2013 by advocates Gyawali and Aryal on the appointment of Khil Raj Regmi as prime minister – more than two years after Regmi had stepped down. The constitutional bench comprising Chief Justice Kalyan Shrestha and Justices Sushila Karki, Baidyanath Upadhyaya, Gopal Parajuli and Om Prakash Mishra quashed the writ petition on the basis that it had become irrelevant as that council of ministers was no longer in place. Kalyan Shrestha and Sushila Karki, however, registered a differing view in the majority's decision and maintained that the move to appoint Regmi as prime minister had been against the interim constitution, the doctrine of separation of power and the principles of check and balance.[37] But it was too little, too late. Sushila Karki, in a BBC interview on 1 July 2016, reiterated that the Nepali judiciary was still paying the price for Regmi's appointment as prime minister while serving as chief justice.[38]

8.4.2 *Protecting Rights, Delivering Justice*

Kalyan Shrestha's Supreme Court tenure has been characterised by a long string of cases in which he upheld the supremacy of constitutional rights and international law. They are many, so this section will offer just a few examples from his decisions on transitional justice, gender equality litigation and socio-economic rights. One central idea guided his judicial decision-making: 'The hope of the justice beggar should not be lost – I could not be a silent spectator in front of injustice. My message

[36] Kalyan Shrestha, personal communication, Kathmandu, 7 August 2018.
[37] https://thehimalayantimes.com/kathmandu/sc-endorses-regmis-appointment-in-executive/.
[38] http://archive.nepalitimes.com/article/from-nepali-press/I-will-not-spare-the-corrupt,3156.

to those seeking the protection and assistance of the Court was this: you can borrow a flame from me to light your stove.'[39]

First, with regard to transitional justice, on 1 June 2007, a division bench of the Supreme Court including Kalyan Shrestha issued a landmark judgment with regard to more than eighty habeas corpus petitions from the families of individuals who had disappeared during the conflict.[40] The Supreme Court ordered the government to enact legislation consistent with international law that would criminalise enforced disappearance, establish a high-level 'Investigation Commission for Disappeared People' for inquiry into past enforced disappearances, and provide interim relief to the families of the victims without prejudice to the final outcome of these cases.[41] Kalyan Shrestha had written the judgment himself and explained the strong words and extensive remedies in this light: 'If the entire state structure is stacked against the victims, what hope do they have?' In his view, the role of the Supreme Court is to offset that power imbalance.

Along the same lines, on 14 January 2013, a single bench of Justice Kalyan Shrestha quashed the order from the Office of the Attorney General, which, on the instructions of Maoist Prime Minister Baburam Bhattarai, had ordered an investigation into the conflict-era murder of journalist Dekendra Thapa. The Court forbade the government to interfere and ordered the police to resume the investigation.[42] On 3 January 2014, a Supreme Court special bench that included Justice Kalyan Shrestha ordered the government to form separate commissions of inquiry, one on truth and reconciliation and another on enforced disappearances, and that the commissions should meet international standards.[43] Finally, on 26 February 2015, a Supreme Court special bench, which included Kalyan Shrestha, ruled that the amnesty provisions in the Truth and Reconciliation Commission Act promulgated in May 2014 were unconstitutional.[44]

Second, Kalyan Shrestha adjudicated on an innumerable set of cases pertaining to fundamental rights. Just to give a few examples, in a 2007 decision, a division bench of the Supreme Court including Justice Shrestha issued an order for the protection of the privacy and identity of women, children, HIV-infected people in cases of rape, incest, divorce, etc., on the basis of an extensive and erudite comparative overview of foreign legal arrangements on the matter.[45] Under the guise of the right to equality, the Supreme Court protected women's reproductive rights and health in the *Prakash*

[39] Kalyan Shrestha, personal communication, Kathmandu, 7 August 2018.
[40] *Rajendra Dhakal and Others v The Government of Nepal*, Writ n. 056-WS-3575. The petition was filed on 21 January 1999 and the decision was handed down on 1 June 2007.
[41] http://nepalconflictreport.ohchr.org/files/docs/2009-03-00_report_icj_eng.pdf.
[42] https://thehimalayantimes.com/kathmandu/cc-recommends-kalyan-shrestha-as-new-cj/.
[43] http://kathmandupost.ekantipur.com/news/2014-01-03/trc-disappearances-ordinance-apex-court-for-2-commissions.html.
[44] www.icj.org/nepal-government-must-implement-landmark-supreme-court-decision-against-impunity/.
[45] *Sapana Pradhan Malla v The Government of Nepal*, Writ n. 063-WS-3561. The decision was handed down on 25 December 2007.

Mani Sharma case, whereby the Court issued an order of mandamus to the government to secure medical treatment for women affected by uterus prolapse.[46] Similarly, in 2009, the Supreme Court issued a landmark judgment, drafted, again, primarily by Kalyan Shrestha, in the case of *Laxmi Devi Dhikta*, in which abortion rights were deemed to be integral to the right against discrimination and the right to equality.[47] The monumental decision of the Court treated reproductive rights as socio-economic rights and ordered the government to guarantee access to safe and affordable abortion services, and compensation for women forced to carry out an unwanted pregnancy.[48] The Supreme Court explicitly recognised women's bodily autonomy and that a foetus does not have the legal status of a human life.

Kalyan Shrestha clearly explained that creating rights is not sufficient and that it is crucial for the courts to foster the ability to enjoy constitutional rights. Pointedly, he said that equality is the only right that a court needs to create such opportunities through an expansive interpretation.[49] Justice Shrestha also highlighted that the court in its constitutional capacity fulfils a discursive function and that, ultimately, judgments are for the public. As such, there is a correlation between the clarity and the implementation of court decisions. Justice Shrestha, however, believes that the implementation of judgments should not be a concern for judges, who should be sufficiently bold to issue the remedies that they deem fit for the case. However, having a string of judgments that remain unimplemented ultimately weakens the standing and institutional strength of the court.

8.4.3 *Institution-Building as Survival*

Kalyan Shrestha introduced pioneering institutional reforms from the beginning of his Supreme Court tenure. He understood that, for the Court to thrive, there was a dire need for resources to finance the modernisation of the court structures and the training of personnel. Thus, he introduced the first Supreme Court Strategic Plan (2004/5–2009/10) as soon as he joined, and then oversaw the Second Strategic Plan (2009/10–2014/15). The acquisition and control of a sizeable budget from the government allowed the Court to develop its structure and deal more efficiently with the caseload. He recalled the dire state of the Supreme Court facilities when he first joined:

> I even had to bring my own water to work – I had a small dark office, a tiny stained desk, and a chair with nails sticking out. No computer, no proper facilities. So I went to visit a number of foreign countries to learn about their courts and understand what resources we needed. When we convinced the government to

---

[46] *Prakash Mani Sharma v Office of the Prime Minister* (Writ n. 064-WS-0230 of year 2060). It was decided in 2066 BS (2009).

[47] *Laxmi Devi Dhikta v Office of the Prime Minister*, 2067, 52(9) NKP 1551 (2009).

[48] www.reproductiverights.org/sites/crr.civicactions.net/files/documents/Lakshmi%20Dhikta%20Factsheet%20FINAL.PDF.

[49] Kalyan Shrestha, personal communication, Kathmandu, 17 June 2019.

give us a budget, well that was a sea change for the Supreme Court, and for the Nepali judiciary more in general.[50]

At the start of his tenure, Justice Shrestha was also instrumental in setting up the National Judicial Academy, which fulfils the training and research needs of Nepali judges and legal professionals.[51] After the Third Strategic Plan, he spearheaded the creation of the Judicial Outreach Programme at district level in collaboration with local non-government organisations (NGOs) and Bar Association local chapters to foster the relationship between the judiciary and local communities across the countries. Finally, as soon as he became chief justice, Kalyan Shrestha used his inherent powers to create the Access to Justice Commission to widen the availability of legal services to the poor and the marginalised.

Efficient, vociferous and unrelenting, Justice Shrestha made an art of nudging the government into action. During our last meeting, he recounted an endearing episode to this effect: after the April 2015 earthquake, the premises of the Supreme Court had been damaged and remained closed for weeks, so one day he became annoyed with the wait, held his bench in the Supreme Court's open air courtyard and called the media to report on his al fresco courtroom to get the government to act.[52] In this respect, Justice Shrestha actively cultivated a good rapport with the media by directly engaging with journalists, not imposing restrictions and never pursuing a contempt of court case against a journalist. He also created the position of media officer within the Court and regular press releases were issued so that the judgments could be appropriately reported and the wider public could be informed about the work of the Supreme Court. He described the relationship between the Court and the media using an old Nepali proverb: 'When the hermit comes across the buffalo, the hermit gets scared. When the buffalo comes across the hermit, the buffalo gets scared.'[53] Justice Shrestha explained that he never pursued a contempt of court charge for inappropriate reporting because he did not want to alienate the media and scare journalists into not reporting cases. But he also drew the line with reporters: judgments are public, the Supreme Court has a spokesperson, and judges cannot comment on individual cases.

While subjected to stringent public scrutiny, Kalyan Shrestha said he suffered remarkably few personal attacks in the media. One of the few instances in which he came under fire was occasioned by the decision of the Judicial Council in March 2016 to recommend eleven individuals (seven appeal court judges and four senior advocates) for Supreme Court appointment, some of which included candidates who had been politically active.

---

[50] Kalyan Shrestha, personal communication, Kathmandu, 7 August 2018.
[51] http://njanepal.org.np/index.php/home.
[52] Kalyan Shrestha, personal communication, Kathmandu, 22 December 2018.
[53] Ibid.

The Judicial Council apparently recommended political figures for the first time. Sapana Pradhan Malla, though highly regarded as one of the most competent female lawyers of her generation, has already played the role as the parliament member from CPN-UML. She is a member of that political party. This means the principle that appointments to the Supreme Court must be non political and not from political cadres has been flouted and creates a precedence for future appointments. What is even more ironic is that it is Chief Justice Kalyan Shrestha, known for his integrity and professionalism, who made this decision under his watch.[54]

The newspaper *Republica* made a similar criticism: 'Hari Krishna Karki, the chairman of Nepal Bar Association, was appointed attorney general by Prime Minister KP Sharma Oli a few months ago and is close to the ruling CPN-UML. Malla was a member of the first Constituent Assembly from the UML under the proportional representation electoral system. Raut is considered close to the main opposition Nepali Congress.'[55] On 1 July 2016, in a BBC interview, Chief Justice Sushila Karki defended the Judicial Council's decision and rebuffed the criticism that it opened the door for politicians to enter the judiciary: 'I do not think so. Our Constitution and laws do not bar those involved in politics from becoming Supreme Court justices. Even so, we have not recommended those who were active in politics as Supreme Court justices.'[56] Eventually, on 1 August 2016, the PHC endorsed the nominations.[57] The issues of politicisation and nepotism in judicial appointments remain hotly contested ones in Nepal, well past Justice Shrestha's tenure. The latest example was the nomination in 2019 of Kumar Regmi and Hari Phuyal, who were perceived as close to the Nepali Congress and UML respectively.[58]

8.5 BACKLASH AGAINST THE TIDAL WAVE OF JUDICIAL ACTIVISM

The main area in which a severe backlash against twenty-five years of Supreme Court-level judicial activism and the emergence of a towering judge of Kalyan Shrestha's stature can be seen is in the way in which Nepal's new constitution frames the position of the higher judiciary. In particular, the 2015 Constitution weakens the overall position of the Supreme Court in at least three respects. The first pertains to judicial review and PIL. Since 1990, many public interest litigants have sought judicial review of legislation from the Supreme Court as their primary remedy. Under the new constitution, this remedy is no longer available except from the newly established constitutional bench. Article 137 creates the Supreme Court's

---

[54] http://archive.nepalitimes.com/regular-columns/Legalese/judicial-match-fixing-Nepal, 674.
[55] http://archive.myrepublica.com/2015-16/politics/story/38016/jc-recommends-11-names-for-justices.html.
[56] http://archive.nepalitimes.com/article/from-nepali-press/I-will-not-spare-the-corrupt, 3156.
[57] http://kathmandupost.ekantipur.com/news/2016-08-01/nominees-endorsed-in-a-first-apex-court-to-have
      -3-female-justices.html.
[58] https://kathmandupost.com/editorial/2019/04/04/imbalance-of-powers.

constitutional bench, which consists of the chief justice and the four most senior justices.[59] The constitutional bench is now the only judicial organ allowed to adjudicate on the validity of legislation on the basis of constitutionality, resolve disputes between the various tiers of government (federal, provincial and local) and determine electoral controversies.

The constitutional bench, after a brief sting under Chief Justice Shrestha, was properly constituted only in September 2017 – two years after the constitution was promulgated. These changes are likely to weaken considerably judicial review, which serves as the main legal mechanism for holding the executive and the legislature to account. In the longer term, it seems likely that reliance on a small constitutional bench will cause the Court's already sizeable constitutional backlog to increase considerably and thus undermine the viability of judicial review and PIL as mechanisms for increasing access to justice and securing legal redress. While the new constitution does extend the ability to entertain PIL petitions to the High Courts and the District Courts, the inability of the lower courts to invalidate primary legislation – the main remedy sought in many PIL cases – renders them an inherently poor venue for effective PIL.

Second, a relaxing of the requirements for impeachment threatens to undermine the independence of the judiciary. The impeachment process may now be initiated by a motion supported by only one-quarter of the total membership of the House of Representatives. If the motion is successful, the accused is immediately suspended from his or her post on an interim basis.[60] This threshold for suspending judges is lower than in any previous constitution.[61] Permanent impeachment then requires a two-thirds vote of the members eligible to vote in both Houses of the Federal Parliament. The easing of the impeachment requirements under article 101 has already led to a failed impeachment attempt in September 2016 against Justice Ananda Mohan Bhattarai,[62] and another in April 2017 against Chief Justice Sushila Karki.[63] Although neither attempt succeeded, these episodes are evidence of politically motivated efforts to thwart the progress that the Supreme Court has made in exercising oversight over the other branches.

Third, the 2015 Constitution retains procedure introduced by the 2007 Interim Constitution. Article 292 requires all nominations to chief justice and all Supreme Court justices, members of Judicial Council, heads or officials of constitutional bodies and ambassadors to be reviewed by the PHC.[64] Article 293 clearly states that

---

[59] Const. of Nepal 2015, article 137.
[60] Ibid. article 101(6).
[61] Ibid. article 101(2).
[62] The impeachment complaint failed to secure the necessary one-fourth support and was quashed by Parliament's Impeachment Recommendation Committee as spurious.
[63] The Supreme Court issued an interim order staying the impeachment motion and reinstating the chief justice. Ultimately, the three main political parties simply agreed to withdraw the impeachment motion as part of a political deal to reshuffle the Cabinet.
[64] Const. of Nepal 2015, article 292.

'constitutional bodies must be accountable and responsible to the Federal Parliament', embedding the principle of parliamentary scrutiny and oversight in the 2015 document.[65] This procedure is redundant as the constitutional bodies, in which the executive is in a majority, already perform the function of vetting candidates and finding agreement among the various institutional actors. The PHC is borrowed from the American model, which aims to ensure parliamentary oversight of presidential nominations. In Nepal, the PHC procedure has been considered a formality until very recently, but, in August 2018, the PHC rejected the nomination of Acting Chief Justice Deepak Raj Joshi in what appeared to be a politically motivated decision by lawmakers from the government's party. Moreover, the effectiveness of the constitutional bodies in dealing with issues pertaining to the judiciary – including misconduct – had already been tested in March 2018, when the Constitutional Council removed Chief Justice Parajuli from his post on the basis of the mandatory age requirement for retirement.

Kalyan Shrestha had a clear sense of the threats to judicial independence that a number of proposals for reforming the judicial branch posed at the time of the constitution-making process. Speaking at a 2010 function, he said:

> One must not lose sight of international values and norms regarding the judiciary. The issue of appointment, promotion and transfer of judges must be handled through proper channels like a Judicial Commission. The commission, he said, can have representations of all major stakeholders so that its decision will not attract wide criticisms. He also said that the practice of parliamentary hearing of judges should be discontinued and that it should be done by the Commission. The major need of the hour is to make the justice-delivery accessible to common people.[66]

A December 2011 report by the International Crisis Group summarises the situation at the twilight of the first Constituent Assembly:

> The issue of the judicial system … remains controversial in legal circles. A constitutional court has been proposed, as well as appointment of judges by an independent body that includes representatives from parliament. This is a considerable change from the original concept, primarily put forward by the Maoists, which would have limited the authority of the Supreme Court; provided that constitutional disputes would be settled by a parliamentary body; and would have made all judges political appointees. The legal community is a significant constituency for politicians to alienate, given the increasing appeals to the Supreme Court on the peace process and politically important issues such as extension of the CA and pardons for crimes committed by party members.[67]

---

[65] Ibid. article 293.
[66] www.ibanet.org/Document/Default.aspx?DocumentUid=A91D8069-9308-4F82-A789 -9AFC9FB740E1.
[67] https://d2071andvipowj.cloudfront.net/b131-nepal-s-peace-process-the-endgame-nears.pdf.

Supreme Court judges continued to speak up against the creation of a separate constitutional court,[68] and, at the last hour of the constitution-making process in 2015, Chief Justice Shrestha renewed his call for the new constitution to respect judicial independence.[69] After years of lobbying by the legal profession, eventually a compromise was reached: the proposal for a separate constitutional court was scrapped, and instead a constitutional bench within the Supreme Court was created. It remains an unsatisfying compromise for many of the judges, and Kalyan Shrestha makes no mystery of his displeasure at the arrangement, which he correctly identifies as an instance of a wider, concerted assault on the Nepali judiciary.

8.6 CONCLUSION: KALYAN SHRESTHA'S LEGACY AND JUDICIAL TRUE NORTH

When I asked Kalyan Shrestha what he thought his legacy was, he responded succinctly: 'my judgments'.[70] My tentative conclusion is to disagree with Justice Shrestha and argue that his legacy may be far more extensive than his judgments. This study has sought to assess the influence of former chief justice Kalyan Shrestha on Nepal's democracy-building and constitutional change at a key juncture in Nepali history. Two sets of conclusions have emerged. First, as an institution-building judge with savvy political instincts, he was instrumental in preserving the independence of the Supreme Court – and ultimately its survival – throughout such a tumultuous decade. Second, the dramatic contextual circumstances of post-conflict Nepal have contributed to the consolidation of Kalyan Shrestha's position as a towering judge. He had the resilience, confidence and moral integrity to stand his ground amidst Nepal's political maelstrom, and he fought back to uphold the constitutional role of the Supreme Court, preserve his professional integrity and, ultimately, protect his core identity as a dispenser of justice. In doing so, he charted a course for other judges to follow. His 'judicial True North', centred on compliance with constitutional rights and international norms, imperviousness to undue polit-ical pressure, and a central concern for the poor and the marginalised, made for an inspiring example of judicial conduct. At the same time, only time will tell whether former chief justice Kalyan Shrestha's judicial compass will serve as a beacon of light for other Nepali judges and will succeed in guiding them through the dark times ahead. Should this be the case, the legacy of this towering judge will be long-standing and pervasive, even reaching beyond the monumental body of landmark case law that he has authored in a decade on the bench of the Supreme Court.

---

[68] https://kathmandupost.com/miscellaneous/2015/07/30/heads-of-constitutional-bodies-demand-greater-autonomy.
[69] http://kathmandupost.ekantipur.com/news/2015-07-24/cj-shrestha-calls-for-judicial-autonomy.html.
[70] Kalyan Shrestha, personal communication, Kathmandu, 7 August 2018.

9

Barak's Legal Revolutions and What Remains of Them: Authoritarian Abuse of the Judiciary-Empowerment Revolution in Israel

Alon Harel

9.1 INTRODUCTION

Much has been written in Israel about the constitutional or, more broadly, the legal revolution instigated to a large extent by the former president of the Supreme Court Aharon Barak, whose name has become identified with the new Israeli jurisprudence. President Barak came to Israel as a refugee after the Holocaust; since then, he has had a meteoric career as a law professor and as a dean at the Hebrew University. He later became Attorney General, a justice on the Supreme Court, and, finally, the president of the Supreme Court. His great success in initiating and entrenching the legal revolution is attributed to his legal talents, his charisma, and his personality, but also to the weakness and erosion in the status of Israeli politicians in the 1980s. He was able to change the course of the jurisprudence not only by developing original new legal doctrines but also by transforming the deferential mentality that characterized the Court and bolstering its self-confidence.[1]

Yet, in recent years, theorists such as Yoav Peled, Doron Navot, Nadiv Mordechay, Yaniv Roznai, and others have been talking about the counterrevolution resulting from the rise of right-wing governments in Israel and the new judicial appointment of judges who are predicted to promote a conservative worldview.[2] Under the conventional story told by legal theorists, the Barak-instigated legal revolution has been eroded and, most likely, is being overturned by a new generation of politicians and newly appointed judges.

---

[1] See, generally, *Nomi Levitsky, Kevodo: Aharon Barak: Biyografyah* [Your Honor: Aharon Barak: A Biography] (Keter, 2001) 183–7 (in Hebrew). Aharon Barak has much confidence in the wisdom of the judiciary. See, e.g., Alon Harel, "Skeptical Reflections on Justice Aharon Barak's Optimism: The Judge in a Democratic Society" (2006) 39 *Israel Law Review* 261.

[2] See Chaim Shain, "The Counter-Revolution Has Been Completed: No Activist Justice" *Israel Hayom* (22.2.2018) (in Hebrew) www.israelhayom.co.il/article/537929; Doron Navot and Yoav Peled, "Towards a Constitutional Counter-Revolution in Israel?" (2009) 16 *Constellations* 429; Nadiv Mordechay and Yaniv Roznai, "A Jewish and (Declining) Democratic State? Constitutional Retrogression in Israel" (2017) 77 *Maryland Law Review* 244.

In this chapter, I shall raise doubts about this claim. More specifically, I argue that there were two legal revolutions in Israel: the judiciary-empowerment revolution (or the institutional revolution) and the liberal (or substantive revolution). I shall also argue that while much of the criticism directed against the Israeli legal revolution is directed against the former (judiciary-empowerment) revolution, the conservative forces in Israel have no urgent interest in overturning the judiciary-empowerment revolution. As a matter of fact, I would argue that the judiciary-empowerment revolution is currently being used by conservative and illiberal groups in Israel to undo the liberal revolution and transform Israel into an illiberal democracy. By illiberal democracy, I refer to a democratic system with regular fair elections that does not respect basic human rights such as freedom of speech, the right to equality, the independence of the judiciary, etc.

The judiciary-empowerment revolution is an institutional revolution that has been designed to increase judicial power in various aspects of social and political life and to increase judicial intervention in various legal spheres: contracts, torts, property law, administrative law, constitutional law, family law, and others. The most salient and controversial aspect of this revolution has been the constitutional revolution empowering the courts to invalidate legislation.

The liberal revolution injected liberal values into judicial decision-making. The Court used its increasing powers and willingness to intervene in order to promote liberal-individualistic values. More particularly, it used its power to protect more vigorously human rights; it entrenched the values of dignity, autonomy, and freedom in interpreting the law; and it also advanced the values of equality and broadened the scope of some positive rights.[3]

Measuring or classifying judges as liberal may often be a complicated task as liberalism has many different dimensions. In Israel, liberal judges are classified, among other things, on the basis of their willingness to protect minorities, to protect women's rights, to grant rights to LGBT, and to be less deferential to the government on issues of immigration, security, and other public policy concerns when those conflict with individual rights. Naturally, some judges may be liberal in some respects and not in others, but it is still possible to identify some judges that are more liberal than others on some or most of these dimensions. President Barak seems to qualify as a liberal justice on most (or all) of these dimensions.[4]

---

[3] For an early description of the liberal revolution, see Menachem Mautner, "The Decline of Formalism and the Rise of Values in Israeli Law" (1993) 17 *Tel Aviv University Law Review* 503 (in Hebrew).

[4] See, e.g., Aharon Barak, "Foreword: A Judge on Judging: The Role of a Supreme Court in a Democracy" (2001) 116 *Harvard Law Review* 19, 20–1. Barak regards the protection of human rights as an integral part of the function of the judiciary. He argues: "[W]ithout human rights there can be no democracy and no protection for democracy." For his liberal jurisprudence, see "Foreword," ns 29–34.

President Barak believes that the two revolutions are interrelated. He believes that judicial powers are inherently conducive to liberal values.[5] The rise of right-wing and conservative forces in Israel and their greater influence on the composition of the judiciary demonstrate that this conviction on the part of retired president Barak was deeply fallacious. In contemporary Israel, it is the judges who are becoming allies of the politicians in undermining the liberal revolution. Ironically, the judges who are responsible for the demise of the liberal revolution often quote President Barak (in particular, his statements advocating the judiciary-empowerment revolution) in support of their conservative and often reactionary judgments.[6] Thus, while the judiciary-empowerment revolution instigated by Barak succeeded beyond expectations, its success has contributed to the failure or, at least, erosion of the liberal revolution.

Section 9.2 provides a (very) brief introduction to the structure and roles of the Israeli courts and to the influence of President Barak on the Court. Section 9.3 analyzes the two Barak-instigated revolutions. Section 9.4 describes the views of the critics of the two revolutions. I argue there that the main target of the critique of Barak was the judiciary-empowerment revolution rather than the liberal revolution. The judiciary-empowerment revolution has been described by its opponents as elitist, antidemocratic, and even authoritarian. Section 9.5 maintains, however, that, when given the power and opportunity, the illiberal new political elites did not focus their attention or make any efforts to undo the judiciary-empowerment revolution. In fact, they have been using the judiciary-empowerment revolution to revoke the successes of the liberal revolution. The main interest of the current political elites is not to limit the power of the Court and return its powers "to the people" (as their rhetoric indicates) but to turn the Court into a faithful (activist) ally of the government in eroding liberal rights. Hence, I conjecture that while the liberal legacy of President Barak may be eroded, his judiciary-empowerment revolution is most likely to have a more enduring effect on the Israeli legal system.

9.2 THE ISRAELI COURT: ITS COMPOSITION AND INSTITUTIONAL STRUCTURE

The Israeli Supreme Court is the highest court in Israel. It has ultimate appellate jurisdiction as well as original jurisdiction in specific areas. It is composed of fifteen judges who are appointed by a judicial selection committee. The committee is

---

[5] See Barak (*supra* n 4) text to which ns 32–5 relate; see also Barak (*supra* n 4) 25–6. Barak argues there that judges are partners in creating the law and not merely agents who defer to the principal and that they should use their powers to protect both formal democracy and substantive democracy as expressed in basic values and human rights. In this respect, Barak is a faithful follower of Ronald Dworkin. See Ronald Dworkin, *Law's Empire* (Harvard University Press, 1986). As I show later, Barak acknowledged his intellectual debt to Dworkin; see Barak (*supra* n 4) text to which ns 33–5 relate.

[6] See, e.g., the decision of Judge Drori (see CC (Jer) 9135–07 *Mashich* v *The Palestinian Authority* (*Nevo*, September 17, 2018) (in Hebrew) and the text accompanying n 61 later in this chapter).

composed of professional (legal) representatives (three Supreme Court judges and two members of the Israeli Bar Association) and four politicians (two members of the Knesset and two ministers, including the minister of justice).

As an appellate court, the Supreme Court has jurisdiction in areas of criminal, civil law and military law. As the High Court of Justice, it has original jurisdiction with respect to petitions against the government and official bodies, including local authorities. The judges typically sit in panels of three judges, but at times, with respect to particularly important decisions, judges sit in larger panels. Petitions to the High Court of Justice have become a primary tool to protect civil and human rights in Israel. Much of the public controversy concerning the Court focuses on its decisions concerning these latter issues, namely decisions it makes when it operates as the High Court of Justice.

The Court has become, since the 1980s, a major player in Israeli political life. This is largely due to the greater willingness of judges to intervene in order to protect individual rights. In 1992, after the enactment of two basic laws, the Court also declared that it has the power of judicial review; it has since used its power of judicial review several times. Also since then, the Court has been consistently subjected to attacks as it is being depicted as too politicized and, in particular, as too interventionist and too liberal.[7]

Barak was appointed to the Supreme Court in 1979 after a very successful career as Attorney General and previously as a professor and a dean at the Hebrew University. Justice Barak was appointed to be president of the Court in 1995 and retired in 2006. President Barak had a crucial role to play in the development of the Court during this period. He was not the only or even the first "activist" judge; president Shamgar, who preceded Barak, was also known to be activist. But the influence of President Barak on the Israeli jurisprudence is greater than that of any other judge.

President Barak is known to have authored important judgments in all fields of law. His judicial approach is grounded in legal realism: law is a means for social change. The judge ought to interpret the law in light of its purposes and, in doing so, balance conflicting considerations. In addition to his judgments (many of which are available in English),[8] President Barak has published numerous books and articles promulgating his judicial philosophy.[9] He is known in the international community

---

[7] Given the intense ideological debates concerning the role of the Court, it is difficult to find a nonideological exposition of Israeli constitutional law. For a useful introduction, see Suzi Navot, *The Constitution of Israel: A Contextual Analysis* (Hart, 2014). For a harsh critique of the Court, see, e.g., Daniel Friedmann, *The Purse and the Sword: The Trials of Israel's Legal Revolution* (Oxford University Press, 2016).

[8] For a major collection of Israeli cases in English, see https://versa.cardozo.yu.edu.

[9] Two of his most influential books are: Aharon Barak, *The Judge in a Democracy* (Princeton University Press, 2006); Aharon Barak, *Purposive Interpretation in Law* (Princeton University Press, 2011). For a critical review of Barak's judicial philosophy, see Harel (*supra* n 1).

as one of the most influential judges, and his judgments, articles, and books have been used extensively in foreign courts.[10]

More than any other judge, President Barak is identified with the Israeli "constitutional revolution." In Section 9.3, I analyze the constitutional revolution and point out that what is often perceived as a single revolution should be conceptualized as two separate revolutions.

9.3 THE TWO ISRAELI LEGAL REVOLUTIONS

This section presents the two Israeli legal revolutions and focuses on President Barak's contributions to them. It is important, however, to recall that President Barak was not the only instigator of the Israeli legal revolutions. As mentioned earlier, Meir Shamgar, who preceded Barak as president in the Supreme Court, as well as other justices contributed to both revolutions. Barak's voice was critical in both revolutions, but other justices as well as other jurists joined President Barak in supporting and entrenching these jurisprudential convictions.

Section 9.3.1 describes the judiciary-empowerment revolution and Section 9.3.2 describes the liberal revolution. Both revolutions are described schematically, as nothing that is being said in this section purports to be original or novel. It is required, however, to establish my claims in Section 9.5.

9.3.1 *The Judiciary-Empowerment (or Institutional) Revolution*

The judiciary-empowerment revolution has been designed to give greater powers to the courts in interpreting legislation, in monitoring the executive's decisions, in providing remedies for violations of rights, in the recognition and enforcement of contracts, in freeing judges from certain doctrinal constraints in both private and procedural law, and, ultimately, after 1992 (after the enactment of two basic laws), in reviewing Knesset legislation. Before I describe some of these changes, let me first make two introductory comments.

First, the judiciary-empowerment revolution instigated by Barak did not focus exclusively on judges; Barak also expressed support for granting greater autonomy and power to government attorneys.[11] It would be fair, therefore, to criticize the title chosen here (the judiciary-empowerment revolution) on the grounds that Barak's real concern was to increase the power of jurists in general or, perhaps, simply to

---

[10]   See, e.g., Jolanta Bieliauskaite and Vyatutas Slapkauskas, "Aharon Barak's Legal Ideology in the Context of European Constitutionalism" (2017) 10 *Baltic Journal of Law and Politics* 183, 187.

[11]   In particular, he is known for maintaining that the Attorney General is entitled to refuse to represent the government when he/she thinks its decision is illegal and, in effect thereby, to veto decisions of the executive. See HCJ 4634/93 *Amitai Citizens for Sound Administration and Moral Integrity v Yizhak Rabin Prime Minister of Israel*, ISrSC 47(5) 441. For a critique, see Evelyn Gordon, "How the Government's Attorney Became Its General," *Azure*, Summer 1998, http://azure.org.il/include/print .php?id=390.

enhance the role of legal rules and principles in policy-making. Second, as I show later, the institutional revolution instigated by Barak did not rest only on the design of new doctrinal tools, some of which are described in this subsection; it ultimately also involved a new temperament – one that is less deferential and more interventionist.

One manifestation of the judiciary-empowerment revolution has been to free the courts from their semantic chains; namely, to allow courts greater freedom to interpret the law in light of its purposes. A famous example is the criminal appeal 787/79 *Mizrachi v State of Israel*.[12] The appellant was an inmate who failed to return to prison after a short vacation. The Israeli criminal law imposes a criminal sanction on prisoners who escape from custody. Given the traditional narrow and formalistic legal interpretation of criminal provisions, the District Court acquitted the inmate on the grounds that failing to return cannot constitute "an escape." In rejecting this formalist interpretation, Justice Barak asserted:

> Criminal law like any other law ought not be interpreted narrowly or broadly but by giving a logical and natural meaning to the language of the law in order to realize the purpose of the legislation. The words of the law are not castles to be conquered with dictionaries but wrapping of a living idea which changes in accordance with new circumstances.[13]

In CA 4628/93 *The State of Israel v Apropim*, President Barak applied the same anti-literalist approach to the interpretation of contracts and maintained that "[a]t times the idea is expressed that it is permissible to depart from the language of the contract if a literal interpretation will lead to an absurd result . . . Literal interpretation leads to absurdity, inconsistency and inconvenience, when it does not achieve the purpose of the contract."[14] President Barak adopted a very similar approach to tort law when he said: "The categories of negligence are never closed, never rigid and never immutable, but are rather determined based on the sense of morality and social justice and society's changing needs."[15] The rejection of literalism and the adoption of functionalist and/or value-based interpretation provided courts much latitude to protect and promote liberal values. For instance, in one case, the District Court determined that the words "man" and "woman" in the Israeli law of succession should also include cases of a man and a man and a woman and a woman. Hence, the male appellant who lives together with another man is entitled to inherit his property.[16]

---

[12]   Cr.A. 787/79 *Mizrachi v State of Israel*, 35(4) PD 421 (1980) (in Hebrew).
[13]   Ibid. 427.
[14]   CA 4628/93 *State of Israel v Apropim* [1995] 49(2) PD 1, 321–2 (in Hebrew) (English translation: versa .cardozo.yu.edu/sites/default/files/upload/opinions/State%20of%20Israel%20v.%20Apropim% 20Housing%20and%20Promotions.pdf) 66.
[15]   Cr.A. 186/80 *Yaari v The State of Israel* [1980] PD 35(1) 769, 779.
[16]   CA (Nazareth) 3245/03 *Estate SR v Attorney General* [2004] PM 2004(2) 721 (in Hebrew).

President Barak was the instigator of the view that rejects literalism and endorses broad and liberal norms of interpretation. He asserted: "Frequently, the court creates, by its very ruling, the right itself. Judging is not merely declarative. It involves creativity."[17] He added: "The judge is not a mirror reflecting the legal picture, but rather an artist who creates the picture with his own hand."[18] Those statements have had large influence on the interpretative norms not only of the Supreme Court but also of the lower courts.

Another major change is the greater willingness of courts to review administrative and executive decisions. Traditionally, there was a strong presumption favoring the legality of executive action, and intervention was restricted to specific and limited causes. President Barak expanded the power of the Court and he did so partly by developing new doctrinal tools. Most significantly, Barak developed the view that unreasonableness on the part of the executive is a sufficient ground for judicial intervention.

Unreasonableness has since become a prominent tool for courts to interfere in executive decisions.[19] President Barak contributed greatly to the development of the unreasonableness doctrine. While traditionally, in order to interfere in an executive decision, petitioners were required to show that the decision was ultra vires or, at least, that the administrative entity had failed to consider relevant considerations or had considered irrelevant considerations, under the unreasonableness doctrine, an executive decision ought, in addition, to meet minimum standards of reasonableness and, if it fails to do so, the Court should intervene. In HCJ 389/80 *Dapei Zahav v The Broadcasting Company*,[20] the Court evaluated the reasonableness of a decision made by the Israeli broadcasting company to deny a firm an opportunity to participate in a bid. In this case, President Barak asserted that unreasonableness could by itself be a ground for invalidating an administrative decision. Barak said:

> The public entity ought to exercise its discretion … in accordance with the public norms that are acceptable in accordance with good governance … These standards require the public entity to act fairly and decently. It is prohibited to act arbitrarily, in a discriminatory manner, in a partial manner … to decide *in a way that is unreasonable*.[21]

In making determinations concerning reasonableness, the Court also developed the concept of proportionality and what it labeled "reasonable weighting" of the

---

[17] HCJ 910/86 *Ressler v Minister of Defence* [1988] PD 42(2), 441, 464.

[18] Aharon Barak, "The Judge-Made Rule and Social Reality" in *Volume in Memory of Yoel Zusman, Supreme Court President* (Daf Hen, 1984) 93.

[19] Margit Cohen, "Unreasonableness in Administrative Law: Comparative Aspects and Some Normative Comments" in Aharon Barak, Ron Sokol, and Oded Shaham (eds.), *Or Book: Collection of Articles in Honor of Justice Or* 773 (in Hebrew) (Sarigim_Leon, Nevo, 2013). See also Daphne Barak-Erez, *Administrative Law*, vol 2 (Israeli Bar-Publishing House 2010) 723–69 (in Hebrew).

[20] HCJ 389/80 *Dapei Zahav v Broadcasting Company* [1981] 35(1) PD 421 (in Hebrew).

[21] Ibid. 435 (my emphasis).

different considerations. The administrative agency ought not only to weigh all relevant considerations and to ignore the irrelevant ones; it also ought to balance all the considerations in a way that reflects their proper or, at least, their reasonable weight. In HCJ 16/96 *Chorev* v *Minister of Transportation*, this principle was used and President Barak maintained:

> The reasonableness of the decision means a proper balancing of the conflicting considerations. The reasonableness of the decision is determined by balancing the conflicting values which compete for seniority in accordance with their weight and settling the conflict. We have therefore a balancing doctrine which is customary in our public law. It is used when there is an authority to make a decision which requires the exercise of discretion and which requires [the official] to balance conflicting values and interests. This is the way this Court acts when the exercise of discretion on the part of public entities harms individuals or the public interest.[22]

The most important and dramatic decision made by President Barak was the decision in CA 6821/93 *United Mizrahi Bank* v *Migdal* where the Court declared its power to invalidate statutes that conflict with the basic laws. This decision was dramatic because the legal tradition in Israel (following the British tradition) cherished the supremacy of the Knesset. Let me provide a very brief introduction to Israeli constitutional law in order to describe the significance of this decision.

Israel has no written constitution. Despite numerous efforts to enact one, it has never been done. Yet, during its history, several "basic laws" have been enacted. Most of the basic laws are designed to specify the institutional structure of the state and the powers of the different branches of government. Only as far back as 1992 did the Israeli Knesset pass two basic laws designed to protect rights: Basic Law: Human Dignity and Liberty, and Basic Law: Freedom of Occupation.[23]

Section 8 of Basic Law: Human Dignity and Liberty declares: "There shall be no violation of rights under this Basic Law except by a law befitting the values of the State of Israel, enacted for a proper purpose, and to an extent no greater than is required." In *United Mizrahi*, the Court was asked to examine whether it has the power to invalidate a regular Knesset law when the law conflicts with a basic law, namely whether it has the power of judicial review. In a decision that can be compared (except maybe for its excessive length) to the famous *Marbury* v *Madison*, the Court declared that it has such a power.[24] Although the Court rarely uses this power, much of the debate concerning the so-called activism of the Court focused on the power of the Court to review legislation. In *United Mizrahi*, Justice Barak maintained:

> Thus, in declaring invalid a law that does not meet the requirements of the Basic Law, the Court enforces the Basic Law. The constitution and the Basic Law

---

[22]　HCJ 16/96 *Chorev* v *Minister of Transportation* [1997] 51(4) PD 1, 37.
[23]　For an English version of the basic laws, see http://knesset.gov.il/laws/special/eng/BasicLawLiberty .pdf; http://knesset.gov.il/laws/special/eng/BasicLawOccupation.pdf.
[24]　*Marbury* v *Madison* (1803) 5 US 137, 138.

themselves legitimize the judicial review of constitutionality ... Thus, judicial review of the constitutionality of the law is the soul of the constitution itself. Strip the constitution of judicial review and you have removed its very life. The primacy of the constitution therefore requires judicial review.[25]

As I said earlier, the power of judicial review has been used rarely by the Court, but the potential use of such a power is always very salient and its (rare) use by the Court often triggers a hostile reaction on the part of politicians, jurists, and some public intellectuals.

It is time to mention an even more radical manifestation of Barak's interventionist view which, so far, has not been exercised either by him or by any other judge. President Barak believes that, at times, the Court has the power to invalidate a law even in the absence of a written constitution:

> Theoretically and as a matter of principle, there exists the possibility that a court in a democratic society declares the invalidity of a law that is contrary to the fundamental principles of the system; even if those fundamental principles are not entrenched in a rigid constitution or in an entrenched basic law. There is nothing axiomatic about the approach that legislation could not be invalidated because of its content.[26]

President Barak was one of the primary instigators (and most likely the primary instigator) of a radical transformation in Israeli law. This section describes a few (but by no means all) prominent developments of Israeli law that are designed to increase the powers of the Court. But it is important to add that the greater interventionism on the part of the Court rests not only on these (or any other) doctrinal changes; it rests primarily on the greater willingness of the Court to use existing legal doctrines and the greater mistrust of the Court (and the public) in the reasonableness of decisions made by the political elites. The public image of the political elites has deteriorated,[27] and, according to some explanations, the Court was pulled in to fill a role that could not be effectively exercised by the executive or legislative branches. Both the doctrinal changes described in this subsection and the greater interventionism on the part of the Court led many to describe the Israeli court as an activist court and even to describe President Barak as "an enlightened despot."[28]

[25]   CA 6821/93 *United Mizrahi Bank* v *Migdal Cooperative Village* [1995] 49(4) PD 1, 267 (1995) (English translation: versa.cardozo.yu.edu/sites/default/files/upload/opinions/United%20Mizrachi%20Bank% 20v.%20Migdal%20Cooperative%20Village_0.pdf).

[26]   HCJ 142/89 *La'or Movement* v *Speaker of the Knesset* [1990] IsrSC 44(3) 529, 554.

[27]   See Simon Fink, "Eroding Israeli Democracy, Public Trust and the Rule of Law," *Times of Israel*, March 22, 2019), https://blogs.timesofisrael.com/eroding-israeli-democracy-public-trust-and-the-rule-of-law/. See also Lahav Harkov, "The Knesset at Age 69: Still Struggling for the Public Trust," *Jerusalem Post*, January 30, 2018, www.jpost.com/Israel-News/Politics-And-Diplomacy/The-Knesset-at-age-69-Still-struggling-for-the-publics-trust-540181.

[28]   See Richard Posner, "Enlightened Despot," *New Republic*, April 23, 2007, 53, www.tnr.com/article/enlightened-despot. See also Barak Medina, "Four Myths of Judicial Review: A Response to Richard

9.3.2 *The Liberal Revolution*

The judiciary-empowerment revolution, according to President Barak, was merely a means to realize substantive values. After all, President Barak, like all contemporary jurists influenced by legal realism, is an instrumentalist; he regards the law as a means by which to realize social goals.[29] Justice, as understood by him, rests on liberal foundations. Among the prominent values regarded by him as embedded in the legal system are the values associated with liberal rights: respecting dignity, promoting autonomy, enhancing equality, and overall cherishing what can be labeled traditional Millian "liberal values." An unambiguous expression of Barak's liberal convictions can be found in Bank Hamizrahi:

> Judicial review of constitutionality is the very essence of democracy, for democracy does not only connote the rule of the majority. Democracy also means the rule of basic values and human rights as expressed in the constitution. Democracy strikes a delicate balance between majority rule and the basic values of society. Indeed, democracy does not mean formal democracy alone, which is concerned with the electoral process in which the majority rules. Democracy also means substantive democracy, which is concerned with the defense of human rights in particular.[30]

In another case, President Barak explained that, in his view, the rights-based constitutional revolution resulting from the enactment of the two human rights basic laws affects all fields of law. In Criminal Appeal 4424/98 *Silgado* v *The State of Israel Justice*, Barak stated:

> With the entrenchment of the basic law: Human Dignity and Liberty, the rights entrenched in it became constitutionalized, ie. having superior normative power. This is the very essence of the constitutional revolution ... As a result we have had constitutionalization of all fields of law. The meaning of it among other things is that constitutional human rights radiate directly or indirectly into every field of the law.[31]

President Barak does not perceive liberal values to be his own private convictions; he regards his *judicial role* as requiring him to protect and expand traditional liberal values. Liberalism, in his view, is not sectarian; it is what unites us as a polity rather than what divides us as members of political parties or as adherents of any particular political or social ideology. He concedes that there could be disputes concerning the meaning and scope of individual rights. But he believes that those values are part of the legal system and that it is part of his role as a judge to defend them. These values include equality, autonomy, freedom of expression, freedom of association, freedom

---

Posner's Criticism of Aharon Barak's Judicial Activism" (2007) 49 *Harvard International Law Journal* 1.

[29] For a discussion and a critique of instrumentalism in contemporary legal theory, see Alon Harel, *Why Law Matters* (Oxford University Press, 2014).

[30] *United Mizrahi Bank (supra* n 25) 270.

[31] *Cr.A. Silgado* v *State of Israel* [2002] 56(5) PD 529, 539–40.

of religion, freedom of movement, fair process, the right to form a family as well as the right to education, the right to work, and the right to a dignified human existence (minimum income).[32]

I have provided some indications as to the prominent role that President Barak has had in implementing and promoting the judiciary-empowerment and the liberal revolutions. Yet, a separate description of the two revolutions does not do full justice to the jurisprudence of President Barak. As I will show, Barak perceived both revolutions as being interconnected. The expansion of the powers of the Court and liberal-individualist values are, in his view, inseparable.

The foreign reader may recall at this point the jurisprudential work of Ronald Dworkin, who perceived the law as a mechanism for protecting rights. This recollection is not an accident; Barak is indeed a faithful follower of Ronald Dworkin. Dworkin expressed this view as follows: "According to law as integrity, propositions of law are true if they figure in or follow from the principles of justice, fairness, and procedural due process that provide the best constructive interpretation of the community's legal practice."[33] Similarly, Barak argued:

> The aim of interpretation in law is to realize the purpose of the law; the aim in interpreting a legal text (such as a constitution or statue) is to realize the purpose that the text serves. Law is thus a tool designed to realize a social goal. It is intended to ensure the social life of the community, on the one hand, and human rights, equality and justice on the other. The history of law is a search for the proper balance between these goals, and the interpretation of the legal text must express its balance.[34]

The law is thus necessarily (or even by definition) fair; it is fair as it results from an interpretation that gives justice and fairness a prominent role. Barak explicitly referred to Dworkin's theory and argued:

> It is not proper to identify the rule of law as merely the principle of the legality of government, with jurisprudential requirements added in. Dworkin has rightly said that we must not be satisfied with the 'rule-book conception' of the rule of law. It must be extended to the 'right conception' of the rule of law ... In my opinion it means guaranteeing fundamental values of morality, justice, and human rights, with a proper balance between these and the other needs of society ... The law exists to insure proper social life. Social life, however, is not a goal in itself, but a means to allow the individual to live in dignity and develop himself.[35]

Hence, it seems that the legal revolution is perceived by President Barak to be a means to what he perceives to be the more important revolution – the liberal

[32] Aharon Barak, *Human Dignity: The Constitutional Value and the Constitutional Rights* (Cambridge University Press, 2015) 174–5.
[33] Dworkin (*supra* n 5) 225.
[34] Barak, *Purposive Interpretation in Law* (*supra* n 9) 122.
[35] Barak (*supra* n 4) 125–6.

revolution. Given that the law is a means to an end – the protection of liberal values – then the liberal revolution is the ultimate goal. This understanding gives rise to the concern that judges are not necessarily or always the best advocates of liberal values. Barak's judicial philosophy rests at least partly on the (unfounded) empirical conviction that the institutional position of judges is more conducive to liberal values.[36] The future developments of Israeli law described in Section 9.5 illustrate that President Barak was wrong and that judges often promote illiberal values.

To sum up, Barak is the instigator of two interrelated revolutions: an institutional (judiciary-empowerment) and a substantive (liberal) revolution. He worked in concert with other judges, but his role in both revolutions cannot be exaggerated; his doctrinal sophistication, his eloquent judgments, his political skills in building coalitions, and his charisma enabled him to be the person who is mostly identified with the new Israeli jurisprudence.

I believe that identifying the two distinct revolutions is important in providing a better understanding of the political developments and the status of the Court. Liberal values had their heydays in Israel in the 1990s. Liberalism was then a dominant force in the Israeli political and public life. Today (2020), liberalism and liberal values have become marginalized and politicized. Liberal values have resonance, but they have to compete with powerful illiberal and authoritarian political ideologies. Given the decline of liberalism as a dominant force in Israeli politics, it is not surprising that the liberal Court is currently perceived not as an impartial protector of human rights but as a political player in the marketplace of ideas. Interestingly, however, as I show in Section 9.4, much of the criticism of the Court has focused on the judiciary-empowerment revolution rather than on the liberal revolution.

9.4 CRITIQUES OF THE REVOLUTION

Barak's revolutions have been subjected to harsh criticism by politicians, legal theorists, public intellectuals, and others. It is beyond the scope of this chapter to summarize this vast literature;[37] critics have come from both leftist and rightist poles of the political map. Our interest here is in a brief exposition of the rightist opposition. Let me, however, first briefly describe some of the most influential leftist critiques.

A prominent leftist critique is that the Court uses its liberalism as a means of acquiring legitimacy. Arguably, with respect to some major issues, in particular the Israeli–Palestinian conflict, the Court is not particularly liberal; instead, it uses a few

---

[36] For a similar critique, see Harel (*supra* n 1).
[37] For two books devoted to criticisms of different aspects of the legal revolution, see Gideon Sapir, *The Israeli Constitution: From Evolution to Revolution* (Oxford University Press, 2018); Friedmann (*supra* n 7).

"liberal" salient decisions to gain legitimacy. Under this view, a more consistent and thorough examination of the judicial decisions shows that the liberal foundations of Israeli jurisprudence are shaky.[38] It has also been argued that the Court does not challenge (and, as a matter of fact, even entrenches) the most fundamental racist premises of the state, namely its characterization as a Jewish state.[39]

Yet, in the Israeli psyche, the Court is identified as a leftist player and the most influential critiques and, in particular, the claim that the Court is too activist are identified with the right.[40] The standard objection of conservative legal theorists and politicians targets the judiciary-empowerment revolution on the grounds that judiciary empowerment is undemocratic and that it undermines the status of the Knesset and the government. It is undemocratic for two reasons. First, it was argued that the judiciary-empowerment revolution unjustifiably limits the powers of the Knesset and thereby does not give effect to popular sentiments.[41] Second, it was argued that the power of judicial review has never been given to the Court and that by declaring it has such a power, the Court performed a judicial putsch.[42] Let me provide a few examples.

Retired President of the Court Justice Landau criticized the decision of the Court to declare that it has the power of judicial review on the grounds that:

> It is hard for me to understand, how we can derive a revolutionary conclusion that elevating the Court above the legislative branch without an express assertion of the constituent assembly but simply because it fails to declare otherwise. Concerning a democratic judicial review, I fail to understand which kind of democracy allows an oligarchic entity such as the Court to scrutinize democratically-accepted statutes.[43]

More relevant to the future are the statements made by Justice Alex Stein before his recent appointment to the Supreme Court in August 2018. In a Facebook post, Justice Stein asserted that "Israeli judicial activism breaks records: There is no real demand for claimants to have standing and everything is adjudicable, there is no 'political question' doctrine. Despite the fact that the Supreme Court rarely disqualifies Knesset laws, its rhetoric is domineering. It assumes authority under

---

[38]   See, e.g., Ronen Shamir, "Landmark Cases and the Reproduction of Legitimacy: The Case of the Israeli High Court of Justice" (1990) 24 *Law and Society Review* 781.

[39]   See, e.g., Oren Yiftachel, "'Ethnocracy': The Politics of Judaizing Israel/Palestine" (1999) 6 *Constellations* 364.

[40]   This claim is also made by prominent jurists. See, e.g., speech by Menachem Mautner at the University of Tel Aviv (in Hebrew), www.youtube.com/watch?v=MaGOlzc8ydM.

[41]   I have argued in the past against this view and argued that it rests on a misunderstanding of what representation means. See Alon Harel and Ofer Malcai, "Populism, Elitism and Private Reason" (unpublished draft).

[42]   See Gideon Sapir, "25 years to the Constitutional Revolution: A Semi Conspiracy of Smuggling a Constitution to the State of Israel," *Mida*, March 26, 2017 (in Hebrew).

[43]   Moshe Landau, "The Supreme Court As Constitution Maker for Israel" (1996) 3 *Mishpat Umimshal* 697, 705 (in Hebrew).

a façade of checks and balances."[44] Prominent ministers in the government have expressed similar sentiments. Among the more vocal ones is Minister of Justice Ayelet Shaked. Her critique rests on her conviction that the public is inherently wise. Minister Shaked believes that "decision-making and governance are not in the hands of the people but in the hands of the justice system"; due to judicial "supremacy," the elected branches "fail to achieve their goals and fulfil the will of the people."[45] In a pointed manifesto, she argued that representatives "ought to express the will of the people" and that the government is "committed to a people who seeks to determine its fate *directly* and through its representatives."[46] In a similar vein, upon the HCJ invalidating the Anti-Infiltration Law for infringing the Basic Law: Human Dignity and Liberty, Minister Miri Regev declared that the HCJ is "disconnected from the people."[47] Minister Naftali Bennet declared: "The Supreme Court has basically turned itself into the sovereign, the highest authority on everything. That's not what they are supposed to do. They are not supposed to govern. We have been elected. They have not."[48] Alongside these statements, a bill has been proposed to curb the powers of the Court, including its authority to invalidate unconstitutional legislation.[49]

Much of the criticisms of the Court were directed against the decision concerning *Bank Hamizrahi* on the grounds that, in enacting Basic Law: Human Dignity and Liberty, the Knesset never intended to grant the power of judicial review to the courts. President Landau argued:

We have not heard about a constitution that was adopted almost secretly. A constitutional revolution must occur publicly and intentionally. A constitution that changes the relations between different branches of government cannot be accepted without legislative deliberation … In order to elevate the constitution

[44] Mordechai Sones, "Israeli Judicial Activism Breaks Records," *Israel National News*, February 28, 2018, www.israelnationalnews.com/News/News.aspx/242505.

[45] Aviel Mageazi, "Minister Shaked: 'It Seems that the Government Has Gone to Court, People Like Me Are Seen As Dark,'" *Ynet*, May 18, 2015, www.ynet.co.il/articles/0,7340,L-4658424,00.html (in Hebrew); Jonathan Lis, "Shaked: 'We Are Proud of Our Supreme Court, Excellent Justices,'" *Haaretz*, May 12, 2015, www.haaretz.co.il/news/politi/1.2634880 (in Hebrew). See also Yonah Jeremy Bob, "Shaked: Judges Are Not the Sons of Light, Legislators Are Not Sons of Darkness," *Jerusalem Post*, December 22, 2017, www.jpost.com/Israel-News/Shaked-Judges-are-not-the-sons-of-light-legislators-are-not-sons-of-darkness-519767 (Shaked suggesting that judges are members of "detached old elites").

[46] Ayelet Shaked, "The Path to Democracy and Governance" (2016) 1 *Hashiloach* 37, 54 (in Hebrew).

[47] See Ido Ben-Porat, "'The Supreme Court Is Detached from the Public,'" *Israel National News*, July 29, 2015, www.israelnationalnews.com/News/News.aspx/198801.

[48] Raoul Wootliff, "Checking Supreme Court's Powers, Bennet Looks to 'Rebalance' Israeli Democracy," *Times of Israel*, November 19, 2018.

[49] See Draft Bill for Amending the Basic Law: Judiciary (Amendment – Judicial Review of Legislation), 5777–2017 (Private Members Bill), No. P/20/4129, main.knesset.gov.il/Activity/Legislation/Laws/Pages/LawBill.aspx?t=lawsuggestionssearch&lawitemid=2013972. The Bill includes an "override clause" that would enable a majority of 61 Knesset Members (out of 120) to override HCJ decisions that invalidated laws on constitutional grounds. See also "What Is the Public's Opinion on the Override Clause?" (press release), *Israel Democracy Institute*, April 29, 2018, en.idi.org.il/articles/23379.

above regular legislation of the legislative branch it is necessary to make it explicit in the constitution itself (supremacy clause).[50]

A conservative professor of constitutional law, Gideon Sapir, maintained similarly that the decision in *Bank Hamizrahi* is ultimately a judicial putsch as the Knesset had no intention of establishing such a power.[51] The most powerful and passionate critic of the Court is Professor Daniel Friedmann, who argued that "what is hidden here is not a struggle for the rule of law, but a struggle for governance itself."[52] Professor Friedmann added his voice supporting the opponents of the revolution: "[A] democratic state is governed by its elected representatives. The fact that they should be subjected to control and supervision does not justify a revolution which leaves all power in the hands of the supervisors."[53]

While some of the liberal decisions of the Court have been criticized on substantive grounds, the main target of Barak's opponents has been the institutional (judiciary-empowerment) revolution rather than the substantive (liberal) revolution. I will show, however, that the attack on the institutional revolution is hypocritical. What ultimately interests the right-wing critics of the Court is the substantive (liberal) revolution and, consequently, upon being given the opportunity, the conservative critics of the Court do not hesitate to act against their own express democratic, anti-elitist rhetoric. The illiberal critics of the Court promote reforms that ultimately strengthen the courts and, most importantly, despite their pretense of promoting democracy (understood as a majority rule), rely on courts and their broad discretion in implementing an anti-liberal agenda.

9.5 ON DEMOCRATIC HYPOCRISY

The primary claim I defend in this section is that the opposition to the judiciary-empowerment revolution is ultimately a tactical and even hypocritical opposition. Once given the opportunity to steer the political wheel and, in particular, to control judicial appointments, the harsh critics of the legal revolution exploit judicial power to promote their own sectarian illiberal agenda. This also implies, I shall argue, that, while the judiciary-empowerment revolution is here to stay, the liberal revolution is under threat and is most likely to be eroded. The long-term legacy of President Barak is the greater influence of jurists on decision-making.

There are, however, two major clarifications concerning the term "hypocritical."[54] First, among the critics of the Court there are some (in particular academic critics

---

[50] Landau (*supra* n 43) 702.
[51] See Sapir (*supra* n 37). The statements by Professor Gideon Sapir and President Landau reflect their lack of familiarity with the US Constitution, which also does not include a specific provision empowering the Court to intervene.
[52] Friedmann (*supra* n 7) 582 (Hebrew version).
[53] Ibid. 595.
[54] I am grateful to Oren Tamir for stressing this point in a detailed comment on this chapter.

such as Daniel Friedmann) who are indeed passionately concerned about the institutional division of labor and the growing powers of the Court. But those critics have little power and their concerns for transforming the institutional division of labor have little influence on decision-makers. Second, I am not arguing that the critics of the Court intend to deceive the public. I believe that many of them simply care much more about their conservativism than about the institutional division of labor and the growing powers of the Court. While they may genuinely believe that the Court is too strong, their actions and decisions reflect their conservative convictions more than their institutional convictions. Hence, it is only progressive activism that gives rise to criticisms on their part, while conservative activism remains invisible. This is particularly true with respect to political figures such as Minister of Justice Ayelet Shaked and other politicians.

At this stage, one could question why the government would ever be interested in interventionist courts if, after all, it can govern by legislation or by using its domination over the executive branch. The answer is that interventionist conservative courts can promote an authoritarian illiberal agenda in places and contexts that have not even been predicted or expected by the government. Instead of restraining the legislature and the executive, they can promote the agenda of the government beyond the boundaries envisaged by the government itself. The powers of the Court and its broad discretion support and reinforce rather than restrain the powers of the two other branches of government. This, of course, undermines the vision of advocates of the doctrine of separation of powers or the advocates of the principle of the rule of law, but this fact does not detract from the great satisfaction of politicians whose agenda is being reinforced by those who are supposed to monitor them.

Let me illustrate this claim by describing a fresh and sensational drama that took place in Israel just a few months ago, before this chapter was written. The Knesset enacted a new basic law that was initiated and supported precisely by those who complained bitterly about the nondemocratic foundations of the constitutional revolution and the earlier two human rights basic laws. Basic Law: Israel as the Nation-State of the Jewish People (2018) was enacted on July 19, 2018 and it was supported *exclusively* by most of the members of the governing right-wing coalition.[55]

The law that is supposed to entrench Israel as a Jewish state was passed by a very small margin (sixty-two in favor; fifty-five against).[56] So while most of the supporters of this basic law complain bitterly about the small margin in which the previous

---

[55] See Basic Law: Israel the Nation State of the Jewish People, knesset.gov.il/laws/special/eng/BasicLawNationState.pdf. For a description of the history of this basic law and evaluation of its implications, see Alon Harel, "Shifting Towards a Democratic-Authoritarian State: Israel New Nation's State Law," *Verfassungsblog: On Matters Constitutional*, July 31, 2018, verfassungsblog.de/shifting-towards-a-democratic-authoritarian-state-israels-new-nation-state-law/.

[56] Jonathan Lis and Noa Landau, "Israel Passes Controversial Jewish Nation-State Bill After Stormy Debate," *Haaretz*, July 19, 2018, www.haaretz.com/israel-news/israel-passes-controversial-nation-state-bill-1.6291048.

basic laws (human rights basic laws) have been passed (and draw the conclusion that they are not sufficiently representational and therefore illegitimate), they have not followed their own judicial philosophy. Short-term interests, hypocrisy, and most likely intellectual dishonesty led the supporters of this basic law to act against their own philosophical inclinations. Ironically, the law that ceremonially opens with a declaration that "the land of Israel is the historical homeland of the Jewish people" and that is regarded by its supporters as representing the shared and unifying values of the state of Israel was supported only by members of the coalition (and not even by all of them). Even the Israeli president, who is a figurehead and, typically, does not engage in political controversies, made no secret of his opposition to this basic law.[57] Hence, politically speaking, there is no way to describe this law except as a sectarian law that divides rather than unites the nation. It is precisely this accusation that was directed by the members of the right-wing coalition against Basic Law: Human Dignity and Liberty. It seems that, after coming to power and having the opportunity to promote nationalist agenda, the conservatives have forgotten their own institutional convictions and, in particular, their opposition to limiting the powers of the legislature and the executive by enacting basic laws – especially, basic laws that do not enjoy broad consensus.

Further, in contrast to the express commitments of right-wing opponents of the Court, Basic Law: Israel as the Nation State of the Jewish People contains vague assertions of the type that the opponents of the Israeli legal revolution typically condemn. Let me provide one example. Section 7 of the Basic Law asserts: "The state views the development of Jewish settlement as a national value and will act to encourage and promote its establishment and consolidation." To fully understand the potential implications of this section, it is necessary to examine its origins.

The ultimate impetus to enact this provision was an early decision of the Court prohibiting discrimination in land owned by the Jewish Agency. Zionism, at its beginnings, cherished the value of settling in the land. The Zionist organizations bought land and promoted Jewish settlement in the land of Israel. After the independence, remnants of this idea were retained in Israel. In particular, the Israel Land Authority leased some of its lands to Jews only, as, legally speaking, the land officially belonged to Zionist organizations and not to the State. In a famous decision HCJ 6698/95 (Ka'adan),[58] which can be compared only with the famous US *Brown v Board of Education*,[59] the Supreme Court decided that this practice is illegal. The Court argued that the Jewish Agency is a public entity and that it therefore has a duty to treat all citizens equally. Since then, there have been persistent efforts to revive the legality of racially homogenous settlements, but so far these have failed.

---

[57]   Toi Stuff, "Israel's President: Nation State Law Is Bad for Israel and Bad for the Jews," *Times of Israel*, September 6, 2018, www.timesofisrael.com/president-nation-state-law-bad-for-israel-and-bad-for-the-jews/.
[58]   HCJ 6698/95 *Ka'adan v Israel Lands Administration* (2000) 54(1) PD 258.
[59]   *Brown v Board of Education* (1954) 347 US 483.

The proponents of Basic Law: Israel as the Nation State of the Jewish People wished to enact a specific provision to allow the establishment of homogenous settlements in Israel; earlier drafts of the basic law contained a specific provision allowing the state to establish such settlements. Yet the proponents of this early draft failed to gain sufficient support for it. Section 7 was enacted precisely because it leaves this decision ultimately to the courts. Leaving such an important issue in the hands of the courts is evidently incompatible with the anti-activist rhetoric of the conservative forces in Israel, yet this is what has been done.

Given the recent judicial appointments, many of which (although by no means all) rest not on the legal competence of the candidates but on their political inclinations,[60] this may indeed be the practical effect of section 7 to the Basic Law. For my purposes, however, the question of how section 7 of the Basic Law will be interpreted is irrelevant. What *is* significant is the willingness to leave this question to the discretion of courts rather than settle it politically as follows from the standard rhetoric of the conservative forces in Israel. When the conservative right-wingers fail to pass a specific provision, they are more than happy to grant discretionary powers to courts with the hope that the courts will promote their ideological convictions. Let me turn to another example illustrating the willingness to use judicial powers to promote illiberal causes.

In what can only be described as one of the most activist private law decisions in the history of the courts in Israel, Judge Drori (of the District Court) used the newly enacted Basic Law: Israel as the Nation State of the Jewish People in a private law dispute. In this decision, Judge Drori discussed the legal responsibility of the Palestinian authority and the Hamas for a terrorist act committed against a Jewish Israeli citizen.[61] Basic Law: Israel as the Nation State of the Jewish People asserts in section 6 a: "The State will strive to ensure the safety of the members of the Jewish People in trouble or in captivity due to the fact of their Jewishness or their Citizenship." Judge Drori used this provision to justify the imposition of punitive damages on the defendants (charged with terrorist acts).

This use of the basic law in the context of private law was not intended and probably also not foreseen by the initiators of the basic law. The primary goal of the basic law was declarative, and it also meant to give the government the power to promote Jewish sectarian causes at the expense of minorities. This decision seems to be a highly activist decision that deviates radically from what the legislature intended or foresaw.

As a matter of fact, we need not speculate much about this question. In reaching this decision, Judge Drori relied heavily on the activist judicial philosophy of President Barak, in particular Barak's promiscuous interpretative approach to

---

[60] See, e.g., Iddo Baum and Bini Aschkenazi, "Ayelet Shaked's Man for Special Tasks Reveals: That's How We Appointed Judges," *The Marker*, July 19, 2019 (in Hebrew), www.themarker.com/law/.premium-1.7539383.

[61] CC (Jer) 9135–07 *Mashich v The Palestinian Authority* (Nevo, September 17, 2018) (in Hebrew).

constitutional texts. To bolster his conclusion that Basic Law: Israel as the Nation State of the Jewish People should be used in this case, Judge Drori cited President Barak who said: "A constitutional text needs to be interpreted with a broad view and with generosity. The approach need not be technical, legalistic or pedantic. A constitutional text determines the framework of governing and authority and the scope of human and civil rights."[62] In using this citation, Judge Drori associates himself with the jurisprudential presuppositions of the judiciary-empowerment revolution instigated by Barak.

An earlier activist decision promoting right-wing causes was the minority decision by Judge Edmond Levi in HCJ 1661/05.[63] This case was a petition of the Israeli settlers in Gaza who faced forced evacuation after the plan to withdraw from the Gaza Strip. The majority in this case refused to interfere in the decision on the grounds that "[t]he law governing the withdrawal is designed to realize the plan of withdrawal dictated by the government. To the extent that this plan means ending the Israeli control on the territory ... it depends on the broad discretion of the government."[64] The Court therefore deferred to the government on the grounds that the decision concerning withdrawal is a political decision that cannot be overturned by the Court. In contrast, the minority justice, Justice Edmond Levi, expressed a highly interventionist approach and was willing to interfere and frustrate the plan of the government. No other justice on the Court has ever dared to consider this possibility. Justice Levi argued:

> The core of the doctrine of judicial review and primarily the heightened restraint that this Court is required to exercise when facing legislation including matters of state is a fundamental principle and this is known. But and this is the fundamental principle of our legal system is that this Court cannot avoid and is not entitled to do so in a decision on some matters only because it is a state or a political matter. It is the character of adjudication that deals with problems of life and those are often accompanied by political concerns.[65]

To the extent that the judiciary-empowerment revolution had been a genuine concern on the part of illiberal political elites, this decision on the part of Edmond Levi should have been condemned as an outrageous form of judicial intervention. Yet, instead of condemning the justice, in January 2012, he was appointed by Prime Minister Netanyahu to head a three-member committee that was to examine the legal aspects of land ownership in the West Bank.[66] No concerns

---

[62]   Aharon Barak, *Interpretation in Law: Constitutional Interpretation*, vol 3 (Nevo, 1994) 83–4 (in Hebrew).

[63]   HCJ 1661/05 *Hof Aza Regional Council v Knesset of Israel* (2005) 59(2) PD 481 (in Hebrew).

[64]   Ibid. 555–6.

[65]   Ibid. 760.

[66]   For his controversial report, see *The Levy Commission Report on the Legal Status of Building in Judea and Samaria*, June 21, 2012, https://web.archive.org/web/20150508072813/http://regavim.org.il/en/wp-content/uploads/2014/11/The-Levy-Commission-Report-on-the-Legal-Status-of-Building-in-Judea-and-Samaria2.pdf.

about his activism were raised by the proclaimed opponents of the interventionist Court.

Perhaps the greater tolerance of interventionist courts can be explained in purely political terms. In recent years, the new minister of justice Ayelet Shaked has succeeded in influencing the composition of the judiciary. She often expresses the view that judges should be less activist and more deferential. In a ceremony after the appointment of two new justices to the Supreme Court, Minister Shaked stated:

> A year ago I started to change the composition of the Supreme Court by appointing four new Justices. Today I have completed the move by appointing two additional Justices. This is part of the move to bring back the Court to perform its important role: interpreting the norm that was endorsed by the legislature and not its replacement ... I have no doubt that their contribution to the Supreme Court will leave a mark in the pages of history of the Israeli legal system.[67]

Yet, a closer look at the appointments promoted by Minister Shaked indicates that her interest was to promote not more deferential judges but more conservative judges. It is not surprising that the decision of Judge Drori has not been conceptualized by her or any other members of her political circles as an activist decision. Activist decisions that are congenial to nationalist causes are not labeled or categorized as activist. They are simply ignored. As I stated earlier, this is not necessarily because Minister Shaked does not care about the institutional division of labor; she may indeed be convinced that the courts should be less activist. Yet, her passion to promote conservative causes distorts her ability or willingness to discern right-wing activism.

I also do not claim that anti-interventionist sentiments have disappeared. As a matter of fact, in these days a new proposal to introduce a Notwithstanding Clause to the Basic Law: Human Dignity and Liberty is being considered in the Knesset. This provision will clearly limit the powers of the Court. I believe that anti-interventionist sentiments will continue to be used by right-wing parties. Yet, they will be used in a selective way: Interventionism will largely be ignored or perhaps even encouraged when it is designed to promote illiberal or authoritarian causes, at which time the principles of the rule of law and the supremacy of courts will be hailed. It will be condemned and repressed when it is being used to promote liberal causes. As a matter of fact, as shown in this section, this is already the prevailing practice of right-wing politicians.

This observation leads me to a further conclusion: Barak's judiciary-empowerment revolution is here to stay. It seems to accord or, at least, not to conflict with the inclinations of the new right-wing political elites. Ironically, however, the judiciary-empowerment revolution may become the greatest enemy of Barak's liberal revolution.

---

[67] Tova Tzimuki, "Shaked: The Move to Change the Supreme Court Is Complete," *Ynet*, February 23, 2018 (in Hebrew), www.ynet.co.il/articles/0,7340,L-5126984,00.html.

One could have thought that the more liberal segments of the Israeli public would indeed condemn Judge Drori or Justice Levi on the grounds that they are too activist; yet this accusation is rarely used by liberal circles. The false perception that the courts are allies of liberal causes in Israel has been internalized by the liberals and, consequently, interventionist decisions may be condemned by liberals as anti-liberal, discriminatory, or unjust, but not as activist. Activism is an accusation that targets only liberal judicial decisions. This may, perhaps, change in the future as courts become more and more nationalist and illiberal.

These observations have important implications with respect to President Barak and, in particular, to his enduring legacy. First and foremost, his legacy will continue to influence the Israeli judiciary. Despite much anti-activist rhetoric, the activism injected by President Barak will have long-term effects on the Israeli legal system. This is because many of today's jurists, including conservative judges, grew up and were educated in the system and, thus, internalized its values. Further, the activism of the Court, in the long run, promotes the interests of right-wing politicians, in particular given the fact that Minister of Justice Ayelet Shaked was very careful to appoint only judges who share her conservativism.

Much more can be learned from this experience. We can conjecture more generally that structural and institutional revolutions may often have longer and deeper influences than substantive revolutions because such revolutions may be supported by many actors in the political system. The judiciary-empowerment revolution initiated by President Barak is here to stay; his substantive-liberal revolution is likely to be overcome by nationalist and authoritarian political forces.

9.6 CONCLUSION

The conservative forces in Israel have been targeting the alleged activism or over-interventionism of the Court for a long time. This chapter puts forward the suspicion that this accusation is being used tactically to undermine the liberal revolution. The primary concern of the authoritarian political elites in Israel is not the too-great powers of the Court or its interventionist inclinations but its liberal values. When an activist judge promotes conservative or illiberal causes, no outcry concerning activism is to be expected. Judicial activism serves as a political tool to condemn not a liberal judiciary but an activist one. As a matter of fact, the judiciary-empowerment revolution instigated by Barak has become a tool with which to undermine the liberal revolution that he also promoted. Consequently, although President Barak may not favor this result, his judiciary-empowerment revolution is here to stay, while his liberal revolution is currently being overturned.

PN Bhagwati and the Transformation of India's Judiciary

Rehan Abeyratne

A constitution is a totally different kind of enactment than an ordinary statute. It is an organic instrument ... it embodies the hopes and aspirations of the people; it projects certain basic values and it sets out certain objectives and goals. It cannot therefore be interpreted like any ordinary statute. It must be interpreted creatively and imaginatively with a view towards advancing the constitutional values.

—Justice PN Bhagwati[1]

10.1 INTRODUCTION

PN Bhagwati, who served on the Supreme Court of India from 1973 to 1986 (including as chief justice from 1985 to 1986) is widely regarded as the most influential jurist in post-independence India.[2] He almost single-handedly reshaped the Indian higher judiciary through his judgments and rhetorical flair. His engagement with the press and civil society, along with his post-judicial career as a global advocate for human rights, made him a well-known figure beyond legal circles and kept him in the limelight long after his retirement from the Court.

The son of Bombay High Court and Supreme Court Justice NH Bhagwati, PN Bhagwati participated in India's independence struggle in his student days.[3] He was inspired by hearing Mahatma Gandhi speak in 1942 during the Quit India Movement and was jailed for organizing student protests.[4] After more than a decade of legal practice in the Bombay High Court – in which he occupied the same chambers as his father once did – he was appointed to the Gujarat High Court

---

[1] PN Bhagwati, "Fundamental Rights in Their Economic, Social, and Cultural Context" (1988) *Commonwealth Secretariat* 57.

[2] George H Gadbois Jr., *Judges of the Supreme Court of India 1950–89* (Oxford University Press, 2011) 205; Abhinav Chandrachud, *Supreme Whispers: Conversations with Judges of the Supreme Court of India 1980–89* (Penguin/Viking, 2018) 28; Anuj Bhuwania, "P.N. Bhagwati's Legacy: A Controversial Inheritance," *The Hindu*, June 27, 2017, www.thehindu.com/opinion/lead/a-controversial-inheritance/article19150883.ece.

[3] Gadbois (*supra* n 2) 204.

[4] Justice PN Bhagwati, *My Tryst with Justice* (Universal Law Publishing, 2013) 33–6.

in 1960.[5] He spent fourteen years on the Gujarat High Court before his appointment to the Supreme Court.[6]

Justice Bhagwati's fame stems primarily from his contributions to fundamental rights jurisprudence, particularly the advent and entrenchment of public interest litigation (PIL).[7] Justice Bhagwati also advanced the cause of criminal justice reform and access to legal aid. Among other posts, he served as Chairman of the National Committee for the Implementation of Legal Aid Schemes during his justiceship.[8] After retiring from the Supreme Court, Justice Bhagwati became a global advocate for human rights. He served on several United Nations (UN) committees and missions, as well as on domestic oversight and academic bodies.[9] Throughout his career, Justice Bhagwati spoke frequently to the press, academia, and the judiciary on the need for innovative judicial solutions to deeply entrenched social problems.[10] He also authored several books, including an autobiography.[11]

That Justice Bhagwati was a towering judge is beyond dispute. More contested is his legacy. In this chapter, I argue that Bhagwati's greatest strength as a justice – unwavering confidence in the rightness of his cause – turned out to be a grave weakness, causing substantial damage to India's higher judiciary. His trailblazing judgments liberalized procedure and broadened the scope of fundamental rights protection in India. However, his aversion to regular procedural and evidentiary rules imbued the Supreme Court and the High Courts of India with tremendous flexibility and independent authority to dictate the terms of public policy – powers they have not always wielded prudently.[12] Many of Bhagwati's landmark judgments also lack firm doctrinal foundations, and entrenched a style of *ipse dixit* judicial decision-making that persists today.

10.2 JUDICIAL LEGACY

An assessment of Justice Bhagwati's legacy must begin with PIL – the transformative series of judicial innovations in the 1980s with which he is synonymous. This section considers the legal aspects of PIL; namely, the procedural, substantive, and remedial changes that it introduced to fundamental rights adjudication in India. Section 10.3.1 will tackle the motivations and politics behind PIL as well as its institutional consequences.

[5] Ibid. 37–40.
[6] Gadbois (*supra* n 2) 204.
[7] Bhuwania (*supra* n 2).
[8] Gadbois (*supra* n 2) 205.
[9] Ibid. 206–7.
[10] See, e.g., PN Bhagwati, "The Role of the Judiciary in the Democratic Process: Balancing Activism and Judicial Restraint" (1992) 18 *Commonwealth Law Bulletin* 1262.
[11] Bhagwati (*supra* n 4).
[12] See, generally, Anuj Bhuwania, *Courting the People: Public Interest Litigation in Post-Emergency India* (Cambridge University Press, 2017).

PIL was a fundamentally new sort of litigation. It moved away from the traditional Anglo-American model in which lawsuits were winner-take-all contests between two parties (or interests), where the judge acted as a passive referee and the courts focused on providing compensation for past wrongs.[13] Under the PIL paradigm, lawsuits would involve a number of affected individuals or groups, judges would assume an active role in shaping litigation, and courts would order various forms of relief in addition to compensation, including prospective relief that would be monitored and reevaluated over a number of years.[14] The Supreme Court's PIL jurisprudence, led by Justice Bhagwati, therefore, affected every stage of litigation – pre-trial standing and filing requirements, the number and types of rights that could be judicially enforced, and post-trial remedies.

10.2.1 *Relaxed Standing and Filing Requirements*

The adoption of more liberal *locus standi* (or standing) rules was Justice Bhagwati's most significant procedural innovation. The Supreme Court's early fundamental rights jurisprudence imposed strict standing requirements that permitted only individuals directly affected by an impugned law to file petitions under articles 32 and 226 of the Constitution.[15] However, these articles do not require such a formalistic approach to standing. They establish the individual right to petition the Supreme Court and the High Courts, respectively, via "appropriate proceedings" to enforce fundamental rights.[16]

The Supreme Court's interpretation of "appropriate proceedings" would shift over time toward more relaxed standing rules. Justices Bhagwati and Krishna Iyer were the principal architects of this shift.[17] In *Mumbai Kamgar Sabha v Abdulbhai Faizullabhai* (1976), Justice Iyer signaled that the Court would alter its standing requirements to advance the public interest. He wrote: "Public interest is promoted by a spacious construction of *locus standi* in our socio-economic circumstances and conceptual latitudinarianism permits taking liberties with individualisation of the right to invoke the higher courts where the remedy is shared by a considerable number, particularly when they are weaker."[18] A few years later, in *Fertilizer Corporation Kamgar Union v Union of India* (1981),[19] Chief Justice Chandrachud's

---

[13]   Clark D Cunningham, "Public Interest Litigation in Indian Supreme Court: A Study in the Light of American Experience" (1987) 29 *Journal of the Indian Law Institute* 494.

[14]   Parmanand Singh, "Human Rights Protection through Public Interest Litigation" (1999) 45 *Indian Journal of Public Administration* 731.

[15]   *Charanjit Lal v Union of India*, AIR 1951 SC 41; *GC College Silchar v Gauhati* University, AIR 1973 SC 761.

[16]   Constitution of India, articles 32, 226.

[17]   Surya Deva, "Public Interest Litigation in India: A Critical Review" (2009) 28 *Civil Justice Quarterly* 19, 23.

[18]   *Mumbai Kamgar Sabha v Abdulbhai Faizullabhai* (1976) 3 SCC 832, 837–8.

[19]   *Fertilizer Corporation Kamgar Union v Union of India* (1981) 1 SCC 568.

majority opinion hewed to the traditional view that standing under article 32 should remain primarily with those individuals whose rights had been directly affected. However, Justice Iyer, joined by Justice Bhagwati, wrote a concurring opinion that advocated for a more functional approach. As he put it, "locus standi must be liberalised to meet the challenges" facing a developing country like India.[20]

This approach would later prevail in the *First Judges' Case* (1981).[21] The Court, per Justice Bhagwati, held that traditional standing rules were no longer appropriate, as they developed "when private law dominated the legal scene and public law had not yet been born."[22] Thus, to adapt to this new era of public law, the Court rejected the traditional view of standing and recognized the right of any member of the public to petition for redress of a wrong to a "person or to a determinate class of persons … [who] by reason of poverty, helplessness or disability or socially or economically disadvantaged position" cannot approach the Court themselves.[23] From formerly requiring direct injury to petition the Court under article 32, the *First Judges' Case* created "representative standing" – it empowered public-spirited citizens and groups to approach the Court in the interest of those unable to petition the Court themselves.

In a related development, Justice Bhagwati did away with filing formalities under article 32. In what would become known as "epistolary jurisdiction,"[24] he would initiate PILs in response to letters or newspaper articles. Upendra Baxi has shown that a majority of PILs (what he calls "social action litigation") filed from 1980 to 1982 were brought by social activists rather than lawyers. Baxi attributes this development to the fact that Justice Bhagwati served as the chairperson of the National Committee for the Implementation of the Legal Aid Scheme in this period. Serving in these dual roles, he converted letters from the public received by legal aid into PILs when he sat as a Supreme Court justice.[25]

Some of the most significant PILs in the 1980s came about through epistolary jurisdiction, where litigation would be initiated by advocates or by judges themselves in response to media reports and letters.[26] For instance, one prominent case reached the Supreme Court due to a series of articles published in the *Indian Express* newspaper that came to Justice Bhagwati's attention.[27] These articles revealed that prisoners had been kept in state custody awaiting trial for so long that, in many cases, the period of detention was longer than the criminal sentence would have been. Justice Bhagwati held on behalf of the Court that this practice violated the right to speedy trial guaranteed under the right to life and liberty under article 21 of the

[20]   Ibid. 584 (Krishna Iyer, J, concurring).
[21]   *SP Gupta v Union of India* (1981) SCC (Supp) 87 (*First Judges' Case*).
[22]   Ibid. 205.
[23]   Ibid. 210.
[24]   Bhagwati (*supra* n 4) 77.
[25]   Upendra Baxi, "Taking Suffering Seriously" (1985) 4 *Third World Legal Studies* 107, 118.
[26]   See, e.g., *Sunil Batra v Delhi Administrator*, AIR 1980 SC 1579; *Dr. Upendra Baxi v State of UP* (1982) 2 SCC 308; *Vikram Deo Singh v State of Bihar* (1988) SCC (Supp) 734.
[27]   *Hussainara Khatoon v State of Bihar* AIR 1979 SC 1369.

Constitution. He further urged the central and state governments to adopt comprehensive legal services for indigent criminal defendants under article 39A: a directive principle that calls for the provision of free legal aid. This case built upon a long line of post-Emergency cases in which the Supreme Court sought to improve prison conditions and uphold the rights of prisoners.[28]

In *Bandhua Mukti Morcha v Union of India* (1984),[29] the Supreme Court, again led by Justice Bhagwati, initiated a PIL in response to a letter it received from a nongovernmental organization (NGO). The letter described the horrific conditions in which bonded laborers worked and urged the Court to end this practice. As we will see, *Morcha* assumed great significance, as it revolutionized the judiciary's evidentiary and pleading rules for PIL.

10.2.2 *Broadening the Right to Life and Liberty*

In the 1980s, the Supreme Court expanded article 21 of the Indian Constitution to encompass due process and socioeconomic rights. This substantive move in the law is often distinguished from PIL, which conventionally refers to procedural innovations. However, Justice Bhagwati saw them as closely intertwined and he gets much of the credit for both developments.

The legal gymnastics required to recognize due process and socioeconomic rights under article 21 were substantial. Article 21 was drafted narrowly to provide: "No person shall be deprived of his life or personal liberty except according to procedure established by law." In *Maneka Gandhi v Union of India* (1978), the Supreme Court revisited its earlier rulings that declined to read a due process requirement into article 21.[30] In this case, Maneka Gandhi, Indira Gandhi's daughter-in-law, alleged that the ruling Janata government had illegally seized her passport under the Passport Act of 1967. She argued that the Act contained no procedural guidelines for how to seize a citizen's passport and that, even if such a procedure existed, it was arbitrary and unreasonable and therefore violated articles 14, 19, and 21 of the Constitution.

Writing for the Court, Justice Bhagwati construed the phrase "personal liberty" to include the right to travel abroad. He said: "[t]he expression 'personal liberty' in Article 21 is of the widest amplitude and it covers a variety of rights which go to constitute the personal liberty of man."[31] Justice Bhagwati further observed that the relevant statute did not provide a reasonable opportunity for the petitioner to be heard before her passport was impounded. He said, therefore, that principles of "natural justice" had to be read into article 21 so as "to invest law with fairness."[32]

---

[28] See Upendra Baxi, *The Indian Supreme Court and Politics: Mehr Chand Mahajan Memorial Lectures* (Eastern Book Company, 1979) 233–45.

[29] *Bandhua Mukti Morcha v Union of India* (1984) 3 SCC 161.

[30] *Maneka Gandhi v Union of India* (1978) 1 SCC 248.

[31] Ibid. 280.

[32] Ibid. 284–5.

The Court held that the Act arbitrarily deprived the petitioner of personal liberty under article 21. In so doing, it adopted a due process standard drawn from the Fifth and Fourteenth Amendments of the US Constitution.[33] Despite the constitutional framers' deliberate omission of the words "due process" and clear precedent to the contrary,[34] the Court here expanded the meaning of article 21 – and thereby expanded its authority – to require the government to show not only that a deprivation of life or liberty is conducted pursuant to a procedure established by law but also that this procedure is reasonable and not "arbitrary, fanciful, or oppressive."[35]

A few years later, the Supreme Court, led by Justice Bhagwati, would expand the scope of article 21 to include socioeconomic rights. To accomplish this feat, Justice Bhagwati interpreted the right to life to encompass some of the Directive Principles of State Policy (DPSPs). The DPSPs are located in Part IV of the Constitution, following the section on fundamental rights. While fundamental rights in Part III – like the right to life and personal liberty in article 21 – can be enforced in court through articles 32 and 226 of the Constitution, the DPSPs are explicitly nonjusticiable. Indeed, article 37 provides that they "shall not be enforceable by any court" even though they are "fundamental in the governance of the country and it shall be the duty of the State to apply these principles in making laws."[36]

As this language suggests, the DPSPs were intended to complement the fundamental rights contained in Part III of the Constitution. The historian Granville Austin put it as follows: "Both types of rights had developed as a common demand, products of the national and social revolutions, of their almost inseparable inter-twining, and of the character of Indian politics itself."[37] He would further credit the directive principles with setting forth "humanitarian precepts that were ... the aims of the Indian social revolution."[38] For instance, the DPSPs provide, among other things, that "the State shall ... direct its policy towards securing ... the right to an adequate means of livelihood" and that the "health and strength of workers ... are not abused."[39]

In *Francis Coralie Mullin* v *Union Territory of Delhi* (1981), the Supreme Court was asked to determine whether a detainee held in preventative detention had the right to meet with his lawyer and family.[40] While the case raised only this narrow issue, the Court, led by Justice Bhagwati, saw an opportunity to expand the meaning of article 21 further. It held that the right to life includes a broader right to "live with

---

[33] Manoj Mate, "The Origins of Due Process in India: The Role of Borrowing in Personal Liberty and Preventative Detention Cases" (2010) 28 *Berkeley Journal of International Law* 216, 249.

[34] *Gopalan* v *State of Madras* (1950) SCR 88.

[35] *Maneka Gandhi* v *Union of India* (1978) 1 SCC at 284.

[36] Constitution of India, article 37.

[37] Granville Austin, *The Indian Constitution: Cornerstone of Nation* (Oxford University Press, 1999) 52.

[38] Ibid. 75.

[39] Constitution of India, articles 39(a), 39(e).

[40] *Francis Coralie Mullin* v *Union Territory of Delhi* (1981) 1 SCC 608.

human dignity."[41] This included "the bare necessities of life such as adequate nutrition, clothing and shelter."[42] In adopting this expansive interpretation, Justice Bhagwati made clear his belief in a flexible, adaptive reading of the Constitution. In his view, "[a] constitutional provision must be construed, not in a narrow and constricted sense, but in a wide and liberal manner so as to anticipate and take account of changing conditions and purposes."[43] The Supreme Court would follow this interpretative approach in later cases to recognize a number of justiciable socioeconomic rights including, inter alia, the rights to work,[44] health,[45] education,[46] food,[47] and shelter.[48] As I have argued elsewhere, while the recognition of these rights is laudable, the doctrinal basis for their *judicial* enforcement is tenuous at best.[49] It goes against the plain meaning of article 37 of the Constitution, and Justice Bhagwati did not provide a persuasive explanation for his departure from the text.[50] This is in keeping with his disdain for legal formalism and desire to untether the Indian legal system from conservative precedents.

Justice Bhagwati explained his departures from traditional rules and doctrines by employing practical reasoning that linked socioeconomic concerns with procedural flexibility. Indeed, as one seminal study of PIL put it, standing rules had to be changed "because the very purpose of the law itself was undergoing a transformation. It was being used to foster social justice by creating new categories of rights."[51] This transformation was closely linked to the changes in the Supreme Court's interpretation of article 21. Justice Bhagwati explicitly made this connection between procedural and substantive innovations in *First Judges' Case*. He noted that fundamental rights were "practicably meaningless ... unless accompanied by social rights necessary to make them effective and really accessible to all."[52] By "social rights," Justice Bhagwati meant DPSPs, which he believed were inextricably linked to the fundamental rights in Part III of the Constitution.[53]

For Bhagwati, the traditional model of litigation was inadequate to protect the public interest from acts that harmed large swathes of the population. Liberal

---

[41]   Ibid. 618.
[42]   Ibid. 618–19.
[43]   Ibid. 618.
[44]   *Morcha* (*supra* n 29).
[45]   *Paschim Banga Khet Mazdoor Samity v State of West Bengal* (1996) 4 SCC 37.
[46]   *Unni Krishnan v State of Andhra Pradesh* (1993) 1 SCC 645.
[47]   *PUCL v Union of India*, Writ Petition (Civil) No. 196 (2001).
[48]   *Olga Tellis v Bombay Municipal Corporation* (1985) 3 SCC 545.
[49]   Rehan Abeyratne, "Socioeconomic Rights in the Indian Constitution: Toward a Broader Conception of Legitimacy" (2014) 39 *Brooklyn Journal of International Law* 1.
[50]   Ibid. 62–6.
[51]   PP Craig and SL Deshpande, "Rights, Autonomy and Process: Public Interest Litigation in India" (1989) 9 *Oxford Journal of Legal Studies* 356, 361.
[52]   *First Judges' Case* (*supra* n 21) 213.
[53]   Ibid. at 214.

standing rules were, therefore, justified not just functionally but also instrumentally –
they permitted the Court to give broader (and, in Justice Bhagwati's view, proper)
meaning to Part III of the Constitution, by supplementing fundamental rights with
directive principles.

10.2.3 *Post-Trial Remedies and Monitoring Mechanisms*

In the post-trial phase, Justice Bhagwati introduced great remedial flexibility in
fundamental rights cases.[54] Following his lead, Indian courts have been willing to
issue a range of remedies, both traditional and innovative, depending on the nature
of the case and the needs of the parties. Remedies are often specific and detailed,
requiring the state to adopt positive measures not only to compensate victims of
fundamental rights violations but also to rehabilitate them over time. This is
achieved through innovations such as continuing mandamus and monitoring agencies that permit courts to issue interim orders and directions in PILs for several years
after cases are heard.

Take, for instance, *Bandhua Mukti Morcha*. The Supreme Court, per Justice
Bhagwati, held in favor of bonded laborers in a stone quarry and recognized a broad
right to work. The Court ordered state authorities to take a number of measures to
rehabilitate the workers and to create a safe work environment going forward.
Authorities were directed to work with NGOs to pay workers a minimum wage,
educate them on their legal rights, provide free education to their children, and
ensure that working conditions are safe, pollution-free, and equipped with proper
medical facilities.[55]

Justice Bhagwati in *Morcha* entrenched two monitoring mechanisms to ensure
the implementation of the Court's orders. First, he initiated continuing mandamus,
which permits courts to enforce their orders on a continuous basis even after
litigation ends.[56] Generally, the mechanism for enforcement is a series of interim
orders that allows the court not only to keep track of whether government schemes
meet judicial guidelines but also to instruct the government on how to execute those
schemes. The second enforcement mechanism adopted in *Morcha* was monitoring
agencies. The Court issued twenty-one directions in that case.[57] Among other things,
It appointed a joint secretary in the Ministry of Labour to visit the stone quarries at
issue and report on the implementation of those directions.[58]

---

[54] Jaime Cassels, "Judicial Activism and Public Interest Litigation in India: Attempting the Impossible?"
(1989) 37 *American Journal of Comparative Law* 495, 505–6.

[55] *Morcha* (*supra* n 29) 219–22.

[56] See Rohan J Alva, "Continuing Mandamus: A Sufficient Protector of Socio-Economic Rights in
India?" (2014) 44 *Hong Kong Law Journal* 207.

[57] *Morcha* (*supra* n 29) 219–22.

[58] Ibid. 222–3.

Justice Bhagwati was also an early advocate for awarding monetary damages in PIL cases.[59] In early constitutional tort cases, the Supreme Court awarded damages to prisoners in Bihar who alleged that they were unlawfully imprisoned[60] or held in pre-trial detention for longer periods than the maximum possible sentence.[61] In another case, the Court found that prisoners had been blinded by the police and awarded them both compensation for the rest of their lives and vocational training in an institute for the blind.[62] While these cases were once the province of private law, they have become constitutionalized and reached the higher judiciary as fundamental rights cases.[63]

Bhagwati further extended constitutional tort jurisdiction to cases between private parties. Consider *MC Mehta v Union of India*.[64] Led by then-Chief Justice Bhagwati, the Supreme Court crafted new remedies for victims of a toxic gas leak from a fertilizer factory. The Court declined to rule on whether the factory's owner, Delhi Cloth Mills Limited, was an agency of the state under article 12 of the Constitution.[65] Since only the state can be liable for fundamental rights violations, the Court could not impose liability on Delhi Cloth Mills Limited or order it to pay damages. However, the Court directed the Delhi Legal Aid and Advice Board to file claims for compensation on behalf of all the victims in "the appropriate court."[66] Thus, even if Chief Justice Bhagwati could not provide a public law remedy, he nonetheless was able to use the PIL mechanism to ensure representation in lower courts for the victims.

Chief Justice Bhagwati also ensured that victims of this accident and all future such accidents would almost certainly prevail in their claims for compensation. At the end of his *MC Mehta* opinion, he declared that hazardous or inherently dangerous activities must be adjudicated under a new, heightened standard of liability. He referred to this new standard as "absolute liability," which holds tortfeasors liable for damages if their hazardous or dangerous enterprise results in injuries, regardless of whether they were at fault.[67] This is more stringent than the strict liability standard established in the classic British case *Rylands v Fletcher*,[68] which exempts defendants from liability when the injury is caused by an act of God

---

[59] See SP Sathe, *Judicial Activism in India* (Oxford University Press, 2002) 232–5.

[60] *Rudul Shah v State of Bihar* (1983) 3 SCR 508.

[61] Jeremy Cooper, "Poverty and Constitutional Justice: The Indian Experience" (1993) 44 *Mercer Law Review* 611, 631.

[62] Ibid.; *Khatri v State of Bihar* (1981) 2 SCR 408.

[63] Rehan Abeyratne, "Ordinary Wrongs as Constitutional Rights: The Public Law Model of Torts in South Asia" (2018) 54 *Texas International Law Journal* 1; Shyamkrishna Balganesh, "The Constitutionalization of Indian Private Law" in Sujit Choudhry, Madhav Khosla, and Pratap Bhanu Mehta (eds.), *The Oxford Handbook of the Indian Constitution* (Oxford University Press, 2016).

[64] *MC Mehta v Union of India* (1987) 1 SCC 395.

[65] Ibid. paras 9–30.

[66] Ibid. para 33.

[67] Ibid. para 31.

[68] *Rylands v Fletcher* [1868] UKHL 1 (Eng.).

or a third party (stranger). Absolute liability has no such exceptions,[69] which means that causation is wholly removed from the analysis – if a dangerous or hazardous activity results in injuries, the defendant will be liable.

Chief Justice Bhagwati's justification for deriving this new doctrine contained his distinctly anti-colonial flavor. Because of their British ancestry and relative narrowness of scope, he viewed traditional tort principles as inapposite in the Indian context. In his words:

> We cannot allow our judicial thinking to be constricted by reference to the law as it prevails in England or for that matter in any foreign country. We no longer need the crutches of a foreign legal order … We in India cannot hold our hands back and I venture to evolve a new principle of liability which English courts have not done.[70]

The doctrine of absolute liability has been hailed as a landmark achievement of Indian jurisprudence. Jamie Cassels, for instance, praised the principle for ensuring "that the full social costs of productions are considered in making risk management decisions."[71]

A more cynical view is that Justice Bhagwati crafted this doctrine to ensure that victims of the Union Carbide (UCC) Bhopal gas leak – the largest chemical disaster in Indian history – would be compensated after he retired from the bench in 1986. *MC Mehta* was decided while the Bhopal litigation was wending its way through the legal system. Tellingly, *MC Mehta* was also decided a day before Justice Bhagwati retired.[72] Following his retirement, Justice Bhagwati served on the legal aid committee formed by the central government to assist Bhopal victims.[73] In 1989, the Supreme Court upheld a final settlement of US$ 470 million between the Indian government and UCC.[74] In its submissions to the Court, UCC argued strongly against the validity of *MC Mehta*, referring to it as "[a] politically motivated judgment that was out of line with Indian law."[75] This was almost certainly a swipe at Justice Bhagwati, whose impartiality in *MC Mehta*, and indeed throughout his judicial career, was suspect. Section 10.3 will consider, among other things, the effect of his political views on PIL jurisprudence.

10.3 INSTITUTIONAL LEGACY

Justice Bhagwati's institutional legacy is a complicated one. On the one hand, his PIL-related innovations reshaped the Indian higher judiciary; on the other hand, he

---

[69] Ibid.
[70] *MC Mehta* (*supra* n 64) para 31.
[71] Cassels (*supra* n 54) 26. For a critique of absolute liability, see Abeyratne (*supra* n 63).
[72] Bhagwati (*supra* n 4) 114.
[73] Gadbois (*supra* n 2) 207.
[74] *Union Carbide Corp.* v *Union of India* (1989) 3 SCC 38.
[75] Cassels (*supra* n 54) 36.

was far less effective in his dealings with colleagues and political leaders, and his penchant for self-promotion often worked to his detriment.

10.3.1 *Institutional Effects of PIL*

Justice Bhagwati, in his tenure on the Supreme Court, sought to exercise a higher degree of judicial review over the actions of elected authorities. By adopting looser standing rules, the Court would enable the public to hold authorities accountable to the judiciary and not merely to the "sweet will" of the authorities themselves.[76] The notion of "representative standing" has become the norm in PIL cases – lawyers, medical practitioners, journalists, and NGOs have filed writ petitions alleging fundamental rights violations on behalf of disadvantaged groups.[77] Moreover, the Supreme Court has appointed *amicus curiae* to represent the interests raised in a PIL if the petitioner fails to act in good faith or does not want to pursue the litigation further.[78] As a result, the Indian judiciary today can hear a substantially higher number of fundamental rights cases, affecting larger communities, than it could before 1980.

This development has been a mixed blessing. While PIL has expanded access to justice, it has also come at a high cost to evidentiary rules and the burden of proof. *Bandhua Mukti Morcha* brought significant innovations with respect to evidence, including appointing socio-legal commissions of inquiry and shifting the burden of proof. As with the changes in pre-trial proceedings, there was a functional, egalitarian rationale behind these innovations. They were designed to democratize the trial process by reducing the expenses of gathering and presenting evidence of widespread fundamental rights violations.[79] As Justice Bhagwati later explained, large fundamental rights cases involving the "poor and oppressed" were "qualitatively different" from the cases traditionally on the Court's docket.[80] These cases required the Court to abandon the *"laissez-faire"* approach.[81] By laissez-faire, Justice Bhagwati meant the traditional, common law approach where the justices passively observed arguments from two opposing sides and adjudicated between them. This calls to mind the oft-repeated analogy of judges to referees or umpires – they do not make the rules; they simply (and neutrally) apply them. Under the PIL model, judges would break this mold and play an active role in trial proceedings.

---

[76] *First Judges' Case (supra* n 21) 212.
[77] Ashok H Desai and S Muralidhar, "Public Interest Litigation: Potential and Problems" in BN Kirpal, Ashok H Desai, Gopal Subramanian, Rajeev Dhavan, and Raju Ramchandran (eds.), *Supreme but Not Infallible: Essays in Honour of the Supreme Court of India* (Oxford University Press, 2000) 163.
[78] See, e.g., *Sheela Barse v Union of India* (1988) 4 SCC 226.
[79] Cooper (*supra* n 61) 625.
[80] PN Bhagwati, "Social Action Litigation: The Indian Experience" in Neelan Tiruchelvam and Radhika Coomaraswamy (eds.), *The Role of the Judiciary in Plural Societies* (Francis Pinter, 1987) 27.
[81] Ibid.

The Supreme Court began appointing socio-legal commissions in the early 1980s. These commissions would investigate facts on the Court's behalf and deliver a detailed report setting out their findings and recommendations.[82] In *Morcha*, the Court, led by Justice Bhagwati, appointed special commissioners to investigate the practice of bonded labor.[83] The Court directed two lawyers (advocates) to visit stone quarries in Faridabad, Haryana. They were asked to interview individuals named in the writ petition in order to ascertain whether they were working at these quarries willingly. The commissioners' report confirmed the existence of bonded labor at these quarries and further observed the laborers' "helplessness, poverty and extreme exploitation at the hands of moneyed people."[84] It concluded: "[P]erhaps beast and animal could be leading more comfortable life [sic] than these helpless labourers."[85] The Court ordered this report to be circulated to all respondents, inviting their responses.

At the same time, the Court appointed Dr. Patwardhan, a professor of sociology from the Indian Institute of Technology, to conduct a "socio-legal investigation" into the working conditions of these bonded laborers. Justice Bhagwati went to great lengths to assure the Haryana government that it should treat this investigation not as a criticism but as an opportunity to remedy existing legal violations. This is an extraordinary gesture, one that seeks to co-opt the state to assist with a legal proceeding in which it is the respondent. At another point in his *Morcha* majority opinion, Justice Bhagwati ventured even further to suggest that PIL was nonadversarial. He encouraged state authorities to "welcome public interest litigation, because it would [allow the government] … to examine whether the poor and downtrodden are getting their social and economic entitlements."[86]

Toward the end of the instructions to Dr. Patwardhan, Justice Bhagwati asked all parties to work together toward a long-term scheme for the bonded laborers. In a subsequent interview, he would describe PIL as a sort of "collaborative litigation" where the petitioner, the government, and the Court work together, rather than as adversaries, to determine the best solutions to major social problems.[87] The *Morcha* case saw "collaborative litigation" in action: the Haryana government assisted in the socio-legal investigation by paying Rs 1,500 to cover Dr. Patwardhan's work.[88]

These new methods of gathering evidence also affected how that evidence was presented. For instance, reports submitted by socio-legal commissioners were collected *ex parte*, with no opportunity for cross-examination.[89] The reports were circulated to all parties who could respond via affidavits to challenge any facts or

---

[82] Ibid.
[83] *Morcha (supra* n 29).
[84] Ibid. 179.
[85] Ibid.
[86] *Morcha (supra* n 29) 182–3.
[87] Cunningham (*supra* n 13) 504 (quoting Justice Bhagwati's interview with Frontline).
[88] *Morcha (supra* n 29).
[89] Cassels (*supra* n 54) 500.

data gathered by the special commissioners. As a matter of constitutional interpretation, this is permissible. Article 32 of the Constitution simply requires petitioners alleging fundamental rights violations to move the Supreme Court by "appropriate proceedings" – a flexible phrase that Justice Bhagwati construed broadly to dispense with formal evidentiary rules. As he put it in *Morcha*, "[i]t is not at all obligatory that an adversarial procedure, where each party produces his own evidence tested by cross-examination ... and the judge sits like an umpire ... must be followed in a proceeding under Article 32."[90]

An important corollary to these new evidentiary procedures was a shift in the burden of proof. In *Morcha*, the Haryana government contended that petitioners (the bonded laborers) had the burden of proving that the state had violated their fundamental rights. Ordinarily, this would be an unremarkable claim – the common law has long recognized that the moving party bears the evidentiary burden in court. But Justice Bhagwati refused to accept this in the context of PIL. Once again, his justification for deviating from this well-established procedural doctrine was both functional and egalitarian. He said: "[S]trict adherence to the adversarial procedure can sometimes lead to injustice, particularly when the parties are not evenly balanced in social or economic strength."[91] For Bhagwati, this sort of injustice, where indigent parties lack the means to submit sufficient evidence, called for him to intervene. He noted that if the Court did not appoint special commissioners and shift the burden of proof, "fundamental rights would remain merely a teasing illusion so far as the poor and disadvantaged sections of the community are concerned."[92] As a result of the *Morcha* judgment, petitioners in PIL cases need not prove fundamental rights violations. The Court, armed with prima facie evidence and recommendations from socio-legal commissioners, may make that determination independently.[93]

What is remarkable about these institutional changes is the extent to which they were driven by one justice's desire to deliver socioeconomic justice. To fully realize fundamental rights, procedures had to be adapted to allow indigent and marginalized groups not only to file writ petitions but also to have the institutional support to investigate and report violations. Access to justice, in this context, is more than a means to achieve greater socioeconomic justice: it is an integral part of socioeconomic justice. And it assumes great importance – greater importance, it turned out, than formal evidentiary rules or the standard burden of proof.

This approach puts enormous strain on defendants – usually, the government. It appears in many cases that judges accept PIL petitions because they are personally moved or troubled by particular issues or events and are, therefore, unlikely to hear evidence from both sides objectively. By calling PIL "collaborative litigation,"[94]

90 *Morcha* (*supra* n 29) 188.
91 Ibid. 189.
92 Ibid. 190.
93 Ibid. 191.
94 Cunningham (*supra* n 13) 504.

Justice Bhagwati essentially admits that the government has no chance of winning a PIL case, so it might as well participate in remedying the injustice alleged.

Another unfortunate effect of Justice Bhagwati's approach is that judges have almost untrammeled power to initiate, mold, and expand litigation as they see fit. The Supreme Court and the High Courts may even initiate PIL proceedings on their *suo motu* authority when the need arises.[95] As Anuj Bhuwania has argued, judges under PIL "could now give free rein to their ideological predilections; their awesome power had no limits except their own sense of judgment."[96] Moreover, as he makes clear, that sense of judgment has often been lacking. The Delhi High Court, for instance, employed PIL as a "slum demolition machine," razing illegal settlements with neither a plan for resettling the residents nor an opportunity for them to be heard in court.[97] In a cruel irony, these communities' fundamental right to shelter – derived from Justice Bhagwati's right to life jurisprudence – was denied in exercising the procedural flexibility he introduced through PIL.

10.3.2 *Relationships with Colleagues and Political Leaders*

Justice Bhagwati's dealings with the political leadership, especially the dominant Indian Congress Party, often worked to the detriment of his reputation and his relationships with judicial colleagues. This began when Bhagwati was on the Gujarat High Court, where he served for fourteen years before his elevation to the Supreme Court.[98] Though he was finally appointed to the Supreme Court in 1973, he was unsuccessfully nominated in 1970 and 1972. In 1970, Chief Justice JC Shah first nominated Bhagwati to the Supreme Court, but the nomination was blocked by Justice JM Shelat.[99] Shelat had previously served as chief justice of the Gujarat High Court, where he developed animus toward Bhagwati. This ill will, at least in part, arose from a speech Bhagwati made to an audience that included Union Law Minister HR Gokhale in which he proclaimed that all judges should be committed to the Congress Party.[100] Bhagwati himself thought that Justice Shelat "blackballed his elevation to the Supreme Court," though he attributed it to a family affair involving Shelat's daughter seeking to marry one of Bhagwati's brothers, who declined the offer.[101]

Justice Shelat may have played a role in blocking Bhagwati's nomination again in 1972.[102] In that instance, the law minister (Gokhale) and former chief justice Gajendragadkar also intervened to stop his appointment in order to ensure that their preferred candidate (and fellow Maharashtrian) YV Chandrachud was appointed

95 See, e.g., *In Re: Networking of Rivers*, Writ Petition (Civil) No. 512 of 2002.
96 Bhuwania (*supra* n 12) 44.
97 Ibid. 80–106.
98 Gadbois (*supra* n 2) 204.
99 Ibid. 194.
100 Chandrachud (*supra* n 2) 22–3.
101 Ibid. 23.
102 Gadbois (*supra* n 2) 195.

first.[103] Since the chief justice is usually chosen by seniority, the prior appointment of Chandrachud, who, like Bhagwati, was relatively young, would ensure that he was chief justice for an extended period.[104] Indeed, Chandrachud went on to become the longest serving chief justice in Indian history. He served in that position for more than seven years; Bhagwati was chief justice for a little more than one year.[105]

Given their closely related careers, it is not surprising that Bhagwati and Chandrachud had an antagonistic relationship. According to Abhinav Chandrachud (YV Chandrachud's grandson), their rivalry perhaps stretched back to their days on the Bombay Bar, where Bhagwati's father – who was a Bombay High Court judge – apparently disliked Chandrachud and other potential rivals to his son.[106] Their animosity toward each other became public on the Supreme Court, such that the Court became divided into two camps: one favoring Chandrachud, the other Bhagwati.[107] Many of the more senior justices were antithetical to PIL – one of them even referred to it mockingly as "publicity interest litigation."[108] For Bhagwati and his allies, these justices were elitist scions of a bygone era, trained at Oxbridge and out of touch with the real India.[109] As for Chandrachud, Bhagwati thought him an ineffectual leader.[110] He further "torpedoed" two of Chandrachud's nominations to the Court and criticized him in judicial opinions in two landmark cases: *Minerva Mills* and the *First Judges' Case*.[111]

Before discussing those cases, it is worth noting that both Chandrachud and Bhagwati were part of the Supreme Court majority that upheld prime minister Indira Gandhi's emergency powers. In one of the darkest moments in post-independence India, the Supreme Court failed to stand against the Gandhi regime's abuses of power during the Emergency (1975–7), when, among other things, she suspended habeas corpus, severely restricted civil liberties and the freedom of the press, and passed four constitutional amendments to curb judicial power.[112] In *ADM Jabalpur* v *Shiv Kant Shukla* (1976),[113] members of the political opposition, who were detained under the 1971 Maintenance of Internal Security Act (MISA), filed petitions for writs of habeas corpus to challenge their detention. A five-judge bench of the Supreme Court (including Bhagwati and Chandrachud) denied their petitions, holding that under a presidentially declared emergency, the government may deny political detainees access to court.

[103]   Ibid.
[104]   Chandrachud was one year older than Bhagwati and was appointed to the Supreme Court at the age of fifty-two. India sets a mandatory retirement age of sixty-five for Supreme Court justices.
[105]   Gadbois (*supra* n 2) 256, 295.
[106]   Chandrachud (*supra* n 2) 21.
[107]   Ibid. 28.
[108]   Ibid. 35.
[109]   Ibid. 37–8.
[110]   Ibid. 27.
[111]   Ibid. 26.
[112]   Mate (*supra* n 33) 243.
[113]   *ADM Jabalpur* v *Shiv Kant Shukla*, AIR 1976 SC 1207.

A few years later in *Minerva Mills* v *Union of India* (1980),[114] the Supreme Court was asked to rule on the constitutionality of article 31-C of the Constitution, which had been inserted via section 4 of the Forty-Second Amendment. This Amendment, one of the most controversial acts during the Emergency, immunized laws aimed at securing any of the DPSPs from legal challenges on the grounds of article 14 (right to equality) and article 19 (right to freedom). Section 55 of the Forty-Second Amendment was also at issue. It explicitly aimed to nullify the *Kesavananda* judgment, which held that there is an unamendable core or "basic structure" of the Constitution.[115] Section 55 provided that constitutional amendments were beyond the scope of judicial review as the constituent power of Parliament was unlimited.

Chief Justice Chandrachud delivered the majority opinion in *Minerva Mills*, which held both these sections unconstitutional. Section 55 violated the Constitution's basic structure by assigning unfettered amendment authority to parliament. As the chief justice said, "a limited amending power is one of the basic features of our Constitution, and therefore, the limitations on that power cannot be destroyed."[116] The Court also struck down section 4, holding that it constituted part of the basic structure and therefore could not be altered by parliament. Section 4 of the Forty-Second Amendment gave the DPSPs primacy over the fundamental rights and therefore ran afoul of the balance between Parts III and IV of the Constitution.[117]

Justice Bhagwati's minority opinion in this case concurred with the majority on section 55 but disagreed on the constitutionality of section 4. For Bhagwati, the fact that the DPSPs in Part IV are nonjusticiable did not diminish their importance vis-à-vis fundamental rights in Part III. Thus, Justice Bhagwati concluded that it was reasonable for parliament to resolve this conflict and to do so in favor of DPSPs.[118]

The charitable explanation for Justice Bhagwati's support of section 4 is that it comports with his career-long concern for social justice. Indeed, his minority opinion in *Minerva Mills* formed the basis for his judgment in *Francis Coralie Mullin*, which recognized a right to live with human dignity under article 21 of the Constitution. The less generous interpretation is that this opinion fits within his long-standing support of the Congress Party and Indira Gandhi in particular. Following the Emergency, Gandhi held national elections in 1977 and lost to the opposition Janata Party. She returned to power in 1980 and received a glowing letter of support from Justice Bhagwati. This letter was later leaked to the press in what was, at the time, the "most scandalous incident" ever involving a Supreme Court justice.[119]

---

[114] *Minerva Mills* v *Union of India* (1980) 3 SCC 625.
[115] *Kesavananda Bharati* v *State of Kerala* (1973) SCC 225.
[116] *Minerva Mills* (*supra* n 114) 643.
[117] Ibid. 654.
[118] Ibid. 713.
[119] Chandrachud (*supra* n 2) 25. However, Bhagwati appears to have been a fair-weather friend. He once referred to Gandhi's prior electoral loss as a "crushing defeat . . . symptomatic of complete alienation between the Government and the people."

Moreover, as Anuj Bhuwania has argued in a revisionist account of the origins of PIL, Bhagwati promoted two planks of Indira Gandhi's attack on the judiciary: the "inaccessibility of the legal system and its alien British form."[120] He then benefited from the solutions, including the expansion of legal aid, that were part of the Emergency policy agenda. Indeed, Indira Gandhi established the Committee on Implementation of Legal Aid Schemes in 1980, on the advice of reports authored by Bhagwati and Krishna Iyer in the 1970s.[121]

Justice Bhagwati was less successful in getting his nominees appointed to the Supreme Court during his stint as chief justice. According to George Gadbois in his seminal study of Indian Supreme Court justices, it was widely known that Bhagwati wanted "activists" who "shared his passion for public interest litigation" to be appointed to the bench.[122] However, the law minister at the time, AK Sen, was "an old school patrician" who did not support Bhagwati's agenda and blocked many of his preferred candidates.[123] In the end, Bhagwati succeeded in having only five of his twelve nominees appointed – an experience he found "absurd and humiliating."[124]

Moreover, his successor as chief justice was the conservative RS Pathak, who refused to let Bhagwati remain in his post as chairman of the legal aid committee following his retirement. Bhagwati later wrote that Pathak's decision to assume the chairmanship for himself "was taken to benefit the holder of the office [of chief justice] rather than to help the impoverished people of the country to realise their basic Human Rights."[125] Given Bhagwati's long-standing commitment to improving access to justice, this was clearly a bitter pill for him to swallow.

10.4 PUBLIC ENGAGEMENT AND HUMAN RIGHTS ADVOCACY

During his judicial career and after his retirement, Justice Bhagwati made many speeches and regularly gave interviews to the press. This public engagement had several aims. First, it served to defend and explain his judicial innovations. In a 1984 speech at Columbia Law School, Justice Bhagwati cited the context in which his judiciary operated to defend a robust judicial role in protecting the rights of marginalized and disadvantaged groups. He made the case that procedural formalism inherited from Anglo-American jurisprudence did not suit the Indian context.[126] He said: "[T]he main obstacle which deprived the poor and disadvantaged of effective access to justice was the traditional rule of standing . . . [I]t effectively barred the doors of the Court . . .

---

[120] Bhuwania (*supra* n 2).
[121] Bhuwania (*supra* n 12) 32–4.
[122] Gadbois (*supra* n 2) 296.
[123] Ibid.
[124] Ibid. 300.
[125] Chandrachud (*supra* n 2) 43.
[126] PN Bhagwati, "Judicial Activism and Public Interest Litigation" (1984–5) 23 *Columbia Journal of Transnational Law* 561.

to large masses of people.["127] In response to criticism of the Court's "judicial activism," Justice Bhagwati argued that it was very much the province of the judiciary to develop new remedies to tackle difficult social problems. In his words, "unorthodox and unconventional remedies" were needed to "initiate affirmative action on the part of the state" to "ensure distributive justice to the deprived sections of the community."[128]

Indeed, Justice Bhagwati welcomed the label of judicial activist. He said in his autobiography that legal formalism "hides the true nature of the judicial process."[129] Citing Lord Reed and Justice Oliver Wendell Holmes, he argued that judges inevitably make law and are, therefore, engaging in activism.[130] The relevant question is to what end that activism is aimed. For Bhagwati, "social activism" – directed towards the achievement of social justice – was most apposite in the Indian context, and that was what he claimed to practice.[131] He tried to convey this message not only to academic audiences but to the broader Indian public as well. For instance, during his tenure as chief justice, Bhagwati penned an article in The Times of India called "The Imperative of Social Justice," in which he explained the importance of the DPSPs and made an impassioned plea for the "equitable distribution of the social, material and political resources of the community."[132] He added that "this social justice ... should be the guiding star in the process of constitutional interpretation."[133]

Second, his public engagement served to promote legal aid and public interest lawyering. As discussed, Justice Bhagwati had supported legal aid initiatives throughout his career and chaired the National Committee for the Implementation of Legal Aid Schemes during his time on the Supreme Court. He further recognized that the success of PIL in bringing social justice depended on lawyers representing the poor. In a speech to the International Bar Association in 1982, Justice Bhagwati urged lawyers to take greater social responsibility in their careers. He said that the judiciary could not succeed in interpreting the law to bring about social justice "unless it has the assistance of a legal profession which is committed to the dynamic concept of the rule of law ... and is keenly aware of the need to mould the law creatively and imaginatively in the service of the weaker section of humanity."[134] In an address to judicial officers, social service organizations, and members of the bar in Thane, Justice Bhagwati encouraged the community-at-large to promote access to justice by asking social workers and students to promote legal literacy.[135]

---

[127]   Ibid. 570–1.
[128]   Ibid. 575–6.
[129]   Bhagwati (supra n 4) 58.
[130]   Ibid. 59.
[131]   Ibid. 62.
[132]   PN Bhagwati, "III – The Imperative of Social Justice," Times of India, September 23, 1986, 1.
[133]   Ibid.
[134]   PN Bhagwati, "The Challenge to the Profession by the Judiciary" (1984) 80 Law & Justice – The Christian Law Review 42, 48.
[135]   "Justice Bhagwati's Stress on Legal Aid to Poor," Times of India, July 26, 1976.

Third, Justice Bhagwati used his public stature, particularly after his retirement, to promote human rights around the world. He served, inter alia, on the UN Human Rights Committee; as regional advisor for Asia and the Pacific for the UN High Commissioner for Human Rights; and as a member of the International Labor Organization's Committee of Experts.[136] He also carried out several missions for the International Commission of Jurists and participated in seven workshops across Asia aimed at developing regional human rights protection mechanisms.[137]

Most importantly for present purposes, Justice Bhagwati worked with the Commonwealth secretariat to organize a series of judicial colloquia to discuss how to apply human rights norms in domestic legal systems.[138] At these events, he rehearsed his usual entreaties to abandon legal formalism, adopt creative judicial approaches, and pursue social justice.[139] These colloquia influenced judges around the world. For instance, Michael Kirby, who served on the High Court of Australia from 1996 to 2009, attended the first colloquium, which was held in Bangalore in 1988. He later wrote that, though he had worked with Bhagwati on several occasions, this event had an "enormous" and "continuing" impact on him.[140] Indeed, Kirby was strongly influenced by Bhagwati's example to evolve the common law in line with international human rights norms – an approach known as the "Bangalore Principles."[141] He further referred to Bhagwati as "my teacher" and praised the latter's influence not only in Australia but in other common law jurisdictions as well.[142]

10.5 CONCLUSION

Perhaps because of this global influence and the adulation that Justice Bhagwati received for his judicial contributions, both from the academy[143] and from society,[144] he did not engage in much critical self-reflection. His writings display a tendency toward self-promotion, even when ostensibly discussing developments in the law. For instance, in a 1985 article on human rights in the criminal justice system, Justice Bhagwati describes positive developments in the treatment of criminal suspects in custody and improvements in their access to justice. Toward the end of the piece, he

---

[136] Gadbois (*supra* n 2) 206.

[137] Bhagwati (*supra* n 4) 134–49, 163–72.

[138] Ibid. 172–82.

[139] Bhagwati (*supra* n 10).

[140] Michael Kirby, "PN Bhagwati: An Australian Appreciation" in Michael Kirby (ed.) *Speeches* (Vol. 42, 1998), www.michaelkirby.com.au/content/volume-42-1998.

[141] Ibid. 7.

[142] Ibid. 8–10.

[143] Shreeraz Latif A Khan, *Justice Bhagwati on Fundamental Rights and Directive Principles* (Deep & Deep Publications, 1996); Mool Chand Sharma, *Justice P.N. Bhagwati: Court, Constitution and Human Rights* (Universal Book Traders, 1995).

[144] Gadbois (*supra* n 2) (noting that, among other awards, Bhagwati received the International Bar Association's highest award and the Padma Vibhushan, India's second highest civilian award).

takes credit for all of this, stating: "This entire human rights jurisprudence has been the result of a most startling and remarkable development of the law following upon the landmark decision in *Maneka Gandhi*."[145] Similarly, in his autobiography, Justice Bhagwati says, "I developed the innovative strategy of public interest litigation" and, later, "[i]t would not be presumptuous on my part to say that my response to [endemic problems in India] . . . was almost unique in the history of the development of law and judicial process."[146] He dismissed criticism, particularly that of his judicial colleagues, as out of touch with reality and wedded to archaic legal doctrines. As he put it in his autobiography, "some of the contemporary judges, trained in the British tradition, are taking a narrow and pedantic view of the judicial function and [are] . . . oblivious to the misery and suffering of . . . large numbers of people."[147]

By contrast, Justice Bhagwati saw himself as deeply committed to improving the lot of those in need. He traced this commitment to his spirituality, writing, "I feel that every human person is an embodiment of the divine and has an immense potential for transformation . . . [M]y ability to put unflinching faith in human goodness is something that has never failed me in my life."[148] This conviction that he was doing the right thing, seemingly guided by a higher power, is evident throughout Justice Bhagwati's writings. His autobiography begins by stating how humbled he feels "to be chosen by the Almighty to be able to contribute in pursuing the path of justice" and concludes with a chapter titled "My Spiritual Journey."[149]

This deep spirituality was essential to Justice Bhagwati becoming such a towering judge for the wellspring of confidence and righteous determination it gave him. But it may also account for his lack of self-reflection and political tact, which left him blind to the dangers of PIL and made him an ineffective institution-builder, particularly during his time as chief justice. He left behind a schizophrenic higher judiciary: one that promotes soaring rhetoric and builds public consciousness for fundamental rights protection while exercising unchecked – and often pernicious – discretion.

---

[145] PN Bhagwati, "Human Rights in the Criminal Justice System" (1985) 27(1) *Journal of the Indian Law Institute* 1, 22.
[146] Bhagwati (*supra* n 4) 66, 71.
[147] Ibid. 91.
[148] Ibid. 4–5.
[149] Ibid. 3, 183.

11

Justice Cepeda's Institution-Building on the Colombian Constitutional Court: A Fusion of the Political and the Legal

David Landau

11.1 INTRODUCTION

The Colombian Constitutional Court is something of an unlikely case for a "towering judge." This is not because of a lack of interesting work – indeed, the Court is one of the most activist in the world. Instead, it is because it is a highly institutionalized body. Unlike some other courts, it has never had the pattern of a single justice dominating legal interpretation. Rather, there have been a number of justices who have made major contributions to the Court's work.[1] In addition, the staff of the Court, especially its clerks who often remain for many years, have been key players in drafting opinions and in ensuring continuity on the Court, since many have been with the institution for far longer than the eight-year, nonrenewable term of any single justice.[2] The internal structure of the Court encourages this kind of fragmentation rather than centralization of power – justices, for example, rotate the presidency so that each holds it for one year, rather than having a single chief justice who dominates that court for a long time as in the United States. Arguably, this high level of institutionalization of the Court has been a key reason why it has maintained a fairly high level of activism for so long, precisely because it has not been dependent on individual personalities.[3]

In this context, I argue here that Justice Manuel José Cepeda Espinosa represents a particular type of impactful judge, which I call a political-legal institution-builder.[4]

---

[1] For some overviews of the Court, see Manuel José Cepeda Espinosa and David Landau, *Colombian Constitutional Law: Leading Cases* (Oxford University Press, 2017); Manuel José Cepeda Espinosa, "Judicial Activism in a Violent Context: The Origin, Role, and Impact of the Colombian Constitutional Court" (2004) 3 *Washington University Global Studies Law Review* 529.

[2] For data on this point, see David Landau, "Beyond Judicial Independence: The Construction of Judicial Power in Colombia" (PhD dissertation, Harvard University, 2015), https://dash.harvard.edu /handle/1/14226088.

[3] Ibid.

[4] In their Introduction to this volume, Iddo Porat and Rehan Abeyratne differentiate "institutionalist" towering judges from "political" or "jurisprudential" towering judges. I would argue that Justice Cepeda belongs largely in the "institutionalist" camp, although, as the categories overlap, which the authors note, he has made substantial contributions along all three dimensions.

His core attributes were a fusion of jurisprudential pragmatism (which has been relatively rare on the Court) and political skill, which he used over time to increase the power of the institution. These attributes focused Cepeda on issues that were otherwise undeveloped in the Court's jurisprudence. For example, Cepeda paid close attention to the design of remedies, and perhaps his greatest contribution to the Court's work were the monitoring mechanisms that he developed for a set of mega-interventions, dealing with internally displaced persons and health, respectively. Moreover, he constructed interventions in ways that built up political support for the Court while dampening the opposition that normally accompanies activism. In so doing, Cepeda played a key role in increasing the power of the institution of the Court.

Cepeda's fusion of political and legal skill in the service of protecting and increasing judicial power is best seen from the standpoint of his entire career, in addition to his relatively brief eight-year term as judge. As a young lawyer, Cepeda was a top advisor to President Gaviria during the drafting of the 1991 Constitution, and he played a role in designing the new institution, in selecting those who would serve as its first justices, and in promoting the new text and the vision of law underlying it. Cepeda then joined the second full Court from 2001 until 2009 – the youngest justice to be appointed to that body – when he reoriented the Court's jurisprudence in ways that made it more effective and more politically sustainable, constructing the basis on which the Court could aggressively enforce socioeconomic rights and effectively check the power of a strong president, Alvaro Uribe. Finally, Cepeda's combination of important political and legal roles continued through his advising and academic work after his term ended, in which he has continued to amplify the Court's major lines of jurisprudence.

The rest of this chapter thus takes a temporal perspective, while stressing the attributes that have allowed Cepeda to play a role that built up the institutional power of the Colombian Court through a combination of legal and political skill. Section 11.2 recounts the key role that Cepeda played, as a very young lawyer, in the design of the Constitutional Court and its major instruments. Sections 11.3 and 11.4 consider his time on the Court. Section 11.3 emphasizes the value of his partial jurisprudential "outsiderness," or his status as a legal pragmatist in a highly formalist legal culture, while Section 11.4, in turn, stresses his political skill, which he used to protect and strengthen the institution of the Court. Section 11.5 very briefly considers his work after serving on the Court, including as constitutional advisor during the recent peace process. Section 11.6 concludes by placing the kind of towering justice that Cepeda represents in a broader and critical perspective.

11.2 A DRAFTER AS (EVENTUAL) JUDGE: CEPEDA BEFORE THE COURT

In recent work, Rosalind Dixon explores the potential role of "drafting judges," who are involved with writing constitutions and later serve on the

Court.[5] Cepeda fits this framework fairly well: as a young lawyer in his twenties, a freshly minted LLM from Harvard Law School and a member of a prominent Liberal family, he served as an advisor to the Virgilio Barco administration in the late 1980s and then the Cesar Gaviria administration after it took office in 1990, in both cases promoting the idea of a new Constituent Assembly to replace the 1991 Constitution, rather than relying on pushing constitutional reforms through Congress as had been attempted throughout previous decades.[6] When the Gaviria administration used a decree to call a Constituent Assembly to rewrite the Colombian Constitution, Cepeda became a key advisor to the Gaviria administration on constitutional issues during the Assembly. In that capacity, he played a major role in formulating and promoting the administration's proposals, which dominated the discussion in the Assembly and were largely adopted in the new constitution.[7]

The 1991 Constitution was adopted during a deep political and economic crisis, including escalating civil conflict with guerrilla and paramilitary groups, endemic drug trafficking, the assassinations of a series of prominent politicians and officials including the initial 1990 candidate for president, and the sense that the existing political institutions were incapable of handling these problems.[8] Cepeda had been one of the key figures who had developed a critique of the role of constitutional law and the Supreme Court in perpetuating these issues. One factor was the overuse of states of exception, which he viewed both as allowing human rights abuses and as increasingly ineffective in dealing with civil disorder.[9] A second was the interpretations given by the Supreme Court, which he critiqued as unduly formalistic, as drawing arbitrary lines, and as failing to give any real meaning to constitutional rights.[10] Overall, the critique was of a constitutional order that enhanced rather than restrained the sense of arbitrariness and lawlessness that pervaded Colombian society in the late 1980s.

---

[5] Rosalind Dixon, "Constitutional Design Two Ways: Constitutional Drafters as Judges" (2018) *Virginia Journal of International Law* 1.

[6] "Los Yuppies Constituyentes," *Semana*, November 12, 1990, www.semana.com/nacion/articulo/los-yuppies-constituyentes/14123-3.

[7] Cepeda himself produced a text that compared the administration's proposals to the final constitutional product, and showed that the administration's ideas were adopted on most (although not all) major points. Manuel José Cepeda, *Introduccion a la constitucion de 1991: Hacia un nuevo constitucionalismo* appx. II (Presidencia de la Republica, 1993).

[8] Renata Segura and Ana Maria Bejarano, "¡Ni una asamblea mas sin nosotros! Exclusion, Inclusion, and the Politics of Constitution-Making in the Andes"(2004) 11 *Constellations* 217, 219–20.

[9] Manuel José Cepeda Espinosa, *Estado de sitio y emergencia economica* (Contraloria General de la Republica, 1985) (critiquing the overuse of states of emergency in Colombia in the decades preceding the constituent assembly).

[10] Manuel José Cepeda Espinosa, *Derecho, Política y Control Constitucional* (Universidad de los Andes, 1986).

Thus, a core part of the Gaviria administration's constitutional vision was to create a new conception of constitutional law that would give constitutional rights more meaning and reality for Colombian citizens.[11] Cepeda played a role in formulating the institutional proposals in this area. One of them was for a new Constitutional Court, which would be tasked solely with constitutional interpretation and would replace those responsibilities of the old Supreme Court. The gist of the proposal was that an institution tasked only with constitutional interpretation would take it more seriously than a Supreme Court composed mainly of specialists in various private law disciplines, and would view constitutional meaning differently.

The second proposal was the creation of a new instrument of constitutional justice that would eventually be labeled the tutela.[12] Since 1910, Colombia has had a "public action" that allows any citizen to launch an abstract challenge to any statute in front of the Supreme Court.[13] The lack of standing requirements or temporal limitations made the public action an unusually strong instrument in comparative terms. But it only allowed for constitutional challenges on abstract issues, rather than concrete violations of rights. The tutela would fill this gap by allowing citizens whose fundamental rights had been violated, whether by state officials or (in limited cases) by private actors, to file an action that would be informal and rapid (decisions needed to be made by a first instance court within ten days).[14] The instrument became the centerpiece of President Gaviria's call for a new conception of law, which sought to use rights to combat the arbitrariness in Colombian society. His sole speech to the Assembly between the times of its inception and closure was devoted in large part to explaining and justifying his proposals for a new Constitutional Court and for the tutela instrument.[15]

Justice Cepeda was involved in the details of the design of both institutions, although the nature of the enterprise makes it impossible to tease out exactly who was responsible for what ideas.[16] What can be said for sure is that both designs reflected carefully on the lessons of comparative experience in a comparative context. The appointment system to the Constitutional Court, for example, reflected in part the limitations of the existing "co-optation" system for judicial appointments in

[11] "Palabras del Senor Presidente de la Republica, Doctor Cesar Gaviria Trujillo, en la Installacion de la Aseamblea Nacional Constituyente, Febrero 5 de 1991" in Manuel José Cepeda, *Introduccion a la constitucion de 1991: Hacia un nuevo constitucionalismo* (Presidencia de la Republica, 1993) 313.
[12] Constitution of Colombia, article 86 (1991).
[13] For the history of this instrument, see Jorge González Jácome, *Entre la ley y la constitucion: Una introduccion historica a la function institucional de la Corte Supreme de Justicia, 1886–1915* (Universidad Javeriana, 2007).
[14] Constitution of Colombia, article 86 (1991).
[15] "Intervencion del Senor Presidente de la Republica, Doctor Cesar Gaviria Trujillo, Ante la Asamblea Nacional Constituyente, Abril 17 de 1991" in Manuel José Cepeda, *Introduccion a la constitucion de 1991: Hacia un nuevo constitucionalismo* (Presidencia de la Republica, 1993) 329.
[16] For reflections on the design of the Court and the tutela in light of Justice Cepeda's constitutional theories, see Manuel José Cepeda Espinosa, "Responsive Constitutionalism" (2019) 15 *Annual Review of Law and Social Science* 21, 29–31.

Colombia, where high court judges under the old constitution had served for life and selected their own successors. Over time, this system was blamed for creating an insular judiciary that was out of touch with social concerns.[17] The new Constitutional Court, based on European models, instead was composed of justices with an eight-year, nonrenewable term. The exact appointment mechanism chosen, however, was not based on any existing model but, rather, was designed to decentralize power and make the Court particularly hard to pack. Thus, three different institutions construct three-member lists for vacancies on the Court: the president, the Supreme Court, and the Council of State (the high administrative court).[18] Each of these institutions controls the lists for three of the nine seats on the Court. Justices are then elected off of each three-member list through a plurality vote in the Senate.[19] The system has worked well in protecting the Court from being packed or pressured by political actors, especially during the administration of Alvaro Uribe (2002–2010). Uribe was able to place two political allies on the Court, but these appointments did not prevent the Court from striking down his attempted constitutional amendment to seek a third consecutive term or from curbing other attempts to expand his power.[20]

Likewise, the design of the tutela was based on careful reflection about other individual complaint instruments found in Latin America and Europe, but it constructed something new rather than merely copying any of these models. The instrument was designed to be more rapid and informal than amparo actions found elsewhere in the region, which were commonly encrusted with procedural formalities.[21] Moreover, the first two levels of any tutela would be heard not by the Constitutional Court but by ordinary courts; the Constitutional Court possessed a certiorari-like discretion as to which tutelas it wanted to revise.[22] This design prevented the Court from being potentially overwhelmed by tutela cases, as had happened in some countries elsewhere, such as in Spain.

After the Constituent Assembly, Cepeda had some involvement in the initial round of appointments to the Court. The early appointments of the executive branch reflected the "new constitutional" ethos of Gaviria and Cepeda; three of the justices on presidential lists, Eduardo Cifuentes, Alejandro Martinez Caballero, and Ciro Angarita Baron, were instrumental in constructing the main doctrines of

[17] Edgar Torres, "Duelo Politico por la guarda constitucional," El Tiempo, June 5, 1991) 3A (arguing that the debates at the Constituent Assembly were dominated by a "harsh judgment" of the work of the old Supreme Court).

[18] Constitution of Colombia, article 239 (1991).

[19] Ibid.

[20] Decision C-141 of 2010 (blocking a constitutional referendum that would have allowed Uribe to run for a third consecutive term in office); Decision C-252 of 2010 (striking down a declaration of a state of economic, social, and cultural emergency issued by Uribe related to the healthcare system).

[21] For an overview of the procedures surrounding these instruments throughout Latin America, see Allan R Brewer-Carias, *Constitutional Protection of Human Rights in Latin America: A Comparative Study of Amparo Proceedings* (Cambridge University Press, 2009).

[22] Constitution of Colombia, article 86 (1991).

the first Court, such as the enforceability of socioeconomic rights via tutela, the availability of the tutela against judicial decisions, the binding effect of constitutional court decisions on other courts, and the reviewability of declarations of state of emergency.[23] These doctrines would become the pillars on which the Court constructed its activist role in Colombia. As importantly, they shifted the discussion toward a more material, rights-centered conception of constitutionalism, heavily infused by international law.

Cepeda did not join the first Court, but he was an important promoter of the 1991 Constitution, the institutions of the Constitutional Court and tutela, and the new vision of law underlying them. He gave speeches to lawyers and others throughout the country explaining the new Constitution and the importance of the tutela instrument.[24] He also authored an array of books on the process through which the new Constitution was written, the meaning of the rights found within it, and the tutela mechanism.[25] These became resources for the new generation of lawyers and judges who were in the process of reworking Colombian law.

11.3 THE VALUE OF THE (PARTIAL) JURISPRUDENTIAL "OUTSIDER"

Justice Cepeda, unsurprisingly, had an elite legal education: he attended the University of Los Andes, one of the most prestigious universities in Colombia, and then received an LLM at Harvard Law School. The degree from Harvard, however, was fairly unusual for his era in Colombia, at a time when the country's elite lawyers were more likely to have international degrees from European law schools, if they studied outside of Colombia.

Cepeda's views on law, which were broadly shared by President Gaviria, proved influential in the framing of the 1991 Constitution and the appointments to the first Constitutional Court. This included the view that constitutional rights should be placed at the center of the Constitution, that judges should strive to make these rights real, and that the law should be used to transform reality and deal with problems such as socioeconomic inequality. This vision impacted the design of

---

[23] See Landau (*supra* n 2) 133. Martinez Caballero and Angarita Baron were initially placed on the Court by the president during its first year of operations using transitional procedures; Angarita Baron, however, was not reappointed to a full eight-year term. Cifuentes was initially appointed by the Attorney General, again using a transitional procedure, but then reappointed to a full term on a presidential list.

[24] Many of these are reprinted in Manuel José Cepeda, *Introduccion a la constitucion de 1991: Hacia un nuevo constitucionalismo* (Presidencia de la Republica, 1993).

[25] Manuel José Cepeda Espinosa, *La Constitución de 1991: Los grandes temas y sus implicaciones para la Enseñanza del Derecho* (Presidencia de la Republica, 1993); *Introducción a la Constitución de 1991: Hacia un Nuevo Constitucionalismo* (Presidencia de la Republica, 1993); *La Carta de Derechos: Su interpretación y sus implicaciones* (Temis, 1993); *Los Derechos Fundamentales en la Constitución de 1991* (Temis, 1993); *La Asamblea Constituyente por Dentro: Mitos y Realidades* (Presidencia de la Republica, 1993).

the tutela instrument as well as several key appointments to the transitional Constitutional Court and the first full Court. The sharp turn in the Court's jurisprudence after 1991 was in part a product of the different kinds of appointments made to the new Constitutional Court as opposed to the old Supreme Court.

But, at the same time, Cepeda's jurisprudential inclinations were different in key ways from the "standard" judicial ideology after 1991. The Constitutional Court under the 1991 text has been much more willing to enforce constitutional rights expansively and to prioritize the rights portion of the Constitution over the organic portion. It has developed as well a commitment to transformative constitutionalism. But the dominant ideology has remained formalist, in much the same way as (in Michaela Hailbronner's account) has been true of the modern German Constitutional Court.[26] The new formalism emphasizes a commitment to methods of interpretation based on the prevalence of constitutional principles over the rest of the constitutional order. It is also scientific in nature, believing that there are "right" answers to legal questions and using tools like proportionality to reach those answers. By a vast margin, the most important foreign academic in modern Colombian legal discourse is Robert Alexy, particularly his promotion of a scientific account of proportionality.

Justice Cepeda's jurisprudential philosophy is quite different. He was influenced by his US legal training and especially by the major structural interventions of the Warren Court. He was heavily influenced by Nonet and Selznick's idea of "responsive law,"[27] as well as by John Hart Ely's conception of "representation reinforcement."[28] In short, Cepeda understood the new formalism and its building blocks, but his own training and inclination were toward a type of legal pragmatism that emphasized the need of a court to respond to social problems in a flexible way, particularly when ordinary democratic processes were not functioning well. His focus was on the concrete impact of the Court's jurisprudence and on its embeddedness in the political system.

The combination of insiderness and outsiderness seems to me to be important in making major contributions to a court. Cepeda's jurisprudence did not seek to overturn many of the lines laid out by the landmark first Colombian Constitutional Court. It instead sought to expand upon those major lines, whether on questions of socioeconomic rights, the use of international law, or the limitations on executive power. But he paid attention to different questions that had previously

---

[26] Michaela Hailbronner, *Traditions and Transformations: The Rise of the German Constitutional Court* (Oxford University Press, 2015) 111–14.

[27] Philippe Nonet and Philip Selznick, *Law and Society in Transition: Towards Responsive Law* (Harper and Row, 1978). Cepeda recently wrote an article on Nonet and Selznick, and their influence on his thinking and career, for the *Annual Review of Law and Social Science* (*supra* n 16).

[28] John Hart Ely, *Democracy and Distrust: A Theory of Judicial Review*, revised edition (Harvard University Press, 1980). Cepeda wrote the preface for a translation of *Democracy and Distrust* (translated by Magdalena Holguín): Manuel José Cepeda Espinosa, "Presentación" in John Hart Ely, *Democracia y desconfianza* (Siglo del Hombre, 1997).

been underdeveloped. Cepeda's jurisprudence is particularly astute on questions of the timing, nature, and justification for judicial review – essentially, on the political context surrounding judicial interventions. I explain these issues in more detail in the remainder of this section and in Section 11.4. Beyond that, he developed a jurisprudence of remedies that is perhaps the Court's most famous contribution to comparative constitutional law and that resulted in some of its most impactful interventions in public policy.

In two major cases, the internally displaced persons (IDP) case T-025 of 2004 and the health case T-760 of 2008, Justice Cepeda authored decisions that committed the Court to sweeping structural orders on major questions. In the IDP case, the Court declared a "state of unconstitutional affairs" involving the roughly four million IDPs in Colombia (10 percent of the Colombian population).[29] The Court joined a large number of pending tutelas filed by IDPs and their representatives, and held that the scope of the problems in the area required not only individual remedies to the plaintiffs but also structural remedies affecting the entire issue. Cepeda's opinion noted that while a law protecting IDPs existed, there were no coherent bureaucratic policy efforts on the question and no budgetary resources. The Court thus ordered the state to undertake to comply with a series of orders to remedy these failures, in order to identify and aid the country's vast population of IDPs.

In Decision T-760, the Court likewise joined a large number of tutelas invoking the right to health and issued an ambitious set of structural orders.[30] Bureaucratic failures in the healthcare system, coupled with patterns in the Court's own jurisprudence, had, since the late 1990s, combined to produce an extraordinary quantity of tutelas just on the right to health – 328,191 cases between 1999 and 2005.[31] The system provided for a complex mix of public and private action. Health insurers were private but required to provide a standard package of benefits defined by the state (the POS) within one of two systems: a contributory system for (generally more affluent) formal-sector workers and a subsidized system for poorer people who were unemployed or worked in the informal sector.[32] However, the state failed to adequately supervise the insurers, and thus many claims that were for items included within the POS were denied, forcing patients to file tutelas in order to get treatment.[33] Likewise, the POS itself was poorly defined and infrequently updated,

[29]   Decision T-025 of 2004, translated in Cepeda Espinosa and Landau (*supra* n 1) 179. Throughout this chapter, I refer to decisions "authored" by Cepeda to refer to decisions where, in Spanish, he acted as *ponente* of the relevant decision. The ponente is charged with drafting the decision, although it should be noted that decisions routinely reflect the input of other justices, must receive a majority vote to be adopted, and, in that very important sense, are the collective product of the institution.
[30]   Decision T-760 of 2008, translated in Cepeda Espinosa and Landau (*supra* n 1) 172.
[31]   See Alicia Ely Yamin and Oscar Parra Vera, "How Do Courts Set Health Policy? The Case of the Colombian Constitutional Court" (2009) 6 *PLos Med* 147, 147.
[32]   Ibid.
[33]   Ibid. 148.

making it increasingly ambiguous to both patients and insurers – again, a source of litigation. Finally, the Court itself greatly increased incentives for litigation when it issued jurisprudence holding that nonPOS treatments (often very expensive treatments for costly diseases) needed to be covered whenever they impacted the right to dignified life of the petitioner, but such treatments should be covered by the state and not the insurers.[34] This holding expanded the contours of the right to health but also caused criticism of the Court for ordering expensive treatments and actually gave strong incentives to the insurers to turn treatments down (in the hopes that they would be found nonPOS), thus sparking even more tutelas. Most of those who sued came from the (relatively affluent) contributory system, even though the subsidized system provided a more limited set of benefits and insured more people, perhaps because the relatively affluent members of the contributory system were more likely to have the knowledge and resources needed to sue.

In this context, Decision T-760 combined novel jurisprudential pronouncements on the right to health with a set of structural orders designed to ameliorate the flaws in the system and overcome the equity bias in the individualized model of enforcement by tutela. The decision for the first time pronounced that the right to health was a "fundamental right" in its own right and not just in conjunction with other rights like the right to health and human dignity. Since only fundamental rights could be enforced by tutela, the decision potentially broadened the enforceability of socioeconomic rights. It also reflected a rejection of the prevailing political discourse surrounding the right to health, which tended to view it as a public service rather than a fundamental right. The orders required the state, inter alia: (1) to unify the contributory and subsidized POS, which was mandated in law with earlier deadlines but had never been carried out; (2) to update and clarify the content of the POS; and (3) to take a series of actions to improve the identification and flow of resources for nonPOS treatments.

The IDP and health decisions were thus quite ambitious. But the concept of a structural order, or even of a state of unconstitutional affairs, was not new in Colombia. The first full Court invented the doctrine to deal with large-scale social problems raised by a series of tutelas. An early use of the doctrine, for example, was in 1997 in a case involving prison conditions.[35] The Court held that prison conditions throughout the country were unacceptable because of overcrowding and other factors and ordered the political system to take steps to remedy the situation. Other cases involved similarly pervasive issues, such as problems in the pension system or regulation of notaries.[36]

---

[34] Julieta Lemaitre and Katharine Young, "The Comparative Fortunes of the Right to Health" (2013) 26 *Harvard Human Rights Journal* 812, 826 (noting that the Court's own reimbursement rule opened up possibilities for "massive corruption and mismanagement").

[35] Decision T-153 of 1996.

[36] Decision T-068 of 1998 (pensions); Decision SU-559 of 1997 (social security); Decision T-1695 of 2000 (notaries); Decision SU-250 of 1998 (notaries); Decision T-590 of 1998 (failure to protect the rights of those defending human rights).

What was new, then, was not the label of a state of unconstitutional affairs or the idea of a structural order but the construction of an effective monitoring and enforcement mechanism for those orders. In the prison case, the Court issued ambitious orders but then failed to follow up or monitor those orders, resulting in a low level of compliance.[37] The IDP and health cases both involved a very ambitious and, overall, fairly successful effort to monitor compliance and issue follow-up orders. The design of remedies was a kind of blind spot in the dominant jurisprudential ideology in Colombia – much more attention had been paid to the interpretation of the Constitution than to the messy, but extremely important, issue of enforcing judgments once issued.[38] The pragmatist inclination and background of Cepeda was better suited to resolving these issues.

In both cases, the Court maintained jurisdiction over the case, actively monitored compliance, and issued a large number of follow-up orders.[39] It put the three-judge panel that issued the original decision in charge of receiving reports and issuing these follow-up orders. The Court also hired a substantial amount of support staff to work full-time on each case. It brought in other state institutions, such as the national procurator and the national ombudsperson, to file reports detailing compliance. It also invited civil society to monitor the state, in each case recognizing civil society commissions composed of a number of different groups. In the IDP case, it included representatives of nongovernmental organizations (NGOs), academics, representatives of the IDP population, and ex-justices; in the health case, it included representatives of patients and other groups such as medical providers.[40] The civil society commissions were invited to report back to the Court, monitor compliance, formulate policy proposals, and participate in public hearings. Especially in the IDP case, the commission became a major player in the follow-up process. On major issues like the construction and application of statistical indicators to measure the depth of the IDP problem, its proposals were routinely accepted in favor of those of the state, and it became a crucial source of information on which the Court relied in drafting subsequent orders.

The Court also relied, across both cases, on periodic public hearings, which were often nationally televised.[41] The hearings included representatives of the state and

---

[37] Cesar Rodriguez-Garavito, "Beyond the Courtroom: The Impact of Judicial Activism on Socioeconomic Rights in Latin America" (2011) 89 *Texas Law Review* 1669, 1694 (finding that the decision "did not include any court sponsored monitoring mechanisms" and instead merely asked the national Attorney General and the national ombudsperson to monitor compliance).

[38] For a generalization of the point that legal pragmatism can point scholars and judges toward traditional "blind spots" in constitutional law such as the design of remedies, see David Landau, "Legal Pragmatism and Comparative Constitutional Law" in Gary Jacobsohn and Miguel Schor (eds.), *Comparative Constitutional Theory* (Edward Elgar, 2018) 208, 225–7.

[39] David Landau, "The Reality of Social Rights Enforcement" (2012) 53 *Harvard International Law Journal* 190, 224.

[40] Ibid. 227–9.

[41] For a description of one of these public hearings in the IDP case, see Rodriguez-Garavito (*supra* n 37) 1669.

members of the civil society commission and other civil society groups and served as often aggressive forums for testing the degree of compliance across different issue areas. They also acted as focal points for public attention and pressure over the state. Finally, based on the information received both in the written reports and at the hearings, the Court issued numerous follow-up orders.[42] The orders fleshed out the (rather broad) initial orders found in each opinion and they also allowed the direction of the case to evolve over time. In the IDP case, for example, the Court began issuing a set of orders protecting the rights of especially vulnerable populations, such as women, children, indigenous groups, and Afro-Colombians, several years after the initial opinion was issued and in light of information it received in its reports and hearings.[43] It required the construction of special programs to protect those groups, as well as other measures.

Cepeda himself has noted that the US structural injunction was an influence on the two decisions.[44] But they adapted the model to a very different context. US structural cases are more decentralized – they are typically handled by trial courts embedded in their local political contexts and involve the reform of local institutions.[45] Both the school desegregation and the prison reform cases, for example, involved schools and prisons located in particular states and cities, not the country as a whole. In contrast, the two Colombian cases were directly executed by the country's high apex court and sought to deal with complex national problems. Thus, the Court had to adopt an especially robust set of mechanisms – the civil society commissions and public hearings, for example – to augment the normal capacities of a court.

Although gauging the overall level of compliance of structural orders is difficult, both of these cases appear to have achieved significant although highly imperfect levels of success. As Rodriguez Garavito and Rodriguez Franco have documented in detail, the remedial design for T-025 produced changes in the design and effort of the bureaucracy, effectively creating a public policy on the issue of internal displacement where one did not exist before.[46] Progress has been slow on many more difficult issues, such as restitution of land, but more rapid on more straightforward issues such as the identification of the displaced population and the provision of emergency assistance to displaced families. In the healthcare case, progress on the Court's major orders was initially very slow. Rodriguez-Garavito has argued that this is because the monitoring scheme in the healthcare case was initially less strong than

---

[42]   http://seguimientot760.corteconstitucional.gov.co/autodeseguimiento.php (health); www .corteconstitucional.gov.co/T-025-04/Autos.php (IDPs).

[43]   Auto 251 of 2008 (focusing on the rights of children).

[44]   Landau (*supra* n 2) 219.

[45]   Malcolm Feeley and Edward Rubin, *Judicial Policymaking and the Modern State: How the Courts Reformed America's Prisons* (Cambridge University Press, 2000) (tracing the history of prison reform litigation in the United States).

[46]   Cesar Rodriguez-Garavito and Diana Rodriguez-Franco, *Radical Deprivation on Trial: The Impact of Judicial Activism on Socioeconomic Rights in the Global South* (Cambridge University Press, 2015).

the one in the IDP case.[47] Additionally, conflicts between civil society groups on the wisdom and direction of the Court's orders initially slowed compliance.[48] But several years after the decision was issued, the Court put renewed effort into the healthcare case and was able to receive substantial compliance on many of the major orders, such as unification of the subsidized and contributory POS, and clarification and revision of the POS.

The two cases are also viewed as landmarks in part because of their broader effects on the political system. The cases highlighted massive failures of state policy and affirmed that those failures touched on central constitutional values. The monitoring schemes helped keep the issues in front of the public eye for a sustained period of time. Over time, the cases and their follow-ups injected a new set of concerns and values into the political process. This eventually produced new legislation that adopted the Court's framing of the two issues. One example is the 2011 Law of Victims and Restitution of Land, which adopted the framing of the Court in labeling those affected by the internal armed conflict as victims who possessed a defined series of rights.[49] The law built heavily on the Court's jurisprudence and adopted new mechanisms for carrying out that jurisprudence, such as procedures for determining reparations and new tribunals to carry out restitution of land. Likewise, the Statutory Health Law of 2015 adopted the Court's framing of the right to health in T-760 as a fundamental right, rather than a public service.[50] Article 1 states that the law is designed to "guarantee the fundamental right to health, to regulate it, and to establish its mechanisms of protection," while article 2 establishes that the "fundamental right to health is autonomous and un-renounceable both individually and collectively." In both cases, then, the decisions eventually played a role in altering political discourse on critical issues.

11.4 POLITICAL SKILL AND THE PROTECTION OF THE COURT

Justice Cepeda had an unusual profile for a justice because of his combination of legal and political skill. His father, Fernando Cepeda Ulloa, is a very prominent political scientist who has authored important works but also held a number of diplomatic and public posts, including ambassador of Colombia to the United Nations (UN), the Organization of American States (OAS), the UK, France, and Germany. Cepeda himself, as noted in Section 11.2, served in the Gaviria administration, first as advisor in front of the Constituent Assembly and later as ambassador to the UN Educational, Scientific and Cultural Organization (UNESCO) and to Switzerland. At the same time, and like his father, he served in prominent academic

---

[47] Rodriguez-Garavito (*supra* n 37) 1694.
[48] Landau (*supra* n 39) 228 (noting that relevant groups had divergent goals and interests regarding the healthcare system).
[49] Law 1448 of 2011.
[50] Law 1751 of 2015.

posts, serving, for example, as dean of the law faculty of Los Andes in Bogotá for several years in the late 1990s. Cepeda's political abilities proved helpful in protecting the institutional power of the Court. Perhaps the best illustration of this were the circumstances at the time when Cepeda was selected to the Court.

The Court, at this point, was in something of a crisis. The country had experienced a very deep recession in the 1998–2000 period, toward the end of the mandate of the first full Court, and the Court had become an active player. Although social rights had played a meaningful role in the Court's jurisprudence from its inception, these rights became much more important during the late 1990s. As Pablo Rueda has explained, during this period middle-class plaintiffs flocked to the courts in droves by filing tutela actions.[51] Many of these plaintiffs were feeling the effects of the crisis and facing losses in pensions, housing, or healthcare. The Court responded by granting relief in many of these cases, abandoning an earlier and more cautious approach to the enforcement of socioeconomic rights that focused on the poorest and most marginalized.[52] There were isolated attempts to stem the tide of these cases, but, overall, the recession put in motion a trend toward the increase of socioeconomic rights cases that has proven irreversible (and has probably increased the Court's popularity).

More politically significant were the Court's larger-scale interventions on economic issues. There were two major sets of cases along these lines. First, due to the macroeconomic crisis, the government proposed a budget that would reduce the real value of many public sector salaries. The Court reviewed the budget and held that it was unconstitutional because public sector employees had an absolute right to maintain the real value of their salaries.[53] The Constitution did not explicitly provide for such an entitlement, but the Court inferred it from a number of provisions. Second, the crisis, coupled with a problematic formula for the determination of interest rates, had a disastrous effect on the formal system for housing finance. Several hundred thousand middle-class debtors were faced with potential foreclosure, but no political response was forthcoming. In the face of this inaction, the Court stepped in with several major decisions that culminated in the nullification and complete rewriting of the mortgage system.[54]

These two decisions created significant blowback against the Court.[55] Both were quite expensive for the state; the salary decision, for example, required a significant

---

[51] Pablo Rueda, "Legal Language and Social Change During Colombia's Economic Crisis" in Javier Couso, Alexandra Huneeus, and Rachel Sieder (eds.), *Cultures of Legality: Judicialization and Political Activism in Latin America* (Cambridge University Press, 2010) 25.

[52] Ibid.

[53] Decision C-1433 of 2000.

[54] Decision C-308 of 1999; Decision C-700 of 1999; Decision C-747 of 1999; Decision C-955 of 2000.

[55] Salomon Kalmonovitz Krauter, "La Corte Constitucional y la Capitalizacion de Intereses" (2000), www .banrep.gov.co/docum/Lectura_finanzas/pdf/K-Corteycapitalizacion.pdf; Sergio Clavijo, "Fallos y Fallas Economicas de la Corte Constitucional: El Caso de Colombia, 1991–2000" (2001), www.hacer.org/pdf/ clavijo.pdf; "¿ Aqui quien manda?" *Semana*, November 27, 2000.

increase in public sector salaries. Critics also argued that the decisions mainly benefited middle-class groups rather than the poor, that they reflected an ignorance of macroeconomic and fiscal policy and thus would have a rash of unintended effects, and that the Court lacked the democratic legitimacy to make interventions into these kinds of issue. The response of some of the justices on the Court reflected a kind of "judicial populism." This was most pronounced on the justice who was instrumental in writing most of the key decisions on the housing crisis. In a newspaper interview, he quoted the most famous populist in Colombian history, Jorge Eliécer Gaitán, to the effect that "the people are more intelligent than their leaders."[56] He became known as the "housing justice" and ran for vice-president and the Liberal Party ticket in the 2002 presidential election, although he lost.[57]

The economic crisis thus reflected a complex political situation for the Court. On the one hand, the Court's judicial interventions raised the salience and popularity of the Court and its major instruments such as the tutela. On the other, the same interventions, especially the structural cases, left the Court in a precarious position vis-à-vis politicians and state officials. The topic became a major issue in the 2001 selection process for new justices to the Court, at which Cepeda was selected. After the 2002 presidential election in which Alvaro Uribe was elected, the new administration showed open hostility toward the Constitutional Court. Uribe's first minister of justice launched probably the strongest assault against the Court in its history, targeting particularly the judicial enforcement of social rights. The attack was ultimately unsuccessful, but it reflected the perilous context within which the Court worked around the time Cepeda was selected to the bench.

At his public hearing for his judicial election before the Senate, he and some other new justices defended the broad outlines of the Court's work as consistent with the Constitution but also suggested that the recent socioeconomic rights jurisprudence needed adjustment. After his selection, Justice Cepeda worked rapidly to make changes to the Court's socioeconomic rights jurisprudence. The most important of these was the issue of public sector salaries. The key change in the Court's jurisprudence, issued in a decision that Cepeda coauthored with another justice, was to hold that the right to maintenance of the real value of public sector salaries was no longer absolute for all public sector workers, only for those making less than twice the minimum wage.[58] For wealthier workers, there was a presumption that their salaries should at least hold value, but this presumption could be overcome with a showing that the state was experiencing a deep financial crisis and that the money that would go to salaries was instead being used for higher priority goals such as social spending.[59] This change in jurisprudence helped to give the government

---

[56]   "Interview with Justice Jose Gregorio Hernandez," *La Republica*, November 12, 2000.

[57]   "El Efecto 'Vice,'" *Semana*, April 8, 2002, www.semana.com/nacion/articulo/el-efecto-vice/50201-3.

[58]   Decision C-1064 of 2001 (coauthored by Justice Cepeda and Jaime Cordoba Trivino), translated in Cepeda Espinosa and Landau (*supra* n 1) 161.

[59]   Ibid.

more flexibility to respond to a deep financial crisis and blunted the critiques against the Court.

The second Court nonetheless deepened rather than abandoning a commitment to socioeconomic rights. But it chose the major cases with somewhat more care. One theme of the Court's new major social rights cases is that they have tended to reorient jurisprudence toward the poor. This is a particularly striking facet of the IDP case, since the internally displaced population in Colombia is, for the most part, extremely poor. But it is also true to a lesser degree of the health case, where some of the Court's core commitments were aimed at the marginalized. For example, one of the key orders in the case was to unify the subsidized package of benefits, which had historically been used by those without formal sector employment, with the contributory package for those with work in the formal sector.[60]

Another example of the reorientation of the Court's social rights jurisprudence toward the poor, and the innovativeness of Cepeda's approach toward social rights, is a decision written by Cepeda in which the Court struck down parts of a major tax reform.[61] The reform, inter alia, broadened the tax base for the value added tax (VAT) by taxing a range of primary necessities that had previously been excluded from the tax. The Court's decision held that taxing decisions could be reviewed for consistency with the socioeconomic rights found in the Constitution. Because the taxation of primary necessities had a disproportionate impact on the poor and was not the product of real legislative deliberation, and because the new resources would not themselves be used to fund social programs for the poor, the Court held that the expansion was unconstitutional.

In addition, the second Court's major cases were carefully chosen to reflect areas where it would be harder to accuse it of supplanting legislative policy choices. In the IDP case, the Court based its intervention on a number of sources, including constitutional rights and international guidelines. But it could also point to the existence of Law 387 of 1997, which provided an expansive set of rights to IDPs. Justice Cepeda's opinion thus framed the case as posing a conflict between executive action and congressional mandates, rather than the judicial imposition of rights:

> This does not mean that, in the present case, the tutela judge is ordering an expense not included in the budget, or modifying the budgetary programming defined by the Legislator. Nor is it the case that new priorities are being defined, or that the policy designed by the Legislator and developed by the Executive is being modified. On the contrary, the Court, bearing in mind the legal instruments that develop the policy for assisting the displaced population, as well as the design of the policy and the commitments assumed by the different entities, is resorting to the constitutional principle of harmonious collaboration between the different branches of public

---

[60] Decision T-760 of 2008. Compliance with this order was achieved by 2012. Presidential Accord 32 of 2012, May 17, 2012.
[61] Decision C-776 of 2003, translated in Cepeda Espinosa and Landau (*supra* n 1) 318.

power, in order to secure compliance with the duty of effective protection of the rights of all residents in the national territory.[62]

Likewise, in the health case, the Court was able to point to a series of mandates in existing legislation that provided support for its actions. For example, unification of the subsidized and contributory package of benefits was required by existing legislation but had been repeatedly put off by executive authorities on the grounds of insufficient resources.[63]

The IDP and health cases were mega-interventions, requiring huge expenditures of funds and bureaucratic resources. The careful selection of issues, on grounds of both the nature of the beneficiaries and the sources of the obligations, helped to blunt resistance to the Court's actions. The IDP case, for example, met with a fairly muted reaction from the Uribe administration, despite its hostility toward the Court as an institution. Unlike in the earlier cases during the economic crisis, there was no significant criticism of the Court for overstepping its bounds. Instead, it helped to spark a conversation, both in the public and in the government, about the shameful situation to which the national IDP population had been subjected. Overall progress on the IDP problem was slow and incremental, but certain issues saw fairly rapid improvement. The budget, for example, increased radically after the Court issued its decision, and bureaucratic attention and coordination also improved.[64] The decision put the government in a position where it was difficult for it to actively resist compliance.

More broadly, the reorientation of the Court's social rights jurisprudence could be viewed as part of a political strategy to protect the Court in a dangerous period, and to allow it to issue decisions curbing the power of an extremely strong president, Alvaro Uribe. Most of Cepeda's term on the Court coincided with the first and second presidential terms of Uribe. As already noted, Uribe opened his first term by making a series of threats against the Constitutional Court. The second Court's reorientation of social rights jurisprudence lowered the levels of political opposition against the court, defanging many of the standard criticisms leveled against it, and increased the Court's public visibility and popularity.

The second full Court was able to issue a series of judgments striking down executive actions that threatened the separation of powers or fundamental rights. The central strategy of the Uribe administration, "democratic security," was premised on taking a tough, militaristic approach against guerrilla groups.[65] The Court struck down laws, emergency decrees, and a constitutional amendment expanding presidential power, putting new restrictions on constitutional rights to freedom of

---

[62]   Decision T-025 of 2004, translated in Cepeda Espinosa and Landau (*supra* n 1) 181.
[63]   Decision T-760 of 2008.
[64]   Rodriguez-Garavito and Rodriguez-Franco (*supra* n 46).
[65]   Ann Mason, "Colombia's Democratic Security Agenda: Public Order in the Security Tripod" (2003) 34 *Security Dialogue* 391.

speech, due process, and freedom of movement, and creating militarized zones in which to fight the armed conflict.

In a decision coauthored by Cepeda and five other justices, the Court placed limits on Uribe's proposed peace process with the paramilitary groups, the Peace and Justice Act.[66] Critics of the law alleged that Uribe was not seeking an authentic peace process; he was merely seeking to provide benefits to criminal groups with which he was accused of having links. The Court upheld the core concept of the Act, holding that providing reduced criminal sentences in return for cooperation with the peace process was consistent with transitional justice models in international law. However, the Court also held that "peace does not justify everything," and placed important conditions on the law.[67] These conditions were generally rooted in international legal norms governing the rights of victims to truth, justice, and reparations. The Court held, for example, that benefits must be conditional on paramilitaries fully confessing to all crimes of which they have knowledge, and that paramilitaries must make greater efforts than called for under the law to give economic reparations to victims.[68] The decision thus placed limits on one of Uribe's core programs and helped to build the legal framework of analysis for victims' rights through which the subsequent peace process with the Revolutionary Armed Forces of Colombia (FARC) would be judged.

The Court, in general, and Cepeda, in particular, were heavily criticized for the 2005 decision allowing Uribe to amend the Constitution so that he could run for a second consecutive term in 2006.[69] The Court was asked to hold that the amendment was unconstitutional both on procedural grounds and on the grounds that it effectively replaced rather than merely amending the 1991 Constitution. Like the Peace and Justice Act decision, it was cosigned by Cepeda and five other justices, a strategy of institutional protection a bit like an occasional use of the per curium by the US Supreme Court.[70] The reasoning of the decision, however, was based on a comparative analysis of presidential systems found elsewhere in Latin America and around the world, as well as consideration of the effects of reelection on the 1991 constitutional design. The Court emphasized the diversity of regional views on the question of term limits and argued, essentially, that allowance of two terms might bend certain aspects of the design but would not break them.

In retrospect, I would argue that the Court's decision not to invoke the substitution of the constitution doctrine in 2005 on the question of a single reelection was reasonable and, in fact, wise, in several senses. First, the doctrine had just been

---

[66] Decision C-370 of 2006, translated in Cepeda Espinosa and Landau (*supra* n 1) 218.

[67] Ibid. 219.

[68] Ibid. 223–4.

[69] Juan Sebastian Jimenez Herrera, "La Reeleccion de Urive fue Inconstitucional y Ilegal," *El Espectador*, April 17, 2015, www.elespectador.com/noticias/judicial/reeleccion-de-uribe-fue-inconstitucional-e-ilegal-articulo-555440.

[70] Decision C-1040 of 2005, translated in Cepeda Espinosa and Landau (*supra* n 1) 343.

invented in a 2003 decision[71] and was still untested – applying it in such a central case, against a president with a popularity rating above 80 percent, would surely have been risky for the future of the doctrine and the Court.[72] Second, the majority is probably correct that allowing two consecutive presidential terms, even in a precarious context, is not necessarily a basic threat to liberal democratic constitutionalism. There are examples of countries both in the region and around the world, such as Argentina, Brazil, the United States, and France, that allow two consecutive terms without having collapsed into authoritarianism. Third, the Court's analysis laid the jurisprudential groundwork for the 2010 decision through which the next Court (after Cepeda's departure) successfully invoked the doctrine to prevent Uribe from once again amending the constitution to allow a third consecutive term in office.[73] The 2010 Court emphasized at the outset of its decision that the 2005 Court had held only that "allowing presidential re-election for a single additional term, subject to a Statutory law aimed at ensuring the rights of the opposition . . ., is not an amendment that substitutes the 1991 Constitution for a completely different text."[74] The 2010 Court thus stressed the limited nature of the 2005 Court's holding in reaching a contrary conclusion, and it noted at several points the ways in which comparative evidence worked differently with respect to three rather than two consecutive terms: there were far fewer examples of successful liberal democratic presidential or semipresidential systems allowing three consecutive terms.[75]

11.5 CEPEDA AFTER THE COURT

Justice Cepeda was elected to the Court quite young and thus ended his term mid-career, in his forties. He has since served as a private lawyer and in academic positions. Additionally, much of his activity after serving on the Court has involved advising the state on constitutional issues and those involving international law, as well as academic activities both inside and outside of Colombia. In this capacity, he has continued to promote the jurisprudence and institution of the Court.

Perhaps Cepeda's most important role, from this perspective, was as a legal advisor to the administration of Juan Manuel Santos (2010–2018) and as a member of the

---

[71] Decision C-551 of 2003.
[72] The Court in fact struck down one provision of the amendment, which allowed the Council of State to write rules protecting the opposition if the political branches failed to act within a defined period of time. This was the first time the substitution of the constitution doctrine was actually used to strike down part of an amendment. Thus, the Court first applied the doctrine on a fairly insignificant issue.
[73] Decision C-141 of 2010, translated in Cepeda Espinosa and Landau (*supra* n 1) 352.
[74] Ibid. 353.
[75] Rosalind Dixon and David Landau, "Transnational Constitutionalism and a Limited Doctrine of Unconstitutional Constitutional Amendment" (2015) 13 *International Journal of Constitutional Law* 606, 632–3 (analyzing the use of comparative evidence in both the first and the second reelection decisions).

technical negotiation team on transitional justice during the difficult peace process with FARC, working on legal and constitutional issues surrounding the system of transitional justice that would judge the ex-combatants.[76] In this sense, Cepeda played a role in crafting (as well as explaining and promoting) the provisions of the peace agreement that created a special set of peace courts and that determined their scope and the substantive legal roles under which they would work.

This was a difficult task because of the political delicacy of the issue and the constraints faced by the negotiators, especially those found in international law and the jurisprudence of the Inter-American Court of Human Rights. The Inter-American Court has long held, mainly in cases involving self-amnesties by military regimes, that the most serious crimes, such as grave war crimes and crimes against humanity, could not be amnestied.[77] The International Criminal Court has also periodically suggested intervention in the event that domestic institutions did not adequately deal with the gravest violations of international law, although it generally took a nuanced and restrained stance.[78] The Colombian Constitutional Court, as already noted, developed a robust jurisprudence surrounding the rights of victims, partly built on international law and partly drawn directly from the Colombian Constitution.[79] The system had to be politically acceptable to both sides while also consistent with these sources of law. This meant thinking creatively about the nature of criminal punishment and about the ways in which the transitional justice system could promote restitution and other goals related to the rights of victims. While the resulting legal framework has faced considerable political criticism within Colombia and been attacked by the new administration that took over in 2018, it has generally succeeded in threading the needle between these constraints and conflicting goals.

Cepeda has, finally, developed an international reputation as a jurist, in part through exporting the lessons of the Colombian case. He is a regular participant and presenter at the Yale Global Constitutionalism Seminar,[80] has served as president of the International Association of Constitutional Law, and has taught classes around the world. He has also authored several books and articles in

---

[76] "Los Cerebros Detras de la Formula de Justicia Para el Proceso de Paz," *Verdada Abierta*, September 23, 2015, at https://verdadabierta.com/los-cerebros-detras-de-la-formula-de-justicia-para-el-proceso-de-paz/.

[77] Christina Binder, "The Prohibition of Amnesties by the Inter-American Court of Human Rights" (2011) 12 *German Law Journal* 1203.

[78] For an analysis, see Mark Kersten, "The Great Escape? The Role of the International Criminal Court in the Colombian Peace Process," *Justice in Conflict*, October 13, 2016, https://justiceinconflict.org/2016/10/13/the-great-escape-the-role-of-the-international-criminal-court-in-the-colombian-peace-process/.

[79] David Landau, "Vulnerable Insiders: Constitutional Design, International Law, and the Victims of Internal Armed Conflict in Colombia" (2018) 57 *Virginia Journal of International Law* 679.

[80] Introduction to this volume (noting that several of the justices in this volume have participated in the seminar).

English on the Court and its relevance. These actions have been important in helping to raise the Court to something of "canonical" status within comparative constitutional law.

11.6 CONCLUSION: THE LIMITS OF THE TOWERING JUDGE IN THE COLOMBIAN CASE

My argument in this chapter is that Cepeda has, throughout his career, played a key role in building the power of the Colombian Constitutional Court through a fusion of political skill and pragmatic legal style. While the Colombian Court has been populated by a number of jurists who have made substantial contributions to the Court's interpretations of the Constitution, it has been much less marked by the kind of political skill and legal pragmatism demonstrated by Cepeda. In addition, Cepeda has been in the unique position of being willing and able to shape and defend the Court and its work from its inception in 1991 up through the present.

Such a role is not, of course, without its potential downsides. The first is that judges of this political-legal type may erode the law/politics distinction, potentially (in the long run) reducing the credibility of the Court. Indeed, this is a major critique of "responsive law," a theory that greatly influenced Cepeda. Cepeda has been criticized, at several points in his career, for being too political. But I would argue that the practical experience in the Colombian case demonstrates a different point: the Court has been consistently at the center of the political storm since its inception, and this has subjected it to sustained critique from the political class and other professionals, especially economists. The latest such storm is the peace process, in which the Court has been forced to issue a large number of decisions with massive legal and social implications. At least in such an environment, a high dose of political skill is primarily an asset to the Court, not a liability: it allows the Court to modulate its interventions in ways that protect the institution and maximize its impact.

A second point goes directly to the scarcity of this kind of political skill. The model of structural social rights interventions developed by Cepeda in the IDP and health cases was a noteworthy advance but also very much an imperfect one. The cases created a large bureaucracy surrounding the Court and one that was working only on one case; it may be, now that more than ten years have passed since each of these decisions was issued, that the bureaucratic inertia surrounding these decisions is outliving their ability to undertake continued interventions. Moreover, the remedial design in each of these cases is extremely costly, such that it would be impossible for the Court to handle more than a couple of these kinds of monitoring mechanism at the same time. The Court has in the past used opportunity constraints as a reason for not developing monitoring mechanisms in other major cases, and has not, at any rate, developed this kind of structure in its subsequent case law.

The weaknesses and the cost of the Colombian structural model demonstrated in the IDP and health cases both create a need for remedial experimentation around new possibilities that might lower the cost and increase the effectiveness of structural interventions in particular contexts. The Court has shown some willingness to do this, but I would argue not enough, in its recent case law. Overall, it has continued to issue structural orders but has shown a reluctance to develop robust ways to monitor their compliance. Given the prevalence of structural problems in the country – surrounding socioeconomic rights and other issues – this is a loss.

The point goes to the different ways in which judges can be "towering." Some of the towering justices studied in this volume overshadowed the institutions of which they were a part, in some sense personalizing constitutional justice within their countries. This kind of dynamic may be desirable only in special contexts or times, for example, as a way to construct or thoroughly reshape constitutional jurisprudence. But an institutionalist judge who can help to steer a court through a political thicket without overshadowing it is a different kind of actor. One would do well to have a Justice Cepeda leading a court in any era.

12

A Towering but Modest Judicial Figure: The Case of Arthur Chaskalson

Dennis M Davis

12.1 INTRODUCTION

In June 1994, Arthur Chaskalson was appointed by President Nelson Mandela as the president of the Constitutional Court of South Africa. This decision preceded the appointment of the other ten members of a court designed to break decisively with South Africa's judicial past.[1] A month later, four sitting judges, as required by the Constitution, were appointed to the Court: Judges Ackermann, Goldstone, Madala and Mohamed. Thereafter, the president appointed the remaining six judges from a shortlist of ten that had been sent to him by the newly established Judicial Service Commission, created in terms of the Constitution to supervise the appointment of judges. From the list of ten, two sitting judges, Judges Kriegler and Didcott, were appointed together with four lawyers who had not, at that stage, been elevated to the bench: Advocate Pius Langa SC and Professors Kate O'Regan, Yvonne Mokgoro and Albie Sachs.[2]

The diverse talents and experience of the new appointees required a formidable leader to create a coherent apex court. Although he had not enjoyed previous judicial experience, Arthur Chaskalson was widely recognised as a pre-eminent legal figure. His record revealed a consistent and tenacious commitment to the fight for justice and democracy in South Africa since his student days at the University of Witwatersrand where he obtained a BCom degree in 1954 and an LLB (cum laude) degree in 1956. He was admitted to the Johannesburg Bar. Over a distinguished legal career, he appeared as counsel in a number of major political trials. The best known of these was the Rivonia trial in 1963/4 in which eight leaders of the African National Congress (ANC), including Nelson Mandela, were convicted and sentenced to life imprisonment.

---

[1] From 1994 to 2001, Arthur Chaskalson was president of the Constitutional Court. Upon the death of Chief Justice Mohamed, who had presided at the Supreme Court of Appeal, the two posts were consolidated and Chaskalson became chief justice.

[2] For a comprehensive, if overly sympathetic account of Chaskalson's career, see Stephen Ellmann *Arthur Chaskalson: A Life Dedicated to Justice for All* (Pan McMillan, 2019) particularly at 413 ff.

More than twenty years later, he was the lead counsel in the so-called Delmas Treason Trial, so named because it was held in the small town of Delmas for the first eighteen months of the trial. In this case, the apartheid government prosecuted key leaders of the United Democratic Front, the informal internal wing of the ANC. It turned out to be the longest running political trial in South African legal history, commencing on 16 October 1985 and ending on 8 December 1988, thereby taking 437 court days to completion.

Perhaps of greater importance to South African law and its future was the decision taken in 1978 by Chaskalson to help set up the Legal Resources Centre, a non-profit organisation dedicated to public interest lawyering in South Africa. Under his leadership, the Centre embarked on a number of critical challenges against pernicious apartheid laws; in particular, the notorious past and influx control laws. Two critical cases were brought by the Legal Resources Centre, *Komani N.O v Bantu Affairs Administration and Board Peninsula Area*[3] and *Oos-Randse Administrasie Raad en Andere v Rikhoto*.[4] The judgments in these two cases rendered it almost impossible to continue with a system that grossly restricted the freedom of movement of the majority of the South African population and under which 1,774,500 black South Africans were prosecuted between 1916 and 1984.[5] Chaskalson's advocacy in persuading a hostile Court to uphold the *Komani* appeal has been heralded. Geoff Budlender, then the attorney in this case, recalls:

> Chief Justice Rumpff – no friend of Mr and Mrs Komani [the couple in question] – became frustrated. 'I think you are leading us down the garden path,' he said to Arthur. But he could not find the flaw in the argument, because there was none. Ultimately, the Appellate Division unanimously decided in favour of Mr and Mrs Komani. It was the result of the most brilliant advocacy I have ever heard.[6]

There had been some considerable debate in legal circles as to who would obtain the nod from President Mandela and thus become the first president of the newly established Constitutional Court. There were two viable candidates: Arthur Chaskalson and Ismail Mohamed. Ismail Mohamed had been appointed to the bench in 1992, admittedly by President FW De Klerk but with the express agreement of Mandela. He, like Chaskalson, had been a leading human rights advocate for many years. Being black, he had suffered egregious discrimination in the earlier years of his legal practice. It was a tough call for President Mandela. It has been suggested that his good friend George Bizos SC had some influence in ensuring that Chaskalson was appointed.

---

[3]   *Komani N.O v Bantu Affairs Administration and Board Peninsula Area* 1980 (4) SA 448 (A).
[4]   *Oos-Randse Administrasie Raad en Andere v Rikhoto* 1983 (3) SA 598 (A).
[5]   For a detailed exposition, see Dennis Davis and Michelle Le Roux, *Precedent and Possibility: The Case and Abuse of Law in South Africa* (Juta, 2008) chapter 4.
[6]   Davis and Le Roux (*supra* n 5) 62.

In his appointment of Arthur Chaskalson as the first president of the Constitutional Court, Nelson Mandela acknowledged Chaskalson's important role as a constitutional and human rights advocate as well as his ability to build institutions. The Legal Resources Centre, for instance, became a formidable vehicle with which to defend human rights and the rule of law in apartheid South Africa, affording legal services to the then disenfranchised citizens of the country. Chaskalson, in an address to the Cape Law Society a few weeks before he died in December 2012, captured the core purpose of the LRC thus:

> Legal aid is crucial to ensure that the constitutional rights to a fair trial and access to courts are rights in substance and not merely rights on paper that are beyond the reach of those who need their protection. It is also important that organs of civil society should cooperate with the legal profession to facilitate the provision of legal services.[7]

It was therefore unsurprising that Mandela turned to Chaskalson to lead the first Constitutional Court. In the decade of this leadership of the Court, Chaskalson repaid the faith shown in him by Mandela. Adept at building institutions, as was evident in his leadership of the Legal Resources Centre, Chaskalson met the challenges of welding a group of judges drawn from very different backgrounds into a Court united in its vision. That vision, which typified Chaskalson's approach to law, was to develop a new constitutional jurisprudence incrementally, being careful not to spell out a comprehensive normative framework in the early years of the Court that might have bound the Court prematurely to a fixed reading of the Constitution. Not only did the Chaskalson Court adopt an incremental approach to legal development but it also sought to ensure that a government, democratically elected for the first time in the country's history, would not be 'second-guessed' in its political choices by the judiciary. For Chaskalson, in keeping with his legal philosophy as revealed during his years at the LRC, the constitutional enterprise was not to be based on the idea of a legal revolution but rather was to be negotiated by way of a careful 'case-by-case' transformation of the apartheid legal system.

12.2 THE FIRST CONSTITUTIONAL COURT

As noted, the composition of the first Court was extremely diverse. As Justice Albie Sachs said later in an interview:

> And then certainly all the judges on the Constitutional Court recognised the need for major transformations in society, not only the ugliness and unfairness and injustice of apartheid and dreadfulness, but the fact that it had left quite deeply entrenched patterns of inequality and disparity. So that was never an issue on our Court, and we came from very different personal backgrounds. It's quite

[7] Cited by Rebecca Davis, *The Daily Maverick*, 3 December 2012.

astonishing, and again, a very different personal phenomenon, that you would have somebody like Yvonne Mokgoro . . . growing up in, what was that called, a location, who studied law and then going on to be assistant nurse and then a part-time prosecutor and then prosecutor and so on, and then someone like Laurie Ackermann, who collected wine labels, and a very cultivated person and totally different social background, and yet Laurie and Yvonne could speak to each other truly as equals on that Court in conceptual constitutional terms.[8]

The judges were able to converse with each other in conceptual constitutional terms. However, welding such a diverse group from different social, economic and legal backgrounds required clear leadership, an attribute that Arthur Chaskalson possessed. His mastery of legal doctrine, his reputation as a lawyer of great stature and his unequivocal stance against a racist past meant that he enjoyed the unqualified respect of all his colleagues. In short, he stood out as their leader. But being a *primus inter partes* was only a start.

A greater challenge was to breathe life into the new Constitution.[9] Again, his background was important. Chaskalson had been, arguably, the most important member of the ANC Constitutional Committee, which formulated the ANC's submissions to the constitutional negotiations of the early 1990s. As a result, he was crucially involved in the drafting of the first post-apartheid constitution. A long-time colleague of Chaskalson, who himself is one of South Africa's most distinguished human rights lawyers, Geoff Budlender said in this regard:

> His hand is clearly visible in the text which was finally approved: his fingerprints are all over the document. You see them in the care precision, and attention to detail; and you see them in the Constitution's recognition that we need to go beyond a typical liberal constitution, which aims to limit the power of the state. Arthur understood that we needed ..'. a constitution which recognises the need to empower the state to address and redress the consequent of centuries of dispossession and discrimination. We needed a constitution which would provide a framework for the democratic transformation which was yet to come.[10]

In this comment, Budlender draws attention to something central to the evaluation of Chaskalson's role: the need for a balance between limiting the power of the state,

---

[8]   Cited by N Bohler-Muller, 'Constitutional Justice Project: Assessment of the Impact of Decisions of the Constitutional Court and the Supreme Court of Appeal on the Transformation of Society: Final Report. Interview with Justice Albie Sachs' (HSRC, 2015) 24.

[9]   Although it falls outside the scope of this chapter, it is important to note that the Constitutional Court was initially required to interpret what was referred to as the Interim Constitution of 1993. This was a constitution that had been negotiated prior to the first democratically held election in 1994 by the existing political parties at that time. It critically required the consent of the ANC and the ruling National Party. After the first democratically held election, parliament began the process of drafting what is now referred to as the Final Constitution. This process culminated in the passing of the Republic of South Africa Constitution Act 108 of 1996 (the Final Constitution).

[10] Geoff Budlender, Funeral Eulogy for Arthur Chaskalson, 3 December 2012. On file with the author.

given the egregious abuses thereof by the racist governments that had preceded democracy, while simultaneously enabling the state to effect democratic transformation of the social, economic and political landscape that had been inherited from apartheid rule.

It was in this period as the leader of the first Constitutional Court that Chaskalson's true influence in the moulding of democratic South African jurisprudence must be analysed.

12.3 THE FIRST CASE

Chaskalson selected the most difficult case through which the Constitutional Court would announce its entrance onto the South African legal landscape. The Court was required to decide the emotive question of whether the death penalty should be available as a sentence in South African criminal law in a democratic country. Given his cautious approach to induced legal development, it might appear surprising that Chaskalson chose the constitutionality of the death penalty as the Court's first case. However, the case was less about dramatic legal innovation and more about asserting a new morality into the legal system, itself derived directly from the text of the Constitution and, in particular, the foundational values of freedom, dignity and equality contained therein.

The death penalty had been used extensively by the apartheid government. From 1959 until 1988, 2,949 people were executed.[11] The importance of this first case was captured in a concurring judgment of Justice Mohamed when he noted:

> The South African Constitution is different: it retains from the past only what is defensible and represents a decisive break from, and a ringing rejection of, that part of the past which is disgracefully racists, authoritarian, insular, and repressive, and a vigorous identification of and commitment to a democratic, universalistic, caring and aspirational egalitarian ethos expressly articulated in the Constitution. The contrast between the past which it repudiates and the future to which it seeks to commit the nation is stark and dramatic.[12]

Although all the judges wrote their own separate judgments, concurring in the result that the death penalty was inconsistent with the Constitution, it was Arthur Chaskalson who penned the comprehensive main judgment. He noted that, during the constitutional negotiations, a Solomonic solution had been adopted by the negotiators. As the two main parties, the ANC and the National Party, could not agree as to whether the death penalty should be expressly dealt with in the Constitution, it had been left to the Constitutional Court to make the decision. Chaskalson was clearly aware, as a pre-eminent human rights

[11] John Battersby, 'Hanging Is Now the Routine at Pretoria Prison', *New York Times*, 1 December 1988.
[12] S v *Makwanyane and another* 1995 (3) SA 391 (CC) at para 262.

lawyer, that his own views about this topic would have been well known. For this reason, he penned a most unusual judicial passage dealing with whether the death penalty breached the constitutional prohibition against cruel inhuman and degrading punishment:

> In the ordinary meaning of the words, the death sentence is undoubtedly a cruel punishment. Once sentenced, the prisoner waits on death row, in the company of other prisoners under sentence of death, for the processes of their appeals and the procedures for clemency to be carried out. Throughout this period, those who remain on death row are uncertain of their fate, not knowing whether they will ultimately be reprieved or taken to the gallows. Death is a cruel penalty and the legal processes, which necessarily involve waiting in uncertainty for the sentence to be set aside or carried out, add to the cruelty. It is also an inhuman punishment for it '. . . involves, by its very nature, a denial of the executed person's humanity', and it is degrading because it strips the convicted person of all dignity and treats him or her as an object to be eliminated by the State. The question is not, however, whether the death sentence is a cruel, inhuman or degrading punishment in the ordinary meaning of these words but whether it is a cruel, inhuman or degrading punishment within the meaning of s 11(2) of our Constitution.[13]

It is clear from this passage that Chaskalson was saying that, from a moral position, the death penalty is inhumane and cruel; it is morally repugnant to any reasonable person. But that was not the question which the Court was required to answer. The judges of the Court needed to eschew their own personal feelings about the matter and decide whether, in terms of the law that they were enjoined to apply, they could come to a similar or different conclusion.

In his judgment, Chaskalson also made another move that held implications for the Court's future jurisprudence. He dealt in detail with the argument that the majority of South African society were in favour of the continuation of the death penalty as part of the criminal justice system, given the level of criminal violence. Thus, he said: 'Public opinion may have relevance to the enquiry, but, in itself, it is no substitute for the duty vested in the Courts to interpret the Constitution and to uphold its provisions without fear or favour. If public opinion were to be decisive, there would be no need for constitutional adjudication.'[14]

---

[13] S v *Makwanyane* at para 26.

[14] S v *Makwanyane* at para 88. At the Court's inaugural ceremony, which took place the day before the death penalty case was argued on 14 February 1995, President Mandela began his speech as follows:

> The last time I appeared in court was to hear whether or not I was going to be sentenced to death. Fortunately for myself and my colleagues we were not. Today I rise not as an accused but, on behalf of the people of South Africa, to inaugurate a court of South Africa has never had, a court on which hinges the future of our democracy.

> Cited by Stephen Ellmann, 'Two South African Men of the Law, Constitutional Conflict and Development: Perspectives from South Asia and Africa' (2014) 28 *Temple International and Comparative Law Journal* 431 at 451.

The *Makwanyane* decision was not the only significant early challenge. In 1994, President Mandela determined that all mothers in prison who had minor children under the age of twelve years be granted special remission of their sentences. The applicant, Hugo, contended that, but for the fact that he was a father of a child under the age of twelve at the relevant date, he too would have been granted remission of the sentence. The Court was required to interpret s 82(1) of the Interim Constitution, namely that the president shall be competent to exercise and perform the following powers and functions: 'to pardon or reprieve offenders, either unconditionally or subject to such conditions, as he or she may deem fit, and to remit any fines, penalties or forfeitures'.

The question arose as to whether these powers were subject to review by the Court, in particular, for want of constitutional compliance. Although the majority judgment was written by Judge Richard Goldstone, it again reflected the determination of the Chaskalson Court to enforce the effect of the Constitution on the exercise of the public power. For this reason, Judge Goldstone found that it would be contrary to the promise of the Constitution if the exercise of the presidential power were not susceptible to review under the Constitution or subject to the discipline of the Bill of Rights.[15] Having made this finding, the majority of the Court followed an extremely cautious approach. Hugo had argued that, in releasing mothers of small children but not fathers, the president had discriminated on the grounds of sex, which constituted a prohibited ground in terms of the equality guarantee set out in s 8 of the Interim Constitution. In effect, the majority judgment held that the president adopted a generic classification in his decision to remit sentences on the basis that women were to be regarded as the primary caregivers of young children. As Judge Johan Kriegler noted in his dissent: 'Reliance on the generalisation that women are the primary caregivers is harmful in its tendency to cramp and stamp the efforts of both men and women to form their identities freely.'[16] *Hugo* provides a clear example of the careful approach taken by the majority of the Chaskalson Court in its early decisions; it asserted the principle of constitutional review but deferred to the executive in respect of the impugned decision.[17]

12.4 SOCIO-ECONOMIC RIGHTS

The South African Constitution included an ambitious set of socio-economic guarantees, including rights to housing, health care, food and water, social security, education and environmental protection.[18] The imperative to ensure that the lives of millions who had suffered egregiously during apartheid would change in terms of

---

[15]   *President of the Republic of South Africa and another* v *Hugo* 1997 (4) SA 1 (CC) at para 28.
[16]   *President of the Republic of South Africa and another* v *Hugo* at para 80.
[17]   Something similar can be determined in *Marbury* v *Madison* 5 US 137 (1803) at 176–7.
[18]   See sections 24, 26, 27, 28 and 29 of the Republic of South Africa Constitution Act 108 of 1996.

the provision of basic goods and services loomed large in the minds of the drafters of the Constitution. The manner in which the Constitutional Court chose to vindicate these rights was as important as any endeavour to breathe life into an ambitious text. The Chaskalson philosophy played a crucial role in the jurisprudence that followed. The Constitutional Court's first encounter with these provisions and thus with a challenge to enforce socio-economic rights came in *Soobramoney* v *Minister of Health*.[19] It involved a claim by a man with a chronic kidney failure to dialysis for which he could not afford to pay. He argued that, in terms of the Constitution, no one may be refused emergency medical treatment. The Court concluded that his chronic illness was not an emergency under the Constitution and that the general health right to health did not support his claim. The hospital in question provided dialysis to patients with chronic renal failure only if they were eligible for a kidney transplant. Soobramoney, because of his other illnesses, was not. The Court concluded that the hospital authority had made a reasonable assessment that it was not prepared to second-guess, particularly given the scarce resources available. Chief Justice Chaskalson wrote:

> These choices involve difficult decisions to be taken at the political level in fixing the health budget, and at a functional level in deciding upon the priorities to be met. A court will be slow to interfere with rational decisions taken in good faith by the political organs and medical authorities whose responsibility it is to deal with such matters.[20]

Shortly thereafter, a second socio-economic rights case came before the Court in *Government of the Republic of South Africa and Others* v *Grootboom and Others*.[21] Here, the Court was confronted with a more difficult problem in that the High Court had already provided relief to the applicants, a group of homeless people who had been evicted from their informal homes situated on private land that had been earmarked for formal low-cost housing.

In this case, applicants relied on s 26(1) and (2) of the Constitution, which read:

(1) Everyone has a right to access to adequate housing;
(2) The State must take reasonable legislative and other measures within its available resources to achieve the progressive realisation of this rights.

The applicants contended that this wording was similar to that contained in the International Covenant on Economic, Social and Cultural Rights (ICESCR). Following the jurisprudence that flowed from the Covenant, a duty was imposed upon the state to fulfil a minimum core obligation to ensure the satisfaction of, at the very least, a minimum essential level for the right; in this case, the right to housing.

---

[19] *Soobramoney* v *Minister of Health* 1998 (1) SA 765 (CC).
[20] *Soobramoney* at para 29.
[21] *Government of the Republic of South Africa and Others* v *Grootboom and Others* 2001 (1) SA 46 (CC).

This argument, if accepted, would prescribe a clear set of obligations upon the state to channel the requisite funds into housing projects.

The Court was clearly determined not to tie the hands of the legislature and the executive. Hence, in its rejection of the 'minimum core' argument, the Court placed emphasis upon the complexity of the task of determining the minimum core obligation for the progressive realisation of the right to access to adequate housing, 'without having the requisite information on the needs and opportunities for the enjoyment of this right'.[22]

Even though the Court was careful not to fetter the economic policy of government, it attempted to give content to the right to housing and the balance of socio-economic rights by concluding that it could not be reasonable for the government to develop a housing plan that made no provision for the neediest of all, such as Mrs Grootboom and her fellow applicants. For this reason, the Court ordered that s 26(2) of the Constitution requires 'the State to devise and implement within its available resources a comprehensive and coordinated programme progressively to realise the right of access to adequate housing ... The programme must include reasonable measures ... to provide relief for people who have no access to land, no roof over their heads, and who are living in intolerable conditions or crisis situations.'[23]

Sadly, this declaration, although important in principle, did not assist Mrs Grootboom, who died some years later without a home. However, this cautious approach to socio-economic rights, and in particular the deference shown to policy choices made by the executive, was to be sorely tested shortly thereafter in *Minister of Health and Others v Treatment Action Campaign and Others*.[24] The Court was required to consider whether the government had violated the constitutional guarantee of health care by failing to establish a national programme that employed the drug Nevirapine to prevent mother-to-child transmission of HIV at birth. The Court was firm. It stated: '[T]he question ... is not whether socio-economic rights are justiciable. Clearly they are. The question is whether the applicants have shown that the measures adopted by the government to provide access to health care services for HIV-positive mothers and their newborn babies fall short of its obligations under the Constitution.'[25]

Again, the Court refused to follow international precedent, in particular the jurisprudence that had been developed by the United Nations Committee on Economic, Social and Cultural Rights in its interpretation of the ICESCR. It made it clear:

The Constitution contemplates rather a restrained and focused role for the Courts, namely, to require the state to take measures to meet its constitutional obligations and to subject the reasonableness of these measures to evaluation. Such determin-

---

[22]   *Government of the Republic of South African and Others v Grootboom and Others* 2001 (1) SA 46 (CC) at para 32.

[23]   *Grootboom* at para 99.

[24]   *Minister of Health and Others v Treatment Action Campaign and Others* 2002 (5) SA 721 (CC).

[25]   *Minister of Health v Treatment Action Campaign* at para 25.

ation of reasonableness may in fact have budgetary implications, but are not in themselves directed at rearranging budgets. In this way the judicial, legislative and executive functions achieve appropriate constitutional balance.'[26]

The Court found that existing government policy was inflexible as it denied mothers and their newborn children in public hospitals and clinics, outside specific research and training centres, an opportunity to receive a single dose of Nevirapine at the time of the birth of a child. This restriction was unreasonable and fell foul of the test for socio-economic rights that the Court had set out in the *Grootboom* case. The Court thus held that the Constitution required the government to devise and implement, within its available resources, a comprehensive and coordinated programme to realise progressively the rights of pregnant women and their newborn children to access to health services to combat mother-to-child transmission of HIV.

Unquestionably, in this judgment, political context mattered even more than usual. The Court was compelled to confront a government that, under the presidency of Thabo Mbeki, not only revealed a deep scepticism about the science relating to AIDS but also had to deal with the minister of health Manto Tshabala-Msimang's claims on national television that she was not prepared to abide by a Constitutional Court decision that gave relief to these applicants.[27]

This decision was the high watermark of socio-economic rights litigation in South Africa. Thereafter, the Court adopted an increasingly pro-executive approach, as is evident in the last major case decided to date by the Constitutional Court in this area, *Mazibuko and others v City of Johannesburg and others*.[28] The Court found that the City of Johannesburg's water policy did not violate the constitutional right to water. Admittedly, Arthur Chaskalson was no longer on the Court, but a number of judges who signed on to the opinion of Judge O'Regan had been on the Chaskalson Court. In this judgment, the Court confirmed that it considered it institutionally inappropriate for a court 'to determine precisely what the achievement of any particular social economic right entails and what steps government should take to ensure the progressive realisation of the right'.[29] As the case dealt with a minimum quantity of water required by the constitutional right to water, it had been hoped that this decision would help broaden the approach to social and economic rights. Sadly, the converse occurred. A number of commentators criticised this decision, contending correctly that the initial potential for ensuring that government policy could vindicate the constitutional vision of responding decisively to the plight of millions of poor people had been curtailed.[30] Chaskalson defended the decision in very

[26] Ibid.
[27] See Theunis Roux, *The Politics of Principle: The First South African Constitutional Court 1995–2005* (Cambridge University Press, 2013) 298.
[28] *Mazibuko and others v City of Johannesburg and others* 2010 (4) SA (1) (CC).
[29] *Mazibuko* at para 61.
[30] See, e.g., Lucy Williams 'The Justiciability of Water Rights: *Mazibuko v City of Johannesburg*' 2010 (18) *Willamette Journal of International Law Dispute Resolution* 211.

much the same way that he had written the judgment in *Soobramaney*; it was not for a court to interfere in the allocation of scarce resources unless it was clear that the government had acted unreasonably.[31]

12.5 AN INSIGHT INTO THE POLITICS OF THE COURT?

Shortly before the Treatment Action Campaign case was argued, the Court had to deal with an interesting question as to whether a Rastafarian who wished to be admitted as an attorney was legally prohibited from being so admitted due to two previous convictions for the possession of dagga (cannabis) and, in the circumstances, where he had expressed his intention as a Rastafarian to possess the same in the future.

Judge Sandile Ngcobo penned a strong judgment in which he emphasized that, in a constitutional democracy that recognised and should thus tolerate diverse religious beliefs, a reasonable accommodation of all faiths should be uppermost in the mind of parliament. When faced with a religious practice that involves some conduct that runs counter to its clear objectives, 'the proper approach under the Constitution is not to proscribe the entire practice but to target only that conduct that runs counter to its objectives'.[32] In Judge Ngcobo's view, the prohibition that had been employed against Prince was 'constitutionally bad' because it prevented the religious use of cannabis even when such use did not threaten the proclaimed interests of government. By contrast, the majority judgment co-authored by Chief Justice Chaskalson found that there was no objective way in which a law enforcement official would be able to distinguish between use of cannabis for religious purposes and use of cannabis for recreational objectives. Thus, the majority held that prohibition of the possession of cannabis was the most obviously effective way of policing the trade and use of the drug.

The result was a five-four split in favour of dismissing Prince's appeal. It is possible that the approach adopted by Chief Justice Chaskalson was mindful of the more controversial case that was on the Court's docket at that time, namely the TAC case, and that a refusal to craft any reasonable accommodation for religious practice by the majority was sourced in a concern to eschew more controversy than was absolutely necessary at that stage. It might have been a case of Chaskalson 'keeping his powder dry' for a more pressing challenge.

This pragmatic interpretation makes sense of the majority judgment, which paid lip service to the idea of diversity as well as circumventing the medical evidence on the record that showed that there was a level of consumption that was unlikely to

---

[31]   Arthur Chaskalson at the SSLJ Seminar: Onrus April 2010. The author was in attendance at this speech.

[32]   *Prince v The President of the Law Society of the Cape of Good Hope and others* (2) SA 794 (CC) at para 79.

pose any risk or harm.[33] However, Chief Justice Chaskalson was also party to two further judgments that showed a clear adherence to social conservatism. In *Jordan and others* v *S and others*,[34] the Court was confronted with a series of challenges to the Sexual Offences Act,[35] in particular the criminalisation of appellants who were brothel owners as well as sex workers. In a minority judgment in Jordan's case, Judges O'Regan and Sachs held that the provision that criminalised the actions of the sex workers but not of their clients constituted unconstitutional discrimination, the salient feature of which was 'that it tracks and reinforces in a profound way double standards regarding the expression of male and female sexuality'.[36] The two justices also disagreed with the majority judgment that the stigma attached to sex work arises not from the law but from social attitudes. In their view, 'by criminalising primarily the prostitute, law enforces and perpetuates sexual stereotypes[,] which degrades the prostitute but does not equally stigmatise the client, if it does so at all'.[37]

The majority judgment, in which Chief Justice Chaskalson concurred, began by holding that the legislature pursued an important and legitimate constitutional purpose in outlawing commercial sex. Thus, it agreed with the state's counsel that one of the most effective ways of curbing sex work was to strike at the supply.[38] Both the appellant's counsel and counsel for the amici had contended that the outlawing of commercial sex by way of the introduction of the Sexual Offences Act served the purpose of imposing the moral views of the apartheid government on the democratic landscape. They further contended that any connection between commercial sex and a range of social ills documented in the judgment was not obvious. The link between prostitution and social ills had often resulted from the criminalisation of sex work in the first place.

The majority judgment completely disregarded these submissions and, without more, accepted that the social ills of violence, drug abuse and child trafficking associated with sex work justified the use of a criminal sanction. As one commentator noted: 'What emerges from the court's instrumentalist account was a very sanitised, pastoral picture of sex, warm, fuzzy, self-focused cuddling not the hot, steamy, edgy stuff that got us into trouble in the first place.'[39]

A similarly conservative approach was evident in *Volks NO* v *Robinson and others*.[40] In this case, the Court was asked to find the Maintenance of Surviving Spouses Act[41] unconstitutional in that it excluded partners in a co-habitation

---

[33] See the minority judgment of Ngcobo J at para 61.
[34] *Jordan and others* v *S and others* 2002 (11) BCLR 1117 (CC).
[35] Act 23 of 1957.
[36] *Jordan* at para 67.
[37] *Jordan* at para 72.
[38] Ngcobo J on behalf of the majority in *Jordan* at para 15.
[39] Nicole Fritz, 'Crossing Jordan: Constitutional Space for (Un)civil Sex?' (2004) 20 *South African Journal of Human Rights* 230 at 235; see also Rosaan Kruger, 'Sex Work from a Feminist Perspective: A Visit to the Jordan Case' (2004) 20 *South African Journal of Human Rights* 138.
[40] *Volks NO* v *Robinson and others* 2005 (5) BCLR 446 (CC).
[41] Act 27 of 1990.

relationship which, it was alleged, constituted unfair marital status discrimination. Significantly, by the time the case reached the Constitutional Court, the respondent had conceded the merits of the equality case. Nonetheless, the majority of the Court rejected this concession. In this case, the respondent and one Shandling had not married but had lived together in a permanent life partnership for some sixteen years prior to the death of Shandling. Following his death, Mrs Robinson submitted a claim for maintenance against the deceased's estate. The executor of the estate (Volks) rejected her claim because she was not a 'survivor' as envisaged in the Act. This decision prompted Robinson to seek an order declaring that she was entitled to lodge a claim for maintenance in the estate or, alternatively, a declaration that the Act was unconstitutional and invalid. Although the majority judgment was written by Justice Skweyiya, the influence of Arthur Chaskalson is not difficult to discern, particularly because when the counsel for the respondent rose before the court to concede the equality challenge, it was Chief Justice Chaskalson who insisted that the concession had not been wisely made.[42]

The essence of the majority judgment was that Mrs Robinson had freely chosen to enter into a life partnership with Mr Shandling 'in which each was free to continue or not and from which each was free to withdraw at will without obligation and without legal or other formalities'.[43] For this reason, the majority found that it was not unfair to distinguish between the survivors of a marriage and survivors of a heterosexual co-habitation relationship.[44]

The judgment was correctly criticised for its unqualified prioritisation of marriage as a foundation of society without any attempt to reference its historically racial and gendered nature, a move that allowed the Court to conclude that it was not unfair to discriminate between relationships that attract legal obligations of support (marriage) and those that do not (a life partnership between a heterosexual couple).[45] There was a dissenting judgment in this case by Judges O'Regan, Mokgoro and Sachs that severely took to task the majority's failure to appreciate the context and thus its seeing of marriage as part of an unfortunate yet legally neutral background.[46]

In contrast to these cautious judgments, the Court developed a more ambitious standard of review in relation to questions of property.[47] This was best illustrated in one of the last cases presided over by Chief Justice Chaskalson, *Port Elizabeth Municipality* v *Various Occupiers*.[48] Here, the Court sought to reconcile the constitutional right to property in terms of s 25 of the Constitution and the right to housing in terms of s 26 of the Constitution. It did so by noting:

---

[42]   Author's interview with Anton Katz SC, counsel for respondent in the case, 23 February 2005.
[43]   *Volks NO* v *Robinson and others* at para 55.
[44]   At para 60.
[45]   See Catherine Albertyn, 'Substantive Equality and Transformation in South Africa' (2007) 23 *South African Journal of Human Rights* 53 at 266.
[46]   *Volks NO* v *Robinson and others* at para 103.
[47]   For a comprehensive explanation, see Roux (*supra* n 27) chapter 8.
[48]   *Port Elizabeth Municipality* v *Various Occupiers* 2005 (1) SA 217 (CC).

The Constitution imposes new obligations on the court concerning rights relating to property not previously recognised by the common law. It counterposes to the normal ownership rights of possession, use and occupation, a new and equally relevant right not arbitrarily to be deprived of a home. The expectations that ordinarily go with title could clash head on with the genuine despair of people in dire need of accommodation. The judicial function in these circumstances is not to establish a hierarchal arrangement between the different interests involved, privileging in an abstract and mechanical way, the rights of ownership over the right not to be dispossessed of a home, or vice versa.[49]

Insisting that eviction from a property on an application by the owner could not take place without the competing parties seeking to engage with each other in a proactive attempt to find an acceptable solution, the Court infused 'elements of grace and compassion into the formal structures of the law'.[50]

At the same time, the Chaskalson Court ensured that no arbitrary eviction from property, including private property, could take place, mindful as it was of apartheid history of land removals. There was a considerable reluctance to apply the Bill of Rights horizontally, that is, to the consequences of the exercise of private power. The distinction that had been embedded in South African law between private and public power was shown to best advantage in *Du Plessis and others v De Klerk and another*.[51] Although the case was litigated under the Interim Constitution, which did not contain express horizontal provisions as later contained in s 8 of the final Constitution, it revealed a clear philosophical division in the Court as to the reach of a constitution. The case turned on whether the protection of the right to freedom of speech and expression under the Interim Constitution should apply to a defamation action between private parties. Arthur Chaskalson concurred in the judgment of Kentridge AJ, the essence of which was that bills of rights 'are ordinarily intended to protect the subject against legislative executive action'.[52] There is nothing in the majority judgment, in which Chaskalson concurred, that recognised the point made by Justice Madala:

Ours is a multi-racial, multi-cultural, multi-lingual society which the ravages of apartheid, disadvantage and inequality are just immeasurable. The extent of the oppressive measures in South Africa was not confined to government/individual relations, but equally to individual/individual relations. In its effort to create a new order, our Constitution must have been intended to address these oppressive and undemocratic practices at all levels. In my view our Constitution starts at the lowest level and attempts to reach the furthest in its endeavours to restructure the dynamics in a previously racist society.[53]

49 *Port Elizabeth Municipality v Various Occupiers* at para 23.
50 Sachs J in *Port Elizabeth Municipality* at para 37; see also Roux (*supra* n 27) at 325–7.
51 *Du Plessis and others v De Klerk and another* 1996 (3) SA 850 (CC).
52 *Du Plessis* at para 45.
53 Ibid. at para 163.

In short, the majority of which Arthur Chaskalson was an important part saw the Constitution through a traditional public law lens, thereby drawing a clear distinction between public and private law. This early judgment set a foundation that has continued, namely, a manifest reluctance on the part of the Court to engage in a significant overhaul of South African private law, which is based on Roman-Dutch law and was bequeathed to South Africa from its colonial past.[54]

12.6 CONCLUSION

The Constitutional Court, however, had to hit the ground running. The people had great expectations and their needs were great, as a result of more than 300 years of colonial and apartheid misrule. Those who worked with him, and I was privilege to be one of them were extremely fortunate to have a person of his calibre at the helm at this critical time.

—Chief Justice Pius Langa[55]

The analysis developed in this chapter reveals that the Court under the leadership of Chief Justice Chaskalson sought to respond to the challenges posed by a new Constitution through the judges' historical experiences of the manner in which law had the capacity to restrain the abuse of political power as well as the arbitrary excess of public power in general. It also adhered to a particular model of legal culture shaped before democracy dawned. It did so initially without much risk, in that the Mandela government was clearly in favour of the abolition of the death penalty and the assertion of the Court's jurisdiction over the executive power of the president.[56] But the Court was prepared later to risk a political backlash when it made its decision in the TAC case. It also developed a coherent jurisprudence to protect homeless people from arbitrary eviction, an approach that was born of a clear recognition of the inhumane effects of the land removals and evictions effected by the apartheid regime. However, even where it held government to its constitutional mandate, the Court was careful to base its judgment on legal principles that were both context-sensitive and modest in the sense of not encroaching on the executive terrain of policy, the ambitious provisions of the Constitution, particularly the clauses guaranteeing substantive equality and socio-economic rights, notwithstanding.

The cautious approach to a thick text is best exemplified in the Court's socio-economic jurisprudence, which was exquisitely careful not to trench on the boundaries of the executive. Even after he retired, Chief Justice Chaskalson tenaciously

[54] For a comprehensive examination of the jurisprudence that followed *Du Plessis* and *De Klerk* notwithstanding the change in the Constitution, see Dennis M Davis and Karl Klare, 'Transformative Constitutionalism and the Common and Customary' (2010) 26 *South African Journal of Human Rights* 403.

[55] Obituary delivered by Chief Justice Pius Langa, 3 December 2012. On file with the author.

[56] Counsel for President Mandela in *Hugo* Gilbert Marcus SC informed me in an interview (19 December 2018) that his client forbade him to argue that the presidential power was not reviewable.

defended the view that courts were not qualified to set a minimum core of each of the socio-economic rights contained in the Constitution. They had neither the expertise nor the knowledge to do so and such over-ambitious jurisprudence would only have compromised the distributive choices made by a democratically elected government.[57]

This level of caution was also evident in Chief Justice Chaskalson's deference to the role of legislative choices. In *UDM v President of the Republic of South Africa (2)*,[58] the Court was concerned with the constitutionality of the so-called anti-defection clause, namely, that a public representative who ceases to be a member of a party loses his or her seat in the relevant legislature. The applicants argued that, given the right to vote and the principle of proportional legislation that was part of the basic structure of the South African Constitution, legislation that sought to abolish the anti-defection clause would compromise this electoral system. Although the judgment was authored by the Court as a whole, the hand of Arthur Chaskalson is clearly evident, particularly in words recalling his early judgment in *Makwanyane*: 'This case is not about the merits or demerits of the provisions of the disputed legislation, that is a political question and is of no concern to this court. What has to be decided is not whether the disputed provisions are appropriate or inappropriate, but whether they are constitutional or unconstitutional.'[59] The Court was criticised for refusing the UDM application, thereby failing to contribute to the curbing of the excessive power of a dominant party.[60]

The Court followed Chaskalson's broad legal philosophy, born of his years as both an advocate at the Johannesburg Bar and head of the Legal Resources Centre. He ensured that the Court attained a legitimacy of its own by exercising its role as a protector of individual rights in, for example, declaring the death penalty to be unconstitutional and protecting homeless people against arbitrary eviction. He also carefully ensured that the Court did not stray into the political domain by pre-empting fiscal and economic policy decisions best left to the executive and the legislature. However, this description of the Court's jurisprudential trajectory was not seamless. When Nelson Mandela, who was fastidiously protective of the Court, was replaced by the more aggressive assertion of executive rule of Thabo Mbeki, the Court acted boldly to safeguard the rights of millions of South Africans who were placed in life-threatening situations because of the Mbeki government's HIV/AIDS policy.

In general, however, it is fair to say that over the decade in which Judge Chaskalson occupied the office of chief justice, the Court developed a

---

[57] Author's interview with Arthur Chaskalson, April 2011.
[58] *UDM v President of the Republic of South Africa (2)* 2003 (1) SA 495 (CC).
[59] Ibid. at para 11.
[60] See Samuel Issacharoff, 'The Democratic Risk to Democratic Transitions' (2013) 5 *Constitutional Review* 1; Sujiit Choudhry, '"He Has a Mandate": The South African Constitutional Court and the African National Congress in a Dominant Political Democracy' (2009) 2 *Constitutional Court Review* 1.

jurisprudence within the confines of an incremental model of legal change while adopting the view that a democratically elected government was to do the heavy social and economic lifting. By contrast, the Court was confident in its protection of certain rights and deferential to political power sourced in the choices of the electorate. It was a judicial model rooted in Arthur Chaskalson's vision of constitutional democracy; after all, he had been a key drafter of the Interim Constitution, which, in large part, was incorporated into the 1996 Constitution. It reflected his approach to law shaped during his time as an advocate of unquestioned technical skill at the bar.

Chaskalson's forensic skill was evident in his conduct of oral hearings. For counsel appearing before him, one of the greatest challenges was to attempt to answer the questions he posed from the bench. Once the first question had been asked, the counsel inevitably knew that, whatever the answer, there would be a series of further questions that would expose their case to the full glare of judicial scrutiny.

The description of this model of constitutional democracy is best left to Chaskalson himself when he delivered the third Bram Fischer Lecture.[61] In this lecture Chaskalson emphasized that, while courts have an important role to play in the transformative process, the doctrine of separation of powers meant that 'countervailing claims of democracy demand that the regulatory role of government in a democratic society be recognised'.[62] He emphasized that the vision of the Constitution requires the energy, commitment and sense of community that were harnessed in the struggle for freedom against apartheid. Thus, 'all of us have an obligation to make the Constitution work and it is in all of our interest that this be done'.[63] Of equal significance was the emphasis placed by Chaskalson on the constitutional right of dignity, which he regarded as crucial in order to accommodate conflicting interests.[64] The emphasis on dignity, sourced in an abiding concern for the individual and his particular reference to the Constitution as being binding all organs of state, without reference to private power, was reflective of the broad approach taken by the Constitutional Court during his ten years in office.

Although the Constitutional Court won universal acclaim for its transformative jurisprudence[65] during the period under review, unlike Chief Justices Bhagwati and Barak, who came to personify the achievements of the Indian and the Israeli apex

---

[61]   Bram Fischer was the lead counsel in the Rivonia case in which Chaskalson was junior counsel. He was eventually imprisoned for his political activities. See, in this regard, S Clingman and Bram Fischer, *Afrikaner Revolutionary* (David Phillip, 2002). Chaskalson was influenced by Fischer's style of advocacy, perhaps by the fact that not only did he acquire the desk used by Bram Fischer as counsel but the desk found its way into Chaskalson's office when he became chief justice of South Africa.

[62]   Arthur Chaskalson, 'The Third Bram Fisher Lecture: Human Dignity as a Foundational Value of Our Constitutional Order' (2000) 16 *South African Journal of Human Rights* 193 at 202.

[63]   Ibid. at 205.

[64]   Ibid. at 201.

[65]   See Roux (*supra* n 27).

courts, respectively, Arthur Chaskalson's name was not synonymous with the South African Constitutional Court. Justices Albie Sachs and Richard Goldstone might have contributed more to the global reputation of the Court. However, ask any serious lawyer in South Africa about the respective influences on the Court and you will be told that the jurisprudential contribution of these prominent jurists pales in significance when compared to that of Chaskalson.

That said, Chaskalson was not one to seek publicity. While he had a formidable and austere personality that commanded respect, he was a shy and socially awkward person who eschewed any kind of profile-raising or media exposure. For this reason, analysts outside South Africa rarely reflect the true nature of his contribution to the post-apartheid judicial enterprise.

However, domestically, Chaskalson had the advantage of enjoying widespread respect for his long and successful career as a human rights lawyer. Thus, far more than his role in drafting the Interim Constitution, his legal career gained him the legitimacy needed to lead the new Constitutional Court. In terms of the dimensions of 'toweringness' described in the Introduction to this volume, Chaskalson may not have propelled the Court into embarking on a coherent progressive agenda, but he was critical to the successful establishment and development of a new apex court that increasingly gained the respect of the country in general and the legal community in particular. He also fashioned the careful and incremental manner in which the Court embraced the challenge of the new Constitution. Viewed in this way, he differed from some of the other towering judges. He was both the intellectual and the social leader of the Court, and he left behind a significant jurisprudential and institutional legacy.

Turning to that legacy, the foundation set by the Chaskalson Court lives on in South Africa, the various vicissitudes of the past decade of Zuma rule notwithstanding. Zuma's presidency between 2009 and 2018, however, posed far greater challenges to the judicial system than those that confronted the Chaskalson Court. Rampant corruption, the capture of key institutions designed to safeguard the constitutional state, the National Prosecution Authority, the South African Police Service, the South African Revenue Service run by Zuma cronies and a majority party whose parliamentary representatives refused to exercise legislative oversight over the executive all contributed to a hollowing out of constitutional democracy.[66] Again and again, the courts, particularly the Constitutional Court, were called upon to determine disputes that were essentially products of a failed political system. Lawfare, the transplantation of political disputes into legal claims, replaced political warfare. Unlike the Mandela era, in which the judgments of the courts were respected by the executive, as the courts held the executive accountable to the strictures of legality, they were consistently attacked for being counterrevolutionaries.[67]

---

[66]   See, e.g., Jacques Pauw, *The Presidents Keepers* (NB Publishers, 2017).

[67]   Gwede Mantashe lambasted the courts for 'acting as if they were the political opposition and in so doing seeking to arrest the functioning of Government'; *Sowetan*, 18 August 2011. Zuma himself gave

Dennis M Davis

The judicial record over this period reveals that the Constitutional Court stood firmly on the side of the Constitution and confirmed its jurisdiction over the executive. In doing so, it continued to perform its role as set out initially by the Chaskalson Court.[68] For this reason, more than any other, it can confidently be claimed that the phrase 'towering judge' is truly apposite when it comes to the evaluation of Arthur Chaskalson's contribution to constitutional democracy in South Africa.

    probably the clearest indicator of the government's aversion to judicial review when he told
    Parliament on 1 November 2011: 'the powers conferred on the courts cannot be regarded as superior
    to the powers resulting from a mandate given by the people in a popular vote. ... Judiciary must
    respect separation of powers'; *PoliticsWeb*, www.politicsweb.co.za/documents/judiciary-must-respect-
    separation-of-powers-jacob.
[68] *Economic Freedom Fighters* v *Speaker of the National Assembly and others* 2016 (3) SA 586 (CC) in
    which the Court upheld the public protector's order that Zuma repay the state for the costs of
    improvements to his private homestead.

13

Chief Justice Sólyom and the Paradox of "Revolution under the Rule of Law"

Gábor Attila Tóth

13.1 INTRODUCTION

László Sólyom was the first chief justice of the Hungarian Constitutional Court between 1990 and 1998.[1] The Constitutional Court, as a member of the third European generation of its kind, was set up to protect the new democratic constitution after the collapse of the Soviet-type autocratic regime. The Court was considered to be the most important guardian of constitutionalism, on account of its decisions favoring human rights and the principles of the rule of law. László Sólyom played a distinguished role in shaping the case law of the Court, and, in an early judgment, he expressed his strong belief in its groundbreaking mission: "The Court must fulfill its task embedded in history. The Court is the repository of the paradox of 'revolution under the rule of law.'"[2]

There is a consensus among constitutional scholars that Sólyom was the most dominant jurist in the short-lived Republic of Hungary. There is, however, much less agreement about his achievements, and scholars arrive at opposing conclusions even regarding their description. For example, Kim Lane Scheppele, a leading expert of Hungarian constitutional law, endorses the Sólyom-led Constitutional

---

[1] László Sólyom was born in 1942 in Pécs and studied law at the University of Pécs. While earning his doctorate, he worked as assistant professor at the Institute of Civil Law in Jena, East Germany. Subsequently, he taught law in Hungary at the ELTE University, Péter Pázmány Catholic University, and Gyula Andrássy German Language University. Sólyom was involved in politics in the 1980s, when he was a member of various organizations, including the environmental group Danube Circle, the Openness Club, and the Hungarian Democratic Forum, a conservative political party. During the transition to constitutional democracy, he took part in the roundtable negotiations. He focused on constitutional adjudication and fundamental rights, especially data protection and freedom of information. In 1989, Sólyom was elected by the parliament to the newly established Constitutional Court, and he served as president of the Court from 1990 to 1998. After the end of his mandate, he continued his academic career. In 2005, he emerged as a candidate for president, nominated by an environmental group and supported by different parliamentary parties, most importantly the then opposition party Fidesz. His five-year term as head of state expired in 2010.

[2] Judgment 11/1992 (III. 5.) HCC.

Court for its judgments establishing the rule of law and democracy.[3] András Sajó, by contrast, warned early on in the given period that the activist Court undermined the rule of law itself by disregarding the written constitution.[4] Bojan Bugarič and Tom Ginsburg are full of praise for "the strong leadership of liberal Chief Justice Sólyom,"[5] whereas János Kis and I have argued that the Sólyom Court was influenced by the conception of the Second Vatican Council, a progressive but nonsecular Catholic view.[6] Scheppele, again, claims that, in the 1990s, the Constitutional Court completed the constitutional transformation and ran Hungary successfully. Bruce Ackerman and Stephen Holmes, by contrast, were doubtful about the initial achievements of the court because of its weak democratic legitimacy.[7] Andrew Arato has observed that Sólyom was on the one hand an admirer of Hans Kelsen's legal positivism, while on the other he mobilized a form of constitutional mythology of origins derived from Carl Schmitt.[8]

This chapter would not attempt to decide between these opposing views on Sólyom. Rather, one of its aims is to show the paradoxes in Sólyom's jurisprudence and personality and through them the challenges of towering judges. Secondly, the aim of this chapter is to examine Chief Justice Sólyom's role in the democratic transformation and consolidation and also in the democratic decline. By focusing particularly on his views and decisions, the analysis may contribute to the understanding of the rise and fall of constitutionalism in Hungary.

I first summarize Sólyom's views on the attributes of the democratic transformation and the status of the Constitutional Court (Section 13.2). Then I turn to the leading judgments and separate opinions of the chief justice (Section 13.3). I offer an explanation of his views on the judiciary, constitutional interpretation, and fundamental

---

[3] Kim Lane Scheppele, "Constitutional Negotiations: Political Contexts of Judicial Activism in Post-Soviet Europe" in SA Arjomand (ed.), *Constitutionalism and Political Reconstruction* (Brill, 2007) 318 and Kim Lane Scheppele, "On the Unconstitutionality of the Constitutional Change: An Essay in Honor of László Sólyom" in Pál Sonnevend, Balázs Schanda, and Zoltán Csehi (eds.), *Viva Vox Iuris Civilis: In Honor of László Sólyom* (Szent István Társulat, 2012) 286–310.

[4] András Sajó, "Reading the Invisible Constitution: Judicial Review in Hungary" (1995) 15 *Oxford Journal of Legal Studies* 253, 266–7.

[5] Bojan Bugarič and Tom Ginsburg, "The Assault on Postcommunist Courts" (2016) 27 *Journal of Democracy* 69–82.

[6] János Kis, *Constitutional Democracy* (Central European University Press, 2003) 295. See also Gábor Attila Tóth, "Unequal Protection: Historical Churches and Roma People in the Hungarian Constitutional Jurisprudence" (2010) 51(2) *Acta Juridica Hungarica* 122–35 and Gábor Attila Tóth, "Lost in Transition: Invisible Constitutionalism in Hungary" in Rosalind Dixon and Adrienne Stone (eds.), *The Invisible Constitution in Comparative Perspective* (Cambridge University Press, 2018) 541–62.

[7] Bruce Ackerman, *The Future of the Liberal Revolution* (Yale University Press, 1992) ch 6 and Stephen Holmes, "Back to the Drawing Board" (1993) 2 *East European Constitutional Review* 21–3. See also Stephen Holmes and Cass R Sunstein, "The Politics of Constitutional Revision in Eastern Europe" in Sanford Levinson (ed.), *Responding to Imperfection: Theory and Practice of Constitutional Amendment* (Princeton University Press, 1995) 300.

[8] Andrew Arato, *Post Sovereign Constitution Making: Learning and Legitimacy* (Oxford University Press, 2016) 174.

rights. Finally, in Section 13.4, I show how Sólyom modified his point of view on key constitutional issues when serving as the head of state between 2005 and 2010, the last years of the Republic of Hungary.

This chapter does not offer simple or easy answers. It does not argue that Sólyom as a liberal thinker and judge consolidated the liberal democracy in Hungary. Nor does it try to convince us that the opposite is true, that is, that Sólyom's judicial activism contributed to the backsliding from the conditions of liberal democracy. Like any remarkable thinker, Sólyom is, of course, complex. Like any constitutional change, transformations to and away from liberal democracy in Hungary are also complex constitutional phenomena. This chapter claims that even though his merits as head of the first Hungarian Constitutional Court should be fully recognized, Sólyom's legacy involves many paradoxical elements. What this study can give is an explanation of the scope, nature, and some causes of the paradoxes. These paradoxes, however, do not detract from the assessment of Sólyom as a "towering judge." Chief Justice Sólyom, as a founder and developer of Hungarian constitutionalism, towered over his peers to distinguish himself not only in the Hungarian context but also worldwide. It is the view of this chapter that his outstanding commitment to constitutionalism and democratic values outshines the flaws and contradictions that will be discussed.

13.2 A CONSTITUTIONAL REVOLUTIONARY

13.2.1 *The Roundtable as "Constituent Power"*

As a representative of a conservative opposition party, László Sólyom was an important participant in the roundtable negotiations over the transition of Hungary into democracy. Thus, he can be considered as one of the founders of the republic and drafters of the constitution. The historical turning point for the transformation from a Soviet-type autocratic regime to constitutional democracy was the autumn of 1989. Departing from both the tradition of revolutionary constitution-making and the models of merely reformatory processes, the peaceful, negotiated regime changes in East Central Europe – along with the previous Spanish and Portuguese experiences – established a new type of constitution-making, labeled "coordinated transition."[9] This means that, with the exception of Romania, the single or dominant party systems collapsed through a series of roundtable negotiations between the old regime and the democratic opposition.

The 1989 roundtables in Hungary and comparable countries in the region were meant to regulate the transition from the old regime to a new one, but they did not

---

[9] Janos Kis, "Between Reform and Revolution: Three Hypotheses about the Nature of Regime Change" (1995) 1 *Constellations* 399 and Andrew Arato, "Post-Sovereign Constitution-Making in Hungary: After Success, Partial Failure, and Now What?" (2010) 26 *South African Journal on Human Rights: Constitution-Making as a Learning Process* 19.

have a mandate for constitution-making. In order for their decisions to take legal effect, those decisions needed to be sent for enactment to the old legislature. The roundtables left the completion of the process to an assembly with the democratic mandate they were lacking.[10] This constitution-making profile can be presented as consisting of two stages. In the first stage, a roundtable agreement determines the ground rules of preparing and holding free and fair democratic elections. The second stage takes place when a body of freely elected representatives adopts, in the sovereign people's name, a new constitution.[11]

In formal terms, the 1989 Hungarian Constitution, drafted by legal professionals at the roundtable, was one of the modifications of the 1949 Stalinist Constitution. The new preamble contained a clear reference to the interim status of the Constitution.[12] In substantive terms, however, the 1989 political transition breathed new life into the Constitution. Since the models of the reshaped Constitution were international human rights instruments, as well as the more recent Western constitutions, it was written in the language of modern constitutionalism: rules for free and fair elections, representative government, a parliamentary system, an independent judiciary, ombudspersons to guard fundamental rights, and a Constitutional Court to review the laws for their constitutionality.[13] Like other East Central European democracies, Hungary followed Western European traditions in establishing a parliamentary system instead of importing a US presidential architecture.[14] A 1990 constitutional amendment made it clear that the prime minister heads the executive and the government is the supreme body of that branch, answerable to parliament.[15]

[10]   Kis characterizes the coordinated transition as an interruption of legitimacy but also a continuity of legality. Kis (*supra* n 9) 317. See also his critical reflections of the legitimacy of the 1989 Constitution: János Kis, "Introduction: From the 1989 Constitution to the 2011 Fundamental Law" in Gábor Attila Tóth (ed.), *Constitution for a Disunited Nation* (Central European University Press, 2012) 1–24.

[11]   In the aftermath of the Polish Round Table Agreement, the old constitution was amended in April 1989, and the first democratic parliament then reshaped the relations between the legislative and the executive branches of the state ("Small Constitution"). The reformed constitution was finally replaced in 1997 by a completely new constitution for Poland. The old constitution of Czechoslovakia was also amended in 1989. The Charter of Fundamental Rights and Basic Freedoms was incorporated in 1991. After the dissolution of the federal state, the Czech Republic and the Slovak Republic each adopted a new constitution in 1992. In Bulgaria and Romania, the second step was made in 1991.

[12]   "In order to facilitate a peaceful political transition to a constitutional state, establish a multi-party system, parliamentary democracy and a social market economy, the Parliament of the Republic of Hungary hereby establishes the following text as the Constitution of the Republic of Hungary, until the country's new Constitution is adopted." Adopted by the National Assembly of Hungary on October 18, 1989 and entered into force on October 23, 1989.

[13]   In more detail, see Gábor Attila Tóth, "Hungary" in Leonard Besselink, Paul Bovend'eert, Hansko Broeksteeg, Roel de Lange, and Wim Voermans (eds.), *Constitutional Law of the E.U. Member States* (Kluwer, 2014) 775–9.

[14]   Lech Garlicki, "Democracy and International Influences" in G Nolte (ed.), *European and US Constitutionalism* (Cambridge University Press, 2005) 264.

[15]   For reconsidering the regional developments between the collapse of communism and the enlargement of the European Union from the point of view of the rule of law and constitutionalism, see Adam Czarnota, Martin Krygier, and Wojciech Sadurski (eds.), *Rethinking the Rule of Law after Communism* (Central European University Press, 2005).

As chief justice and a constitutional scholar, Sólyom claimed subsequently that the roundtable constitution was a final one, even if its preamble declared an interim status. He argued that there was no need to complete the constitution-making project because the 1989 constitutional text substantially fulfilled the requirements of constitutionalism. Although he showed that he was very aware of the legitimation problems by admitting that the process "did not originate among the people," Sólyom characterized the roundtable as "constituent power."[16] There are several Constitutional Court judgments from the initial period referring to the roundtable documents as legal sources of the original meaning of the constitution or the framers' original intent.[17]

Importantly, Hungary was the only post-communist country that omitted the second step, as it did not adopt a formally new constitution in that period (prior to 2011). Although the 1989 Constitution was amended several times – for example, to qualify Hungary to join the European Convention of Human Rights, NATO, and the European Union – the country did not accomplish the symbolic mission: it failed to adopt a final constitution, a step that would have demonstrated a completion of the democratic transition. This failure may seem unexpected because, compared to those of other European states, the 1989 Hungarian Constitution was easy to amend. Despite the fact that the Constitution could not be modified or amended by the ordinary law-making procedure according to a simple majority rule, it was regarded as relatively flexible rather than rigid, in the sense that it did not render any provision or principle unamendable, and it required only the votes of two-thirds of members of the one-chamber legislative body. Neither a referendum nor any other form of ratification (e.g., approval by the subsequent parliament) was required for the adoption of a new constitution or a constitutional amendment. However, the increasingly hostile political environment and the divergent, often diffuse constitutional conceptions prevented a consensus or even compromises on a formally new constitution.[18]

In substantive terms, Sólyom was correct to describe the amended constitution of the old regime as a complete text consistent with the abstract principles and institutions of modern constitutionalism. In other words, the 1989 roundtable constitution was suitable as a framework for liberal democracy. In procedural terms, however, Sólyom's revolutionary claim can be seen as both counterfactual (because the roundtable did not have constitution-making power) and normatively

[16] László Sólyom, "The Role of Constitutional Courts in the Transition to Democracy, with Special Reference to Hungary" in Saïd Amir Arjomand (ed.), *Constitutionalism and Political Reconstruction* (Brill, 2007) 283–314, 305. For a critical analysis, see Andrew Arato, *The Adventures of the Constituent Power* (Cambridge University Press, 2017) part II.3 and Arato (*supra* n 8) 173–4.

[17] Gábor Attila Tóth, *Túl a szövegen: Értekezés a magyar alkotmányról* (Osiris, 2009) 73–5; László Sólyom, *Pártok és érdekszervezetek az alkotmányban* (Rejtjel, 2004) 15–25; László Sólyom, *Az alkotmánybíráskodás kezdetei Magyarországon* (Osiris, 2001) 333.

[18] Andrew Arato, "The Constitution-Making Endgame in Hungary" (1996) 4 *East European Constitutional Review* 31–9.

problematic. The roundtable constitution was democratic in its content but without democratic confirmation. The constitution-making process would have required a completion by a democratically elected assembly.

13.2.2 *The Constitutional Court as "Constituent Power"*

László Sólyom expressed another powerful argument on the constitution-making authority. He insisted that the Constitutional Court has to fulfill its task embedded in history to complete the democratic regime change. In Sólyom's view, the Court was in an exceptional situation to develop "unwritten constitutional principles, substitute rules, and creative interpretations."[19] In a judgment, he expressed that the "revolution under the rule of law" means, among other things, that "in the process of the peaceful transition, beginning with the new Constitution, the Constitutional Court must, within its competences, in all cases unconditionally guarantee the conformity of the legislative power with the Constitution."[20] By referring to exceptional historical circumstances, he went further and sought to justify a "revolutionary legitimacy" for the Constitutional Court. In this way, he affirmed a quasi-constituent power for the Court.[21] Sólyom's approach thus vindicated even the status of a substitute constitution-making authority, much beyond the role of final constitutional arbitrator.[22]

Constitutional transformations are, of course, inseparable from institutional changes. Judicial protection of the Constitution in Hungary and elsewhere in the region was closer to the centralized German model than to the US judicial review.[23] This meant that the Constitutional Court was institutionally separated from the ordinary court system and had unique *erga omnes* constitutional interpretative authority. One of the main reasons for this was that the transition was characterized by a deep mistrust of the judiciary among the new elites and the masses, as it was considered to be a means of oppression from the previous regime.[24]

---

[19] Sólyom (*supra* n 16) 305.
[20] Judgment 11/1992 (III. 5.) HCC. See also Gábor Attila Tóth, "The Bitter Pills of Political Transition" in A Jakab, P Takács and A Tatham (eds.), *The Transformation of the Hungarian Legal Order 1985–2005* (Kluwer Law International, 2007) 281–6.
[21] Arato (*supra* n 8) 174, 199–200.
[22] That is crucially different from Dworkin's theory, which argues for constitutional review only by saying that democracy does not insist on judges having the last world in constitutional issues; it does not insist that they must not have it. Ronald Dworkin, *Freedom's Law: The Moral Reading of the American Constitution* (Oxford University Press, 2005) 7.
[23] From a theoretical and a critical point of view, see Wojciech Sadurski, *Rights before Courts: A Study of Constitutional Courts in Post-Communist States of Central and Eastern Europe* (Springer, 2005). See also Herman Schwartz, *The Struggle for Constitutional Justice in Post-Communist Europe* (University of Chicago Press, 2000).
[24] András Sajó, "The Judiciary in Contemporary Society: Hungary" (1993) 25 *Case Western Reserve Journal of International Law* 293, https://scholarlycommons.law.case.edu/jil/vol25/iss2/14.

As a member of the third generation of European constitutional courts, the Hungarian institution followed the modern constitutional model of democratic change.[25] Famously, the Austrian, German, and Italian constitutional courts were (re)established after the fall of totalitarian regimes, in the late 1940s and the early 1950s, then the Spanish and Portuguese courts were set up after the fall of the regimes of Franco and Salazar in the late 1970s; these were followed by the constitutional courts of post-Soviet democracies, along with the post-apartheid South African Constitutional Court, from the early 1990s.[26] Finally, after the bloody breakup of Yugoslavia, the newly independent states established their own constitutional institutions, including constitutional courts.

Sólyom strongly believed in constitutional hierarchies. He easily associated the centralized model of constitutional adjudication, the separation from the ordinary court system, and the *erga omnes* constitutional interpretative authority with judicial superiority. Similarly to the Kelsenian hierarchy of legal norms, with the constitution at its peak, in the field of institutions, the constitutional court is the highest in rank. Sólyom acknowledged the constitution-making authority of parliament but also degraded it by viewing it as being motivated by actual political interests. Thus, representative forms of democratic decision-making were regarded with ambiguity. Sólyom believed that the symbolic completion of the democratic transition with a brand-new constitution was unnecessary because the Court as the highest-ranking constitutional body could replace the constitution-making authority by its principled judgments.

Looking back from the present, one may conclude that the activism of the Sólyom Court was unjustified and that the young constitutional democracy should have secured itself in nonjudicial ways. I think, however, that this would be a simplistic conclusion. It must be admitted, on the one hand, that constitutional theory or comparable case studies could hardly support Sólyom's view that a constitutional court may vindicate the status of a substitute constitution-making authority. But, on the other hand, countless empirical cases from countries in democratic transition teach us that apex courts play a distinctive, incomparable role in establishing the rule of law and protecting fundamental rights. Judicial activity of a certain kind was indeed inevitable in Hungary since the interim, often amended constitution

---

[25] Originally, Favoreau distinguished "three waves" of constitutional justice, starting with the Austrian and Czechoslovak constitutional courts from the 1920s, then the reestablishment of the Austrian court together with setting up the German court, and, finally, the Spanish, Portuguese, and East-Central European courts. Louis Favoreu, *Les Cours Constitutionnelles* (Presses Universitaires de France, 1986). See also Louis Favoreu and Wanda Mastor, *Les cours constitutionnelles. Connaissance du droit* (Dalloz, 2011) As for the first three generations of constitutional courts, see László Sólyom, "The Role of Constitutional Courts in the Transition of Democracy: With Special Reference to Hungary" (March 2003) 18 *International Sociology* 133–61, 135.

[26] For the case of Hungary, see Catherine Dupré, *Importing the Law in Post-Communist Transitions: The Hungarian Constitutional Court and the Right to Human Dignity* (Hart, 2003). See also László Sólyom and Georg Brunner, *Constitutional Judiciary in a New Democracy: The Hungarian Constitutional Court* (University of Michigan Press, 2000).

required that the first Constitutional Court play a stabilizing role. The judgments of the Constitutional Court can be seen as attempts of the main force of consolidation to create a new constitutional culture not only within the state institutions but also within the whole of society.[27] Even if these understandable attempts were not fully successful, the attempt should be understood in the conditions of the time.

13.3 CHIEF JUSTICE WITHOUT PRECEDENT

13.3.1 Creating a Jurisprudence from Scratch

The Constitutional Court seemed to be the most important institutional guarantee of constitutionalism, on account of its decisions favoring human rights and the principles of the rule of law.[28] The lack of an entirely and formally new constitution increased the responsibilities of the Constitutional Court as both the ultimate interpreter of constitutional principles and fundamental rights and the most crucial constitutional check on the powers of parliament. The 1990 starting point for

[27] See a debate on this between Scheppele and Arato: Scheppele (*supra* n 3 (both works)) and Arato (*supra* n 8) 86, 173–5. As regards the legitimacy of this kind of judicial attitude, many advocates of powerful constitutional courts engaged in endless debates with scholars such as Bruce Ackerman who were doubtful about the initial achievements of the courts because of their weak democratic justification. Although it also touched on the very nature of East-Central European coordinated transitions, this discussion can be placed within the general debates on the final guardians of the constitution. The main question was supposedly which organ possesses the "final word" in matters of constitutional justice. In this way, the rival scholars were revolving judicial interpretive authority as well as its mandate to review the constitutionality of legislative acts. This problem has its roots in the Kelsen-Schmitt debate on the guardians of the constitution. Hans Kelsen, "Wesen und Entwicklung der Staatsgerichtsbarkeit" [1927] in Peter Häberle (ed.), *Verfassungsgerichtsbarkeit* (Darmstadt, 1976) and Carl Schmitt, *Der Hüter der Verfassung* (Duncker & Humblot, [1931] 1996). Subsequently, Bickel introduced the concept "countermajoritarian difficulty" in liberal democracies. Alexander Bickel, *The Least Dangerous Branch: The Supreme Court at the Bar of Politics* (Bobbs-Merrill, 1962) Contemporary discussions are explainable in the light of the Ely-Dworkin and Dworkin-Waldron debates on the legitimacy of judicial review. John Hart Ely, *Democracy and Distrust: A Theory of Judicial Review* (Harvard University Press, 1980); Ronald Dworkin, *Taking Rights Seriously* (Harvard University Press, 1977); Ronald Dworkin, *Law's Empire* (Hart, 1998); Jeremy Waldron, *Law and Disagreement* (Clarendon Press, 1999); and a partly revisited view, Jeremy Waldron, "The Core of the Case Against Judicial Review" (2006) 115 *Yale Law Journal* 1346. See also the last word from Ronald Dworkin, *Justice for Hedgehogs*,(Belknap Press, 2011) 483–5. Meanwhile, Habermas presented a model of discourse between courts and representative bodies: Jürgen Habermas, *Faktizität und Geltung, Beitrage zur Diskurstheorie des Rechts und des demokratischen Rechtsstaats* (Suhrkamp, 1992). Recently, many new scholarships have emerged, offering, on the one hand, justificatory perspectives, e.g., Mattias Kumm, "Institutionalising Socratic Contestation: The Rationalist Human Rights Paradigm, Legitimate Authority and the Point of Judicial Review" (2007) 1(2) *European Journal of Legal Studies* 1–32, and, on the other, intense critiques such as: Mark Tushnet, *Taking the Constitution Away from the Courts* (Princeton University Press, 1999); Ran Hirschl, *Towards Juristocracy: The Origins and Consequences of the New Constitutionalism* (Harvard University Press, 2007); and, particularly, Tom Gerald Daly, *The Alchemist: Questioning Our Faith in Courts As Democracy-Builders* (Cambridge University Press, 2017).

[28] Spenzer Zifcak, "Hungary's Remarkable, Radical, Constitutional Court" (1996) 1(3) *Journal of Constitutional Law in Eastern and Central Europe* 1–56. See also Dupré (*supra* n 26).

constitutional jurisdiction meant that neither domestic precedents nor a doctrinal framework elaborated on by academics guided the Court. Chief Justice Sólyom, aided by his distinguished expertise and striking judicial ambition, had a chance to dominate the inceptive period of adjudication. He was the only judge who promptly realized that constitutional principles and fundamental rights are interpretive concepts. They are at the core of the text of the constitution and the basis of the jurisdiction of the Court. As a matter of substance, the Court initiated a process of creating from case to case a coherent system of fundamental rights. As a matter of interpretive methods, Sólyom acknowledged in one of his interviews that the Court took on itself the task of providing a moral reading of the underlying principles of the Constitution.[29]

In the absence of domestic precedents, the Sólyom Court used many international and foreign standards of judicial review as precedents. The Court protected fundamental rights effectively with the help of the proportionality principle, and the *allgemeine Handlungsfreiheit* imported from the European Court of Human Rights and the Federal Constitutional Court of Germany (General Personality Right Case),[30] as well as the *clear and present danger* scrutiny derived from the US constitutional adjudication (Hate Speech Case I).[31] More importantly, the Sólyom-led Court placed human dignity at the center of its judicature in an unprecedented way. With only mild exaggeration, we could say that the early reading of the constitutional text gave rise to applied theories of justice and human dignity in Hungarian constitutional jurisdiction. Theories of justice were meant to determine the results compatible with the constitutional text. In its first landmark judgment, in 1990, the Constitutional Court abolished the death penalty.[32] The

---

[29] László Sólyom and Gábor Attila Tóth (interview), "A nehéz eseteknél a bíró erkölcsi felfogása jut szerephez. Sólyom Lászlóval, az Alkotmánybíróság elnökével Tóth Gábor Attila beszélget" in Gábor Halmai (ed.), *The Constitution Found? The First Nine Years of the Hungarian Constitutional Review of Fundamental Rights* (Indok, 2000) 389.

[30] Judgment 8/1990 (IV. 23.) HCC.

[31] Judgment 30/1992 (V. 26.) HCC.

[32] Judgment 23/1990 (X. 31.) HCC. Sólyom expressed in *obiter dicta* that he was applying the "invisible" constitution:

> The Constitutional Court must continue its effort to explain the theoretical bases of the Constitution and the rights included in it and to form a coherent system with its decisions in order to provide a reliable standard of constitutionality – an "invisible Constitution" – beyond the Constitution, which is often amended nowadays by current political interests; and because of this "invisible Constitution" probably will not conflict with the new Constitution to be established or with future Constitutions. The Constitutional Court enjoys freedom in this process as long as it remains within the framework of the concept of constitutionality. (Judgment 23/1990 (X. 31.) HCC, concurring opinion by Chief Justice Sólyom)

This doctrine became the benchmark of Hungarian constitutionalism after the democratic transition thanks to some leading judgments under Sólyom's name. The doctrine was understood as a tool for implicitly amending the text of the constitution in the name of constitutional ideas, as happened in the Capital Punishment Case. In this respect, the Court's approach was not in line with the famous phrase from Chief Justice Marshal that it must never be forgotten that it is the Constitution that judges

interpretation of the right to human dignity, both as a moral value and as a constitutional right, served as an example for the Ukrainian, Lithuanian, Albanian, and South African Constitutional Courts.[33] The chief justice emphasized that the constitutional concept of human dignity is more than a declaration of moral value; it is a value a priori and beyond law, a source of rights; therefore, the Court's task is to transform many of its aspects into a true right. The reasoning went on with the idea that

> [t]he right to human dignity has two functions. On the one hand, it means that there is an absolute limit which may not be transgressed either by the State or by the coercive power of other people – *i.e.* it is a seed of autonomy and individual self-determination withdrawn from the control of anybody else by virtue of which, according to the classical wording, man may remain an individual and will not be changed into a tool or object ... The other function of the right to dignity is to ensure equality.[34]

Sólyom held that the system of fundamental rights has its *hierarchical* nature. First, the chief justice and his fellow justices declared that human life and dignity have the greatest value in the constitutional order. Furthermore, "the rights to human life and human dignity form an indivisible and unrestrainable fundamental right which is the source of and the condition for several additional fundamental rights."[35] Subsequently, the Court added that the freedom of expression, the so-called "mother right" of fundamental rights of communication (freedom of the press and all media, as well as freedom of information), also takes a special place in the hierarchy of rights. Although this privileged place does not mean that this right may not be restricted – unlike the right to life or human dignity – it nonetheless necessarily implies that the freedom of expression must give way to only a few rights; that is, the laws restricting this freedom must be strictly construed.[36] Finally in this line, the Court stated further that this second-best status in the hierarchy of rights also applies to the freedom of religion, because "in a certain sense, religion is part of human dignity."[37]

13.3.2 *Contradictions in the Jurisprudence*

Despite the clarification of dignity-based constitutional freedoms and equality, the Court had a Janus-faced constitutional adjudicatory record. By way of examples

are expounding. *McCulloch v Maryland*, 17 US 316 (1819) at 408. János Kis argues that the invisible constitution metaphor was applied to critically revise the text of the Constitution. Kis (*supra* n 6) 253–9. For a different, praiseful summary, see Scheppele (*supra* n 3 (both works)); for another critical analysis, see Sajó (*supra* n 4). See in detail Tóth, "Lost in Transition" (*supra* n 6).

[33] *The State v T Makwanyane and M Mchunu* CCT/3/94, Judgment of June 6, 1995. Lithuania, Case No. 2/98. Judgment of December 9, 1998; Albania, Case No. 65. Judgment of December 10, 1999; Ukraine, Case No. 11-rp/99. Judgment of December 29, 1999.
[34] Judgment 23/1990 (X. 31.) HCC, concurring opinion by Chief Justice Sólyom.
[35] Judgment 23/1990 (X. 31.) HCC.
[36] Judgment 30/1992 (V. 26.) HCC.
[37] Judgment 4/1993 (II. 12.) HCC.

from the case law, here I pair crucial dignity-based principles of fundamental rights with differing judgments to show both sides of the coin.

Under the human dignity-based conception of equality, everyone has a right to equal respect and treatment. The Court developed a standard for prohibition of discrimination according to which all people must be treated as equal, as persons with equal dignity; the right to human dignity may not be impaired by law; and the criteria for the distribution of the entitlements and benefits shall be determined with the same respect and prudence and with the same degree of consideration of individual interests.[38] We can call this a comparative standard: individuals and members of particular groups have certain rights because others, in a comparative situation, also enjoy them. The Court connected the requirement of preferential treatment to this principle. The right to equal personal dignity requires that goods and opportunities must be distributed with equal concern to everyone. If, however, a just social purpose may be achieved only if equality in the narrower sense cannot be realized, then a preferential treatment shall not be declared unconstitutional (Family Protection Case).[39]

Notwithstanding the developed standards of constitutional equality, the Court never declared unconstitutionality based upon suspect classification or the special needs for protection of vulnerable groups. It did not clash with the legislature in order to support women's rights. In cases where it found gender-based discrimination, it was mostly against men.[40] In a similar fashion, the Court slightly preferred a pro-life approach in abortion cases. Although not going against the rather pro-choice public opinion, it maintained in practice an intermediate regulation between the conflicting alternatives. The Sólyom-led Court recommended that parliament introduce criminal sanctions against those women who terminate their pregnancies even in the first trimester (Abortion Case II).[41] The reasoning envisaged that the extension of human rights protection to the embryo and fetus "would be comparable only with the abolition of slavery, or would be greater than that" (Abortion Case I).[42]

As to same-sex couples, the landmark judgment implicitly established the category of *separate and unequal*. Even though the decision required legal recognition of same-sex partnership, it emphasized that same-sex couples might not get married; moreover, when it comes to regulating their partnership, the differences between such relationships and marriage, flowing from "nature" as well as from traditions, was to be maintained (Same-Sex Partnership Case I).[43]

---

[38] Judgment 9/1990 (IV. 25.) HCC.

[39] Judgment 9/1990 (IV. 25.) HCC. For the theoretical foundation, see Ronald Dworkin, *Sovereign Virtue: The Theory and Practice of Equality* (Harvard University Press, 2000). Sólyom argued that the Constitutional Court had adapted Dworkin's theory of equality. László Sólyom, "The Hungarian Constitutional Court and the Social Change" (1994) 19 *Yale Journal of International Law* 222, 229.

[40] Kriszta Kovács, "Think Positive, Preferential Treatment in Hungary" (2008) 5 *Fundamentum* 48.

[41] Judgment 48/1998 (XI. 23.) HCC.

[42] Judgment 64/1991 (XII. 17.) HCC.

[43] Judgment 14/1995 (III. 13.) HCC.

It is well known that many hundreds of thousands of Roma living in Hungary have to face social difficulties, prejudice, and segregation. Despite several petitions, however, the constitutional problems relating to the exclusion and discrimination of Roma remained absolutely hidden from the public eye, and the Court hesitated to intervene.[44] In one case, the petitioner argued that, in the course of employment, she found herself in an unfavorable situation due to the fact that her name revealed her mother's Roma origin. The chief justice dismissed her petition on procedural grounds since she did not question explicitly a specific legal rule, only the application of a legal provision in a concrete case. According to the procedural order that dismissed the claim, the law on changing names "has no relevant constitutional relationship with the right to work and non-discrimination clauses" of the constitution.[45] Thus, the discriminatory regulation behind the surface of the ostensibly neutral law could not be unveiled. The Court applied neither the concept of dignity-based equality, nor that of preferential treatment, nor yet the principles of liberty rights in cases of vulnerable groups.

The counterpart of the dignity-based conception of equality and dignity-based individual freedom is that the scope of rights is independent of egalitarian, distributive principles. Individuals have fundamental rights and freedoms not because others, in a comparative situation, enjoy them but because, as human beings, they deserve certain treatment. In an early decision, the Court claimed that from freedom of speech to right to privacy, each liberty right originates from the notion of human dignity. As an example, the Court clarified all the relevant notions concerning personal freedom of religion. "The individual freedom of conscience and religion acknowledges that the person's conviction, and, within this, in a given case, religion, is a part of human dignity, so their freedom is a pre-condition for the free development of personality."[46] In addition to this, the Court's concept concerning the neutrality of the state originates from the notion of equal liberty of conscience. The requirement of religious neutrality of the state means separation of the state from churches. This separation means that the state must not be institutionally attached to any church or churches; that the state must not identify itself with the teachings of any church; that it must not interfere with the internal working of any church; and especially that it must not take a stance in matters of religious truth. From this, it follows that the state must treat all churches equally (Churches Case I).[47]

By implementing the principle of separation of church and state, the Court concluded that this does not mean that the state must disregard the special characteristics of religion and church in its legislation. Additionally, "treating the churches equally does not exclude taking the actual social roles of the individual churches

[44] In detail, see Tóth, "Unequal Protection" (*supra* n 6).
[45] Order 924/I/1996 HCC.
[46] Judgment 4/1993 (II. 12.) HCC.
[47] Judgment 4/1993 (II. 12.) HCC.

into account."[48] According to this interpretation, it became possible to treat preferably those churches that had been operating for a long period of time. Thus, numerous cases shutting up the communist past and laying the foundations for the future ended with a favorable outcome for historical churches. Within the scheme of reprivatization, only historical churches were returned some of their real estate in the course of property compensation. Other institutions were given only very limited compensation for their nationalized real estate. Following this, the Court declared it constitutional that churches are exempted from the general statutory ban on acquiring soil.[49] The Court upheld that obligatory lustration extends, besides state leaders and professional politicians, to persons who carry out "public-opinion-forming tasks." However, contrary to journalists, for example, a decision exempted church leaders from lustration.[50] Similarly, practicing clergymen did not have to serve mandatory military service because this so-called "positive discrimination" ensured the believers' free exercise of religion.[51] In order to fulfill their role emanating from the free exercise of religion, "positive discrimination" is to be secured for church-run schools and kindergartens as compared to not-for-profit public education institutions run by foundations or associations. As a result, only church-run schools have the right to an auxiliary subsidy above the normative state allowance.[52]

One of the leading judgments on church status explicitly and purposively provided preferential treatment for historical churches vis-à-vis other churches, religious groups, and communities.[53] Following the *ratio decidendi*, the Court declared constitutional the governmental decree on army chaplain service, a decree that provided for the free exercise of religion and spiritual care only for members of the four "historical churches (Catholic, Calvinist, Lutheran, Jewish)." The Court came to the conclusion that the privileges of historical churches are not unconstitutional but "refer to the real historical role and social significance of such churches."[54]

We can see that, in the cases of selected churches, the judges applied the concept of preferential treatment, but it is not clear what type of inequality can be found at the starting point. The Court accepted the premise that historical churches have outstanding social weight, and that they have a crucial role in the field of spiritual care and, also,

---

[48]   Judgment 4/1993 (II. 12.) HCC.
[49]   Judgment 4/1993 (II. 12.) HCC; Judgment 35/1994 (VI. 24.) HCC.
[50]   Judgment 31/2003 (VI. 4.) HCC. This judgment overruled a former one that stated that certain organizations of churches and their representatives "surely take part in forming the public opinion" (Judgment 60/1994 (XII. 24.) HCC.).
[51]   Judgment 46/1994 (X. 21.) HCC. Mandatory military service ceased to exist in 2005 by constitutional amendment.
[52]   Judgment 22/1997 (IV. 25.) HCC.
[53]   András Sajó argued that the 1989 Constitution provided for the separation of the State and the Church; however, the Court's judgment treated other countries' century-old compromises as models, e.g., Austria, Germany. András Sajó, "A 'kisegyház' mint alkotmányjogi képtelenség [the 'small church' as constitutional nonsense]" (1999) 3(2) *Fundamentum* 96.
[54]   The empirical findings did not show the degree of exercise of religion; only the formal affiliation with churches. Judgment 970/B/1994 HCC. For a critical account, see Kis (*supra* n 6) 282.

socially and culturally. At the same time, the Court influenced communal practice in such a way that some churches were granted exceptionally favorable conditions for their spiritual and other activities. Here, tradition appears in the strong sense, meaning that tradition is an unconditionally obligatory norm. This type of traditionalism supports maintaining the tradition even if it violates the egalitarian principle of dignity.

In all likelihood, the leading role of the Sólyom-led Court in democratic transition, as well as some of its landmark judgments on fundamental rights stemming from egalitarian liberal theoretical roots, led to the widespread but incomplete understanding that the Court could be characterized ideologically as liberal. I think that it is better to say that the fundamental rights case law of the Sólyom-led Court has two contrasting aspects: establishment of a human-dignity-based constitutional concept of freedom and equality, acknowledgment of the separation of state and church, and respect for freedom of speech, religion, and other liberty rights on the one hand; and restrictive views on the social role of women and families, zealous protection of the life of the embryo and the early fetus, and denial of equal respect to same-sex couples while privileging traditional marriage and churches on the other.

I argue elsewhere that the interpretive practice of the Sólyom Court can be easily associated with a Christian moral and political worldview; specifically, that of the Second Vatican Council.[55] The roots of the Janus-faced nature of the first Constitutional Court's record thus can be found embedded in the teaching of the Second Vatican Council. Many of the Council's sweeping reforms are incorporated into the Declaration *Dignitatis humanae*. It recognizes the inviolable human rights based on the dignity of the human person and claims that "constitutional limits should be set to the powers of government in order that there may be no encroachment on the rightful freedom of the person and of associations." The declaration spells out that the dignity of the human person, and of the person in community, requires religious freedom.[56] By contrast, the famous encyclical *Humanae vitae*, representing a view that the Council's reforms went too far, affirms the church's orthodox view of marriage, marital relations, and family planning. It allows sex between a man and a woman for procreation and within the institution of holy matrimony. It bans "artificial" birth control, all forms of contraception, and abortion, even for therapeutic reasons.[57] I think that this duality within the teaching of the Second Vatican Council is what most closely explains the contrasting aspects of the first Hungarian Constitutional Court.[58]

---

[55] Kis (*supra* n 6) 295 and Tóth (*supra* n 6 (both works)).

[56] Declaration on Religious Freedom. Dignitatis Humanae: On the right of the person and of communities to social and civil freedom in matters religious. December 7, 1965.

[57] Encyclical Letter Humanae Vitae of the Supreme Pontiff Paul VI. July 29, 1968. In fact, Pope John XXIII convened the Second Vatican Council in 1962. He died before the council finished its work, which was then overseen by his successor, Paul VI. The encyclical did not accept the conclusions of the Birth Control Commission, established by his predecessor, that family planning and contraception were not inconsistent with Catholic doctrine.

[58] The judicature was far from linear also in the sense that in cases of transitional justice – specifically the retroactive punishment of previous political crimes – the Court dissociated itself from natural law and positioned itself as strictly positivist. A famous phrase from the leading judgment says: "Legal

The landmark judgments on fundamental rights also led to the prevailing understanding that the Sólyom Court was methodologically activist. As Andrew Arato noted, "while there have been many activist courts in history, it would be hard to find another major jurist who so explicitly affirms the power and authority of a court to freely interpret the law of the constitution."[59] Two notes should be added here. First, interpretive activism is a concept that is too complex and ambiguous to simply stick as a label on a court or judge. Realizing that, in certain cases, the abstract moral norms of the constitution require a moral interpretation is one – I believe, right – judicial attitude; assuming the role of the constitution-making power is another – in my view, mistaken – position. Therefore, the case law of the Sólyom Court may receive criticism on the ground that it approved not only the former but also the latter strategy. Second, in fact, after the initial three or four years of its jurisdiction, the Court became much more self-restrained. Bruce Ackerman foresaw this.[60] The period when the Court was willing to extend the scope of fundamental rights in the name of human dignity was over after a short time.

13.4 THE GUARDIAN OF THE CONSTITUTION

László Sólyom served as head of state between 2005 and 2010. The former leader of the supreme judicial body, considered as the guardian of the constitution and to be maintaining the rule of law in Hungary, also assumed a crucial role in his new capacity during a deep crisis and the final phase of the Republic.[61] His presidency proved once again that formal power written in the constitution can differ from actual power. President Sólyom was frequently in political conflict with the prime minister.[62] The scope-of-authority controversies revealed a

certainty based on formal and objective principles [of the rule of law] is more important than necessarily partial and subjective justice" (Judgment 11/1992 (III. 5.)). With the help of an entirely formalistic concept of the rule of law, the Court was presumably trying to prevent a political and legal witch-hunt. From a comparative perspective, it did not adopt the German Constitutional Court's reception of the Radbruch Formula (in cases connected to Nazi crimes), which says, in short, that legal norms lose their legal validity when they are extremely unjust. In this way, the Hungarian Constitutional Court preferred the apparently value-neutral category of the rule of law to justice as a matter of value judgment.

[59]   Arato (*supra* n 8) 184–5.

[60]   Ackerman (*supra* n 7) 110 and Kis (*supra* n 6).

[61]   The election process was far from following the rule of law. Even though the Constitution made it clear that the parliament shall elect the president of the republic by secret ballot, the leader of the Fidesz parliamentary caucus checked every vote before the MPs entered the booth. In fact, the whip sent back any MP who voted "wrongly" to change his vote. https://hungarianspectrum.wordpress.com/2012/04/07/zsofia-mihancsik-two-old-new-presidents-mesterhazy-and-solyom-2/.

[62]   The Hungarian Constitution copied the German Chancellor-led system with a weak president elected by the parliamentary representatives. However, serious conflicts emerged between the president and the prime minister over appointment-related issues and competences to represent the country abroad.

characteristic uncertainty in the Hungarian parliamentary system.[63] His claims
to real power as the head of state and the repository of national sovereignty led
to constitutional struggles. He sought to expand his authority as the guardian of
the constitution. His maneuvers, on the one hand, demonstrated the president's
moral integrity above the ordinary course of political fights between the governing party and the opposition.[64] His critics, on the other hand, formed a
judgment that the head of state had begun to represent an alternative government program: he strongly criticized the government's economic policy,
launched his own foreign policy, and created political conflicts with neighbor-
ing countries.[65]

During this half a decade, Sólyom vetoed, using his powers as president, as many
acts as his two predecessors had in the previous one-and-a-half decades.[66] The
Constitutional Court, in line with the presidential motions for *ex ante* constitutional review, became very active again between 2006 and 2010, almost paralyzing
the legislature by declaring an unprecedented number of newly adopted acts
unconstitutional and void. Sólyom, who had formerly represented the view,
following Kelsen and Heller, that the guardian of the constitution was the
Constitutional Court, seemed to borrow ideas from Carl Schmitt in claiming

[63] Gábor Attila Tóth, "From Uneasy Compromises to Democratic Partnership: The Prospects of
Central European Constitutionalism" (2011) 13(1) *European Journal of Law Reform* 53–69, 84–8.
See also Norman Dorsen, Michel Rosenfeld, András Sajó, and Susanne Baer, *Comparative
Constitutionalism: Cases and Materials* (Thomson-West, 2003) 269 ff.

[64] Under article 29(1) of the Constitution, Hungary's head of state "manifests the unity of the nation and
safeguards the democratic operation of the State." Based on that constitutional authorization, the
president might make an independent political decision when grave disruptions arose in the democratic functioning of the governance system that required an intervention by the head of state to
eliminate them. Sólyom was convinced that his decisions are moral issues representing value
judgments.

[65] See, e.g., the judgment of the European Court of Justice in the case of *Hungary v Slovak Republic*,
C-364/10, October 16, 2012. On the invitation of a civil association based in Slovakia, László Sólyom
was scheduled to go to the Slovak town of Komárno on August 21, 2009 to take part in the ceremony
inaugurating a statue of Saint Stephen, the founder of the Hungarian State. The Slovak government
prohibited the president of Hungary from entering Slovak territory. Sólyom was informed about the
prohibition while on his way and thus he could not enter the Slovak territory. Hungary brought an
action before the European Court of Justice, complaining that the Slovak Republic had infringed the
free movement provisions of the EU law. The Court, dismissing the action brought by Hungary,
expressed the view that even though Union citizens are entitled by EU law to move and reside freely
within the territory of Member States, under international law, Member States reserve the right to
control the access of a foreign head of state to their territory, regardless of whether that head of state is a
Union citizen. Free movement clauses thus do not apply to the visit made by the head of state of
Hungary to the territory of Slovakia.

[66] Article 26(1) of the Constitution held that the President of the Republic shall ratify and order the
promulgation of a law. Article 26(2) laid down the political veto: "Should the President of the
Republic disagree with a law or with any provision of a law, prior to ratification, he shall refer such
law, along with his comments, to the Parliament for reconsideration." Article 26(4) formulated the
constitutional veto: "Should the President of the Republic have reservations about the constitutionality of any provision of a law, he may refer such law to the Constitutional Court for review."

that the head of state (sovereign) had the authority to be the ultimate guardian of the constitution.[67]

Consider the early years of the Republic of Hungary, when serious conflicts emerged between the head of state and the prime minister over appointment-related issues and the competences of the president as commander-in-chief of the armed forces. The Sólyom-led Constitutional Court then interpreted the president's power restrictively, maintaining that the constitution clearly provided a pure parliamentary system and that the government was the sole executive branch.[68] Later, when the president refused to sign the dismissal of the chairman of national television initiated by the prime minister, the Constitutional Court tailored the president's right of refusal to appoint extremely narrowly. According to its reasoning, the president "stands outside the executive power" and "no construction may be derived from the constitution according to which the government and the president jointly head the executive branch, making consensus-based decisions in a mutually limiting and counterbalancing manner."[69]

As head of state, Sólyom initiated an overruling of or at least a distinguishing from those precedents. In 2007, he did not intend to award a former prime minister (Gyula Horn) with the Order of Merit of the Republic of Hungary on the recommendation of the current prime minister. He referred to the fact that Horn had not changed his views on the 1956 revolution, in which he had taken part on the Soviet side, fighting against the Hungarian revolutionaries. Sólyom argued that Horn's opinions conflict with constitutional values and that, despite his merits, he could not give the award to Horn. Sólyom thus filed a petition with the Constitutional Court seeking an abstract interpretation of the Constitution. In his opinion, "the moral integrity of the head of state may be jeopardized if he is not given true discretionary powers in making a decision under his powers following from the constitution." In its decision, the Constitutional Court deferred to the presidential petition by ruling that

> the President of the Republic has actual discretionary powers in conferring orders and awards ... In the case of a recommendation for an award that violates the constitutional values of the Republic of Hungary, it is the President's right not to sign the recommendation, refusing to confer the award. The refusal to confer an award ... protects in this case the constitutional values of the Republic of Hungary.[70]

The judgment of the Constitutional Court thus restricted not merely the prime minister's competence but also its own authority. The head of state successfully assumed control over the constitution.

---

[67] See in detail, David Dyzenhaus, *Legality and Legitimacy: Carl Schmitt, Hans Kelsen and Hermann Heller in Weimar* (Oxford University Press, 1997).

[68] Judgment 48/1991 (XI. 23.) HCC. See Sólyom and Brunner (*supra* n 26) 159.

[69] Judgment 36/1992 (VI. 10.) HCC. See Dorsen, Rosenfeld, Sajó, and Baer (*supra* n 63) 268.

[70] Judgment 47/2007 (VII. 3.) HCC.

In the very final phase of the Republic of Hungary, however, the guardian of the constitution proved to be powerless. In 2010, the then-opposition party, Fidesz, won a landslide victory in the parliamentary election. In the first months of its term, the two-thirds parliamentary majority adopted a range of amendments to the Constitution pertaining, among other things, to the representative bodies, the judiciary, and civil liberties. It changed the jurisdiction of the Constitutional Court by reforming the election process, limiting its competences, and adding seven justices to the bench. It established a powerful media authority to supervise and sanction the content of the broadcast media, print, and internet outlets. On top of this, it announced its intention to draft a brand-new constitution. The new prime minister, Viktor Orbán, personally established an advisory council and named its members, who were to elaborate the text.[71]

Sólyom expressed an unfavorable opinion regarding the constitutional amendments and sent back to parliament for reconsideration several pieces of legislation, although he did not turn to the Constitutional Court on key issues. As he explained, he couldn't send constitutional amendments to be checked by the Constitutional Court because a series of binding decisions excluded the possibility of any judicial review of amendments.[72] Subordination of both the Court and the president to the two-thirds parliamentary majority seemed to be a new direction. Previously, as chief justice and a constitutional scholar, Sólyom expressed theoretical belief in the possibility of constitutional review of constitutional amendments and clearly affirmed the need for procedural review.[73] In an early interview, he emphasized that even if an unacceptable constitutional amendment cannot be reviewed by the Court, a moral critique remains: resignation.[74] In the cases of the 2010 unconstitutional amendments,

---

[71]   The new constitution, called Fundamental Law, was adopted in 2011. See Kriszta Kovács and Gábor Attila Tóth, "Hungary's Constitutional Transformation" (2011) 7 *European Constitutional Law Review* 183–203 and Gábor Attila Tóth (ed.), *Constitution for a Disunited Nation* (Central European University Press, 2012).

[72]   For a detailed analysis, see Arato (*supra* n 8 and n 16).

[73]   László Sólyom, *Az alkotmánybíráskodás kezdetei Magyarországon* (Osiris, 2001) 276–81. Arato argues that the ambivalence of this statement (theoretical belief in the possibility of review of amending power versus subordination of the Court to parliament) reflects the unresolved tension in Hungary between constitutionalism and parliamentary sovereignty. Arato (*supra* n 8) 198. See also László Sólyom and Kriszta Kovács (interview), "Az Alkotmánybíróság többé nem az alkotmányvédelem legfőbb szerve. Sólyom László volt köztársasági elnökkel Kovács Kriszta beszélget" (2013) 1 *Fundamentum* 19–30.

[74]

    [We, the Court] recognize the constitution above us as an absolute standard, the creation of which is in the hands of parliament. This is one kind of self-limitation and consciousness of the fact that we do not stand above parliament, but are a part of the constitutional system. The majority of the Constitutional Court does not aspire to review the constitutionality of constitutional amendments, although theoretically it could be justified. Of course not by a positivistic method: in our constitution there are no elevated, so-called eternal rules as in Germany, by which we could evaluate the amendment. In the case of unacceptable constitutional amendment moral critique remains: one resigns. (Sólyom and Tóth (*supra* n 29) 389; Arato's translation (*supra* n 8) 198)

Sólyom, as the guardian of the constitution, chose neither to develop a new standard of review of constitutional amendments nor to resign. His harsh critics conclude that, in this way, the president assisted the adoption of an unconstitutional constitution and the rise of an authoritarian system. Other observers, in contrast, have used Sólyom's repeated critical statements on the emerging constitutional system as a reliable source of constitutional reasoning.[75] In any case, the ruling party did not seem to be fully satisfied with Sólyom's presidency; therefore, he was not nominated for a second term of office.

13.5 CONCLUSION

I think that it is undisputed that none of the founders of the Republic of Hungary had a greater impact on Hungarian constitutionalism than László Sólyom. He qualifies as a towering judge in the political, institutional, and jurisprudential senses.[76] Professor Sólyom promoted a constitutional change from autocracy to democracy and sought to integrate the country into the European community of constitutional democracies. As chief justice, he leaves a lasting legacy in terms of a constitutional institution that he created and developed: the Constitutional Court of the Republic of Hungary. Sólyom also leaves a jurisprudential mark on constitutionalism in Hungary through the legal and intellectual force of his leading judgments.

It will remain a subject of debate, however, whether he found the best constitutional tools for creating and saving the delicate unity of the short-lived republic.[77] Sólyom's jurisprudence and legacy are full of contradictions. He was correct to describe the 1989 Constitution as a complete list of principles and rights being in conformity with modern constitutionalism. However, he ignored the fact that the roundtable constitution lacked democratic confirmation and that a democratically elected assembly should have completed the constitution-making process. The Sólyom-led Constitutional Court aimed to play a stabilizing role and was the main force of constitutional consolidation by importing standards of apex courts of mature liberal democracies and measures of international human rights institutions. Furthermore, Sólyom's development of a new understanding of human dignity and fundamental rights by way of moral reading of the constitution can be considered as a towering achievement. But, at the same time, this study rejected Sólyom's view that a constitutional court may vindicate the status of a substitute constitution-making

---

[75] László Sólyom, *Das Gewand des Grundgesetzes. Zwei Verfassungsikonen – Ungarn und Deutschland* (Berliner Wissenschafts-Verlag, 2017); László Sólyom, "The Rise and Decline of Constitutional Culture in Hungary" in Armin von Bogdandy and Pál Sonnevend (eds.), *Constitutional Crisis in the European Constitutional Area: Theory, Law and Politics in Hungary and Romania* (Hart–Beck, 2015) 5–32.

[76] See the Introduction to this volume.

[77] Compare this phrase with the initial words in Joel Richard Paul, *Without Precedent: Chief Justice John Marshall and His Times* (Riverhead Books, 2018) 1.

authority. I also argued that the Sólyom-led court could not be characterized simply as liberal because its interpretive practice was associated with a nonsecular moral and political worldview. Finally, I showed how Sólyom modified his point of view on key constitutional issues when serving as the head of state in the last years of the Republic of Hungary. To put it short, we should accept that different facets of a complete oeuvre do not necessarily amount to a coherent view. We see parallels and paradoxes rather than a baroque harmony.

The democratic decline in Hungary is the subject of more comprehensive analyses than the one this chapter can afford. What I would like to emphasize here, however, is that it would be a grave error to simply consider Sólyom's actions on the first Constitutional Court as failures that directly led to the rise of authoritarianism. Compare the case of the Hungarian Constitutional Court with that of the Polish Constitutional Tribunal. Even though the latter, lacking a towering leader comparable to Sólyom, moved forward slowly, both institutions were rendered ineffective in a similar fashion, by politically expedient modifications to anything from the personal composition ("court packing"), to the competences, to the institutional and financial independence.

We may find the roots of democratic decline in personal attitudes, impersonal institutions, and global tendencies, rather than in judicial review. The autocratic turn in Hungary was a result of maneuvers by antidemocrats to subvert democratic institutions. The liberal democracy was torn apart, too, because its constitution proved too fragile during the crisis. (Remember the flexible constitution allowing its modification by the votes of two-thirds of members of the one-chamber parliament and the disproportionate electoral structure.) Together, institutional shortcomings, political polarization, and a financial shock have precipitated a cumulative process that eroded the trust in civil constitutionalism and led to an authoritarian leadership.[78]

Today, authoritarian leaders are invoking the conception of a Constitution adopted by popular will, as famously embodied in the idea of "We the people," to limit the role of the constitutional judiciary. Authoritarian regimes reportedly replace "juristocracy" with "parliamentary sovereignty," and ostensibly introduce "political constitutionalism" instead of "legal constitutionalism." But weaker constitutional ties mean that it is not only the judiciary but also other democratic institutions and public deliberation that are undermined. It becomes possible to sidestep principles of democratic representation and participation if the popular will is not legally constructed or channeled but is, rather, the echo chamber of a dominant leader. As the 2011 Hungarian Constitution demonstrates, authoritarian leadership emerges at the expense of not only constitutional judiciary but also democratic parliamentarianism.

---

[78] See also the case of Poland: Wojciech Sadurski, *Poland's Constitutional Breakdown* (Oxford University Press, 2019).

14

The Socialist Model of Individual Judicial Powers

Bui Ngoc Son

14.1 INTRODUCTION

The Socialist Republic of Vietnam is a socialist country ruled by a single party, the Communist Party of Vietnam. The constitutional framework is based on the 2013 Constitution, the fifth constitution (the four previous documents were enacted in 1946, 1959, 1980, and 1992) in the country under communist rule.[1] This framework denies the doctrine of separation of power in favor of the Leninist doctrine of democratic centralism: power is concentrated, in theory, in the hands of the National Assembly, while other major institutions (the government, the president of state, the Supreme People's Court, and the Supreme People's Procuracy) are subordinate to the former.[2] In reality, political power is concentrated in the Communist Party.[3] The centralist constitutional system has consequences for the judicial system.[4] Judicial review is absent: courts are not allowed to review the constitutionality of legislation. Rather, legislative constitutional review is adopted. The National Assembly reviews the constitutionality of its own laws and governmental regulations. Its Standing Committee has the final word on constitutional interpretation,[5] though these powers have never been used. Judicial independence[6] is guaranteed in theory. For instance, article 103 of the 2013 Constitution provides: "During a trial, the Judges and Assessors are independent and shall obey only the law. Agencies, organizations or individuals are

---

[1] For Vietnamese constitutional history, see Mark Sidel, *The Constitution of Vietnam: A Contextual Analysis* (Hart Publishing, 2009).

[2] Vietnam's Constitution (2013), articles 69 and 70.

[3] Hai Hong Nguyen, "Resilience of the Communist Party of Vietnam's Authoritarian Regime since Doi Moi" (2016) 35(2) *Journal of Current Southeast Asian Affairs* 31.

[4] On the Vietnamese judiciary, see P Nicholson, "Renovating Courts: The Role of Courts in Contemporary Vietnam" in Jiunn-rong Yeh and Wen-Chen Chang (eds.), *Asian Courts in Context* (Cambridge University Press, 2014).

[5] Vietnam's Constitution (2013), articles 70 and 74.

[6] On the issue of judicial independence in Vietnam, see P Nicholson and NH Quang, "Independence, Impartiality and Integrity of the Judiciary in Vietnam" in HP Lee and Marilyn Pittard (eds.), *Asia-Pacific Judiciaries: Independence, Impartiality and Integrity* (Cambridge University Press, 2017).

prohibited from interfering in a trial by Judges and People's Assessors."[7] But the judiciary's dependence on the political power of the Party and the government is clear, especially in politically sensitive cases.[8] The centralist constitutional framework provides more space for the exercise of individual judicial powers, especially by the chief justice.

In July 2007, the National Assembly of Vietnam selected Mr. Truong Hoa Binh, a police and security leader with a background in water resources, to be the chief justice of the Supreme People's Court. He then became a powerful leader of the judiciary for nearly a decade until 2016 when he was appointed first deputy prime minister of the government. If a "towering judge" is understood as a judge who plays a dominant role in the judiciary, then he can be considered one. How and why did a policeman with no previous experience in the court system become an influential chief justice?

A socialist model of individual judicial powers is needed to explain this phenomenon. Constitutional inquiries into judicial powers in a democracy tend to differentiate institutional accounts from individual accounts of judicial power.[9] Yet, the socialist model is characterized by the *institutionalization of individual judicial powers*. The logic runs as follows: One of the instrumental functions of court design in the socialist state of Vietnam is to make sure that the judiciary is under the control of the government and the Communist Party. This can be achieved by empowering the chief justice and placing them under the control of the government and the Party. The chief justice in Vietnam, therefore, becomes towering not because of their jurisprudential excellence but because of the institutional arrangement. The judicial institutional design in this socialist state naturally results in a towering chief justice, and Chief Justice Truong Hoa Binh is a *paradigmatic* example of this institutional design. Personally, he achieved this towering position by using his institutionalized and informal powers to carry out judicial reform policy and spread the Party's views on judicial reform.

This chapter relies on the chief justice's writings and speeches, local written material, and personal conversations with a variety of local jurists in Vietnam. Following this introduction, Section 14.2 articulates the socialist model of individual judicial power, Section 14.3 considers the practice of this model with the case of Mr Truong Hoa Binh, Section 14.4 analyses this practice and how it culminated in a towering judge, and Section 14.5 concludes.

---

[7] Vietnam's Constitution (2013), article 103.
[8] John Gillespie, "The Emerging Role of Property Rights in Land and Housing dispute in Hanoi" in Hue-Tam Ho Tai and Mark Sidel (eds.), *State, Society and the Market in Contemporary Vietnam: Property, Power and Values* (Routledge, 2013) 103; Mark Sidel, "Property, State Corruption, and the Judiciary: The Do Son Land Case and Its Implications" in Hue-Tam Ho Tai and Mark Sidel (eds.), *State, Society and the Market in Contemporary Vietnam: Property, Power and Values* (Routledge, 2013) 124.
[9] Kevin M Stack, "The Practice of Dissent in the Supreme Court" (1996) 105(8) *Yale Law Journal* 2238.

14.2 MODELING INDIVIDUAL JUDICIAL POWER

14.2.1 *Individual Judicial Power in Constitutional Theory*

Constitutional theory has been conventionally occupied by the institutional question of whether and how courts should exercise judicial review power.[10] These debates are largely *normative*, assuming courts to be *collective* entities and tending to focus on *democratic* institutional settings.[11] Normative constitutional theorists are less interested in exploring and explaining how and why judicial power is exercised by individual judges in a particular institutional setting, especially a nondemocratic one.

There is, however, a body of scholarship investigating and theorizing about individual judicial powers as exercised. G Edward White and Theodore W Ruger discuss the exercise of judicial power by the chief justice in the United States.[12] Kim Lane Scheppele examines two *constitutional court presidents*: László Sólyom of the Hungarian Constitutional Court and Valerii Zorkin of the Russian Constitutional Court.[13] Focusing on the case of the Brazilian Supreme Court, Diego Werneck Arguelhes and Ivar A Hartmann argue that the *pedido de vista* (the power "to request more time to study the files of a given case") can function as "an individual power, unconstrained by the Court's internal rules of procedure."[14] In another study, Werneck Arguelhes and Leandro Molhano Ribeiro draw again on the Brazilian experience to address theoretical issues on individual judicial powers. They develop a typology of three powers,

> by means of which Justices within collegiate judicial bodies can influence the legal status quo and the behaviour of actors outside the court, either directly or indirectly: (i) *agenda setting* (deciding what the court will decide); (ii) *position taking* (speaking on behalf of the court, thus signalling a potential judicial decision in specific directions); and (iii) *decision making* (resolving cases, controversies, and matters of dispute brought to the court).[15]

---

[10] Jeremy Waldron, *"The Core of the Case Against Judicial Review"* (2006) 115 *Yale Law Journal* 1346; Richard H Fallon, "The Core of an Uneasy Case for Judicial Review" (2008) 121 *Harvard Law Review* 1693.

[11] Keith E Wittington, "Constitutionalism" in Keith E Whittington, R Daniel Kelemen, and Gregory A Caldeira (eds.), *The Oxford Handbook of Law and Politics* (Oxford University Press, 2008) 282.

[12] G Edward White, "The Internal Powers of the Chief Justice: The Nineteenth Century Legacy" (2006) 154(6) *University of Pennsylvania Law Review* 1464; Theodore W Ruger, "The Chief Justice and the Institutional Judiciary: Foreword" (2006) 154 *University of Pennsylvania Law Review* 1323.

[13] Kim L Scheppele, "Guardians of the Constitution: Constitutional Court Presidents and the Struggle for the Rule of Law in Post-Soviet Europe" (2006) 154 *University of Pennsylvania Law Review* 1758.

[14] Diego Werneck Arguelhes and Ivar A Hartmann, "Timing Control Without Docket Control: How Individual Justices Shape the Brazilian Supreme Court's Agenda" (2017) 5(1) *Journal of Law and Courts* 105.

[15] Diego Werneck Arguelhes and Leandro Molhano Ribeiro, "'The Court, It Is I'? Individual Judicial Powers in the Brazilian Supreme Court and Their Implications for Constitutional Theory" (2018) 7(2) *Global Constitutionalism* 240. Italics in original.

National and comparative constitutional studies of individual judicial powers suggest important insights. First, courts are more than a collective entity: individual judges can play an important role in exercising the judicial power. Second, judicial powers are more than judicial decision-making: courts and individual judges have nonadjudicative powers to influence the whole judicial system, other institutions, and the society. Yet, constitutional theory about individual judicial power is largely informed by the experience in constitutional democracy. The shared assumption tends to be that constitutional democracy is committed to the separation of powers, which provides the institutional guarantee for judicial independence and constitutional review. The exercise of individual judicial powers in authoritarian regimes[16] may not fully resonate with the positions advanced by democratic constitutional theory.

14.2.2 *The Socialist Model of Individual Judicial Powers*

The socialist model of individual judicial powers is underpinned by a distinctive socialist constitutional principle called "democratic centralism," which is the antithesis of liberal separation of powers. This principle aims to combine two competing "democratic" and centralist elements in institutional design: powers are centralized in the hands of a legislature, variously called the Supreme Soviet (Soviet Union), the National Assembly (Vietnam), or the National People's Congress (China). In theory, this "democratic" and centralist constitutional arrangement subordinates all central institutions to the supreme legislature: all central institutions are subject to the supervision of the legislature, while the latter is free from institutional checks by the former. In practice, however, the socialist regime is placed under the leadership of a communist party, and, therefore, the legislature is the platform that institutionalizes party policies and decisions. Consequently, democratic centralism turns out to actually mean the concentration of power in the Communist Party.

"Democratic centralism" generates two important consequences for the courts. First, courts as a subordinate institution are not allowed to review the constitutionality of legislative and government action. Second, courts are not merely forums in which to pursue justice; they are also instruments through which the Party and the government seek to control society.

To control the court system, the Party and the government must control its highest body. The Supreme People's Court becomes, in practice, a weak institution externally and a strong institution internally. Externally, the Court is subordinate to the Party and the executive, operating as an instrument for the latter to control the society and the behavior of its citizens to make sure that Party policy is implemented consistently throughout the society and that citizens cannot use the courts to

---

[16]   For courts in authoritarian regimes, see, generally, Tom Ginsburg and Tamir Moustafa, *Rule by Law: The Politics of Courts in Authoritarian Regimes* (Cambridge University Press, 2008).

challenge Party and government actions. Internally, the Supreme People's Court is a very powerful institution: it centrally controls the whole judicial system.

To control the Court, the Party and the government must control its leader. The chief justice is, therefore, an instrument for the Party and the government to control the Supreme Court, and hence the whole court system. Consequently, the chief justice is a weak figure externally – roughly the same rank as a government minister – but, internally, the most powerful figure within the judicial system.

The Party and the government, however, do not control the Court and the chief justice by personal fiats. Authoritarians in the post-Cold War era no longer exercise their powers personally as in previous times. Recent scholarship on "autocratic legalism," "stealth authoritarianism," and "abusive constitutionalism"[17] suggests that to gain international and domestic legitimacy and to conceal authoritarian purposes, authoritarians and would-be authoritarians now use law and constitutions to institutionalize their power.

Vietnamese authoritarianism operates in the same manner and for the same reasons. The "democratic" and centralist mechanisms of the court system and the chief justice particularly must be institutionalized. The principle of democratic centralism is formally established as a constitutional principle. Vietnam's 2013 Constitution provides: "The State shall be organized and operate in accordance with the Constitution and law, manage society by the Constitution and law, and implement the principle of democratic centralism."[18] The Constitution and other organic laws create a centralist constitutional system with the National Assembly located at the top and the government and the Supreme People's Court subordinate to it. The chief justice is selected by the National Assembly and answerable to this institution.

Various judicial acts in Vietnam create a centralized court system in which the Supreme People's Court is vested with the powers to supervise and manage the work of other courts. These include Law No. 33/2002/QH10 of April 2, 2002, on Organization of the People's Courts, and its replacement, Law No. 62/2014/QH13 dated November 24, 2014, on Organization of People's Courts.[19] The latter largely retains the powers of the Supreme Court and of its chief justice provided in the former but includes more powers. Article 27 of the 2014 Law on Organization of People's Courts unrestrainedly lists fifteen points regarding the powers of the chief justice. These powers empower the chief justice in their individual capacity to pervasively influence the structure, the work, and the personnel of the judicial system.

[17] Kim Lane Scheppele, "Autocratic Legalism" (2018) 85 *University of Chicago Law Review* 545; Ozan O Varol, "Stealth Authoritarianism" (2015) 100 *Iowa Law Review* 1673; David Landau, "Abusive Constitutionalism" (2013) 47 *UC Davis Law Review* 289.
[18] Vietnam's 2013 Constitution, article 8.
[19] Law No. 62/2014/QH13 dated November 24, 2014, on Organization of People's Courts, article 20.

These powers are very broad and cannot be captured by Arguelhes and Ribeiro's three-part typology. This typology is informed by the principle of separation of powers, which assumes that courts have only adjudicative powers. Within a socialist centralized constitutional system, the legislative, executive, and judicial powers are distributed among the three state branches but not clearly separated. Powers are shared among and cooperatively exercised by the state institutions. Consequently, a supreme court may have powers that are equivalent to those of the executive. In fact, the powers of the chief justice listed in article 27 are mainly executive powers, and, through the exercise of these powers, there is potential for the chief justice to become a towering judge.

To be sure, the chief justice also has what Arguelhes and Ribeiro call *decision-making* power or the capacity to influence the decision on specific legal cases. This includes the capacity to influence the cassational review practiced by the Supreme People's Court. The Judicial Council of the Court has the power "to review according to cassation or reopening procedure in accordance with the procedural law judgments and decisions of courts which have taken legal effect and are protested against."[20] The chief justice can influence decision-making through the power to request cassational review. In addition, through chairing the meetings of cassational review by this body, the chief justice can influence judicial decision-making.[21]

However, the main powers of the chief justice enumerated in article 27 are the executive ones: the power to influence the structure, the operation, and the personnel of the judicial system. The power of agenda-setting in Arguelhes and Ribeiro's typology is only one among the lavish executive powers that the chief justice in Vietnam enjoys. The 2014 Law on Organization of People's Courts elevates the chief justice by generously vesting this individual with executive powers. These *executive powers* can be further divided into three categories: structural, functional, and personnel.

Structural executive power refers to the chief justice's capacity to influence the organizational institutional design of the court system; for instance, to create a new court or dissolve the current court. In this regard, the law empowers the chief justice to submit to the National Assembly Standing Committee for a decision on the establishment or dissolution of superior courts, local courts, military courts at regional level, and on the establishment of other specialized tribunals of people's courts; to submit to the National Assembly Standing Committee for approval of the organizational structure, duties, and powers of the assisting apparatus of the Supreme People's Court; and to decide on the organization of specialized tribunals.[22]

---

[20]   Ibid. article 22.
[21]   Ibid. article 27.
[22]   Ibid.

The functional executive power of the chief justice refers to their individual capacity to influence the working of the Supreme People's Court and of the whole judicial system. This includes the power to organize the adjudicating work of the Supreme People's Court; to chair meetings of the Judicial Council;[23] to direct the overall assessment of adjudicating practices; and to pronounce judicial precedents.[24]

The chief justice also enjoys extensive power to affect the composition of personnel in the court system. The chief justice is empowered to submit to the National Assembly for approval of the appointment, relief from duty, or dismissal of judges of the Supreme People's Court; to propose that the president appoint, relieve from duty, or dismiss deputy chief justices of the Supreme People's Court and judges of other courts; to appoint, relieve from duty, or dismiss other staff members; to decide on the allocation of payrolls, the number of judges, and the budget funds for the operation of courts; to set the payrolls of military courts in conjunction with the minister of national defense; to decide on the rotation and transfer of judges; and to organize the training and retraining of judges and assessors and other court staff.[25]

To implement these powers, the chief justice can issue legal rules that have normative, general legal effects. They can issue legal documents according to their competence in accordance with the Law on Promulgation of Legal Documents.[26] According to this law, the chief justice can issue a legal instrument called a "circular" to implement their powers.[27]

Apart from the institutionalized individual powers, the chief justice in Vietnam also enjoys what Arguelhes and Ribeiro call *position-taking* or speaking on behalf of court. But the function of this power is quite different in Vietnam compared with other polities. Arguelhes and Ribeiro anticipate the signaling function of this power, stating:

> Courts can influence the outside world by taking a public stance that signals, to different actors, a potential favourable or unfavourable decision in the future. If we assume that courts operate in a strategic environment, then the behaviour of different institutional actors is influenced by what they anticipate as the future behaviour of the other actors (judicial or otherwise) with whom they now engage.[28]

Within the united and centralized institutional framework, the chief justice in Vietnam does not need to signal the Court's views to political institutions as they are externally weak and cannot exert substantive influence on the behavior of the political institutions. Rather, the position-taking in Vietnam has two functions:

---

[23] The Judicial Council is a body of the Supreme People's Court; it consists of thirteen to seventeen members, hears appeals, and supervises the work of the court system. Ibid. article 26.

[24] Ibid. article 27.

[25] Ibid.

[26] Ibid.

[27] Law No. 80/2015/QH13 dated June 22, 2015 of the National Assembly on promulgation of legal documents, article 22.

[28] Arguelhes and Ribeiro (*supra* n 15) 243.

signaling and propagandizing. First, it sends a signal to the society that the Court is committed to reforms. Second, it spreads and promotes the judicial public views about judicial reform to the society. This is aimed to legitimatize the existing judiciary and to gain public support for possible judicial reforms.

In short, the Law on Organization of People's Courts institutionalizes significant power in the chief justice. Any individual assuming this position can legally influence the workings and the structure of not only the Supreme People's Court but also the whole judicial system, and hence become a towering judge. In addition, the chief justice enjoys a position-taking power. While every chief justice has an institutional base from which to become a towering justice, how they can achieve this and their degree of success depend upon their use of institutionalized and informal powers to contribute to the institutional development of the judiciary.

14.3 THE SOCIALIST MODEL IN PRACTICE

14.3.1 A Policeman Turned Towering Judge

Truong Hoa Binh was born on April 13, 1955 in Long An, a province in southern Vietnam.[29] He attended the professional school of the Ministry of Public Security from 1974 to 1975 and received an undergraduate education in water resources at the Ho Chi Minh City University of Technology from 1977 to 1981.[30] He also obtained a master's degree in law from the Institute of People's Public Security, but the date is not publicly known.[31] When he was appointed as deputy prime minister of the government, the online newspaper People's Public Security reported that he has a PhD in law,[32] but the official websites of the government and the People's Supreme Court do not report this qualification.[33]

Before holding this highest position in the judiciary, he served for many years in the police and security force at both local and central levels. He held different positions in the public security departments of Ho Chi Minh City and achieved the highest position in the city's police and security force in 1988. From 2001 to 2004, he served as the leader of another institution in the city, the procuracy, an institution for supervising law enforcement, which Vietnam borrowed from the Soviet Union. He then returned to pursue his career in the public security force at the central level,

[29] His brief biography is referenced on the government's website: Tóm tắt tiểu sử Phó Thủ tướng Chính phủ Trương Hòa Bình [Brief Biography of Deputy Prime Minster of the Government Trương Hòa Bình], http://chinhphu.vn/portal/page/portal/chinhphu/tieusulanhdao?personProfileId=7978&govOrgId=2856 (hereinafter, "Trương Hòa Bình").
[30] Ibid.
[31] Trương Hòa Bình.
[32] Chân dung các thành viên Chính phủ khóa mới [Portraits of New Government Members] [Báo Công an nhân dân điện tử, April 8, 2016], http://cand.com.vn/Su-kien-Binh-luan-thoi-su/Chan-dung-cac-thanh-vien-Chinh-phu-khoa-moi-388518/.
[33] Trương Hòa Bình.

holding various positions, and was promoted to deputy minister of public security in 2006. From there, he entered the judicial system as the chief justice in 2007 and was reelected in 2011. He held this post until 2016 before being elected first deputy prime minister of the government, the position that he currently holds at the time of this writing (2020). Apart from holding these positions, Truong is concurrently a deputy of the National Assembly terms X, XI, XII, XIII, and XIV.[34]

Truong's affiliation with the Communist Party of Vietnam (CPV), the single ruling party in the country, is an important factor in his various state positions. He is a son of a family that was active on the communist side during the Vietnam War. His father, Trư ơ ng Văn Bang, held important positions in the Indochina Communist Party, the former name of the CPV, such as leader of the party committee in Saigon [the former name of Ho Chi Minh City] before the 1975 national unification. His mother, Nguyễn Thị Nho [or Nguyễn Thị Một], was a member of the Communist Party from 1935 to 1936, served as chief of the Southern Party Committee in 1955, was imprisoned and tortured by the Southern government in 1959, but remained loyal to the Communist Party.[35] Truong Hoa Binh himself has been an official member of the CPV since 1974. He has been elected to powerful positions in the central institutions of the Party, including: member of the Central Committee terms X, XI, and XII; secretary of the Central Committee term XI; and member of the Politburo term XII.[36] He is the only chief justice in Vietnamese history to enjoy membership in the Politburo, the highest and most powerful body of the CPV, which currently includes eighteen top leaders in the state and Party bodies.

14.3.2 *The Hero of Judicial Reform*

After Truong was appointed as the deputy prime minister, the local media portrayed him as a hero, which was a turning-point in judicial reform in Vietnam.[37] In addition, he also actively used the position-taking power. Let us consider some examples.

14.3.2.1 Structural Reform

The structure of the court system experienced significant change under Truong's leadership. First, a four-level court system (including the Supreme People's Court,

---

[34] Trư ơ ng Hòa Bình.
[35] H.Hiệp, Tiễn đồng chí Nguyễn Thị Một về nơ i an nghỉ [To See Comrade Nguyễn Thị Một in the Peaceful Place] [*Sài Gòn Giải Phóng*, April 20, 2013], www.sggp.org.vn/tien-dong-chi-nguyen-thi-mot-ve-noi-an-nghi-250487.html.
[36] Trư ơ ng Hòa Bình.
[37] Tân Phó Thủ tư ớng Trư ơ ng Hòa Bình: Ngư ời tạo nên như ng thay đổi bư ớc ngoặt trong cải cách tư pháp [New Deputy Prime Minister Trư ơ ng Hòa Bình: The Person Who Created Fundamental Changes in Judicial Reform], [*Báo Lao Động*, April 11, 2016], https://laodong.vn/thoi-su/tan-pho-thu-tuong-truong-hoa-binh-nguoi-tao-nen-nhung-thay-doi-buoc-ngoat-trong-cai-cach-tu-phap-539334.bld.

superior courts, provincial courts, and district courts) was created in 2015 to replace the previous three-level system (the superior courts are the addition). In the previous system, local courts were organized parallel to the local administrative systems, which resulted in courts being dependent on local governments. The new four-level court system attempted to enhance judicial independence by opening the door for separating courts from the administrative system. While the provincial courts and the district courts are still organized according to the corresponding administrative units, the superior courts are arranged in different regions, independent from the administrative system. Second, two specialist tribunals were created in the provincial courts in 2016: the Family Tribunal and the Juvenile Tribunal. Truong explained that these two new tribunals indicate the effective implementation of the Party's policy and the state's law regarding the care and protection of family and children and confirm "Vietnam's strong commitment to protecting children."[38] He was perhaps speaking to the domestic audience (as well as to the Party and the government) about the political and legal legitimacy of the two new judicial institutions, and to an international audience about Vietnam's judicial reform to implement human rights commitments.

14.3.2.2 Functional Reform

Under Chief Justice Truong's leadership, many sensitive corruption cases were handled. From 2006 to 2015, courts at different levels tried 4,323 corruption cases.[39] This is attributed to the fact that the chief justice was determined to implement the principle of judicial independence. In an interview, he said: "The Constitution clearly provides that courts shall try independently."[40] It is reported that "this is the principle that he has fiercely implemented as the leader of the court system."[41] Truong believes that two important steps should be taken to implement this principle: fighting against corruption and implementing adversarial trials. On the first step, he said: "I myself and the staff of judges must be conclusive in fighting against corruption."[42] As to the latter, he said: "My experience is that previously courts tried cases according to the indictments and profiles, but now adversarial trials are the priority."[43] In addition, under his leadership, several unjust

---

[38] Thành lập Tòa Gia đình và Người chưa thành niên đầu tiên tại Việt Nam [The Creation of Family Tribunal and Juvenile Tribunals in Vietnam] (*Đại Đoàn Kết*, April 4, 2016], http://daidoanket.vn /chinh-tri/lap-toa-gia-dinh-va-nguoi-chua-thanh-nien-dau-tien-tai-viet-nam-tintuc95474.
[39] Nhiều vụ án lớn, trọng điểm tham nhũng được xét xử kịp thời, nghiêm minh [Many Major Corruption Cases Have Been Handled On Time and Seriously], [Công an TP Hồ Chí Minh, March 14, 2016] http://congan.com.vn/tin-chinh/chinh-tri-thoi-su/nhieu-vu-an-lon-trong-diem-tham-nhung-duoc-xet-xu-kip-thoi-nghiem-minh_15988.html.
[40] Ibid.
[41] Ibid.
[42] Ibid.
[43] Ibid.

decided cases were retried, and the victims received a state apology and compensation.[44]

Chief Justice Truong is also remembered for creating the judicial precedent system in Vietnam. Courts were traditionally not allowed to develop judicial precedent as a matter of socialist legal positivism. Yet, since 2016, Vietnam has created an active precedent system according to which the Supreme People's Court centrally issues judicial precedents drawing from previous valid judgments and decisions, and all local courts must study and apply these precedents. Currently (February 16, 2020), the court has issued twenty-nine precedents that have been widely applied by local courts throughout the country. The creation and development of the judicial precedent system is associated with the name of Chief Justice Truong. He has been very enthusiastic about the application of precedent in Vietnam. He considers judicial precedent to have international value, practiced in both common law and civil law jurisdictions, and believes that the application of precedent in the Vietnamese court system will help correct the shortcomings of legislation, unify legal application, and ensure the stability, transparency, and predictability of judicial decisions.[45] He issued a decision to launch the Precedent Project in 2012. In 2015, the Judicial Council of the Supreme People's Court issued a resolution, signed by him, which formally creates the precedent system in Vietnam. Shortly thereafter, in 2016, the chief justice issued a decision to pronounce the first set of six precedents. For the first time, precedents were released in socialist Vietnam. I have explained elsewhere that the creation and function of the Vietnamese judicial precedent system is a major judicial reform, which greatly expands the "living" constitutional power of the judiciary to protect justice, interpret law, and make law.[46]

14.3.2.3 Position-Taking

Truong Hoa Binh has also been very active in speaking on the judiciary's views in different fora: the meetings of the National Assembly, the meetings of the Supreme Court, the general meetings of the judicial branch, the meetings of the Party, and through the media. In terms of substantive content, he communicates the courts' views about "new" judicial ideas and judicial reform policy and achievements.

---

[44] Báo cáo công tác của Chánh án TANDTC nhiệm kỳ 2011-2016: Phản ánh đầy đủ tình hình thực hiện nhiệm vụ của Tòa án [Report of the Chief Justice of People's Supreme Court: Sufficiently Reflecting the Work of the Courts] [*Báo mới*, March 22, 2016] https://baomoi.com/bao-cao-cong-tac-cua-chanh-an-tandtc-nhiem-ky-2011-2016-phan-anh-day-du-tinh-hinh-thuc-hien-nhiem-vu-cua-toa-an/c/18945906.epi.

[45] Trương Hòa Bình, Thực hiện tốt nhiệm vụ phát triển án lệ, bảo đảm áp dụng thống nhất pháp luật trong hoạt động xét xử của tòa án nhân dân [Carrying Out Work to Develop Precedent and Ensure Legal Application in the People's Courts' Decisions], Trường Đại học Kiểm sát Hà nội, https://tks.edu.vn/thong-tin-khoa-hoc/chi-tiet/120/764.

[46] Bui Ngoc Son, "The Socialist Precedent" (2019) 52(3) *Cornell International Law Journal* 421.

Consider, for instance, his writing for the *Communist Review*, the official journal of the Communist Party. He has spoken about the idea of judicial independence in Vietnam and how the country can implement this notion.[47] Citing data from the Comparative Constitutions Project,[48] for instance, he began one article by stating that "judicial independence (including independence of judges) is a core element written in constitutions and laws of many countries in the world."[49] He then moved on to articulate how the idea of judicial independence is understood in Vietnam. He said: "In Vietnam, the State power is unified with delegation, coordination and control among legislative, executive and judicial bodies. In relations with other power branches, judicial independence is demonstrated most apparently in non-interference in the work of courts, judges and trials of judges."[50] He was speaking here of the functional (not structural) position of judicial independence, which is sensible within the unified constitutional framework in Vietnam. To implement this principle, he believes that a correct understanding of courts exercising judicial powers to protect justice is necessary. He also suggests further institutional reforms regarding "capacity, ethics and enhanced responsibility of judges and People's Assessors"; judges' appointments, movement, discipline, and award; security of judges' tenure; security of judges' salaries, age of retirement; judicial administrative management; and ensured funding for courts.[51]

In addition to judicial ideas, Truong has spoken on judicial reform policy. As he was both the leader of the Supreme People's Court and a major figure in the Communist Party, his position-taking in this area aims to signal that judicial reform is under the leadership of the Communist Party and consistent with the Party's policy for judicial reform. For example, to justify the need to revise the law on the court system, he said: "Judicial reform in general and court reform in particular are important affairs in the process of reformation of the political system and building and consolidating the socialist rule of law state, which has been confirmed in many documents of the [Communist] Party."[52] He then articulated several principles for judicial reform, including "institutionalizing the Party's policy regarding judicial

---

[47] Truong Hoa Binh, "Độc lập tư pháp trong Nhà nước pháp quyền XHCN, bảo đảm cho Tòa án thực c hiện đúng đắn quyền tư pháp" ["Judicial Independence in the Socialist Rule-of-Law State to Ensure Courts Duly Exercise Judicial Power"] *Tạp Chí Cộng sản* [September 9, 2014], https://nhandan .com.vn/chinhtri/doc-lap-tu-phap-trong-nha-nuoc-phap-quyen-xhcn-bao-dam-cho-toa-an-thuc-hien-dung-dan-quyen-tu-phap-212835/.

[48] On this project, see Comparative Constitutions Project, https://comparativeconstitutionsproject.org.

[49] Truong Hoa Binh (*supra* n 47).

[50] Ibid.

[51] Ibid.

[52] Trương Hòa Bình, Đổi mới tổ chức và hoạt động của Tòa án nhân dân với mục tiêu xây dự ng nền tư pháp trong sạch, vững mạnh, dân chủ, nghiêm minh, bảo vệ công lý [Reforming the Structure and Operation of the People's Courts with the Goal to Build a Transparent, Strong, Democratic, and Just Judiciary which Can Protect Justice] Cổng thông tin điện tử Tòa án Nhân dân tỉnh Quảng Nam (Toà án Quảng nam, April 19, 2014), https://toaanquangnam.gov.vn/doi-moi-to-chuc-va-hoat-dong-cua-toa-an-nhan-dan-voi-muc-tieu-xay-dung-nen-tu-phap-trong-sach-vung-manh-dan-chu-nghiem-minh-bao-ve-cong-ly/.

reform, which includes the requirement to build transparent, strong, democratic, just judiciary which can protect justice and serve the people and the Socialist Fatherland of Vietnam."[53] Thus, he aligned the Court's view with the Party's view in his position-taking.

Last but not least, Truong has spoken of the achievements of judicial reform. For example, he stated: "Judicial reform has achieved many new renovations. These renovations are among historic events in the development of the national judiciary, which has fundamentally reformed the people's courts system in the construction of the Socialist Rule of Law State."[54] Thus, Truong disseminated the official view that reforms introduced to the court system have been successful and fundamental to the development of the rule of law in Vietnam.

14.4 ANALYSIS

14.4.1 *The Chief Justice as an Executive Leader*

Why was a policeman with no previous judicial experience selected as the chief justice? The position of chief justice in Vietnam is not primarily an adjudicative position, although the chief justice can sit on the Judicial Council, hear legal cases, and request a cassational review. Rather, his main function, as provided by law, is to manage the work of the Supreme People's Court and control the whole judiciary through various executive powers. According to the law, a justice must have an LLB in law and acquire professional judicial training,[55] but the chief justice is not required to have these qualifications and experience. Hence, the chief justice is not always a judge and is not necessarily selected from among the community of justices.

The chief justice in Vietnam is more like an executive leader. The logic is that the regime needs to control the court system through nominating and controlling its leader. This can be achieved by nominating a leader from one of the most powerful departments of the government (the Ministry of Public Security) to hold the highest position in the court system, which, as discussed, is similar to other government departments. In addition, to ensure that the candidate is under the control of the Party as well, he must be chosen from among the top party leaders.

14.4.2 *Towering Through Implementing Judicial Reform Policy*

As the leader of the judiciary, Chief Justice Truong Hoa Binh could have enjoyed all the powers provided by law and have naturally become a towering justice who dominates not only his court but also the whole judicial system. However, he

---

[53] Ibid.
[54] Tân Phó Thủ tướng Trương Hòa Bình (*supra* n 37).
[55] Law on Courts, article 67.

became a towering figure by using his institutionalized powers to implement judicial reform policy.

The judicial reform policy was endorsed by the Party. Chief Justice Truong individually contributed to the formation of Party policy on judicial reform, including policies to hear grave corruption cases, to reform the court structure, and to vest more power in the judiciary. But what made this justice such a towering figure is that he was determined to implement these policies, and this implementation has led to positive outcomes. This, in turn, has created a positive image among the public about the court system and the chief justice himself. The chief justice's desire to leave a mark on the judiciary determined the timing of several institutional reforms to the court system. For example, the precedent system was created in 2015, and the first set of precedents was issued in April 2016, shortly before he was promoted to become deputy prime minister in July of the same year. Chief Justice Truong left a valuable legacy of precedents in the judiciary, which has been actively continued by his successor, Nguyen Hoa Binh. The creation of the two specialist tribunals in 2016 can also be explained by the justice's incentive to leave a legacy in the court system before moving on to another post.

In addition to carrying out judicial reform policy, Truong Hoa Binh has been active in using the position-taking power to propagandize and to inform society about the achievements of judicial reforms and the direction the judiciary would take moving forward. What he has said about judicial independence reflects neither his personal views nor those of the Court. Rather, these are the Party's views or the juridical views of legal scholars endorsed by the Party, which are presented in Party documents or even confirmed in the Constitution and law. The chief justice's position-taking has two aims. First, by speaking on these issues, the chief justice selectively disseminates the Party's views on judicial reforms to create a positive impression among the public about the judiciary (e.g., courts will protect them) and to encourage public support for judicial reform policy. Second, the chief justice's position-taking is not purely propagandist; it is also meant to signal to the public what the Party and the courts are going to do. When the chief justice has spoken on judicial independence, the message that he wanted to send to the public may be that more corruption cases will be tried, among other things.

14.5 CONCLUSION

This chapter discussed the social model of individual judicial powers. The model features the institutionalization of individual judicial powers: these powers are officially provided by the Constitution and related constitutional law. This institutionalization is due to socialist constitutional principles, which have deeply shaped the Vietnamese constitutional system. The socialist model is exemplified by Chief Justice Truong Hoa Binh. The institutional framework created a powerful position, that of chief justice, and, in theory, anyone appointed to this position would naturally become a "towering" judge. The current chief justice, Nguyen Hoa Binh, can also be considered a towering judge. The institutional infrastructure is already there. The actual manifestation of a towering judge would depend on personal practice: determination in implementing judicial reform policy; personal use of position-taking power; management of the highest court's work; and political relationship with key Party members. I conclude with a reflection on the question of why we should study towering judges. At least in the case of Vietnam, the study of towering judges is not to understand how individual judges behave but to understand how judicial power is employed and structured institutionally, and how individuality influences the use and structure of that judicial power.

15

The Civil Law Tradition, the Pinochet Constitution, and Judge Eugenio Valenzuela

Sergio Verdugo

15.1 INTRODUCTION

Civil law jurisdictions are not fertile ground in which to produce or identify *towering* judges. The formalistic judicial style of the civil law tradition discourages the personalization of the courts,[1] and some countries even promote the anonymity of judicial decisions and prohibit the publication of judicial dissenting opinions. It is probably not accidental that this book does not explore the experience of any civil law judge from Western Europe.[2] Even though judicial doctrines in the civil law tradition may still help to shape relevant aspects of the legal system, and there seems to be a growing trend allowing the publication of separate opinions,[3] the identities of the judges that authored those doctrines many times remain anonymous or are forgotten over time. In these kinds of civil law system, key legal actors can probably identify who the influential judges are, but it is perhaps hard for those individual judges to build a broader long-term reputation, as the court is frequently seeing as speaking with one voice. As a result, as Pasquale Pasquino has suggested, judges in countries like France, Italy, and Germany "have no public persona."[4]

---

[1] I use a weak approach to the idea of legal formalism. I do not mean a comprehensive legal theory but a judicial inclination to emphasize the role of legal texts in adjudicating cases, presenting the arguments in an apolitical way, seeking consistency of legal concepts, coherent systematization of legal issues and relevance of linguistic conventions, while avoiding writing morally charged or politically inclined arguments. Perhaps the most accurate way to describe this is by saying that the civil law tradition invites judges and legal actors to be "conceptualistic, not pragmatist." See Víctor Ferreres Comella, "Commentary: Courts in Latin America and the Constraints of the Civil Law Tradition" (2011) 89 *Texas Law Review* 1967.

[2] As Abeyratne and Porat say in the Introduction, Section V.A: "Nine out of the fourteen jurisdictions covered in this volume are common law or common law affiliated systems."

[3] The Venice Commission identified thirty-six states of the Council of Europe that "explicitly regulate separate opinions" and eleven that "do not permit them or have no relating provisions." Venice Commission, "Report on Separate Opinions of Constitutional Courts – CDL-AD(2018)030" 4.

[4] Pasquale Pasquino, "E Pluribus Unum: Disclosed and Undisclosed Vote in Constitutional/Supreme Courts" in Jon Elster (ed.), *Secrecy and Publicity in Votes and Debates* (Cambridge University Press, 2015) 204.

Despite the limitations just described, which oversimplify a diverse group of jurisdictions, this chapter claims that civil law judges can *tower* over other judges and examines one set of conditions under which this happens. I argue that, although the civil law features may limit the possibility of identifying towering judges in courts like the French *Cour de Cassation*,[5] and towering judges are expected to arise less often in civil law jurisdictions, centralized constitutional courts in civil law countries situated in politically fragile contexts[6] may produce the conditions for a towering judge to appear, and may help the legal community to recognize that judge as such.

I do not claim that having towering judges is necessarily a desirable thing in every context, as an excessive personalization of judicial institutions may carry some problems that I cannot examine here. My purpose is to explain *how* the legal features of the civil law tradition may not prevent the existence of constitutional towering judges in scenarios of institutional fragility, producing recognizable legacies that the community can associate with the identity of a specific judge, although perhaps not the high visibility of judges such as Aharon Barak and Earl Warren. I will claim that judges do not need to achieve the public stature of people like Barak or Warren to become *political* towering judges. As stated in the Introduction to this volume, a political towering judge needs to promote a particular agenda or change,[7] having a substantial impact on his or her constitutional system and individually distinguishing from his or her colleagues.[8]

This chapter elaborates an example to illustrate my claim: the experience of Eugenio Valenzuela, a judge who served in the Chilean Constitutional Court in the 1980s and who helped to advance the democratization agenda in the context of General Pinochet's dictatorship – a regime that had ruled the country since September of 1973. At that time, the formal independence of the Chilean Constitutional Court was weaker than that of the Chilean Supreme Court, as constitutional judges of that time lasted for eight renewable terms, and the dictatorship controlled the judicial appointments either directly or indirectly. However, while the Supreme Court aligned with the dictatorship's plans by promoting an apolitical judicial ideology that provided a sense of legal legitimacy to the regime,[9] the Constitutional Court challenged the

---

5 A useful example is Lasser's book, which shows how the French *Cour de Cassation* and the French judicial system, unlike its American counterpart, aims for a different type of legitimacy, one that is based not on participatory and deliberative values but on a unified institutional approach that avoids judicial transparency. Mitchel de SO-l'E Lasser, *Judicial Deliberations: A Comparative Analysis of Transparency and Legitimacy* (Oxford University Press, 2009).

6 I am borrowing Sam Issacharoff's expression. See Samuel Issacharoff, *Fragile Democracies: Contested Power in the Era of Constitutional Courts* (Cambridge University Press, 2015).

7 Introduction, Section III.

8 Introduction, Section I.

9 See Lisa Hilbink, *Judges beyond Politics in Democracy and Dictatorship: Lessons from Chile* (Cambridge University Press, 2007).

autocrats by helping to create the conditions that were going to end in Pinochet's defeat. The Constitutional Court behaved differently from the Supreme Court possibly because of two factors: first, the presence of Judge Valenzuela; and second, the institutional arrangements that centralized the judicial review power of legislation in the Constitutional Court, which provided the opportunity for Judge Valenzuela to act. These factors, along with the authoritarian context and the democratization agenda that many politicians were promoting, partly explain why the Constitutional Court, and not the Supreme Court, defied the Pinochet regime.[10]

This chapter will also show that Judge Valenzuela's legacy has two distinguishable dimensions. First, a *legal* aspect, consisting of a flexible and democratic way of interpreting the constitutional text enacted by the dictatorship that challenged the authoritarian originalism that prevailed at that time.[11] Second, a *political* dimension, consisting of the onset of a gradual and incremental way to advance democratization. The Chilean way for transitioning to democracy, unlike other countries that replaced their constitutional texts in post-authoritarian scenarios (e.g., Spain 1978, Brazil 1988), consisted of an evolving constitutional transformation that gradually eliminated authoritarian enclaves.[12] Valenzuela played a role in that strategy by turning the Pinochet Constitution against the interests of Pinochet.

This chapter proceeds as follows. Section 15.2 elaborates on the idea of a *towering* judge in the context of the civil law tradition and explains my claim. Section 15.3 briefly elaborates on the political context in which Judge Valenzuela worked and summarizes the Constitutional Court's main institutional features, aims, and procedures. Section 15.4 explains how the Constitutional Court helped to advance the democratization agenda against the interests of the incumbent regime. Section 15.5 elaborates on the persona of Judge Valenzuela and describes how he *towered* over other judges and how the legal and political communities have recognized his political legacy. Section 15.6 concludes.

---

[10] I offer a more complete explanation elsewhere: Sergio Verdugo, "Making Sense of the Chilean 1980 Constitutional Court" [2020] On file with author. See another explanatory account, compatible with the one that I offer in this chapter, in Robert Barros, *Constitutionalism and Dictatorship: Pinochet, the Junta, and the 1980 Constitution* (Cambridge University Press, 2002).

[11] The *legal* dimension that I conceptualize in this chapter is a less demanding version of the "jurisprudential dimension" that the Introduction associated with some towering judges. As I will show, although the doctrinal legacy of Judge Valenzuela was relatively relevant, it was not as meaningful as the jurisprudential dimension or "intellectual mark" described by the editors of this volume (Introduction, Section III).

[12] Elsewhere, I have summarized the democratization reforms that ended with the authoritarian enclaves. See Sergio Verdugo, "The Role of the Chilean Constitutional Court in Times of Change" in Richard Albert, Carlos Bernal, and Juliano Zaiden Benvindo (eds.), *Constitutional Change and Transformation in Latin America* (Hart Publishing, 2019) 206–10.

15.2 SOME THEORETICAL REMARKS ON THE POSSIBLE DIMENSIONS OF THE TOWERING JUDGES AND THE LIMITS OF THE CIVIL LAW TRADITION

There are different ways in which a judge can *tower* over other judges. A judge can become towering because of the influence that his or her doctrinal views have and the intellectual mark they leave – the *jurisprudential* dimension[13] – including the way that his or her judicial opinions frame essential legal and political debates over time. This dimension usually also involves the judge acquiring public visibility, at least within the legal community. A judge like Aharon Barak, for example, framed long institutional discussions that are still important in Israel. A judge can also become towering because of his or her agenda, which impacts the constitutional system in meaningful ways. The judge can become an institution-builder – the *institutional* dimension[14] – sometimes protecting the court's independence, and sometimes they can push for significant changes – the *political* dimension.[15] These kinds of judge may appear in foundational moments and use those moments as opportunities to contribute to shaping the political or legal landscape of their countries. Chief Justice Arthur Chaskalson of the South African Constitutional Court is perhaps a textbook example of this. It is also possible that, in these sorts of scenarios, judges can also champion liberal or democratic values in fragile institutional systems, such as judge László Sólyom did in the 1990s in Hungary.[16] Even though some of these judges' doctrines may not last long in some cases due to political backlashes,[17] scholars will continue to pay attention to and debate the legacies of these judges and to cite their judicial decisions, and history books and comparative constitutional projects like this volume will continue to discuss their rulings and even their separate opinions.

Many times, towering judges are also associated with progressive doctrines that require the elaboration of innovative tools of interpretation. Over time, their decisions may become the "canon" for a democratic or human rights normative approach.[18] Judges that are also talented lawyers are perhaps better positioned to

---

[13] Introduction, Section III.
[14] Introduction, Section III.
[15] Introduction, Section III.
[16] Kim Lane Scheppele, "Democracy by Judiciary: Or, Why Courts Can Be More Democratic than Parliaments" in Adam Czarnota, Martin Krygier, and Wojciech Sadurski (eds.), *Rethinking the Rule of Law After Communism* (Central European University Press, 2005) 25–60; Kim Lane Scheppele, "Guardians of the Constitution: Constitutional Court Presidents and the Struggle for the Rule of Law in Post-Soviet Europe" (2006) 154 *University of Pennsylvania Law Review* 1757.
[17] See examples of political backlashes or failed judicial experiences in Stephen Gardbaum, "Are Strong Constitutional Courts Always a Good Thing for New Democracies?" (2015) 53 *Columbia Journal of Transnational Law* 285; Tom Gerald Daly, *The Alchemists: Questioning Our Faith in Courts As Democracy-Builders* (Cambridge University Press, 2017).
[18] On the possibilities of judicial decisions becoming "canons," and what a canon means, see the useful discussion in Michaela Hailbronner, "Constructing the Global Constitutional Canon: Between Authority and Criticism" (2019) 69 *University of Toronto Law Journal* 248.

gain a good reputation and to influence their peers.[19] Becoming the leader of a personalized court –or personalizing the court – can also help, as it is probably easier for a broader audience to associate the court's outcomes with the persona of a specific judge in these cases. Even though these conditions may not be necessary – or sufficient – for a judge to become towering, they can help us to identify who the towering judge is, if there is one.

As I said in the introduction to this chapter (Section 15.1), towering judges are probably more easily found in common law jurisdictions rather than in civil law systems because judicial institutions in common law countries tend to be more personalized. Textbooks in common law jurisdictions typically refer to the doctrines of particular judges, and those doctrines are subject to academic scrutiny evaluating the consistency of those judges' approaches. Apex court judges are usually more influential than law professors in developing legal interpretations, and litigants discuss whether previous opinions authored by particular judges apply to their specific procedures, and expect those previous rulings to control the actual cases they litigate.

On the contrary, law textbooks in civil law countries typically avoid personalizing the doctrines of the court, and even though judges tend to cite previous judicial decisions, they usually do not associate them with the personal identity of a judge and prefer to quote "the court" as an institutional actor that speaks with a single and unified voice. The judicial culture in many civil law countries still seeks to legitimize the judicial role by elaborating on the appearance of strict adherence to the written law – including the codes. If there is only one correct judicial answer to any legal issue, then the court should limit its function to identifying what that answer is and applying it to the case with a unitary voice. The law should not have contradictions; if judges are the loyal agents of the law, then they should not show conflicting views. Most civil law judges present their arguments using an apolitical narrative. Sometimes the role of leading legal scholars commenting on the written law can be quite influential in the elaboration of consistent legal concepts and in building or systematizing legal categories.[20]

Some courts, such as the French *Conseil Constitutionnel*, release brief anonymous decisions that avoid deeply elaborating moral arguments. And like the French *Conseil*, a group of civil law jurisdictions – mainly from Western and Northern Europe – prohibit the publication of dissenting or separate opinions, and some possess a judicial tradition that disincentivizes the existence of dissenters even in politically charged cases.[21] Even in jurisdictions such as Germany, where the

---

[19] See Mark Tushnet's argument in Chapter 2 in this volume.

[20] John Henry Merryman and Rogelio Pérez-Perdomo, *The Civil Law Tradition: An Introduction to the Legal Systems of Europe and Latin America*, 3rd edition (Stanford University Press, 2007).

[21] The literature is too extensive to cite. See, e.g., Pasquino (*supra* n 4). Exceptions exist, of course, and we should probably remove the Brazilian Supremo Tribunal Federal from this list. Diego Werneck Arguelhes and Leandro Molhano Ribeiro, "'The Court, It Is I'? Individual Judicial Powers

publication of judicial dissenting opinions has been allowed since 1971 and the
Constitutional Court has been regarded as "transformative,"[22] it is not easy to
identify an influential and visible judge that towered over others.[23] In these conditions, it is hard in a civil law jurisdiction to identify important and visible judges like
the American "great judicial dissenters."[24] If we also consider that constitutional
judges in civil law countries usually serve short, fixed, and nonrenewable terms, we
can appreciate that they also have less time, influence, and opportunities to become
towering figures and to be recognized as such by their legal communities.

Even though these features may limit the possibilities for towering judges to be
recognized as such in civil law jurisdictions that possess a legal culture of judicial
secrecy and that value the idea that courts should have a unified voice, civil law
judges may still *tower* over their colleagues inside closed chambers, while releasing
anonymous opinions that will influence the political or legal landscape of the
country or frame debates in significant ways. Their peers, and possibly some key
legal actors, will know who the towering judges are. However, it may be harder for
a legal scholar or a historian to find proof of how that judge *towered* over others. In
the end, the towering judge may retire; his or her legacy will be remembered but not
his or her identity. Indeed, we can quickly identify influential judicial doctrines as
belonging to a particular court, but we will probably know little – if anything – about
the doctrine's real judicial author. If a concept of what a towering judge is requires
a long-lasting reputation outside the judicial sphere, then judges in civil law
jurisdictions certainly have a disadvantage over common law judges.

Nevertheless, I argue that a particular type of court (i.e., the centralized constitutional court) working in a specific kind of context (i.e., a foundational moment),
within the civil law tradition, can provide a fertile ground for a towering judge to
appear. Judges integrating these kinds of court are likely to have the opportunity,
and many times the obligation, to be involved in politically salient and morally
complex cases, and their identities can be associated with their decisions because
of the high visibility that these cases possess. If the court or legal system allows the

---

in the Brazilian Supreme Court and Their Implications for Constitutional Theory" (2018) 7 *Global Constitutionalism* 236.

[22] Michaela Hailbronner, "Transformative Constitutionalism: Not Only in the Global South" (2017) 65 *American Journal of Comparative Law* 527.

[23] There is a comparative constitutional law literature on judicial dissent that engages with this and other related topics. See, e.g., Lee Epstein, William M Landes, and Richard A Posner, "Why (and When) Judges Dissent: A Theoretical and Empirical Analysis" (2011) 3 *Journal of Legal Analysis* 101; Sergio Verdugo, "Aportes Del Modelo de Disidencias Judiciales al Sistema Político" (2011) Año 18, N° 2 *Revista de Derecho (Coquimbo)* 217; Santiago Basabe-Serrano, "Determinants of Judicial Dissent in Contexts of Extreme Institutional Instability: The Case of Ecuador's Constitutional Court" (2014) 6 *Journal of Politics in Latin America* 83; Lydia B Tiede, "The Political Determinants of Judicial Dissent: Evidence from the Chilean Constitutional Tribunal" [2016] *European Political Science Review* 377; Katalin Kelemen, *Judicial Dissent in European Constitutional Courts: A Comparative and Legal Perspective* (Routledge, 2018).

[24] Kelemen (*supra* n 23) 63–6.

judges to sign their opinions and even publish their separate votes, it will be easier to identify particular judges' ideas, even if the number of rulings released is relatively small.

When politically charged cases are submitted to courts, it is hard for civil law judges to avoid giving answers to complicated constitutional questions. The centralization of the judicial review power might put more pressure on constitutional judges when they need to answer politically charged constitutional questions in cases that are critical for the development of the political system. This should not surprise us, as one of the aims of proposing the creation of centralized courts was to prevent regular judges from answering hard constitutional questions.[25] True, scholars like Tom Daly have nonetheless suggested that courts in democratization scenarios should select their battles prudently and find the correct timing to advance normatively desirable political principles.[26] However, as Víctor Ferreres Comella claims, centralized constitutional courts usually cannot select the cases they decide and, although it is not impossible, it is hard for those courts to develop self-restraint doctrines to avoid solving critical political conflicts.[27] Indeed, justifying deferential theories such as the political question doctrine and elaborating a sort of Bickelian judicial "passive virtues" idea,[28] or pursuing strategies such as avoidance[29] or deferral,[30] might be a difficult task for a constitutional court to accomplish without abandoning the formalistic nature of judicial reasoning in these countries. As a result, when a single court that is separated from the regular judiciary centralizes the judicial review power over legislation, it is common for that court to attract the attention of critical political and social actors interested in the judicial outcomes. Moreover, if the court also has *ex ante* judicial review powers – that is, the authority to review legislative bills before their promulgation – those courts will be pushed to

---

[25]   See John Ferejohn and Pasquale Pasquino, "Constitutional Adjudication: Lessons from Europe" (2004) 82 *Texas Law Review* 1671; Víctor Ferreres Comella, "The Rise of Specialized Constitutional Courts" in Tom Ginsburg and Rosalind Dixon (eds.), *Comparative Constitutional Law* (Edward Elgar, 2011) 265–77. Also, see Hans Kelsen's reasons for preventing regular judges from engaging in constitutional issues in the context of the Austrian Court: Hans Kelsen, "Judicial Review of Legislation: A Comparative Study of the Austrian and the American Constitution" (1942) 4 *Journal of Politics* 183. But Kelsen was also skeptical of the power of centralized courts engaging with abstract principles or fundamental rights. Hans Kelsen, "La Garantía Jurisdiccional de La Constitución" ([1928] 2008) 10 *Revista Iberoamericana de Derecho Procesal Constitucional* 3.

[26]   Daly (*supra* n 17) 280–6.

[27]   Víctor Ferreres Comella, "The Consequences of Centralizing Constitutional Review in a Special Court: Some Thoughts on Judicial Activism" (2004) 82 *Texas Law Review* 1705; Víctor Ferreres Comella, *Constitutional Courts and Democratic Values: A European Perspective* (Yale University Press, 2009).

[28]   On the idea of the judicial passive virtues, see the seminal work by Alexander M Bickel, "Foreword: The Passive Virtues" (1961) 75 *Harvard Law Review* 40.

[29]   Erin F Delaney, "Analyzing Avoidance: Judicial Strategy in Comparative Perspective" (2016) 66 *Duke Law Journal* 1.

[30]   Rosalind Dixon and Samuel Issacharoff, "Living to Fight Another Day: Judicial Deferral in Defense of Democracy" (2016) *Wisconsin Law Review* 683.

evaluate the work of sitting legislatures, many times getting involved in partisan politics[31] and sometimes becoming a sort of "third chamber."[32]

The existence of a fragile democratic system, a post-authoritarian context, or a vulnerable democratization agenda aimed at avoiding authoritarian turns provides foundational moments that judges can use to secure a legacy that will be remembered by legal scholars and politicians, even though other judges may prefer not to cite them in their judicial decisions. These contexts of fragile political systems may provide the ground for great judges to appear. In this book, David Landau's account of Judge Manuel J Cepeda[33] and Gábor Attila Tóth's study of Judge László Sólyom[34] are useful examples to illustrate this, as both judges served on centralized constitutional courts in a context of vulnerable or fragile democracies in civil law countries.

However, the conditions listed earlier in this section may also push courts to become submissive institutions that align with the goals of incumbent regimes. After all, incumbent regimes have many ways to control courts and discipline judges.[35] In Chile, for example, the autocratic regime did not need to intervene in the regular judiciary, as the Supreme Court had spontaneously aligned with the dictatorship's goals by, for example, not investigating human rights violations.[36] Nevertheless, those conditions can also provide an opportunity for constitutional courts to challenge powerful political actors by releasing impactful and consequential judicial decisions. This is what happened in Colombia when the Constitutional Court prevented former president Álvaro Uribe from triggering "a significant erosion of democracy"[37] by stopping him

---

[31] Alec Stone, "The Birth and Development of Abstract Review: Constitutional Courts and Policymaking in Western Europe" (1990) 19 *Policy Studies Journal* 81, 84; Juliane Kokott and Martin Kaspar, "Ensuring Constitutional Efficacy" in Michel Rosenfeld and András Sajó (eds.), *The Oxford Handbook of Comparative Constitutional Law* (Oxford University Press, 2012) 807.

[32] Pasquale Pasquino, "Constitutional Adjudication and Democracy: Comparative Perspectives: USA, France, Italy" (1998) 11 *Ratio Juris* 38, 48; Ferejohn and Pasquino (*supra* n 25) 1675; Tom Ginsburg and Zachary Elkins, "Ancillary Powers of Constitutional Courts" (2009) 87 *Texas Law Review* 1431, 1437.

[33] See Chapter 11 in this volume.

[34] See Chapter 13 in this volume.

[35] The literature identifies diverse strategies that those regimes can employ. See a useful example in the way the Polish Law and Justice Party controlled the Constitutional Tribunal of that country in Wojciech Sadurski, "Polish Constitutional Tribunal under PiS: From an Activist Court, to a Paralysed Tribunal, to a Governmental Enabler" (2019) 11 *Hague Journal on the Rule of Law* 63–84.

[36] Jorge Correa Sutil, "The Judiciary and the Political System in Chile: The Dilemmas of Judicial Independence During the Transition to Democracy" in Irwin Stotzky (ed.), *Transition in Latin America: The Role of the Judiciary* (Westview Press, 1993) 90–101. Also, Hilbink (*supra* n 9); Lisa Hilbink, "Agents of Anti-politics: Courts in Pinochet's Chile" in Tom Ginsburg and Tamir Moustafa (eds.), *Rule by Law: The Politics of Courts in Authoritarian Regimes* (Cambridge University Press, 2008) 102–31.

[37] David Landau, "Abusive Constitutionalism" (2013) 47 *UC Davis Law Review* 189, 201–3. Also, Samuel Issacharoff, "Constitutional Courts and Consolidated Power" (2014) 62 *American Journal of Comparative Law* 585, 600–4.

from reforming the Colombian 1991 Constitution to be able to run for a third presidential term.[38]

A critical question that needs further research is how those judges can secure that the incumbent regimes will obey their decisions. I do not aim to reply to that question here.[39] Instead, in the remainder of this chapter, I explore the example of Judge Valenzuela to show how a civil law judge integrating a constitutional court in an authoritarian context can champion democratic values and explain how that judge *towered* over the others.

15.3 THE 1980 CONSTITUTION AND THE CHILEAN CONSTITUTIONAL COURT

The first Chilean Constitutional Court, created in 1971 by the constitutional reform pushed by former president Eduardo Frei Montalva, had closed after the 1973 military coup.[40] A military junta ruled the country between 1973 and 1990, committed gross human rights abuses, and implemented a right-wing Chicago-style economic program. The regime had promised to restore the rule of law and to establish a "democratic" system safeguarded by the military, although it took seventeen years for an elected civilian administration to return to power. Pinochet was the commander of the army, the head of the executive branch, and a member of the Junta, an institution that concentrated the legislative power. The Junta also comprised navy and air force commanders and the "general director" of the police. Pinochet did not rule with absolute power, though, as the regime established critical norms such as the Junta's decision-making procedure, which required all of its members to agree unanimously to adopt key political decisions.[41] Also, Pinochet was somehow forced to uphold the credibility of the regime's initial promises, as both the opposition and the regime's civilian supporting coalition had expected the military to return to their barracks in the future.[42] However, no clear

---

[38]   On this decision, see also Carlos Bernal, "Unconstitutional Constitutional Amendments in the Case Study of Colombia: An Analysis of the Justification and Meaning of the Constitutional Replacement Doctrine" (2013) 11 *International Journal of Constitutional Law* 339.

[39]   I developed an answer to this question somewhere else. See Sergio Verdugo, "How Can Judges Challenge Dictators and Get Away with It?" [2020] On file with author.

[40]   About the experience of that court, see Enrique Silva C, *El Tribunal Constitucional de Chile (1971–1973)*, vol 38, 2nd edition (2008), Cuadernos del Tribunal Constitucional 1977; Sergio Verdugo, "Birth and Decay of the Chilean Constitutional Tribunal (1970–1973): The Irony of a Wrong Electoral Prediction" (2017) 15 *International Journal of Constitutional Law* 469.

[41]   See, generally, Robert Barros, "Dictatorship and the Rule of Law: Rules and Military Power in Pinochet's Chile" in José María Maravall and Adam Przeworski (eds.), *Democracy and the Rule of Law* (Cambridge University Press, 2003) 188–220; Robert Barros, "Personalization and Institutional Constraints: Pinochet, the Military Junta, and the 1980 Constitution" (2001) 43 *Latin American Politics and Society* 5.

[42]   An interesting example of the political attitudes of many right-wing civilian politicians is the political agreement that they achieved with the opposition seeking to reform the Constitution – later rejected

deadlines existed and, in Pinochet's words, the government "only had goals, not deadlines."[43]

In 1980, the Pinochet regime enacted a constitution that reshaped the political system, aimed partly at legitimizing the regime's institutions while also making credible the regime's promises.[44] According to the 1980 Constitution, a referendum in 1988 was going to decide whether Pinochet's "presidency" was going to be extended or not. Pinochet was initially skeptical of this referendum, but one of his key advisors convinced him that it was important to legitimize his "presidency" with votes.[45] The constitutional plan was then designed for Pinochet to win the 1988 referendum.[46] Pinochet had easily approved the 1980 Constitution through a controlled referendum that did not meet minimum democratic guarantees,[47] and he expected to repeat that strategy for the 1988 plebiscite. The political rights of his opponents were severely limited, and no electoral court was going to supervise that new plebiscite.

Among the many institutional changes that the Pinochet Constitution implemented, it created the second Chilean Constitutional Court. The judges of that Court worked for it only part-time without exclusivity, and the dictatorship controlled all the appointments, either directly or indirectly. The Junta, General Pinochet, the National Security Council and the Supreme Court, an institution that had proven its loyalty to the regime,[48] all had the power to appoint judges to the Constitutional Court. Constitutional judges were supposed to serve eight-year terms; at the end of their terms – and before the elections of the future Congress – institutions controlled by the regime would decide whether to renew their tenures. Given these conditions, any way to evaluate the formal independence of the 1980 Court will probably conclude that that Court was hardly independent. Take, for example, Brinks and Blass's proposal on how to measure judicial empowerment.[49] For their model, the Chilean Court had low *ex ante* autonomy because of who the appointers were and, although the Court had some degree of *ex post* autonomy, its authority was too narrow to be able to "reshape the political landscape."[50]

by Pinochet. See D Matías Tagle (ed.), *El Acuerdo Nacional. Significados y Perspectivas* (Corporación Justicia y Democracia, 1995).

43 Cited by Verónica Valdivia Ortiz de Zárate, "'¡Estamos En Guerra, Señores!' El Régimen Militar de Pinochet y El 'Pueblo', 1973–1980" (2010) 43 *Historia* 136, 167. My translation.

44 See Jeffrey M Puryear, *Thinking Politics: Intellectuals and Democracy in Chile, 1973–1988* (Johns Hopkins University Press, 1994) 129; Heraldo Muñoz, *The Dictator's Shadow: Life Under Augusto Pinochet* (Basic Books, 2008) 127–8.

45 Ascanio Cavallo, Manuel Salazar, and Oscar Sepúlveda, *La Historia Oculta Del Regimen Militar. Historia de Una Época, 1973–1988* (Editorial Grijalbo, 1997) 127–8.

46 Genaro Arriagada, *Pinochet: The Politics of Power*, trans. Nancy Morris, Vincent Ercolano, and Kristen A Whitney (Unwin Hyman, 1988) 46.

47 Claudio Fuentes, *El Fraude* (Hueders, 2013).

48 Grupo de los 24, "Las Críticas Del Grupo de Los 24" 7; Alejandro Silva Bascuñán, "Las Fuerzas Armadas En La Constitución" (1985) 37(38) *Revista de Derecho Público* 137, 155.

49 Daniel M Brinks and Abby Blass, "Rethinking Judicial Empowerment: The New Foundations of Constitutional Justice" (2017) 15 *International Journal of Constitutional Law* 296.

50 Ibid. 318.

The lack of sufficient judicial independence should not surprise us. Courts can be useful for autocrats,[51] and the Chilean Constitutional Court of 1980 was no exception. Indeed, the Court was supposed to become a one-sided constitutional insurance for the regime.[52] That insurance consisted of a long-term mission to supervise the legislation enacted by future elected Congresses,[53] and a short-term mission to rubber-stamp the legislation passed by the Junta, thus providing the regime a sort of legal legitimacy. For that purpose, the regime designed an *ex ante* mandatory judicial review power, partly inspired by the French abstract organic law review model, and expected the Court to "remain in line" with the policies and interests of its leaders.[54]

15.4 CHAMPIONING DEMOCRACY IN AN AUTHORITARIAN CONTEXT

Initially, the Constitutional Court served the aims of the regime by rubber-stamping the legislation enacted by the Junta,[55] contributing to banning political organizations that threatened the dictatorship,[56] solving some legal disagreements among the Junta's advisors, and becoming a deferential or even obedient institution.[57] When the Court thought that a judicial decision could make the Junta uncomfortable, it respectfully addressed the issue in a nonconfrontational way and one time even used informal channels to communicate with the Junta, to avoid any possible confrontation.[58] This first period of the 1980 Court is important as it helps to understand better how the Court built its credibility with the Junta, probably gaining the confidence of the regime. Had the Junta not trusted the Court, it would probably have never submitted the bills that the Court later challenged.

---

[51] See, e.g.: Julio Ríos-Figueroa and Paloma Aguilar, "Justice Institutions in Autocracies: A Framework for Analysis" [2017] *Democratization*; Tom Ginsburg and Tamir Moustafa (eds.), *Rule by Law: The Politics of Courts in Authoritarian Regimes* (Cambridge University Press, 2008).

[52] On the idea of a one-sided insurance, see Rosalind Dixon and Tom Ginsburg, "The Forms and Limits of Constitutions as Political Insurance" (2018) 15 *International Journal of Constitutional Law* 988.

[53] See, e.g., Amaya Alvez Marín, "Forcing Consensus: Challenges for Rights-Based Constitutionalism in Chile" in Colin Harvey and Colin Schwartz (eds.), *Rights in Divided Societies* (Hart Publishing, 2012) 252; Felipe Meléndez Ávila, "La Influencia Del Control Preventivo En El Diseño Normativo Del Régimen Presidencial Chileno" (2017) 21 *Anuario Iberoamericano de Justicia Constitucional* 81, 96.

[54] Carlos Huneeus, *The Pinochet Regime* (Lynne Rienner, 2007) 399.

[55] Patricio Navia, "The History of Constitutional Adjudication in Chile and the State of Constitutional Adjudication in South America" (1999) 2 *Asian Journal of Latin American Studies* 1, 27.

[56] See Eduardo Aldunate, "Chile" in Markus Thiel (ed.), *The "Militant Democracy" Principle in Modern Democracies* (Routledge, 2009) 59–74.

[57] Teodoro Ribera, "El Tribunal Constitucional y Su Aporte al Desarrollo Del Derecho. Aspectos Relevantes de Sus Primeros 59 Fallos" (1989) 34 *Centro de Estudios Públicos* 195; Patricio Zapata, "¿Alternativas Menos Drásticas? Notas Sobre El Uso y Abuso de Prevenciones, Exhortaciones y Consejos Por El Tribunal Constitucional Chileno" (2001) 63 *Revista de Derecho Público* 601.

[58] Robert Barros, *La Junta Militar. Pinochet y La Constitución de 1980*, trans. Milena Grass (Editorial Sudamericana, 2005) 320–3.

Since 1985, the Constitutional Court, with the leadership of Judge Valenzuela, adopted a more independent attitude and significantly contributed to framing the conditions that allowed the opposition to the Pinochet dictatorship to win the 1988 plebiscite and put an end to the military regime. The most crucial case came that year when the Court reviewed the regulation establishing the Electoral Court. The Constitution established that the Electoral Court was going to be implemented after, and not before, the 1988 referendum, and the Junta enacted a bill that tried to lock in the detail of that rule. Nevertheless, the majority decision, written by Valenzuela, made a creative interpretation of the Constitution and established that political electoral principles demanded implementation of the Electoral Court before the 1988 plebiscite was going to take place, and not after.[59]

In his decision, Valenzuela identified a tension between parts of the Constitution and established that the Electoral Court should be implemented before the 1988 plebiscite by using abstract constitutional principles that seemed to oppose the specific rule. This argumentative strategy was surprising, as originalism and literalism were the prevailing legal tools of interpretation at that time.[60] Some civilian advisors and members of the dictatorship's supporting coalition shared Valenzuela's approach to the constitutional question,[61] and Judge Valenzuela knew about this.[62] These facts are relevant because they show that Valenzuela's position was not an isolated doctrine but an idea that could be defended from *within* the regime's supporting coalition. Also, Valenzuela's position was consistent with the regime's legitimization narrative consisting of the need to restore a civilian democracy, and by a constitution that was drafted partly as a result of this narrative. Sure, Valenzuela was brave. But he was not alone.

An interesting question is why the Pinochet regime did obey the Constitutional Court's decision on the Electoral Court statute. Although I cannot fully respond to that question here, secondary evidence suggests that Pinochet believed that he was going to win the plebiscite in any event,[63] probably influenced by his advisors and by the polls that the regime took at that time.[64] Elsewhere, I argue that the costs of disobeying the decision were high.[65]

---

[59] TC (1985) rol 33.

[60] Patricio Zapata Larraín, *Justicia Constitucional* (Editorial Jurídica de Chile, 2008) 203–9.

[61] Carlos Cruz-Coke, "La Sentencia Del Tribunal Constitucional de 24 de Septiembre de 1985" (1985) 37(38) *Revista de Derecho Público* 143.

[62] In a paper published in 2003, Valenzuela stated that political actors from diverse tendencies and the "immense majority of constitutional scholars" were supportive of his position. See Eugenio Valenzuela Somarriva, *Contribución Del Tribunal Constitucional a La Institucionalización Democrática*, vol 30 (Tribunal Constitucional, 2003) 23.

[63] J Esteban Montes and Tomás Vial, *The Constitution-Building Process in Chile: The Authoritarian Roots of a Stable Democracy* (International IDEA, 2005) 12; Roberto Garretón, "Chile: Perpetual Transition under the Shadow of Pinochet" in Ximena Barra (ed.), *Neoliberalism's Fractured Showcase* (Brill, 2011) 78; Patricia Arancibia Clavel, *Carlos F. Cáceres. La Transición a La Democracia 1988–1990* (Libertad y Desarrollo, 2014) 58–9.

[64] Peter M Siavelis, *The President and Congress in Postauthoritarian Chile: Institutional Constraints to Democratic Consolidation* (Penn State University Press, 2000) 13.

[65] Verdugo (*supra* n 39).

Later, Valenzuela voted in favor of all of the rulings that helped to democratize the other aspects of the 1988 plebiscite regulations, drafting most of them. In 1986, the Court reviewed the regulations of the electoral register and the Electoral Service agency. It decided to cut down the Electoral Service's director's power to cancel citizens' electoral inscriptions, arguing that that power violated due process.[66] In 1987, the Constitutional Court prevented the Junta from promulgating several questionable rules included in the new statute regulating the political parties.[67] That ruling strengthened the possibilities for the factions that opposed the dictatorship to organize their campaigns more effectively. For example, it declared the unconstitutionality of a norm aimed to expand the regime's power to ban political associations;[68] and it removed the prohibition of using the name, abbreviations, or symbols of political parties that were already dissolved (a ban that, in practice, targeted the Communist and Socialist Parties).[69] The Constitutional Court also prevented the Junta from establishing that only "natural persons" could provide funding to political parties (harming the creation of new parties);[70] and it determined that the Junta's power to regulate political parties should be interpreted narrowly, obliging the Junta to defer to the parties regarding critical organizational party rules.[71]

Then, the Constitutional Court had to review a new electoral regulation enacted by the Junta, and Valenzuela managed to convince sufficient judges to protect the political rights of citizens that were not affiliated to the existing political parties. The new regulation tried to limit independent citizens' political rights by imposing rules such as preventing them from becoming *apoderados* – that is, individuals that check and review the voting procedure. The Court declared that some of these rules violated equality.[72] The Court also forced the Junta to specify the dates of the presidential elections (Pinochet could lose the plebiscite, and the regime needed to organize presidential elections in that scenario) and the plebiscite.[73] The Junta had decided that the referendum was going to take place between thirty and sixty days after the regime had officially announced the regime's candidate. Valenzuela obliged the Junta to publicly establish the date with some time in advance, helping the "No" campaign to be organized more effectively.[74] The Junta obeyed the Court's decision and amended the electoral regulation as a result.[75]

With these decisions, Valenzuela's jurisprudence succeeded to secure favorable electoral conditions for Pinochet's opponents, who used the opportunity to organize

---

[66] TC (1986) rol 38, at pp. 6–7.
[67] TC (1987) rol 43.
[68] TC (1987) rol 43, at pp. 14–15.
[69] TC (1987) rol 43, at pp. 16–17
[70] TC (1987) rol 43, at pp. 17–18.
[71] TC (1987) rol 43, at pp. 18–22. See Ribera (*supra* n 57) 218.
[72] TC (1988) rol 53.
[73] TC (1988) rol 53.
[74] See Cavallo, Salazar, and Sepúlveda (*supra* n 45) 477–9.
[75] Ribera (*supra* n 57) 220. The Court reviewed the modification in TC (1988) rol 56.

a sophisticated and well-planned "No" campaign.[76] Pinochet was defeated in the end.

15.5 ON JUDGE VALENZUELA, HIS APPOINTMENT, AND HIS LEGACY

As I explained in Section 15.1, the depersonalization of the courts in the civil law tradition sometimes makes it hard for towering judges to be noticed. In other words, even if a towering judge rises, and other judges follow this judge, it may be hard to identify or demonstrate how that judge *towered* over his or her colleagues. However, I have also argued that a foundational moment like the one consisting in advancing democracy in the context of an authoritarian regime, along with the centralization of the judicial review power in a single constitutional court, may produce the opportunity for a towering judge to be noticed in a civil law jurisdiction.

Judge Valenzuela was not an outsider of the regime – the National Security Council appointed him along with Judge Enrique Ortúzar, who was a close advisor of Pinochet and had chaired the committee that wrote the first draft of the 1980 Constitution. Before the National Security Council discussed Valenzuela's nomination, Pinochet tried to convince the Council to appoint another lawyer – Avelino León Hurtado, a well-known commentator on the Civil Code – but the Junta opposed León Hurtado's nomination because of his advanced age.[77] Mónica Madariaga – Pinochet's secretary of justice, who advised him in judicial matters – recommended Pinochet to appoint Valenzuela. Valenzuela was at that time a lawyer of the *Consejo de Defensa del Estado*, an administrative agency that litigates in favor of state interests. Valenzuela resigned from the *Consejo*, but Madariaga, who was impressed by him, was keen to retain him and so offered him a position in the Court.[78] Valenzuela had no clear partisan background, but he was supposed to be a reliable lawyer with a promising legal career, and Madariaga seemed to trust him.

When the Junta submitted to the Constitutional Court the bill regulating the Electoral Court, the judges were divided on how to rule that case. It is helpful to note that, unlike its French counterpart, the Chilean Constitutional Court allows the publication of dissenting opinions, and the identity of who wrote the decisions many times appears at the bottom of the documents that include the rulings. That way, along with using secondary evidence, it is not hard to identify voting coalitions. We know that Valenzuela convinced some of his colleagues to support his views[79] and wrote most of the decisions that I explained in Section 15.4.

Valenzuela's positions divided the Constitutional Court into two groups. The first faction, led by Judge Ortúzar, was loyal to the regime and used a formalistic

---

[76] See Eduardo Engel and Achilles Venetoulias, "The Chilean Plebiscite: Projections Without Historical Data" (1992) 87 *Journal of the American Statistical Association* 933.

[77] Cavallo, Salazar, and Sepúlveda (*supra* n 45) 392, 472.

[78] Ibid. 472.

[79] Huneeus (*supra* n 54) 399–400; Hilbink (*supra* n 9) 140.

approach to constitutional interpretation with literalistic and originalist techniques aimed at implementing the Junta's will. The other faction, led by Judge Valenzuela, elaborated creative legal techniques to avoid literal interpretations that could lead to undemocratic outcomes and enforced a more liberal approach to the 1980 Constitution.[80] By doing this, Valenzuela ignored the literal meaning of the constitutional rule and broke with a long Chilean judicial tradition that emphasizes a formalist reading of the legal texts.

In an interview commenting on his decision on the Electoral Court, Valenzuela said: "Rosende [one of the regime's more influential lawyers] wanted the plebiscite to be like 1980, and he thought he could manipulate us. But we argued that to be compatible with the Constitution, the plebiscite had to be transparent."[81] Valenzuela was also aware of how the decisions helped the dictatorship's opposition: "Few people knew it at the time, but we changed the course of Chilean politics. We made the process something people could believe in."[82]

Valenzuela's positions were not only remarkable in the cases where he advocated for creating unfavorable electoral conditions for Pinochet, as he also showed hints of independence at least since January of 1985. At that time, he wrote a dissenting opinion against the Constitutional Court's decision legitimizing the ban of the Communist and Socialist Parties along with other left-wing political organizations.[83] Another interesting case that was going to test the Court's commitment to democratic principles came in 1987. The dictatorship was prosecuting Clodomiro Almeyda – a former secretary of state of the Socialist Allende's presidency and a founding member of the Socialist Party – who had returned to Chile after being exiled. The Pinochet regime's secretary of interior asked the Court to declare that Almeyda had violated the constitutional rule that prohibited promotion of the Marxist ideology. Although Valenzuela could not convince his colleagues to favor Almeyda in this case,[84] he filed a dissenting opinion.[85]

Three additional facts helped to make visible Valenzuela's work in advancing democracy. The first was the only noticeable measure that the Pinochet regime took against the Constitutional Court: when Judge Valenzuela's term ended, the National Security Council decided not to renew his term, and Valenzuela was forced to retire from the Court.[86] The National Security Council could not

[80] Druscilla L Scribner, "The Judicialization of (Separation of Powers) Politics: Lessons from Chile" (2010) 3 *Journal of Politics in Latin America* 71, 85.

[81] Cited by Pamela Constable and Arturo Valenzuela, A *Nation of Enemies: Chile Under Pinochet* (Norton, 1991) 303. My translation.

[82] Ibid. 304.

[83] The regime had already dissolved those parties, but some regime supporters had asked the Court to enact a formal judgment on the matter, probably to legitimize the ban. TC (1985) rol 21.

[84] Cavallo, Salazar, and Sepúlveda (*supra* n 45) 479.

[85] TC (1987) rol 46, at pp. 66–84.

[86] Sergio Díez, *Reflexiones Sobre La Constitución de 1980* (El Mercurio – Aguilar, 2013) 391.

reappoint Judge Ortúzar because he had reached the age limit (seventy-five), so it replaced both Valenzuela and Ortúzar, with two right-wing appointees.[87]

The second fact is that, later, civilian politicians acknowledged Valenzuela's actions and even rewarded him. In 1997, the Senate needed to appoint one judge to the Constitutional Court, but right-wing senators were divided and could not achieve an agreement.[88] While some argued that appointing Valenzuela might politicize the Court, others claimed that Valenzuela could help the Court to become a more credible institution.[89] Left-wing senators knew that a left-wing judicial nomination was not feasible; they decided to team up with the right-wing faction that was supporting Valenzuela, and voted in favor of Valenzuela's nomination. Thus, Valenzuela's appointment was due to a bipartisan agreement that succeeded in reaching twenty-eight votes against the right-wing nominee, who got seventeen votes.[90] Later, Valenzuela was invited by the Senate to give his opinion on the reforms that President Lagos was promoting to put an end to the authoritarian enclaves of the 1980 Constitution.[91] Although it is hard to know the exact impact of Valenzuela's views on the outcome of the 2005 reform, it is easy to notice that, at least, the final institutional design of the Constitutional Court coincided with most of Valenzuela's recommendations.[92] In 2005, the Senate reappointed Valenzuela with thirty-five votes (out of thirty-nine),[93] but Valenzuela retired a year after.

The third fact that helps to demonstrate how Valenzuela's reputation grew is that the legal community currently cites and discusses his judicial opinions. Although the Constitutional Court has cited Valenzuela in only a few rulings that use the non-literalist tool of interpretation that Valenzuela promoted in the 1980s[94] and only a few advocates have mentioned Judge Valenzuela's decisions to explain a constitutional approach to political equality,[95] his rulings have influenced many legal scholars. Those scholars typically cite the rulings as landmark examples of how to challenge a literal and originalist interpretation of the Constitution by advancing a "systematic" interpretation that treats political principles as relevant democratic ends.[96]

---

[87]   See Mary Helen Spooner, *The General's Slow Retreat: Chile After Pinochet* (University of California Press, 2011) 24.

[88]   Manuel Antonio Núñez, "Sobre La Designación de Los Magistrados Del Tribunal Constitucional Chileno" (1998) Número Especial *Revista Chilena de Derecho* 211.

[89]   Díez (*supra* n 86) 390.

[90]   Senate's 30th session, March 5, 1997.

[91]   Biblioteca del Congreso, "Historia de La Ley N° 20.050" 29–43.

[92]   Ibid. 31, 90, 102, 243, 301, 302. Also, see Javier Couso Salas and Alberto Coddou MacManus, "La Naturaleza Jurídica de La Acción de Inaplicabilidad En La Jurisprudencia Del Tribunal Constitucional: Un Desarío Pendiente" (2010) 8 *Estudios Constitucionales* 389, 394–5.

[93]   Senate's 35th session, March 9, 2005.

[94]   See, e.g., TC (1992) rol 141.

[95]   See, e.g., TC (1992) rol 160, TC (1996) rol 245, TC (1998) rol 282. Also, TC (2005) rol 460.

[96]   José Luis Cea Egaña, "Influencia Del Tribunal Constitucional En El Proceso de Institucionalización Política" (1988) 15 *Revista Chilena de Derecho* 205, 205–11; Cruz-Coke (*supra* n 61) 143–8; Zapata Larraín (*supra* n 60) 201–9.

Other scholars have claimed that Valenzuela's opinion on the Electoral Court bill was "courageous,"[97] "brilliant,"[98] and "beautiful."[99] These kinds of approach have been popularized among Chilean legal scholars, mainly due to Patricio Zapata Larraín's treatment of the Electoral Court case.[100] Another relevant example of a contemporary work highlighting Valenzuela's jurisprudence is a paper written by former Chief Justice Marisol Peña, who celebrated Valenzuela's judicial opinions and his judicial style.[101] Former judge Peña never cited Valenzuela in her judicial opinions, but she did cite him in her academic writings. Other scholars writing from a historical or political science perspective have also given credit to Valenzuela. To name only one, Óscar Godoy Arcaya claims that Valenzuela's decision on the Electoral Court was a "decisive step towards the transition."[102]

15.6 WHY IS EUGENIO VALENZUELA A TOWERING JUDGE AND WHAT CAN WE LEARN FROM THIS?

Judge Valenzuela *towered* over his colleagues of the Constitutional Court of 1980 because he succeeded in building the necessary judicial majority to confront the dictatorship in cases that were crucial for advancing the democratization agenda. In doing that, he defeated the faction led by Enrique Ortúzar, he did not follow the conventional formalistic approaches to legal interpretation, and he succeeded in building a reputation that transcended the closed chambers of the Court.

Valenzuela's legacy has two dimensions: a *legal* one and a *political* one. The *legal* aspect consists of his way of approaching and interpreting the Constitution using an anti-formalism technique that diverged from the conventional ways of reading the Constitution in the 1980s. Although some contemporary scholars highlight Valenzuela's approach, judges rarely cite Valenzuela's judicial opinions. Thus, it should be noted that Valenzuela's legal influence does not achieve the required intellectual mark to fit with the jurisprudential dimension conceptualized in the Introduction to this book. If Valenzuela left a "mark," it was due to the *political* dimension of his work, which had a significant impact in helping to put an end to the dictatorship and to advance democracy.

Perhaps Valenzuela differs from other towering judges discussed in this book, at least because of two reasons. First, as already explained, although legal scholars

---

[97]   Cea Egaña (*supra* n 96).

[98]   Zapata Larraín (*supra* n 60) 203.

[99]   See Mario Verdugo's work, cited by ibid. 207.

[100] Patricio Zapata Larraín, *La Jurisprudencia Del Tribunal Constitucional. Parte General* (Biblioteca Americana – Universidad Andrés Bello, 2002) 48–55; Zapata Larraín (*supra* n 60) 201–9.

[101] Marisol Peña, "El Perfil de Un Juez Constitucional: El Ejemplo de Eugenio Valenzuela Somarriva" in José García and Rafael Pastor (eds.), *Grandes Jueces Chilenos* (Ediciones Jurídicas de Santiago – Universidad Autónoma de Chile, 2017) 107–24.

[102] Óscar Godoy Arcaya, "La Transición Chilena a La Democracia: Pactada" (1999) 74 *Estudios Públicos* 79, 92.

have studied and discussed Valenzuela's opinions, other judges have rarely cited his decisions; even when they do cite his views, they do not identify Valenzuela as the author. This last fact is probably associated with the features of the Chilean civil law tradition, which encouraged the depersonalization of judicial rulings. After all, Chilean judges rarely give credit to a concrete judge for a judicial doctrine that they cite, and they prefer to quote the formal institutional author – "the Court." Second, unlike other judges discussed in other chapters of this book, Valenzuela did not participate in an elevated number of decisions. Indeed, the official statistics show that the 1980 Constitutional Court released an average of 9.6 rulings each year from 1981 to 1989.[103] If a judge needs to participate in numerous cases to become a towering figure, and if other judges need to cite those decisions while giving credit to their author, then Valenzuela can hardly be considered a towering judge.

On the other hand, if a judge does not need to participate in an elevated number of decisions to become towering, and if there are other ways in which a judge can be recognized besides other judges citing his or her judicial opinions, then there is an argument that can be made to recognize Valenzuela as a towering judge, and the way in which Valenzuela's jurisprudence influenced the political history of the country compensates for the small number of rulings in which he was involved.

Judge Valenzuela's example shows one path that a civil law judge can take to become a towering figure. His experience shows that the depersonalization of judicial institutions associated with the civil law tradition may not prevent a judge from becoming towering when foundational moments occur in fragile political scenarios.

---

[103] Tribunal Constitucional, "Cuenta Pública Del Presidente Del Tribunal Constitucional 2016" 179–80.

16

Towering versus Collegial Judges: A Comparative Reflection

Rosalind Dixon

16.1 INTRODUCTION

There is clear value to focusing on 'towering' judges: the topic invites us to think about some of the most significant judges on constitutional courts worldwide, and how those judges have helped shape their country's constitutional jurisprudence and broader framework. It likewise invites us to consider the factors that predict (positive) judicial influence of this kind, and constitutional law and institutional practice at a more particularistic level.

But the topic also raises definitional challenges: what dimensions of influence are most relevant or important in this context? Should an individual judge's influence be measured in objective or subjective, national or international, or relative or absolute terms? What is the relevant time frame for measuring such influence?

Each of the preceding chapters answers these questions somewhat differently. A key aim of this chapter is thus to explore these questions as axes of both similarity *and* difference among the various contributions to the volume. Another is to provide greater analytic clarity in thinking through these questions and to invite further reflection and study of their relationship to questions of audience and substance: should we measure judicial influence within a given constitutional polity or globally? And does a towering judge have to adopt a specific substantive jurisprudential approach? While these are distinct issues, there may ultimately be important connections between the two questions.

In addition, there may be dangers, as well as virtues, in focusing on the notion of a towering judge. The idea of a towering judge may tend to privilege chief justices over other leading judges, and male over female justices. Moreover, towering or dominant judges will not always be a good thing for the courts on which they serve or for constitutional jurisprudence. A scholarly focus on such judges may thus also have dangers: it may appear to celebrate this kind of judicial leadership style, when in fact collegial, non-dominant forms of judicial leadership are more desirable.

The chapter explores these questions and themes, largely by drawing on the examples and insights offered in earlier chapters: it is in this sense designed to provide a conclusion to the volume. In certain contexts, however, it draws on additional comparative examples to support the definitional issues and dangers it draws attention to; and these examples are largely focused on the United States, South Africa and Australia – as examples well known to many readers but especially the author.[1]

The remainder of the chapter proceeds in three parts. Section 16.2 explores the challenges of defining a judge as 'towering' in nature, and specifically (a) the relevant notions of judicial influence involved; (b) its temporal aspects; and (c) the relative versus absolute nature of the concept. Section 16.3 explores the individual, contextual and institutional factors that may explain or predict when a judge will assume towering status or influence of the relevant kind. Section 16.4 explores potential downsides to dominant or towering judges, from both an internal and an external perspective, then offers a brief conclusion as to the advantages and disadvantages of a scholarly focus on the notion of the towering judge.

16.2 DEFINITIONS

Towering: Extremely tall, especially in comparison with the surroundings; Of great importance or influence. (Oxford English Dictionary)

What is meant by a 'towering' judge? Common usage of the word 'towering' suggests two possibilities: a judge who is important, leading or especially significant in some absolute sense; or a judge who is especially significant or dominant *compared to other judges*, either at a given point in time or across history. On this view, as Mark Tushnet notes, there 'cannot be a towering judge without there being other judges over whom [they tower]'.[2] Most contributors to the volume also adopt some variant of the second, more relative approach: they treat a judge's 'towering' status as the product of both their absolute and their relative influence.

16.2.1 Forms and Definitions of Influence

The most important form of influence for any judge will undoubtedly be jurisprudential, or how a judge's opinions shape various areas of law. Most contributors are

---

[1] See, e.g., Rosalind Dixon and George Williams (eds.), *The High Court, the Constitution and Australian Politics* (Cambridge University Press, 2015); Rosalind Dixon, 'Weak-Form Judicial Review and American Exceptionalism' (2012) 32 *Oxford Journal of Legal Studies* 487; Rosalind Dixon (ed.), *Australian Constitutional Values* (Hart, 2018); Rosalind Dixon, 'A Minimalist Charter of Rights for Australia: The UK or Canada as a Model' 37 *Federal Law Review* 335; Rosalind Dixon and Theunis Roux (eds.), *Constitutional Triumphs, Constitutional Disappointments: A Critical Assessment of the 1996 South African Constitution's Local and International Influence* (Cambridge University Press, 2018); Rosalind Dixon, 'Constitutional Design Two Ways: Constitutional Drafters As Judges' (2017) 57 *Virginia Journal of International Law* 1.

[2] Chapter 2 in this volume.

constitutional scholars and thus choose to focus on constitutional jurisprudence as
the key test of a judge's jurisprudential influence. But other areas of law, including
private law, could also be equally significant for some judges. There may be
important spillovers between a judge's contribution to public and private law: it
may enhance their reputation and authority in both areas, in ways that allow them to
make greater contributions to both areas of law.[3]

Judges may also exert other forms of influence: over a court's relationship with the
public and/or political branches; and over the court's own broad institutional
features or design. They may do so in myriad ways: in how they write and frame
their opinions, in the cases they take, through various public speeches and engagement with the media, through influence on the training and appointment of judges
as well as court budgets and independence, and the structure and jurisdiction of
various courts.

The contributions to the volume also consistently note all three forms of judicial
influence – namely, jurisprudential, political and institutional – on the part of
towering judges, though they take differing approaches to the relative priority of
these different forms of influence.[4]

They likewise raise, but do not fully answer, important questions about the
relationship between these different forms of influence. Does it matter to a judge's
later jurisprudential influence whether they have both a broad public profile and
recognition within the legal professional community? Does it matter that they have
some broader claim to understand, or be part of, the creation of the court – or its key
institutional features? The answers to these questions will inevitably be contextual
and depend on the specific legal traditions and culture of a country at a given point
in time. But there is also some evidence that the three forms of influence may be
mutually reinforcing.[5]

The relative importance of each dimension may likewise depend on the composition of a court at a given time: if there are other judges on a court who exercise
significant influence along some of these dimensions, a judge may assume towering
status only if they have meaningful influence across a greater number of dimensions.
But if there are few other leading judicial figures on a court, influence on just one
dimension might be enough to give a judge towering status. In this sense, the

---

[3]   This was arguably the case for some of the leading common law judges, such as Lords Atkin, Denning,
      and Chief Justice Dixon: see Chapter 7 in this volume (citing Chan's identification of these judges as
      towering common law judges). It may also explain the relationship between public and private law
      decisions of a range of courts, including the Hong Kong Court of Final Appeal: see, e.g.,
      Rosalind Dixon and Vicki Jackson, 'Hybrid Constitutional Courts: Foreign Judges on National
      Constitutional Courts' (2018) 57 *Columbia Journal of Transnational Law* 283.
[4]   In this volume, see, e.g., Chapter 5 (noting Kennedy's jurisprudential legacy and contribution to
      constitutional drafting and the reform of Irish courts), Chapter 11 (discussing Justice Cepeda's
      contributions as both a designer and a defender of the court), and Chapter 12 (noting President
      Chaskalson's role in leading the country's first Constitutional Court).
[5]   See, e.g., accounts of Mason and Cepeda in Chapters 3 and 11 in this volume, respectively.

multidimensional nature of judicial influence may itself suggest the need for some degree of relative, not just absolute, judgement in assessing towering status.

Overlaid with these questions are also important questions about audience and substance: should we, for example, assess a judge's claim to towering status in purely 'objective' terms, or terms that give weight to the opinions of some relevant set of the legal and political actors? Several contributors note broad consensus on the dominance of particular judges – such as Barak and Sólyom – during their time in office.[6] Tom Daly, in contrast, suggests that Justice Hugh Kennedy, the first chief justice of an independent Ireland, is a candidate for towering judicial status yet is 'overlooked'; 'there is little chance that you will hear Kennedy's name' outside or even within his home country.[7]

Judges in this category could potentially be considered important or even 'towering' on some measure but still *insufficiently recognized as such by key national and international actors* to count as towering in the relevant sense.

This may also suggest an important role for constitutional scholars and teachers in constructing the status of a towering judge: who we focus on as significant jurists may affect their later (subjective) claim to towering status.[8] The same is true for later lawyers and judges. We should, however, perhaps be more cautious about a judge's own claim to towering status – or the significance of a judge's own statements and writings about their role.[9] Engaging in a comparative study of the most self-promoting judges would be interesting, but it would be a very different project from a study of influential or towering judges. Indeed, in a collegiate court, the most influential judges may often be those who combine a strong sense of professional ambition with a sense of, or at least outward presentation of, personal humility. Otherwise, they may find it hard to command the support of judicial colleagues.[10]

Overlaid with this question – of objective versus subjective definition – are also important questions about audience and substance: questions of *political* audience can be critical in determining whether certain polarising judges are deemed 'towering' or dominant in the relevant sense. So, too, can questions about geographic audience: should we, for example, measure judicial influence within a given constitutional polity or globally? Some judges may have a limited national reputation but broad international recognition, whereas others may be broadly recognised

[6] Chapters 9 and 13 in this volume.
[7] Chapter 5 in this volume.
[8] See, e.g., the treatment of Valenzuela by Chilean scholars: Carlos Huneeus, *The Pinochet Regime* (Lynne Rienner, 2007); José Luis Cea Egaña, 'Influencia Del Tribunal Constitucional En El Proceso de Institucionalización Política' (1988) 15 *Revista Chilena de Derecho* 205; Chapter 15 in this volume.
[9] This might affect how we weigh judicial interviews and autobiographies. In this volume, compare Chapter 8 (relying on first-hand accounts and interviews) and Chapter 10 (exploring Bhagwati's autobiography but from a more critical perspective).
[10] The judges included in our list include several that meet this description. My own dealings with Chief Justices Li and Mason and Justice Cepeda certainly confirm this. Neo and Tan also recount remarkable humility on the part of Chief Justice Chan; see Chapter 7 in this volume (suggesting that he was unsure as to whether his judgments had 'contributed anything to the development of the law').

within their own constitutional system but have a more limited global reputation. Others, still, may have a large national and international reputation.

Chan, Shrestha and Valenzuela, for instance, are widely known in their own constitutional systems but have more limited recognition elsewhere,[11] whereas Barak, Bhagwati, Cepeda, Chaskalson and Mason are broadly known to a global constitutional audience as well as to lawyers and scholars in Israel, India, Colombia, South Africa and Australia.[12] For some, such as Mason, their international reputation has been formally recognised, and amplified, by appointment as a judge of other courts of appeal, including the Hong Kong Court of Final Appeal (CFA).[13] For others, such as Bhagwati and Cepeda, it is a product of a range of roles within the international system.[14]

This is also a reason why common law judges may have an advantage in claiming towering status: they are more likely than civilian judges to be cited by judges in other common law systems. This influence may be declining, as national systems develop a more distinctive common law. But it also helps to explain the broad consensus on the status of earlier common law judges such as Holmes, Brandeis and Cardozo,[15] or Lord Atkin, Lord Denning or Chief Justice Dixon.[16]

This raises the question of whether 'towering judges' must be nationally recognised as having a significant jurisprudential impact or may be nationally *or* internationally significant. Is it merely an accident, for example, that the contributors to the volume do not focus on judges with a significant global but more limited national reputation (such as Australia's Justice Michael Kirby and Germany's Dieter Grimm[17])? Or does this reflect something definitional about the character of a towering judge?

Another important question relates to the substance of a judge's influence: Iddo Porat suggests that the towering judge is necessarily a judge committed to the liberal-cosmopolitan project.[18] Malagodi cites Justice Shrestha's role in promoting

---

[11] Chapters 5, 7, 8, and 15 in this volume. Malagodi herself suggests that the Nepali CJ has a significant international reputation, but that again depends on questions of geographic reach and audience – or on what international circles one is focused; see Chapter 8 in this volume.

[12] Chapters 3, 9, 10, 11 and 12 in this volume.

[13] Chapter 3 in this volume. See also discussion in Dixon and Jackson (*supra* n 3).

[14] Chapters 10 and 11 in this volume.

[15] Tushnet (Chapter 2 in this volume), citing Justice Roberts in Felix Frankfurter, 'Mr Justice Roberts' (1955) 104 *University of Pennsylvania Law Review* 311, 312.

[16] Neo and Tan (Chapter 7 in this volume), citing ' In Conversation: An Interview with the Honourable Attorney-General, Mr Chan Sek Keong' (1993) 14 *Singapore Law Review* 1. But see Chapter 3 in this volume (rejecting Dixon's status as a towering judge based on the decline in legalist as opposed to more realist or functionalist approaches to interpretation).

[17] See, e.g., Robin Fitzsimons, 'Michael Kirby: Reformer, Monarchist, Blogger and Dissenter', *The Sunday Times*, 19 February 2009, www.thetimes.co.uk/article/michael-kirby-reformer-monarchist-blogger-and-dissenter-qm9c2vkjzzf; Gruber Foundation, '2010 Justice Prize: Michael Kirby: Laureate Profile', https://gruber.yale.edu/justice/2010/michael-kirby; Dieter Grimm, *Constitutionalism: Past, Present, and Future* (Oxford University Press, 2016); Hertie School, 'The EU's "Legitimacy Deficit"', 7 February 2017, www.hertie-school.org/en/events/event-highlights/2017/dieter-grimm/. Compare with local criticism and controversy: AJ Brown, *Michael Kirby: Paradoxes and Principles* (Federation Press, 2011).

[18] Chapter 1 in this volume.

compliance with international norms in Nepal as one important part of his claim to towering status.[19] Chin Leng Lim points to the 'perfectionist' approach of Chief Justice Andrew Li and Justice Kemal Bokhary toward the Hong Kong Basic Law – that is, their commitment to promoting 'civic virtue' and/or rights in the process of construction – as key to their towering status.[20] Daly emphasizes the connection between a judge's towering status and their contribution to normatively attractive constitutional ideals – such as constitutional independence, democratic transition and constitutions as peace settlements.[21]

But others have reservations about that view. I would argue, for example, that Justice Scalia could be considered a modern towering judge in the United States,[22] which necessarily implies that it is possible for judges to have towering status and adopt a more limited view of judicial power, entailing a relatively formalist, non-cosmopolitan approach to constitutional construction.

Neo and Tan likewise identify the Singaporean chief justice as a candidate for towering influence, based on both his jurisprudence and his broader institutional role, but they suggest that this influence is at once towering and 'Burkean minimalist' in nature.[23] Dennis Davis suggests that Chief Justice Arthur Chaskalson was a towering judge, despite his commitment to judicial restraint and even socially conservative values, in certain cases.[24] Bui even suggests that the chief justice of Vietnam, Truong Hoa Binh, can be considered a towering judge when his influence was often in the service of the goals of 'democratic centralism' (and especially the kind of centralisation of power) favoured by the government.[25]

There may, however, still be an important *connection* between a judge's claim to towering judicial status and their substantive judicial philosophy or orientation: broadly speaking, judges who adopt a liberal-cosmopolitan approach to constitutional construction are more likely to be known, and cited, by foreign judges. First, they seem more likely to move in the same circles or networks.[26] Second, their interpretive approach will often be more directly relevant to other judges with the same approach – where foreign law plays a role. All else being equal, this can also mean that they are more likely to be globally *influential* than judges with a more conservative or nationalistic judicial philosophy. If global reputation is part of what defines a judge as a 'towering' member of his or her court, then a liberal-cosmopolitan set of values and approach to constitutional construction will thus increase the chances of assuming that status.

---

[19]   Chapter 8 in this volume.
[20]   Chapter 6 in this volume.
[21]   Chapter 5 in this volume.
[22]   Tushnet (Chapter 2 in this volume) ends his survey of the United States in 1955, at the time of Frankfurter's statement.
[23]   Chapter 7 in this volume.
[24]   Chapter 12 in this volume.
[25]   Chapter 14 in this volume.
[26]   Anne-Marie Slaughter, 'Judicial Globalization' (1999) 40 *Virginia Journal of International Law* 1103.

16.2.2 *Time*

A second important definitional question relates to time, or the temporal frame, in which we make judgements about a judge's influence and significance: towering figures in history are generally not easily forgotten. They may prevail in either the short or the long run, but they must have an influence that either endures or is *remembered* as significant.

This further suggests two variants to the idea of a 'towering' judge: 'short-run' and 'long-run' towering judges. Short-run towering judges will have significant influence on the court on which they serve but diminishing influence over time, whereas long-run towering judges may have more limited contemporaneous influence but greater long-term jurisprudential impact (for example, if they are persistent dissenters during their time on the court but are followed by later judges).[27] The *most* influential judges will tend to be towering in both the short and the long term.

On this view, there are also important differences among the various judges examined earlier in the volume. Barak and Sólyom were arguably some of the most influential short-run towering judges during their times on the court, but they have lost influence over time.[28] Tushnet suggests that Justice Felix Frankfurter has suffered a similar fate.[29] Judges such as Cepeda, Chaskalson and Mason, in contrast, have seen their influence persist since leaving the bench.[30]

This also raises complex questions about how and *when* we judge the status of a towering judge. In the short run, it suggests that we may make provisional assessments of a judge's influence as significant or dominant. But it also suggests the need to revisit these assessments later, usually well after a judge has left a court, to allow for a greater understanding of their long-term influence on later judges and political actors.

Judgements of this kind will not be truly long-term judgements: there is always the scope for later legal and political changes either to undermine or to amplify a judge's legacy. But they should allow some assessment of a judge's enduring influence and thus *sufficient* time for assessment of this kind. Often, this will require the passage of decades, rather than years, from the time of a judge's retirement.

A further complexity relates to when – within a judge's period of service on a court – it is meaningful to identify a judge as having 'towering' status. A towering judge does not typically come to a court fully formed: generally, they require some

---

[27] Compare Andrew Lynch, *Great Australian Dissents* (Cambridge University Press, 2016). A dissenter might also have more short-run influence over public attitudes or views of a court, as with Scalia. See Bruce Allen Murphy, *Scalia: A Court of One* (Simon and Schuster, 2014); Steven G Calabresi, 'The Unknown Achievements of Justice Scalia' (2016) 39 *Harvard Journal of Law and Public Policy* 575.

[28] Chapters 9 and 13 in this volume, respectively.

[29] Chapter 2 in this volume.

[30] In this volume, Chapter 11; Chapter 12 ('The foundation set by the Chaskalson Court lives on in South Africa, the various vicissitudes of the past decade of Zuma rule notwithstanding'); Chapter 3 (suggesting that the Brennan and Gleeson Courts largely continued Mason's jurisprudential approach and that differences in these courts were 'more a matter of tone and style than of substance').

period in which to develop their judicial voice (or to persuade others to follow it) before they assume a dominant role on a court. This means that there may be periods in a judge's history during which, even though they *later* assume towering status, their status as a towering judge may be incipient but not yet fully established or developed. It would therefore also be inaccurate to treat their early decisions as having towering status.[31]

Of course, one could take the opposite view: one of the ways we may be able to determine whether a judge has towering status is to consider early decisions of theirs that at the time looked inconsequential but later assumed outsized jurisprudential significance because of their authorship.[32] On this view, the later transformation of a decision from inconsequential to consequential – simply by reason of its authorship – may be one of the more important indications that a judge has assumed towering status.

Long-run influence also raises complex issues of *causation*: a judge may have either a positive or a negative long-run influence on the development of the law; and influence that is either explicit or implicit. We should be cautious in assessing claims of both explicit and implicit positive influence: explicit citation may ultimately be a form of justification for a later practice rather than a cause of or influence on its development. Implicit forms of influence are even more difficult to establish with confidence. Similarity alone is generally insufficient to show positive influence: a later judge may adopt the relevant approach in spite of, and not because of, its earlier antecedents,[33] or may develop the approach independently, without reference to earlier precedents.[34]

16.2.3 *Relative versus Absolute Influence*

A third issue relates to the rivalrous quality of a judge's claim to towering status. Can there be only *one* towering judge on a court at a time? My own view is that there may be more than one dominant judge on a court at a given time but only under special conditions: for example, two judges might share a claim to towering status because they consistently write together *or* because they occupy dominant but distinctly polarised positions at opposite ends of a court.

---

[31] For example, the early versus later decisions of Sir Anthony Mason in Australia on questions such as the implied freedom of political communication, though his career also cannot be 'perfectly bifurcated' into stages: see Chapter 3 in this volume.

[32] This is true of some decisions of Sir Owen Dixon in Australia. See, e.g., Michael Wait, 'The Slumbering Sovereign: Sir Owen Dixon's Common Law Constitution Revisited' (2001) 29 *Federal Law Review* 57.

[33] This is arguably one way of characterizing the relationship between judgments of Justice Murphy and Chief Justice Mason on the scope of implied rights under the Australian Constitution.

[34] This might be one reason for caution in accepting Daly's claim that Kennedy was an influence on the development of later 'activist' decisions of the Irish Supreme Court: compare Chapter 5 in this volume.

In the United States, for example, Chief Justice Earl Warren and Justice William Brennan were arguably judges who were towering in this joint sense: together, they helped shape and define the reputation and jurisprudence of the Warren Court, very often through joint opinions.[35] Mark Tushnet suggests Justice Hugo Black as another candidate for joint towering status in this same period.[36]

There are also, arguably, recent examples of pairs of towering but polarised justices: Justices Scalia and Ginsburg, or Scalia and O'Connor, for example. During his time on the US Supreme Court, Scalia was the leader of its conservative wing and the prominent advocate of an 'originalist' approach to constitutional construction, whereas O'Connor was the leading voice for a more moderate, hybrid approach to construction emphasizing judicial standards over rules, and minimalist, contextualist judgments.[37] Ginsburg, in turn, became the lead voice for the liberal-progressive wing of the Court, its commitment to a broad view of civil rights and liberties, and an anti-subordination reading of the Constitution. She was an opponent of key Scalia opinions, adopting a narrower, more formalist, originalist approach to these questions.[38]

In Australia, there are likewise historical examples of this same pattern: in the early to mid-twentieth century, Justice Evatt was arguably the leading progressive judicial voice on the High Court of Australia, whereas Sir Owen Dixon was the leading proponent of a more orthodox, 'legalist' approach to constitutional construction.[39] In the early twenty-first century, these roles remained constant but were occupied by Justices Michael Kirby and Bill Gummow.[40]

The idea of two rival towering judges, however, necessarily invites questions about audience: Scalia, for instance, is arguably the dominant judicial figure for late-twentieth-century legal and political conservatives in the United States,[41] but many politically liberal scholars and commentators reject the significance (and

---

35 See G Edward White, *Earl Warren: A Public Life* (Oxford University Press, 1982) 185; Bernard Schwartz, *Super Chief: Earl Warren and His Supreme Court – A Judicial Biography* (New York University Press, 1983).

36 Chapter 2 in this volume.

37 See, e.g., M David Gefland and Keith Werhan, 'Federalism and Separation of Powers on a "Conservative" Court: Currents and Cross-Currents from Justices O'Connor and Scalia' (1989) 64 *Tulane Law Review* 1443; Murphy (*supra* n 29).

38 See, e.g., Scott Dobson (ed.), *The Legacy of Ruth Bader Ginsburg* (Cambridge University Press, 2015); Reva B Siegel, 'Equality and Choice: Sex Equality Perspectives on Reproductive Rights in the Work of Ruth Bader Ginsburg' (2013) 25 *Columbia Journal of Gender and Law* 25.

39 See Gabrielle Appleby, 'The Gavan Duffy Court' in Rosalind Dixon and George Williams (eds.), *The High Court, the Constitution, and Australian Politics* (Cambridge University Press, 2015) 141; Helen Irving, 'The Dixon Court' in Rosalind Dixon and George Williams (eds.), *The High Court, the Constitution, and Australian Politics* (Cambridge University Press, 2015) 179.

40 See Rosalind Dixon and Sean Lau, 'The Gleeson Court' in Rosalind Dixon and George Williams (eds.), *The High Court, the Constitution, and Australian Politics* (Cambridge University Press, 2015) 284. Gummow is complicated in this context in that he exercised his role in a more collegial way, along with Hayne, Gaudron and, at times, Heydon and Gleeson.

41 See Calabresi (*supra* n 29); Steven G Calabresi and Justin Bragg, 'The Jurisprudence of Justice Antonin Scalia: A Response to Professor Bruce Allen Murphy and Professor Justin Driver' (2015) 9

desirability) of his jurisprudential influence.[42] Justice Ruth Bader Ginsburg, in contrast, has become a public icon on the left – indeed, she is arguably the leading popular towering judge globally[43] – but she is widely reviled by the political right, including for her comments about President Trump.[44] In the United Kingdom, as Hunter and Rackley note, Lady Brenda Hale has likewise made a significant impact in areas such as family law, tort, refugee, welfare and criminal law.[45] Yet political conservatives have repeatedly criticised her appointment and judgments as 'hardline', 'radical' and 'ass[inine]'.[46] This also highlights the importance of *who* decides whether a judge counts as dominant or 'towering' in the relevant sense.

16.3 EXPLANATORY OR PREDICTIVE FACTORS

What does this say about the qualities that are likely to define a towering judge? What is the role of individual skill and disposition or other personal characteristics such as gender? What about institutional position or role? Are chief justices, for example, more likely than other justices to exert this kind of outsized influence, and, if so, is this because of their institutional position or rather a mix of institutional stature and ingoing judicial reputation? If towering judges are *dominant* judges, their identity will likewise be what Tushnet calls 'colleague-dependent'.[47] Other factors may include the broader legal and political environment in which a judge serves.

16.3.1 *The Individual Judge and Their Institutional Position*

Some of the factors that affect a judge's capacity to influence a court will be absolute or personal in nature – for example, the legal skill and creativity of a judge, their

---

New York University Journal of Law and Liberty 793; Richard F Duncan, 'Justice Scalia and the Rule of Law: Originalism vs the Living Constitution' (2016) 29 *Regent University Law Review* 9; 'A Tribute to Justice Scalia', *The Federalist Society*, 14 May 2016, https://fedsoc.org/commentary/videos/a-tribute-to-justice-scalia.

[42] See Jedediah Purdy, 'Scalia's Contradictory Originalism', *The New Yorker*, 16 February 2016, www .newyorker.com/news/news-desk/scalias-contradictory-originalism; Erwin Chemerinsky, 'The Jurisprudence of Justice Scalia: A Critical Appraisal' (2000) 22 *University of Hawaii Law Review* 385; Marie A Failinger, 'Not Mere Rhetoric: On Wasting or Claiming Your Legacy, Justice Scalia' (2003) 34 *University of Toledo Law Review* 425.

[43] See *On the Basis of Sex* (2018) (a biographical film based on the life of Ginsburg); *RBG* (2018) (a documentary film based on the life of Ginsburg); Lauren Kelly, 'How Ruth Bader Ginsburg Became the "Notorious RBG"', *Rolling Stone*, 27 October 2015, www.rollingstone.com/culture/culture-features/how-ruth-bader-ginsburg-became-the-notorious-rbg-50388/.

[44] See Ian Tuttle, 'Ruth Bader Ginsburg Isn't Even Pretending to Be Impartial', *National Review*, 20 May 2015, www.nationalreview.com/2015/05/notorious-rbg-ian-tuttle/; Cheryl K Chumley, 'Ruth Bader Ginsburg, You Must Recuse', *The Washington Times*, 27 June 2017, www .washingtontimes.com/news/2017/jun/27/ruth-bader-ginsburg-you-must-recuse/.

[45] Chapter 4 in this volume.

[46] Chapter 4 in this volume.

[47] Chapter 2 in this volume.

capacity to craft well-reasoned and well-written judgments, and their broader interpersonal and political skills. For a judge to be a leading or towering judge, they will
likely need to have a high degree of absolute and relative skill along all, or at least
most, of these dimensions.

Daly, for example, notes Kennedy's place among the global judiciary's most
'powerful intellectual forces' and his significant diplomatic and tactical skills.[48]
Landau suggests that Manuel Cepeda 'had an unusual ... combination of legal
and political skill' for a judge.[49] Tóth calls Sólyom a 'remarkable thinker'.[50] Verdugo
notes other scholars' praise of a particular opinion of Valenzuela as 'courageous',
'brilliant' and 'beautiful'[51]. Neo and Tan note the reputation of Chan Sek Keong as
a 'piercing intellect' with 'encyclopaedic knowledge' of the law, but they also discuss
his enormous productivity and strategic abilities.[52] Hunter and Rackley likewise note
Brenda Hale's 'acknowledged expertise' in a range of legal areas, the power of her
reasoning and her notable productivity and engagement – both in judgment writing
and in an extrajudicial context.[53] Davis notes Chaskalson's role as a public interest
lawyer and ANC advisor but also his 'unquestioned technical skill at the Bar'.[54]
Appleby and Lynch praise Sir Anthony Mason's 'vision' and 'statesmanship'.[55]

In prior work, I have suggested that this is one reason why 'drafter-judges' – judges
who have demonstrated and honed their legal and political skills in the process of
formal constitutional change – may be especially likely to be leading or influential
judges.[56] There are also a number of drafter-judges included in the volume –
including Kennedy, Barak, Cepeda, Chaskalson and Sólyom.[57] Other judges,
such as Chief Justice Chan, had alternative forms of prior political experience.[58]
But other factors may also be relevant in this context, including a judge's formal
training and education and their mix of 'insider' and 'outsider' status.[59]

Another factor is the length of time a judge serves on a court.[60] A long period of
judicial service gives a judge additional time to hone and refine their skills and to
exert a jurisprudential and institutional influence.[61] Long-serving judges may also

---

[48] Chapter 5 in this volume.
[49] Chapter 11 in this volume.
[50] Chapter 13 in this volume.
[51] Chapter 15 in this volume.
[52] Chapter 7 in this volume.
[53] Chapter 4 in this volume.
[54] Chapter 12 in this volume.
[55] Chapter 3 in this volume.
[56] Dixon, 'Constitutional Design Two Ways' (*supra* n 1).
[57] Chapters 5, 9, 11, 12 and 13 in this volume, respectively. Sólyom was also later elected as President of
      Hungary.
[58] Chapter 7 in this volume.
[59] Compare Dixon and Jackson (n 3); Landau (n 4).
[60] Compare Chapter 2 in this volume.
[61] This was arguably the case for Sir Anthony Mason, who was a junior justice on the Barwick Court and
      did not share the broad approach of that court but who, over time, served with far more legally and
      ideologically sympathetic judges and refined his skills as an institutional leader. Compare Chapter 3

have an advantage over judges who serve for lesser periods because they have a greater opportunity to claim authorship or ownership over a joint line of reasoning.

It is thus unsurprising that several towering judges in the volume served for long periods of time: Barak served for twenty-eight years (eleven years as chief justice and seventeen years as a puisne justice)[62] and Mason served for twenty-two years (eight years as chief justice and fourteen years as a puisne justice).[63]

Hale was close behind with a tenure of sixteen years (three years as president of the Supreme Court and thirteen as an ordinary member of the Court/legal committee).[64] Other judges served only much shorter periods: for example, Chan served for six years as chief justice,[65] Binh served as chief justice for nine years[66] and Cepeda served for eight years (and as president for one year).[67] But, in several cases, this reflected norms of mandatory retirement or judicial term limits, which reduced the significance of time as a factor in judicial dominance.[68]

What is perhaps most striking about this volume's list of towering judges, however, is that they are disproportionately *male*. Of the nineteen judges nominated as candidates for towering status in the preceding chapters, only one (Lady Brenda Hale) is female.[69]

As Hunter and Rackley note in their study of Lady Hale, this reflects broader societal attitudes toward female leadership: 'influence and individualism ... have gendered associations: they are qualities (usually) identified and celebrated in men, and not identified or celebrated in women'.[70] This is true of both the identification and the celebration of female leadership.

One possibility is that the gender imbalance in the volume's list of towering judges reflects a systematic – and gendered – set of mistakes on the part of contributors, or at least editors, in inviting a focus on certain judges – that is, a gendered failure to *identify* or focus on towering female judges or to at least recruit scholars willing and able to write about those judges. There is now a long list of female judges worldwide who could be considered highly influential, including in the relevant jurisdictions – for example, Justices O'Connor and Ginsburg in the United States,[71] Chief Justice

in this volume; Michael Kirby, 'Sir Anthony Mason Lecture 1996: A F Mason – From *Trigwell* to *Teoh*' (1996) 20 *Melbourne University Law Review* 1087.
[62] Chapter 9 in this volume.
[63] Chapter 3 in this volume.
[64] Chapter 4 in this volume.
[65] Chapter 7 in this volume.
[66] Chapter 14 in this volume.
[67] Chapter 11 in this volume.
[68] Judicial term limits, for example, explain why Cepeda served for only eight years on the Court and Chaskalson for twelve years; Chapters 11 and 12 in this volume, respectively. This is one reason why Jackson and I suggest that service on a foreign court after retirement may be significant: it creates a form of global senior status, which allows a judge's influence to continue; compare Dixon and Jackson (*supra* n 3).
[69] Chapter 4 in this volume.
[70] Chapter 4 in this volume.
[71] See Joan Biskupic, *Sandra Day O'Connor: How the First Woman on the Supreme Court Became Its Most Influential Justice* (Ecco, 2005); Dobson (*supra* n 40); Siegel (*supra* n 40).

McLachlin and Justices Wilson, L'Heureux-Dube and Abella in Canada,[72] Justice Mary Gaudron in Australia[73] and Justice Kate O'Regan in South Africa.[74] Other potential candidates for the title of 'leading' female justices elsewhere include Dame Sian Elias in New Zealand,[75] Lady Mabel Agyemang in Gambia,[76] Florence Arrey of Cameroon[77] and Desiree Bernard of Guyana.[78]

Another possibility, however, is that the failure is not simply one of perception and that gender-based differences do exist in the willingness or ability of female judges to assume towering or *dominant* – as opposed to leading – status on a court. Female judges might be willing to play a highly influential role on a court but less willing than equivalent male judges to assert a claim to dominance or pre-eminence. Or they might be equally willing to assert such a claim but less likely to succeed in doing so – without triggering an adverse response from colleagues.[79]

The first explanation finds some support in experimental evidence about the willingness of women to engage in rivalrous or competitive behaviours that involve attempts to dominate others rather than achieve high levels of absolute performance.[80] But great care should be taken in applying these findings to female

[72]   See Elizabeth Halka, 'Madam Justice Bertha Wilson: A Different Voice in the Supreme Court of Canada' (1996) 35 *Atlanta Law Review* 242; Constancy Blackhouse, *Claire L'Heureux-Dube: A Life* (University of British Columbia Press, 2017).

[73]   See Pamela Burton, *From Moree to Mabo: The Mary Gaudron Story* (University of Western Australia Publishing, 2010); Michael Pelly, 'Mary Gaudron Was Her Own Judge on the Bench', *The Australian*, 29 October 2010, www.theaustralian.com.au/business/legal-affairs/mary-gaudron-was-her-own-judge-on-the-bench/news-story/6e4f4472ad0c73c6fe63114435240c29. Later Australian female members of the High Court have also had significant jurisprudential influence.

[74]   See Kate O'Regan, 'Human Rights and Democracy: A New Global Debate: Reflections on the First Ten Years of South Africa's Constitutional Court' (2004) 32 *International Journal of Legal Information* 200; Elrena van der Spuy, 'Interview with Judge Kate O'Regan' (2015) 53 *South African Crime Quarterly* 59.

[75]   See 'Elias – Top Judge and Judicial Activist', *New Zealand Herald*, 29 March 2005, www .nzherald.co.nz/who-runs-nz/news/article.cfm?c_id=1500896&objectid=10117345.

[76]   Lady Mabel Agyemang has also served on the judiciaries in Swaziland and Ghana. See Linda Jele, 'Judge Mabel Agyemang Leaving the High Court', *Times of Swaziland*, 14 September 2010, www .times.co.sz/News/19414.html; Judge Mabel Agyemang, 'Foreword' in Gretchen Bauer and Josephine Dawuni (eds.), *Gender and the Judiciary in Africa: From Obscurity to Parity?* (Taylor and Francis, 2016).

[77]   See 'Florence Rita Arrey: Outstanding Legal Mind', *Cameroon Tribune*, 3 February 2018, www .cameroon-tribune.cm/article .html/16334/en.html/article-CT; Eleanor Ayuketah, 'Constitutional Council: A Woman of Substance in the Eleven-Man Council', *CRTV*, 6 March 2018, www.crtv.cm/2018/03/constitutional-council-woman-substance-buried-eleven-man-council/.

[78]   See Dhanpaul Narine, 'Justice Desiree Bernard: Blazing a Trail!', *The West Indian*, 28 October 2017, https://guyaneseonline.files.wordpress.com/2017/11/profile-justice-desiree-bernard-by-dr-dhanpaul-narine.pdf; Latoya Giles, 'CCJ Honours First Female Judge, Justice Desiree Bernard', *Kaieteur News*, 20 February 2014, www.kaieteurnewsonline.com/2014/02/20/ccj-honours-first-female-judge-justice-desiree-bernard/.

[79]   In equilibrium, this might also lead to them being less willing to do so in the first place.

[80]   Muriel Niederle and Lise Vesterlund, 'Do Women Shy Away from Competition? Do Men Compete Too Much?' (2007) 122 *Quarterly Journal of Economics* 1067; Muriele Niederle and Lise Vesterlund, 'Gender and Competition' (2011) 3 *Annual Review of Economics* 601.

judges: female judges are not typical female subjects, in part because discrimination often forces female lawyers to downplay traditional 'female' or feminine characteristics and encourages the selection of female lawyers with more 'masculine' behaviours or career profiles.[81]

The latter explanation, however, seems more plausible: male lawyers and judges may be willing to recognise female judges as important judicial minds and even as equals. But they may have deep-rooted, unconscious resistance to the idea of female judicial dominance – especially if it stems from a claim of superior legal or political skills rather than some formal institutional role (such as the role of chief justice).[82] (The same might also be true for openly LGBTQI judges or judges from a minority racial or ethnic background, though we have fewer examples worldwide against which to test this hypothesis.[83])

The female judge listed as a towering judge in this volume, Lady Brenda Hale, is a former chief justice and thus has a distinctive *institutional* claim to exert some form of judicial leadership. It is also striking the degree to which contributors *generally* chose to focus on chief justices as candidates for towering status. Only four out of the nineteen judges nominated by the contributors to the volume as having towering status were not chief justices.

---

[81]   Elizabeth Cruikshank, *Women in the Law: Strategic Career Management* (Law Society, 2003) 91; Brenda Hale, 'Equality and the Judiciary: Why Should We Want More Women Judges?' (2001) *Public Law* 489.

[82]   Compare studies on male attitudes to high-earning females: Claire Cain Miller, 'When Wives Earn More Than Husbands, Neither Partner Likes to Admit It', *New York Times*, 17 July 2018, www .nytimes.com/2018/07/17/upshot/when-wives-earn-more-than-husbands-neither-like-to-admit-it.html; Marianne Bertrand, Jessica Pan and Emir Kamenica, 'Gender Identity and Relative Income Within Households' (2015) 130 *Quarterly Journal of Economics* 571. See also reports that resistance to women, including in the judiciary, increases as women progress: Sally J Kenney, 'Choosing Judges: A Bumpy Road to Women's Equality and a Long Way to Go' (2012) *Michigan State Law Review* 1499, 1508.

[83]   On the lack of sexual and racial diversity on courts, including constitutional courts, worldwide, see, e.g., Leslie Moran, 'Judicial Diversity and the Challenge of Sexuality: Some Preliminary Findings' (2006) 28 *Sydney Law Review* 565; Angela Onwuachi-Willig, 'Representative Government, Representative Court: The Supreme Court as a Representative Body' (2005) 90 *Minnesota Law Review* 1252 (on the US Supreme Court); Nadia Khomani, 'Recruitment of Black and Asian Judges Too Slow – Lord Chief Justice', *The Guardian*, 20 July 2017, www.theguardian.com/law/2017/jul/20/ recruitment-of-black-and-asian-judges-too-slow-lord-chief-justice (on UK courts); Ray Steinwall, 'Addressing Cultural Diversity in the Australian Judiciary', *Diversity Council of Australia*, 30 April 2014, www.dca.org.au/blog/addressing-cultural-diversity-australian-judiciary (on Australian courts). But, for notable exceptions, see regarding Edwin Cameron (Constitutional Court of South Africa): Minoshni Pillay, 'Gay Rights Activists Urged to New Efforts Against Discrimination', *SABC*, 10 December 2018, http://affinity.org.au/gay-people-exist-and-you-cant-change-us-michael-kirby-delivers-stirring-speech-on-lgbtqia-rights-2/; Susanne Baer (German Federal Constitutional Court): 'Germany's First Openly Gay High Court Judge Speaks at University of Michigan', *Watermark Online*, 31 January 2018, www.watermarkonline.com/2017/01/31/germanys-first-openly-gay-high-court-judge-speaks-at-university-of-michigan/; and on race, Thurgood Marshall, Sonia Sotomayor and Clarence Thomas (US Supreme Court): Jessica Campisi and Brandon Griggs, 'Of the 113 Supreme Court Justices in US History, All But 6 Have Been White Men', *CNN*, 5 September 2018, https:// edition.cnn.com/2018/07/09/politics/supreme-court-justice-minorities-trnd/index.html.

Clearly, formal leadership of a court is neither a necessary nor a sufficient condition for a judge to be a towering judge. There are notable individual judges who have had a towering jurisprudential influence without occupying the office of chief justice – for example, Justice William Brennan on the US Supreme Court,[84] Justice Kemal Bokhary on the Hong Kong CFA[85] and Eugenio Valenzuela on the Chilean Constitutional Court.[86] There are likewise many chief justices who have had limited jurisprudential influence,[87] and others who have notably failed to defend a court against outside criticism and attack.

The role of chief justice will also vary by jurisdiction: the legal committee of the House of Lords, for example, had a long tradition of allowing judges to speak individually both within and for the Court, and thus the role of president of the Court had limited significance at least for an external audience.[88] It is perhaps thus unsurprising that some of the towering jurisprudential influences on the court in recent decades, such as Lords Hoffman and Steyn, or in earlier periods, such as Lords Diplock, Reid and Denning, have not been the formal institutional head of the court.[89] It may be that *formal* leadership of the UK Supreme Court was less important to the jurisprudential contribution and standing of justices such as Lord Bingham – or even Lady Hale.[90]

But in some countries, at least, the role of chief justice may make some judges especially *well positioned* or likely to become towering judges: they generally have some role in the management of the court as an institution. There may be a norm that it is largely or even exclusively the role of the chief justice to speak publicly for the court.[91] This means that the chief justice will tend quite naturally to be the lead

---

[84] See Lino A Graglia, 'The Legacy of Justice Brennan: Constitutionalization of the Left-Liberal Political Agenda' (1999) 77 *Washington University Law Quarterly* 183.

[85] Chapter 6 in this volume.

[86] Chapter 15 in this volume.

[87] See, e.g., Brian Galligan, 'The Barwick Court' in Rosalind Dixon and George Williams (eds.), *The High Court, the Constitution, and Australian Politics* (Cambridge University Press, 2015) 201; Nicholas Aroney and Haig Patapan, 'The Gibbs Court' in Rosalind Dixon and George Williams (eds.), *The High Court, the Constitution, and Australian Politics* (Cambridge University Press, 2015) 220.

[88] See Patrick O'Brien, 'Judges and Politics: The Parliamentary Contributions of the Law Lords 1876–2009' (2016) 79 *Modern Law Review* 786.

[89] See Paul S Davies and Justine Pila (eds.), *The Jurisprudence of Lord Hoffman: A Festschrift in Honour of Lord Leonard Hoffman* (Hart, 2015); 'Law Lord Known for Liberal Outlook', *BBC News*, 26 November 2003, http://news.bbc.co.uk/2/hi/uk_news/3239726.stm; Martin Childs, 'Lord Steyn: Judge Who Opposed Tony Blair and George Bush Over Iraq War and Guantanamo', *Independent*, 3 December 2017, www.independent.co.uk/news/obituaries/obituary-lord-steyn-died-judge-who-opposed-iraq-war-and-guantanamo-blair-bush-a8089426.html. See also Chapter 4 in this volume.

[90] For discussion, see note x later in this chapter.

[91] For a defence of this view, see, e.g., Sir Anthony Mason, 'No Place in a Modern Democratic Society for a Supine Judiciary' (1997) 35 *Law Society Journal* 51; Adam Liptak, 'Chief Justice Defends Judicial Independence After Trump Attacks "Obama Judge"', *New York Times*, 21 November 2018, www.nytimes.com/2018/11/21/us/politics/trump-chief-justice-roberts-rebuke.html. Other courts also seem to have acted consistently with this view: see, e.g., the role of Asshiddiqie on the Indonesian

candidate for the status of towering judge. Indeed, in Vietnam, Bui Ngoc Son suggests that the broad executive powers enjoyed by the chief justice – which include influencing the 'structure, operation and personnel of the judicial system' – mean that the chief justice 'naturally becomes a towering judge'.[92]

For female judges, having the role of chief justice may thus be especially important to their chances of assuming towering status; yet, in many countries, female judges have only recently begun to be appointed as chief justice.[93]

16.3.2 *Other Judges and the Broader Institutional Context*

Other factors affecting a judge's claim to towering status will likely be far more contextual in nature – for example, the degree to which their preferred legal or constitutional outlook is shared by others on the court and the degree to which other judges are willing to follow and join them.[94] In the short run, at least, a towering judge will arise only if other judges are willing to follow that judge's approach rather than compete with them for leadership status. This will also depend on a mix of the ideological and jurisprudential sympathies among members of a bench and the skills of a leading judge in persuading others.

In the United States, Mark Tushnet examines the role of Chief Justice Charles Evans Hughes as a potential towering judge. Hughes was also extremely influential in persuading Justice Owen Roberts to reverse his position on the scope of the Due Process and Commerce Clauses and to uphold key parts of the New Deal legislative agenda. This, Tushnet suggests, depended on a range of factors: Hughes's intellect, advocacy skills and willingness to do 'the work' of legal reasoning and argumentation but also the fact that Roberts himself recognized Hughes's 'superior intellect' and

---

Constitutional Court, discussed in Stefanus Hendrianto, *Law and Politics of Constitutional Courts: Indonesia and the Search for Judicial Heroes* (Routledge, 2018).

[92] Chapter 14 in this volume.

[93] See, e.g., the large number of historical first female chief justices on courts globally in recent years: 'Balochistan High Court in Pakistan Gets 1st Woman Chief Justice', *Hindustan Times*, 1 September 2018, www.hindustantimes.com/world-news/balochistan-high-court-in-pakistan-gets-1st-woman-chief-justice/story-genMELc7S64WmJckPurSqM.html; Carmel Rickard, 'First Woman Chief Justice Sworn in for Ethiopia', *African Lii*, 1 November 2018, https://africanlii.org/article/20181101/first-woman-chief-justice-sworn-ethiopia; Paul Kar, 'Susan Kiefel Becomes Australia's First Female Chief Justice of the High Court', *The Guardian*, 30 January 2017, www.theguardian.com/australia-news/2017/jan/30/susan-kiefel-becomes-australias-first-female-chief-justice-of-the-high-court; 'Susan Denham to Become Ireland's First Female Chief Justice', *The Journal*, 19 July 2011, www.thejournal.ie/susan-denham-to-become-ireland%E2%80%99s-first-female-chief-justice-181629-Jul2011/; 'First Woman Chief Justice of Nepal, Sushila Karki, Takes Oath', *Indian Express*, 11 July 2016, https://indianexpress.com/article/world/world-news/first-woman-chief-justice-of-nepal-sushila-karki-takes-oath-2907173/; 'Majara Appointed New Chief Justice', *Lesotho Times*, 4 September 2014, http://lestimes.com/majara-appointed-new-chief-justice/; 'First Woman Chief Justice Appointed in Seychelles', *Seychelles News Agency*, 7 August 2015, http://m.seychellesnewsagency.com//articles/3484/First+woman+Chief+Justice+appointed+in+Seychelles.

[94] Compare Chapter 3 in this volume.

was persuaded by his arguments.[95] This involved Hughes deploying a mix of legal and interpersonal skills and Roberts being open to argument and persuasion.

A receptive political climate may likewise affect a judge's claim to towering status. As Tushnet notes, certain periods lend themselves more to long-term towering judicial influence than others, including the early period of a court's existence or periods of major constitutional change or transition.[96] Judges who serve in periods of this kind have a far greater opportunity to contribute to foundational precedents or precedents that determine the direction of the law in the long run. They also have greater opportunities to contribute to institutional reform and design. They may even have a different psychology or attitude than other judges: they may more readily see themselves as contributing to a broader process of constitutional change or transition.[97]

Thus, two of the judges included in the volume, Kennedy and Chaskalson, served during or immediately after the adoption of a new constitution: the 1922 Irish Constitution and the 1993 and 1996 South African Constitutions, respectively. Others served during important periods of constitutional change or transition, such as following the adoption of major constitutional amendments or reforms. For example, Sólyom became chief justice in 1990, after the series of constitutional reforms adopted as part of the transition from Soviet rule and the 1989 Roundtable Talks in Hungary. Similarly, Barak assumed the role of chief justice in 1995, soon after the passage of the 1992 Basic Law on Human Dignity and Liberty and the Basic Law on Freedom of Occupation. Further, Chief Justice Li and Justice Bokhary served on the Court in the period after the Sino-British handover and the coming into force of Hong Kong's Basic Law and Bills of Rights, or the 'founding era' of Hong Kong's adoption of a 'one country, two systems' model.[98]

Sergio Verdugo identifies Judge Eugenio Valenzuela as having towering status in significant part because his decisions 'contributed to framing the conditions that allowed the opposition to the Pinochet dictatorship to win the 1998 plebiscite and put an end to the military regime'.[99] Malagodi likewise identifies Chief Justice Shrestha as a towering judge, in part because his tenure on the Court coincided with the end of a ten-year civil war (from 1996 to 2006) and an extended period of constitutional drafting (2008 to 2015). Mason became chief justice around the time of the passage of the Australia Acts, which severed formal legal ties between Australia and the United Kingdom and made the High Court Australia's final court of appeal.[100]

---

95 Chapter 2 in this volume.
96 Ibid.
97 Compare Sir Anthony Mason, 'Future Directions in Australian Law' (1987) 13 *Monash University Law Review* 149, on the psychological significance of the Australia Acts. See also Chapter 13 in this volume.
98 Chapter 6 in this volume.
99 Chapter 15 in this volume.
100 Australia Act 1986 (Cth); Australia Act 1986 (UK).

Another external or contextual factor is the degree to which a towering judge faces a favourable versus a hostile political context. Political hostility can, in some cases, offer opportunities to achieve 'towering' status: it allows a judge to demonstrate political and leadership skills by defusing a conflict or defending the Court in the face of opposition.[101] Judges may also be able to frame their decisions in ways that increase or decrease the degree of political opposition to their decisions.[102] This was arguably true for Justice Manuel Cepeda, who was appointed to the Court at a time of relative institutional crisis but who approached his role in a way that successfully defused that crisis.[103] Malagodi likewise points to the role played by Chief Justice Shrestha in 2015 – in helping to broker a compromise with the government about the role and independence of Nepali courts – as evidence of his towering status.[104]

But political crisis or opposition also carries with it risks for a judge's reputation and legacy. It can mean that a court's decisions are more readily overturned or that its jurisdiction is pared back in ways that undermine the long-term legacy and towering status of a judge. As a general matter, an unfavourable political environment will make it less likely that a judge will achieve short- or long-run towering status. For example, it makes it less likely that a judge's decisions will be implemented or that their influence will be seen as positive.

A final contextual factor that may affect the perception of a judge as towering is the way in which the political culture approaches leadership: in some eras, there has been a focus on collective decision-making, whereas in others, there has been a greater focus on individual or personalised forms of leadership. Changes of this kind arguably inform the focus of this volume and also the perception of judges as dominant in different periods.

16.4 CONCLUSION: BENEFITS AND DANGERS OF A FOCUS ON TOWERING JUDGES

In many legal systems, the focus has long been on courts as collective bodies. In some civil law systems, there is little or no dissent or concurrence by individual judges; the court speaks with one voice.[105] Similarly, in socialist law systems, there is often an emphasis on collective over individualised notions of legal and political action.[106] A focus on individual judges is therefore something quite new: often, the unsigned or unanimous nature of judgments will make such a focus extremely

---

[101] Compare Chapter 8 in this volume.
[102] See especially Chapters 11 and 15 in this volume.
[103] Chapter 11 in this volume.
[104] Chapter 7 in this volume.
[105] See, e.g., European Court of Justice traditions inflected by civilian practices of many member states: David Edward, 'How the Court of Justice Works' (1995) 20 *European Law Review* 539.
[106] See William Partlett and Eric C Ip, 'Is Socialist Law Really Dead?' (2016) 48 *New York University Journal of International Law and Politics* 463.

difficult, but there is still clear value to scholarship that takes a more granular, individualised approach to analysing judicial behaviour.[107]

In the common law world, however, legal and cultural tendencies are different. We start with a fascination with individual judges and their jurisprudence and approach. In fact, we often need to be reminded that courts are a 'they[,] not an it'.[108] There is thus already a danger to scholarly work that focuses on the individual judge rather than on courts as a collective body. A focus on individual 'towering' judges may also carry even greater dangers: it may risk privileging chief justices over other leading justices, male over female justices, and individual over collegial approaches to decision-making.

Why is this kind of individualistic focus dangerous? First, if truly dominant, a towering judge may undermine the role of independent judicial judgment in the development of constitutional precedents. This danger may seem quite modest: most judges are intelligent and independent-minded and enjoy significant institutional protections from both the elected branches and *each other*. They are, thus, quite likely to follow their *own* professional judgement when deciding how to interpret and apply the law.[109] But the *quality* of judicial reasoning may still suffer if a single judge is perceived to be dominant within a court as well as outside it. Other judges may be too quick to join that judge's opinion, without fully testing all aspects of the reasoning and analysis.[110]

Second, a towering judge may so dominate public perceptions of the role of a court that they undermine the institutionalisation of judicial review as a practice or leave courts vulnerable to attack in key periods when a towering judge has left the court. Consider the role of 'per curiam' opinions as a means of protecting a court from attack.[111] Some courts have little or no tradition of dissent, whereas others have a long tradition of judges writing separate concurring and dissenting opinions. Almost all courts, however, have some tradition of issuing 'per curiam' opinions. Often, they use such opinions to rebut a perception of partisanship on the part of certain justices or to underscore the importance of compliance with the court's decision, where one or both those facts might be thought to be in doubt. Collegial decision-making by a court might also be thought more broadly to advance these same goals – to increase public confidence in a court as a legal institution and increase pressure on the elected branches to comply with court decisions.

Take events in Israel since the retirement of Chief Justice Aharon Barak: it is widely agreed that, since Barak left office, the 'Barak-instigated legal revolution has

---

[107] Chapter 14 in this volume.
[108] Lewis A Kornhauser and Lawrence G Sager, 'Unpacking the Court' (1986) 96 *Yale Law Journal* 82.
[109] But see Dyson Heydon, 'Judicial Activism and the Death of the Rule of Law' (2003) 47 *Quadrant* 9.
[110] Compare Chapter 3 in this volume (noting commentary suggesting that the HCA under Dixon's leadership 'was arguably unbalanced by Dixon's unquestioned dominance and its intellectual conformity').
[111] See, e.g., Steven L Wasby, Steven Peterson, James Schubert and Glendon Schubert, 'The Per Curiam Opinion: Its Nature and Functions' (1992) 76 *Judicature* 29.

been eroded'.[112] One explanation for this is simply that there has been a conservative political backlash against the liberal and judicial-empowerment dimensions to Barak's jurisprudential legacy. Another, advanced by Harel, is that political conservatives have reacted to the substance of Barak's approach but sought to use the new forms of judicial power he helped create to advance quite different (far more illiberal) political ends.[113] In either event, the Court has been subject to institutional attack – including through the process of judicial appointment and proposals to create new forms of formal legislative override. It also seems plausible that attacks of this kind have been easier, or less costly, for the government and the Knesset, in part, because no other judge from the same era has had the same stature as Barak in seeking to defend the Court from such attacks.

This is one reason why I would question whether all the judges included in this volume are in fact *towering* judges in the sense of being judges who (at least publicly or visibly) tower *over* others, as opposed to leading collegial judges who have contributed to a well-respected court. Almost all the judges on our list are *leading* judges: they have been party to leading decisions and significant institutional players nationally and internationally. But some have adopted a sufficiently collegial approach so that it is hard to identify them as the dominant intellectual or institutional influence on the courts on which they served, at least not with any confidence or until sufficient time has passed for otherwise confidential insights into the judicial decision-making process to have been revealed.

Dennis Davis's description of Chaskalson's contribution to South African constitutional jurisprudence is especially notable in this context. For instance, regarding *Makwanyane*[114] and the Court's decision to strike down the death penalty as unconstitutional, Davis notes how it was 'Chaskalson who penned the comprehensive main judgment'.[115] But in other cases, such as the constitutionality of a legislative anti-defection clause (*UDM*[116]), Davis suggests that 'the hand of Arthur Chaskalson [was] clearly evident' though the decision was written by the Court collectively.[117] This analysis may well be accurate; it undoubtedly reflects Davis's considerable insider knowledge as a High Court judge and leading ANC intellectual with close ties to Chaskalson and other members of the Constitutional Court. But is not an analysis that could have been widely made with any confidence by members of the broader society, or political branches, at the time.

There are several other leading judges who could be viewed as candidates for inclusion in this category of 'great' collegial, as opposed to towering, judges – for example, Cepeda, Li and Mason.

---

[112] Chapter 9 in this volume.
[113] Ibid. Compare also Oren Tamir, 'Abusive "Abusive Constitutionalism"' (working paper 2019, on file with author), https://hls.harvard.edu/dept/graduate-program/oren-tamir/.
[114] *S v Makwanyane and another* 1995 (3) SA 391 (CC).
[115] Chapter 12 in this volume.
[116] *UDM v President of the Republic of South Africa (2)* 2003 (1) SA 495 (CC).
[117] Chapter 12 in this volume.

As the various contributors note: key decisions authored by Cepeda were 'co-signed by Cepeda and five other justices, a strategy of institutional protection a bit like an occasional use of the per curiam by the US Supreme Court'.[118] Li often authored the lead opinions of the Hong Kong CFA[119] but also many joint and unanimous judgments.[120] Under the leadership of Sir Anthony Mason, the High Court of Australia 'tended more often to express its reasoning in unanimous and joint judgments' than in most previous eras.[121] Mason himself cites *Cole v - Whitfield*,[122] a unanimous decision of the Court, as his greatest jurisprudential legacy;[123] and many commentators have noted the 'collegial spirit' among members of the Court while Mason was chief justice.[124] And in the United Kingdom, Hunter and Rackley suggest that one of the distinguishing features of Lady Hale as a towering (feminist) judge is that 'through her judgments, judicial leadership and extrajudicial activities[, she] … sought to bring people together and to create conditions in which others are enabled and empowered'.[125]

In most, if not all, these cases, I would suggest that this kind of collegial approach also reflected a self-conscious *choice* on the part of relevant (leading) judges to exercise a form of self-restraint in judgment writing and individual public influence. Some judges may simply be ordinary members of a collegial court who join others for reasons for comity, convenience or expertise. Others, such as Cepeda, Chaskalson, Li and Mason, have certainly had the legal and political skills to dominate a court but have chosen not to do so – arguably, out of a commitment to the value of collegial judging. This is also exactly what the idea of 'leading collegial judge' embodies.

Hunter and Rackley link this kind of collegiality to broader gender-based theories and understandings of leadership: they suggest that feminist leadership is inherently a form of leadership that 'values and supports community, connections, collegiality and inclusivity'.[126] Others might raise questions about the extent to which such leadership should be identified as female, feminine or feminist.[127] In each case, however, there is clear value to seeing judicial leadership within a broader collegial and institutional context and to understanding that judicial influence is a product of *both* the quality of an individual judge's reasons and their capacity to work effectively

---

[118] Chapter 11 in this volume.
[119] Chapter 6 in this volume ('key judgments of the Court were delivered in Li's name').
[120] Simon NM Young, 'Constitutional Rights in Hong Kong's Court of Final Appeal' (2011) 27 *Chinese (Taiwan) Yearbook of International Law and Affairs* 6, 79.
[121] Chapter 3 in this volume.
[122] *Cole v Whitfield* (1988) 165 CLR 360.
[123] 'In Conversation: An Interview with Sir Anthony Mason' (1996) 17 *Singapore Law Review* 3, 6.
[124] Chapter 3 in this volume.
[125] Chapter 4 in this volume.
[126] Ibid.
[127] For a critique of cultural feminist accounts that link feminism to feminine values of care and collaboration, see, e.g., Catharine A Mackinnon, *Toward a Feminist Theory of the State* (Harvard University Press, 1989).

with other judges to see those reasons prevail or become law in either the short or the long term.

In concluding this fascinating volume on towering judges, I therefore end with a note of caution. We should all welcome the provocation offered by the editors and the many rich portraits of constitutional judges offered by the contributors as important sources of comparative study and reference. Paying attention to individual judges and their jurisprudence invites a fine-grained and complex account of different constitutional systems. It also provides insights into the necessary conditions for 'successful' forms of constitutional decision-making.

But we should also be careful to maintain a distinction between studying and celebrating the idea of a towering judge: in studying such judges, we should continue to question both *how* and *why* these judges are regarded as significant and, even more importantly, why other judges who may be just as important are not included in this list.

Doing so does not diminish from the importance of this volume. Rather, it helps to avoid the dangers of an overly narrow, individualised and even gendered conception of institutional leadership, when the best forms of leadership may be far more collegial, collaborative and pluralistic. The volume should be read as the beginning rather than the end of an important comparative conversation about leading judges, and judicial models, worldwide.

Appendix

Judge	CJ?	Term	Gender
Charles Evans Hughes (United States)	Y	1910–16 CJ – 1930–41	M
Owen Roberts (United States)	N	1930–45	M
Hugo Black (United States)	N	1937–71	M
Earl Warren (United States)	Y	CJ – 1953–69	M
William Brennan (United States)	N	1956–90	M
Anthony Mason (Australia)	Y	1972–86 CJ – 1987–95	M
Brenda Hale (UK)	Y	2004–20 CJ – 2017–20	F
Hugh Kennedy (Ireland)	Y	CJ – 1924–36	M
Andrew Li (Hong Kong)	Y	CJ – 1997–2010	M
Kemal Bokhary (Hong Kong)	N	Permanent – 1997–2012 Non-permanent – 2012–Present	M
Chan Sek Keong (Singapore)	Y	2006–12	M
Kalyan Shrestha (Nepal)	Y	2005–15 CJ – 2015–16	M
Aharon Barak (Israel)	Y	1978–95 President – 1995–2006	M
PN Bhagwati (India)	Y	1973–85 CJ – July 1985–December 1986	M
Manuel José Cepeda Espinosa (Colombia)	Y	2001–9 President – June 2005–April 2006	M
Arthur Chaskalson (South Africa)	Y	President – 1994–2001 CJ – 2001–5	M
Laszlo Sólyom (Hungary)	Y	1989 President – 1990–8	M
Truong Hoa Binh (Vietnam)	Y	CJ – 2007–16	M
Eugenio Valenzuela (Chile)	N	1980–9 1997–2006	M

Index

Pang Khang Chau, 140–1
Parajuli, Gopal, 166
Parliamentary Hearings Committee (PHC),
    171–2
Pasquino, Pasquale, 290
Passport Act of 1967 (India), 199
Pathak, R. S. (Chief Justice) (India), 211
Pázmány, Péter, 255
Peace and Justice Act, Colombia, 231
*Peck Constance Emily v Calvary Charismatic
    Centre Ltd.*, 139
Peled, Yoav, 174
Peña, Marisol (Chief Justice) (Chile), 306
PHC. *See* Parliamentary Hearings Committee
Phuyal, Hari, 170
PIL. *See* public interest litigation
Pinochet, Augusto, 291–2, 298–300. *See also*
    Valenzuela, Eugenio
Constitutional Court of Chile under, 298–300
Pius, Gilbert Louis, 140
Platonic Conception, of constitutional rights
    in Australia, 32
    definition of, 32
    global community of judges and, 33
    global constitutionalism and, 22, 29–33
        community of judges and, 33–4
        judicial function in, 30
    in Hungary, 30–1
    in India, 31–2
    in Israel, 31
    judicial function in, 30
Platonic Theory of Ideas, 29
Plyler v. Doe, 50–1
Polish Round Table Agreement, 258
political constitutionalism, 25, 274
political rights, 124–5
political "towering" judges, 10–11, 215, 306
popular sovereignty, in Australia
    through legal independence from U.K., 70
    Mason's embrace of, 67
populism movements
    Constitutional Court of Colombia and, 228
    global constitutionalism with, 23–4
Porat, Iddo, 17, 34–5, 97, 215, 312
Port Elizabeth Municipality v Various Occupiers,
    248–9
positivist courts, in Australia, 10
Powell, Lewis F. (Justice) (U.S.), 50
Prakash Mani Sharma case, 167–8
precedent system, in Supreme People's Court of
    Vietnam, 285
private law, in South Africa, reform of, 250
property rights, in South Africa, 248–9
proportionality doctrine, 34–5

public interest lawyers, promotion of, 212
public interest litigation (PIL)
    Bhagwati and
        entrenchment of, 14
        as institutional legacy of, 205–8
        in judicial philosophy, 196–9
    Supreme Court of Nepal and, 156, 170–1
public law
    Chan Sek Keong and, 142, 145, 152–3
Pusey, Merlo, 45

Rajkumar, Prasad Shah (Justice) (Nepal), 163–4
Rana, Rajkumar (Advocate) (Nepal), 164
rational judicial leadership, 57
Reed, Stanley, 50
reform, judicial
    by Kennedy, H., 103–5
        under Courts of Justice Act 1924, 103
        for lower courts, 104
        natural law influences on, 108
    by Shrestha, 168–70
        Constitutional Bench, 170–1
        of impeachment requirements for justices,
            171
        through Supreme Court Strategic Plans,
            168–9
Regmi, Khil Raj (Chief Justice) (Supreme Court of
    Nepal), 155–6, 163–4, 165–6
Regmi, Kumar, 170
Republic (Plato), 29
Republic of Ireland Act 1948, U.K., 110
Reynolds v. Sims, 49
Reynolds v Times Newspapers Ltd., 147
Ribiero, Leandro Molhano, 277
right to life, interpretation of, in India, 200
Rivonia trial, 236–7
Roberts, Owen (Justice) (U.S.), 3–4, 40–6
    New Deal crisis cases, 41–6
Roosevelt, Franklin Delano, 41–6
Rosen-Zvi, Issachar, 27
Roznai, Yaniv, 174
Rueda, Pablo, 227
Ruger, Theodore W., 277
rule of law
    global, community of judges under, 34
    for Kennedy, H., 115
Rylands v. Fletcher, 203–4

Sachs, Albie (Justice) (South Africa), 238–9
Sajó, András, 109, 256, 267
Santos, Juan Manuel, 232–3
Sapir, Gideon, 188
Scalia, Antonin (Justice) (U.S.), 55
Scheppele, Kim Lane, 9, 108–9, 255–6, 277

For EU product safety concerns, contact us at Calle de José Abascal, 56–1°,
28003 Madrid, Spain or eugpsr@cambridge.org.

www.ingramcontent.com/pod-product-compliance
Ingram Content Group UK Ltd.
Pitfield, Milton Keynes, MK11 3LW, UK
UKHW020401140625
459647UK00020B/2593